THE GIANT BOOK OF
VILLAINS

THE GIANT BOOK OF
VILLAINS

Edited by
Ian Schott, Damon Wilson,
Rowan Wilson and Colin Wilson

‖ •PARRAGON• ‖

This edition published and distributed by Parragon

This edition first published by Magpie Books Ltd in 1994,
a division of Robinson Publishing

Magpie Books Ltd
7, Kensington Church Court
London W8 4SP

A copy of the British Library Cataloguing in Publication
Data for this title is available from the British Library.

Typeset by Hewer Text Composition Services, Edinburgh
Printed and bound by Firmin-Didot (France),
Group Herissey. No d'impression : 28863.

Contents

· *World Famous* ·

DICTATORS

Ian Schott

INTRODUCTION

Dictator: "a ruler who is not restricted by a constitution; a tyrannical ruler". This loose definition might bring a hundred names to mind. Many have ruled without the slightest regard for legal niceties, using force as their first and last resort. What distinguishes the gentlemen in this book is their reputation for excess; the public flaunting of their cruelty, their acute vanity and their grotesque disregard for the people they claimed to represent. It is tempting to consider the Idi Amins, or Saddam Husseins of this world as being freaks, personifications of evil. Sadly, while their stories will show you how far sheer ruthless ambition will take a man, they also demonstrate how complex human evil is; all too often the world not only stood by and watched these tyrants evolve, but even fed them and helped them grow into fully fledged monsters.

chapter one

PAPA DOC: VOODOO GANGSTER

In the late Summer of 1963, fifty badly trained soldiers, a motley bunch of exiles and dissidents, straggled through the humid, mountainous sub-tropical forest that spans the border between Haiti and the Dominican Republic. This pathetic army, weighed down by the CIA supplied weapons it barely knew how to fire was supposed to constitute a force capable of liberating Haiti from the regime of Doctor Francois Duvalier, better known as Papa Doc. It was the fourth such sad little invasion, and got as far as the others. Outnumbered and shot to pieces at its first encounter with Duvalier's forces, the expedition might simply have been another tragi-comic episode in Haiti's sorrowful history, were it not for the frightening postscript. One of the dead invaders was a Captain Blucher Philogenes, a former officer in Duvalier's army, who had frequently boasted that he was immune to bullets. On the specific orders of Duvalier, a Lieutenant Albert Jerome cut the head off the corpse. Packed in ice, it was delivered by a specially arranged airlift to the Palace. A weird rumour began to spread. In the still of the night, they said, Papa Doc would sit, staring desperately into the cold, lifeless eyes of his dead enemy, trying to learn what those still living planned.

There are many bizarre stories from Haiti, which has obstinately remained a cradle of witchcraft and superstition in the age of science. Duvalier was notorious for his use of Voodoo to manipulate the fears of his people. But this is not only the story of a mysterious bogeyman who wove a net of spells over Haiti. This is the story of a man who triumphed by doing nothing; who in fifteen years of absolute rule over a country, achieved absolutely nothing except the further abasement of an already degraded people; whose promises meant nothing, and who left nothing behind except terror. Most dictators at least manage to build a row of public toilets. More galling even than the sheer misery of the people is that this incompetent tyranny was sponsored to the tune of hundreds of millions of dollars in aid blackmailed from the American Government, eighty per cent of which went straight into the pockets of the foul brood in charge. As the International Commission of Justice said in words which barely concealed their incredulous shock at the blatant criminality:

"In today's world there are many authoritarian regimes. Generally speaking they are the reflection of some ideology. The tyranny that oppresses Haiti does not even have that excuse; its sole object is to place the country under tribute in order to ensure the future affluence of those now in power".

Haiti has never been served well by its rulers, white or black, who have traditionally acquired power by violence and are obliged to maintain it with fear. Barely five minutes of its strange and violent history have been devoted to the welfare of the population rather than the enrichment of the powerful. The best the people could hope for in the 1957 elections was a benign criminal who might allow them a few crumbs off his table. In the unassuming, bespectacled and soft spoken Dr Francois Duvalier, they found an outright gangster. They had always given their rulers names, but Duvalier did not even give them that privilege. He christened himself "Papa Doc", and in a clear sign of what was to come announced:

"As President I have no enemies and can have none. There are only enemies of the nation . . ."

The implication was terrifying. He was the people; they had no voice other than him, and he considered every murder to be sanctioned by them. They were his property, and he would end up selling their own blood to keep his pockets full.

Duvalier had campaigned as the saviour of the masses, the wretched black peasants who had suffered at the hands of its mulatto elite since Haiti became the first, black independent State in 1804. Over ninety per cent of the population were illiterate, most earning the equivalent of £1 per week or less, and few having an average life expectancy over thirty-five. Papa

Doc was a champion of traditional Haitian culture, and stressed the importance of this as a means to creating a nation with an identity. He was an acutely vain man, who considered himself an exceptional intellectual. The only clarity in his speeches came when he praised himself. Otherwise they were incomprehensible goobledegook, stuffed full of confused mystic twittering. Two crucial influences he had often paraded were the idea of "negritude" and, of course, the ancient folk-religion of Haiti, Voodoo.

To understand these better, it is helpful to know a little of Haiti's remarkable history.

Haiti shares the Caribbean island of Hispaniola with the Dominican Republic. It is a lush but wild country, which was once the single richest colony on earth. The island was initially conquered by the Spanish, who within eighteen years of Columbus' discovery of America, had worked the native population of Arawak Indians to death, in their search for gold. The Spanish also bequeathed a variety of European diseases to the Indians, which killed off those they had overlooked.

After a period as a haven to pirates, the island came under French control as an affluent plantation worked by slaves imported from West Africa. The Africans brought their tribal customs and gods with them. Christianity had little impact. The teachings of the Catholic missionaries, full of rituals, resurrection, saints and hell were simply absorbed into their folk-beliefs to create the heady brew that is Voodoo. In Voodoo, the Catholic creed, the Apostles creed and the Hail Mary are all used in the ceremonies. The Virgin Mary appears as Grande Erzulie, Goddess of Fertility. The Cross of Christ is a symbol of Baron Samedi, lord of the dead. Saint Peter is Papa Legba. God exists, but he is aloof, remote and indifferent. Those who practice Voodoo are appealing the lesser spirits or "loas" to help them with the daily requirements of life – food, sex, shelter, disease and protection from enemies – when no other power on earth will. There are two types of these spirits: "Rada" which are African, and "Petro", which are particularly Haitian and much more violent and unpredictable. Voodoo priests are known as "Houngans". Papa Doc became a houngan early on in his evolution. In addition there are sorcerers called "bocors" who specialize in practising the magic that is part of the religion. They cast the spells and curses, the "ouanga". The peasant's biggest moment is death. He may mortgage and sell all that he possesses to ensure a proper funeral, when his personal god will be removed from his body and return to mystical Guinea. The houngan will be well paid to ensure that his corpse does not become the zombie slave of an enemy.

Duvalier employed both priests and sorcerers to scan the future, and used his personal influence over the hundreds of local bocors to maintain his hold on the people of the most remote regions. He moved from practising Voodoo to dabbling in black magic. Contrary to popular belief, Voodoo does not normally do deals with the devil. Reputable houngans reject "magie noire"; they know that in order to practise it one must make a bargain with evil spirits and ultimately be destroyed.

The first slave rebellions of 1791 began in an atmosphere of tropical storms and night-time voodoo sacrifices; the first slave leader was a famed voodoo priest, a giant, called Brookman. It was under Toussaint Louverture that the slaves gained their freedom, only to lose it when Napoleon sent 43,000 troops to restore slavery. The French imported dog: from Cuba which they trained to pursue and kill the blacks, but even this unspeakable cruelty could not stem the tide. Dessalines, the great Haitian hero who Papa Doc was so fond of comparing himself to, so thrashed the French that they surrendered to the British rather than face the fury of his ragged army. When Boisrond Tonnere, one of Dessalines' officers, came to write the Act of Independence in 1804, he famously said:

> "To write this Act of Independence we must have a white man's skin for parchment, his skull for an inkwell, his blood for ink and a bayonet for a pen . . ."

The violent racism of a world still dependent on slavery isolated Haiti which was an unwanted example of a free black nation. It was crippled by debt, and fell under the heel of a string of black tyrants. Between 1843 and 1915 alone, there were twenty-two dictators. Most were assassinated by their successors. The more educated mulatto elite, the half-breeds, with Negro mothers and white fathers tended to be born into more favourable circumstances and became the aristocracy, with the blacks an embittered majority. Hence, in the twentieth century, the evolution of the idea of "negritude" – the attempt to raise the pride and consciousness of the negro majority, who for so long had felt cursed by their colour. Unfortunately, under Duvalier this became an excuse to tell the people that only he knew what was good for them. He was never slow to play the race card to justify his atrocities or explain why his country was in a mess;

it could always be blamed on the racism of another nation. On the advice of friends, Duvalier also married a mulatto.

Francois Duvalier was born in 1907 in a tin-roofed shack a few streets away from the National Palace. He was the son of a primary school teacher and a bakery employee. His early childhood was spent in an atmosphere of continuous revolution and tyranny, as the British, French, Germans and Americans played poker with Haiti, each underwriting their favoured dictators. After would-be Emperor Guillame Sam was impaled on the railings of the French Embassy, the US finally sent in the marines, who remained until 1934. Their occupation was widely resented, and there were frequent suicide bombings, but they left hospitals, telephones, bridges and schools.

Duvalier was a quiet, forgettable pupil during his early education and afterwards went on to medical school. He had become involved on the fringes of student politics and protests. Significantly, he fell under the influence of Lorimer Denis, a twenty-four year old voodoo mystic and mainspring of the "Negritude" movement, and began to write for "*Action National*", the nationalist newspaper. In his articles he criticized the US occupation, and praised the flowering of traditional Haitian culture hoping that "A man will come to correct injustice and set things right".

The moment the Marines went, the population went on an illogical orgy of destruction, tearing up the bridges and telephone systems their white rulers had left. It was this instinctive and irrational hatred that Duvalier was later able to harness. So strife-torn were the years that followed that in the words of one of Duvalier's associates "Francois was the only one of his generation who never knew the inside of a prison". Duvalier kept his head down, and worked on his strategy of doing nothing which was later to serve him so well. He continued to dabble in "Haiti's traditional culture" and became a houngan or Voodoo priest by virtue of his knowledge. He also continued to write, under an assumed name, but was incapable of doing anything without the help of the voodoo mystic, Denis. His articles vowed to restore the National pride of Haiti, and contained the same vain boast that he would repeat all his life; "We swear to make our motherland the Negro miracle". Duvalier worked in a series of government hospitals as a consultant, and in 1943 was chosen to work alongside some US doctors on a project intended to wipe out the terrible, contagious disease called "yaws" that afflicted over seventy per cent of the population. It was on the evidence of this association that the

Americans later thought he might be a suitable candidate for their support.

From here, having done only what he was told, he made it, without doing anything, to the position of Director of Public Health, where he did nothing. He had been fortunate that his self-styled reputation as an "intellectual" had secured him a prominent position in the new Nationalist party; his position in the Government came by default, when the current dictator failed to rig the elections sufficiently and was forced to buy the Nationalists' support in a coalition with a few ministerial goodies. Here, while all around him indulged in frenzied activity and disastrous blunders, Duvalier's revolutionary policy of doing nothing came into its own. It continued to be his most successful tactic, and ensured he kept his job, and eventually was promoted to Cabinet Minister for Public Health and Labour. As he never directly expressed a view, he made no enemies; and as he did nothing, there was no action he could be criticized for. It was ingenious.

Under Dumarsais Estime, who had won power with the support of the army, a new class of black elite, like Duvalier, began to emerge, breaking into business and government, and challenging the mulattos. Unfortunately, those obtaining power were no better to their fellow men, and displayed prodigious indiscipline and greed. The mulattos persuaded the army to round on their former ally and in 1950, Colonel Paul Magloire became the umpteenth dictator in Haiti's short history.

Duvalier's inexorable rise to the top was halted. Thwarted, he finally did something and left the Government before Magloire could devise an unpleasant end for him. He went back to treating yaws. He acquired a lasting distrust of the Army, and was further embittered by the sight of new favourites overtaking him. His behaviour became paranoid and he took to constantly switching plates with his dinner companions to avoid poisoning.

Magloire had a reputation as a playboy. Haiti became a decadent and sexy international attraction. The international literati – Noel Coward, Truman Capote and Graham Greene – flocked to it. The lavish excesses of its leader and the lingering smell of corruption and violence stimulated the jaded appetites of the tourists that thronged to its capital, Port-Au-Prince. The Americans were already providing considerable financial support, but in return asked that Haiti should be maintained a Communist-free zone. Magloire was only too happy to oblige, and took it further by shooting anyone suspected of promoting unrest.

In 1954 Magloire lined up his sights on Duvalier, who spent the next couple of years in hiding, dressed as a woman. There was considerable political unrest in the country, and though Duvalier had done very little, if anything, to agitate, the Government needed an enemy to blame for the spreading dissent. Hence Duvalier, whose contribution to democracy had been to write a few half-baked articles was built up into the big, bad wolf, and found himself acknowledged as the leader of the opposition. His enemies created him as a plausible leader. In 1956, he dropped his skirts and came out of hiding, disassociating himself from the continued killings and bombings. It was, predictably, nothing to do with him. Although by this time he was probably doing something, namely using Voodoo to frighten the peasants into economically ruining the Government, he had changed his tack. Before, he had done nothing. He was still true to those values, but now he told other people to do things, like bomb and shoot. He was still untarnished by action.

Magloire fled to Jamaica, and elections were called. Reporters frankly found Duvalier a bit odd. He was unable to answer their questions regarding what he stood for, preferring to offer them a bit of mystic philosophy here and there. The election campaign was a virtual civil war; there were six changes of leader in the course of it. In one incident, over 1,000 of Duvalier's opponents were massacred in Port-Au-Prince. The results were a final proof of his magical powers; in some areas his vote alone was double the entire population. Such popularity is traditional among Haitian dictators.

The elections also marked the death of Duvalier's longtime guru, Lorimer Denis. People whispered that Duvalier had given his friend to the Voodoo spirits in order to ensure his election as President.

There were two priorities facing the new President of Haiti: firstly to guarantee that he was well paid for the job, and secondly, that he could keep it. The people thought that the President's chair had an evil spell over it. His solution to both was to turn to America.

The key was Communism. Cuba was shortly to fall to Castro, and Duvalier was quick to exploit the US fear of Communism spreading through the Caribbean: "Communism has established centres of infection – no area in the world is as vital to American security as the Caribbean . . ." he reminded the US, adding that he hoped Haiti could become the "spoiled child" of America.

For the next fifteen years he continued to flirt with Communism to keep the dollars coming. By 1960, quite apart from the vast loans he had extorted, the US had given Duvalier $22 million. In addition, on his election he had promised Cuba's dictator, Batista that he would, for a price, not help Castro's Communist rebels. Batista's henchmen got a million dollar kickback for arranging the deal, Duvalier personally got $3 million, and Haiti got the few cents left over. The President was off to a flying start. After Cuba became Communist he had the Americans over a barrel. His country didn't need any industry when he could make millions of dollars from doing nothing. The Duvalier philosophy began to pay off.

Loans were received from the US for educational and health projects and the little that was left after everybody had taken their cut was wasted on grandiose plans – hotels and jet airports, which were never finished. Over fifty per cent of the country's entire budget came from the US, and American experts estimated that Duvalier's personal income could have funded a comprehensive aid programme for the entire nation. Within a few years of his election, the annual bill for his personal security amounted to a staggering $28 million, half of the country's yearly expenditure. His Secret Police, the Ton Ton Macoute cost another $15 million.

He resented any notion that the US should supervise the funds it gave to Haiti, and encouraged left-wing, student disturbances to give the Americans the jitters. He even dressed his troops up to look like Castro's gaily coloured revolutionaries. The Cuban Missile Crisis, when the Americans discovered that Russia was building missile launching sites on Cuban soil, within spitting distance of Florida, played straight into his hands. After deliberating, he came out in support of the US who were forced to keep paying him. When President Kennedy cut off aid he threatened to "bring him to his knees", and reputedly put a "ouanga" on him. Weirdly enough, Kennedy was shot shortly afterwards.

All this may falsely give the impression that he was doing something. In reality, he still did absolutely nothing but had discovered that he only had to imply that he might in the future do something, like vote Communist, and everybody paid him to stay completely still.

The magazine, *Newsweek*, described him as "Big Brother masquerading as the Mad Hatter", a reference to the dark suits and top hats he took to wearing and said:

> "He moves hyperslowly, speaks in a whisper; his eyelids droop. Wearing a slightly bemused unshakeable

half-smile, he does nothing for disconcertingly long periods of time and Haitian people, susceptible to the unusual, are awed . . ."

He improved his absolute stillness by taking increasingly large doses of Voodoo, consulting the entrails of goats and speaking to the Gods as he sat in his bathtub wearing a top-hat. "Haitian democracy is defined and refined as a national discipline within the revolution", he gibbered to passing journalists.

America provided the major part of his income. The rest had to be extracted from people by less glamorous means. He put this in the capable hands of Clement Barbot, under whom evolved the Ton Ton Macoute, the Secret Police force. An old Haitian tale features a giant bogeyman who strides from mountain to mountain stuffing little boys and girls into his knapsack or "macoute". Hence he is called Uncle Knapsack, or Ton Ton Macoute. These human bogeymen had a uniform of dark glasses and machine guns. There were up to 10,000 of them, unrestrained by any law. Technically, any Government employee could join; extortion was a civil service perk.

The Government's potential sources of revenue were the sale of gambling and hotel concessions, and monopolies on everything from sugar and cement to matches. Each time these changed hands vast amounts of money fell into the pockets of Duvalier and Barbot. Within a few months, Barbot had sold and resold the gambling concession three times, even though it was still owned by an Italian. Barbot was a chillingly efficient henchman, but was arrested and imprisoned when he yet again sold the gambling concession, and didn't cut Duvalier in on the deal. He told the purchasers that Papa Doc needed the money to build a hospital.

Barbot, a thoroughly evil man in his own right, later escaped and became Duvalier's most hated enemy. He told the *Washington Post* that Duvalier had informed him that he, personally, wished to kill three hundred people a year. The peasants of Haiti said that Barbot too had magical powers, and could assume the shape of a black dog at will. Duvalier panicked and ordered all black dogs to be shot on sight.

His successor as favourite was Luckner Cambronne, a bright young man who declared that "a good Duvalierist stands ready to kill his children, or children kill their parents". No-one ever defined Duvalierism better.

Cambronne was charged with raising funds for Papa Doc's pet project, Duvalierville, a new town to commemorate his

> ¨Duvalier has performed an economic miracle. He has taught us to live without money and eat without food. Duvalier has taught us how to live without life . . .¨

greatness. Cambronne set about his task with zeal, using every means imaginable, including tolls, threats, beatings and torture. Even school children were mugged for donations to "The National Renovation Fund", a bottomless pit from which the money poured into the private bank accounts of officials. Cambronne had one inspired idea for fund raising. Thousands of people received extortionate bills for using telephones that had never worked or, in some cases, had never been installed. Cambronne explained that, when all the bills were paid, the telephone service would be restored to working order.

Duvalierville was supposed to be finished in six months. At the end, there was only a pile of rubble and a sign swinging in the wind, the name already fading.

Tourism, another vital source of income plummeted by seventy per cent. Duvalier launched a $40,000 drive to bring the tourists back. Typically, he ruined it by simultaneously stringing up the decomposing body of one of his opponents opposite the "Welcome to Haiti" sign at the airport. Poverty and despair were joint kings of Haiti.

When aid and hard currency became hard to obtain, he compelled peasants to donate blood in exchange for a few days wages. This was then sold in America for $20 a litre.

To keep power, he again enlisted the help of the Americans. Because of the previous occupation, the mere sight of a marine was enough to send the Haitians screaming into the undergrowth. They regarded the Americans with superstitious terror. Duvalier persuaded the Americans to send a small unit of marines over to train his own forces. Once they were there, he clung onto them. Their presence, however neutral, gave his regime an almost divine authority.

Opposition was outlawed. A state of emergency was declared, with a permanent curfew. The homes of potential opponents were bombed. He could have no enemies, and so he told the world's press that there were only two political prisoners in Haiti and one was a friend of his.

Jacques Alexis, Haiti's foremost novelist and a committed Communist, had once been a hero of Duvalier's. He was now an obstruction to the inevitable progress of Duvalierism. He was accused of being behind the left-wing unrest which Duvalier himself had encouraged. Alexis left Haiti to attend a conference. Forbidden to return, he tried to slip in over the border but was caught by the Ton Ton Macoute. Under their encouragement, the peasants and children, the very people he had fought for, tore out his eyes and stoned him to death.

Under pressure from the US Duvalier held a "sneak" election in 1961, after which he declared himself President for another six years, because irrespective of whose name the people chose to write on their ballot papers, his name appeared on every one. This was true; the ballot papers issued to voters had his name printed at the bottom. He told the people: "I am and I symbolize an historic moment in your history as a free and independent people. God and the people are the source of all power. I have taken it, and damn it, I will keep it forever . . ."

He helpfully explained his success as a divine sign; "I am already an immaterial being". He had a very royal habit of addressing himself in the third person, as if talking about a disembodied, holy spirit. ". . . this giant capable of eclipsing the sun because the people have already consecrated me for life . . ."

At the next election he was the only candidate, and he thereafter regarded elections as an unnecessary activity, and declared himself President for life. Finally he changed the Constitution to ensure the dynastic succession of his equally loathsome son, Baby Doc.

He split his time between practising Voodoo and writing tributes to himself for the press to print: "Duvalier is the professor of energy, electrifier of souls . . . powerful multiplier of energy . . . renovator of Haitian Fatherland . . . synthesizes all there is of courage, bravery, genius, diplomacy, patriotism and tact . . ."

Whatever this homicidal fruitcake was taking, it was fairly potent. His reputed use of Voodoo was the strongest means to maintain a hold over Haiti. Catholic priests were persecuted and expelled. The Vatican excommunicated the Haitian authorities. In response, Duvalier's Militia chief held a Voodoo ceremony on the steps of the Cathedral, smearing them with pigs blood. The funeral procession of Clement Joumelle, a prominent opponent,

---

"Some people get crazy. They are not responsible for their actions and anyway, I am a doctor . . ."

was hijacked by the Ton Ton Macoute, who drove off with the body and refused to let a Catholic priest bless the internment. It transpired that Joumelle's heart had been removed to make a powerful "ouanga". There were stories of Duvalier burying people alive at the foot of a giant cross in the Bel Air region of Haiti, and sacrificing babies, which had become plentiful and cheap in a nation so poverty stricken that mothers openly sold their children for forty cents.

The opposition dug up Duvalier's father and extracted his heart to put a spell on Papa Doc's powers, splattering human excrement over the corpse and tomb. It didn't work.

In spite of these blood-curdling events, the average Haitian is easygoing and abhors physical violence, venting their anger in highly coloured curses and threats which are rarely carried out. The violence of the few oppresses the many, who have such a bloody history that they are profoundly fatalistic and cynical about all governments, and tend to simply endure the latest horrors.

There were more orthodox, but equally bizarre attempts to dethrone Papa Doc. Shortly after he took power, a mere eight men rode into town, took the main barracks and narrowly failed to capture the Palace and President. This was the famous "Dade County Sheriff's Invasion," so-called because the "army" included a couple of Florida deputy sheriffs. They did have reinforcements of sixteen in reserve, but these never made it from Miami. The Haitians were terrified of the white invaders, who found the defending forces armed with wooden sticks and broom handles; Duvalier didn't trust them to have guns, which most couldn't shoot anyway. It was a long time before the Haitians realized the size of the invading force. Even so, it took all the available troops to winkle them out. Afterwards, Duvalier, who had been frantically packing his bag posed in full army uniform, helmet and gun as a triumphant warrior who had seen off an army of thousands. An "international conspiracy"

He founded the "Praise Papa Doc" movement and published a staggering bit of self-flattery, called "Catechisms of the Revolution", a parody of the Catholic prayer book with himself as the Holy Trinity. The Lord's Prayer began:

"Our Doc, who art in the National Palace for life, hallowed be thy name by present and future generation. Thy will be done in Port-Au-Prince and in the Provinces . . ."

had been defeated. It transpired that the mercenaries were only going to receive $2,000 apiece. Some had invested their own savings in the invasion.

The US, which desperately hoped Duvalier would simply be overthrown, ended up supporting his regime with aid, whilst the CIA tried to undermine him through supporting the sad little efforts of the rebels. Nothing worked.

His death in 1971, from diabetes and heart failure, did not spell the end of the misery for Haiti. Jean Claude "Baby Doc" Duvalier succeeded him. This witless youth, the only son among five children, enjoyed the nicknames at school of "Fat Potato" and "Baskethead". So thick was he that he compelled the teachers to stop publicizing his grades at school. He was terrified at the prospect of stepping into his father's shoes, took an overdose of valium and missed the funeral. He devoted his time to fast cars and sex, leaving Mama Doc to get on with the serious business of looting the country. He didn't miss out, however. By the time of his overthrow in 1986, he had diverted at least $120 million into his pockets. His wife had flowers flown in from Miami at $50,000 a shot. Her jewellery required a mobile vault. She was utterly loathed by the people.

Amidst popular unrest, the Duvalier clan finally left Haiti aboard as US Airforce plane, which dropped them off in France, which, along with Libya, is a trash-can for used dictators. They live in Parisian suburbs, or are tucked away on the right wing coast of the South. There, in fashionable restaurants, nightclubs and hotels, you may find any number of redundant tyrants, wandering around with suitcases stuffed full of swag. They are good news for French business. Baby Doc lives in Cannes, the wealthy sun-spot on the Riviera. He sits alone in restaurants, and at night drives his BMW pointlessly up and down the sea front. Every six weeks, his courier disappears and comes back with a car-load of cash, reputedly $100,000.

In 1991, Haiti's first ever truly democratically elected President, Father Jean-Bertrand Aristide took office. Seven months later, this popular Roman Catholic priest was forced out of office and into exile by a military coup. He had threatened the accumulated privilege of the few. It remains to be seen whether he will have a second chance to change Haiti. Communism can no longer be a valid threat, and perhaps that is why the world is slightly less interested in the outcome. After all the damage of the past, it would be an unfortunate time to stop caring.

chapter two

THE EMPEROR CALIGULA: BLOOD AND POISON

W hatever the public thought, the Roman Emperors were not particularly interested in the virtues of restraint. Caligula's predecessor Tiberius, in whose loving care he spent a large portion of his early life, went into semi-retirement on the island of Capri where he established a colony of vice that beggars description. A lecher's Disneyland supervised by a Minister for Pleasures, and staffed with the selected youth of both sexes, its features included wall-to-wall pornography and round-the-clock, highly theatrical debauchery throughout the surrounding countryside. Children dressed as nymphs and satyrs sported in the woods; boys, whom Tiberius had chosen as "minnows" stocked his swimming pool. Even babies had their uses. One wonders what "Hello" magazine would have made of it all. Caligula spent five years on Capri under the personal tuition of this old goat, whose clinical pursuit of excess was only to be outdone by the bestial behaviour of his pupil.

Caligula was born on 31 August AD 12. He was one of six children. Augustus, then in his seventies, was still ruling. He had pursued a fruitful policy of "first among equals" with the Senate, and under him the Roman Empire had expanded into a miracle of political and military engineering, extending from the French coast to Palestine and Syria, from Africa and Egypt to Spain and Belgium boasting over 6,000 miles of frontier.

Caligula can have barely known anyone to die of natural causes. His mother and her parents, sisters and brothers were banished, murdered or condemned for treachery or promiscuity. His father was poisoned, his brothers disgraced. His brother Drusus had been starved to death in prison, trying

Sabbatai Zevi, who was born and brought up in Smyrna, was a Jew who considered, for reasons best known to himself, that he was the Messiah. From 1651 until 1665 he travelled around the large Jewish communities of the Middle East claiming not only that he was the Messiah but also that he would usher in the millennium quite specifically in the year 1666. By 1665 he had convinced a large number of other people of this notion and his disciples spread the word with great enthusiasm to many others.

By the time he returned to his native Smyrna in 1665 he received a hero's welcome. Everyone went mad. All the natives prepared for a speedy exodus to the Holy Land, considering that the Age of the Messiah was about to descend upon them. Businessmen everywhere were so sure of the correctness of their facts that they neglected their trade and began to sell up, in preparation for the imminent return to Jerusalem.

A necessary first step to the Age of the Messiah was that the Sultan of the Ottoman Empire had to be deposed. Following this simple logic, and knowing that they could not fail, Sabbatai and his followers all landed on the Dardanelle Coast early in 1666 and were promptly arrested by local policemen and dragged to Constantinople in chains and pitiful ignominy.

This did not however dampen the ardour of his followers who decided that the fact that he had not been massacred straight away was even clearer proof that he must be the true Messiah. A constant procession of adoring visitors streamed through the prison in Constantinople where Sabbatai played it up no end and continued to disseminate tales of his miraculous endeavours.

Contemporary reports indicate that in large commercial towns all over Europe, where the Jews led the business world, stagnation of trade took a terrible toll on all local enterprise. Citizens everywhere packed up their linen and their dry goods in order to prepare for the imminent journey home.

The Sultan had to think up a sophisticated way of coping with the problem without making Sabbatai into an instant martyr. He thus attempted to convert Sabbatai to Islam. Almost immediately the plan worked. Curiously many of his original followers could not accept Sabbatai's mistake and resolved it in their own minds by continuing to pursue their original conviction with a somewhat muddled vigour. They also converted in their hundreds.

frantically to prolong his life by eating the stuffing from his mattress. Parentless, the remaining children were shipped from one relative to another. Around about the age of seventeen, Caligula began to sleep with his sisters. Drusilla was the first and favourite. She was about fourteen at the time that they were discovered in bed together by his great-aunt Antonia. He later had the other two, Livilla and Agrippina. Caligula regarded this incest as an exceptional experience. Years afterwards as Emperor, he asked Parsiensus Crispus, one of Rome's best known wits if he had enjoyed sex with his sisters. "Not yet . . ." came the tactful reply.

An evil shadow hung over his branches of the family tree. His character, which the Romans hoped would be influenced by his noble bloodline, was instead distilled from the poison of his upbringing. The final products of the Imperial stable were not thoroughbreds, but maggot-ridden corpses, with only the diseased and deranged surviving.

In AD 37 Tiberius finally died. In his final years he had appointed an ambitious outsider, named Macro, to the position of Captain of the guard. Macro was so desperate to ensure his future that he encouraged his wife to sleep with Caligula. It was Macro who helped Caligula to climb over the final corpses between him and the throne.

Tiberius fell seriously ill at Misenum on the Bay of Naples, not far from his beloved Capri. Macro rushed to join Caligula at his deathbed, and they removed the Imperial signet ring from Tiberius' finger. Long before he died, agents were dispatched to the outposts of the Empire to proclaim Caligula Emperor. They knew that Tiberius had made a will and that they must secure power before the contents became public. Tiberius nearly scuppered their plans by suddenly reviving and demanding his ring back, but Caligula and Macro ended his long goodbye, smothering him with his own bedclothes.

Life under Tiberius had been grey, grim and repressive. He had only been prevented from killing many more of his enemies by the influence of his popular astrologer Thrasyllus, who kept predicting a longer life for him, thus convincing him he could afford to take the murders steadily. This saved many people from certain death. Now the Romans wanted to celebrate. Only Caligula prevented them from throwing Tiberius' body into the Tiber. By the time his will was read, Caligula was already Emperor. The will actually named Caligula as joint heir along with another relative, Tiberius Gemellus. It was not a happy document for Gemellus, bequeathing him only and his family inevitable death at Caligula's hands.

In his opening speech Caligula promised co-operation and respect with the Senate, humbly casting himself as their junior. He had grown into a big, tall, balding man, with a thin neck, thin legs and thin hair. He had hollow eyes and temples, a bulbous nose and a withdrawn lower lip. He was not pretty. He had been epileptic as a boy, and was quarrelsome as an adult, and had become a haunted insomniac. The isolation and fear of his childhood had taught him the virtues of hypocrisy. He wept at Tiberius funeral. Whatever madness and revenge he had in mind he kept it under control and devoted himself to restoring the memory of his tragic, ghostly family. A little later he would appease those unquiet ghosts with rivers of blood.

His mother had games and sacrifices in her honour. He made a pilgrimage to retrieve her ashes from exile and lay them beside Augustus. Coins had her image on them. He named the month of September after his father Germanicus. The laws that the Senate had passed against the descendants of Germanicus were rescinded. This had never happened before. Not content, he bestowed titles on all surviving members of his family, and had his sisters made honorary Vestal Virgins. They were even included in the oath of Imperial allegiance; "I shall not hold myself or my children dearer than I do Gaius Caligula and his sisters".

Declaring an end to the puritan days of Tiberius, Caligula welcomed back the political exiles. An end was promised to treason trials. The files on suspects, he said had been destroyed. The games, banned by Tiberius were re-staged in spectacular fashion by Caligula; the new Temple of the Divine Augustus was dedicated with the sacrifice of four hundred bears and lions apiece. Caligula threw money about in lavish style, giving each member of the Imperial guard the equivalent of a year's income. His behaviour was extravagant and emotional; he was very much the gay, generous public figure that the people wanted, inclined to grand spontaneous gestures which warmed the heart. Early on, he awarded an ex-slave 800,000 sesterces because he heard that she had refused to inform on her former employer, even under torture. The average income was about 1,000 sesterces so this made her a multi-millionaire. Perhaps Caligula was trying to tell the Romans that he thought loyalty was a rare quality among them.

In the words of Suetonius; "So much for the prince; now for the monster".

A few months into his reign he fell very ill and nearly died. During his illness, a prominent citizen, Publius Politus, tried to prove his love for Caligula by publicly vowing that he would willingly sacrifice his life to ensure the Emperor's recovery. Not to be outdone, another, Atanius Secundus announced he would happily fight a gladiator. Recovering, Caligula generously gave them the opportunity to fulfil their hypocritical promises. Publius was dressed up in sacrificial garments and dragged through the streets by slaves, to be hurled off the Tarpeian rock and into the Tiber. Atanius, who had never held a sword, got his fight, and to the death.

He began to interpret the most innocent behaviour as veiled treason. Silanus, the father of his dead wife, suffered from seasickness and politely declined to go on a boat-trip with Caligula, who divined from this that Silanus was hoping for a ship-wreck and instantly dispatched troops to murder him. In despair, Silanus slit his own wrists.

The unlucky Tiberius Gemellus, who Tiberius had named as joint heir with Caligula, caught an unpleasant cold. In Caligula's presence, he treated himself with some cough medicine. Caligula presumed this was an antidote to poison, which demonstrated that Gemellus distrusted him. "An antidote!" he said "How can one take an antidote against Caesar?" In any case, he was sure that Gemellus had prayed for his death, and had both him and his family killed.

Macro, who had helped him to power, and been his constant companion, adviser and sycophant, went the way of all flesh, described by Caligula as ". . . the teacher of one who no longer needs to learn". As he had been sleeping with Macro's wife, he executed him for pimping.

During his illness Caligula had made Drusilla his heir. To make things more convenient, he freed her from her legal marriage and hitched her to a male lover of his, Marcus Lepidus, who became the heir-designate, though he was eventually executed for treason. Caligula was partial to both sexes. His sisters were his favourite women, but he liked others, particularly if they could be stolen. At a wedding he famously accused the bridegroom of "making love to my wife", and married the poor woman, Livia Orestilla, himself. He quickly divorced her and married Lollia Paulina, who was also the wife of another man. She lasted a few months. When he divorced her he forbade her to ever have sex again. With men, he adored the company of actors, and took several of the more famous ones as lovers, reflecting his childish addiction to the spectacle of the games and the theatre.

An invitation to Caligula's bed could not be refused, and many happily dived in, looking for influence rather than pleasure. This was highly risky. He was fond of telling them that "you'll lose this beautiful head when I decide".

He had no concept of the value of money and it is hard to grasp the mountainous scale of his extravagance. Tiberius, miserly by nature, had left nearly three billion sesterces, the equivalent of six years revenue in the state coffers. Caligula got through it in a year, throwing it at favourites. He required daily amusement, and there were constant games, races and parties. He spent ten million sesterces, the annual tribute of three provinces, on a single dinner. The various kings deposed by Tiberius were restored, and their lost revenues returned to them. One received a hundred million sesterces, a quarter of the entire Empire's annual revenue.

These were the good times. In the Summer of AD 38, Drusilla died. Caligula was too distraught to attend her funeral, at which she was accorded the highest honours ever awarded to a woman. During a period of mourning he imposed on the city, Caligula made it a capital offence to laugh in public or private. Then he disappeared from Rome, returning with wild hair and eyes to demand that his dead sister be made a Goddess. One quick-witted sycophant was given eight million sesterces for claiming he saw her ascend to heaven. The frightened Senate awarded her her own Shrines and priestesses and placed her golden image in the Senate house. It didn't avert the attentions of Caligula who told them that he had spoken to the ghost of Tiberius, who had told him: "Show no affection for them and spare none of them. For they all hate you and pray for your death, and they will murder you if they can."

Producing the secret files of Tiberius he claimed to have destroyed, he investigated the public trials of his family under Tiberius and discovered that the same senators who grovelled to him now had accused and passed sentence on his dead relatives.

The killings that followed had a richly theatrical flavour to them. Parents were forced to attend the execution of their children, and Caligula would sometimes invite them to dine with him afterwards. One senator, thrown to the lions, insisted on proclaiming his innocence. He was rescued, only for his tongue to be cut out before he was thrown back. Caligula had the limbs and bowels of another stacked in front of him. He favoured slow killings, ordering the executioner to "strike so that he may feel he is dying". The realization that he was running out of money gave added impetus to the endless treason trials. He increased his income by lopping off heads and confiscating estates. When one victim was discovered to have been bankrupt, Caligula regretfully said "he might just as well have lived". The money problem became particularly acute while he was on a trip to Lyon in Gaul. Informed that he had bankrupted the State, he sold off his Divine Sister's possessions. This proved so successful he had the contents of the Palace shipped from Rome, and proceeded to stage a series of auctions. The country's richest men were herded into these, where Caligula would compel them to buy family souvenirs at vastly inflated prices, introducing each item with a tag like "this belonged to my mother", or "Augustus got this from Anthony". He was a brilliant auctioneer, and cunningly exploited the fear of his audience. Back in Rome, he auctioned off victorious gladiators to selected purchasers. One man, who dozed off for a few moments, woke to find he had purchased thirteen gladiators at a cost of nine million sesterces.

On another occasion in Lyon, when he was gambling and running low on cash he ordered the Public Census list of Gaul to be brought to him and selected a few wealthy men from the list of inhabitants. Ordering their deaths, he gleefully pointed out to his gambling companions that "while you play here for a few denarii, I have just made a hundred and fifty million".

The Senate was so terrified that it refused to meet, and when it did, spent all its time pathetically praising Caligula in the hope that he would spare them. "Let them hate me, so long as they fear me," he said. It wasn't simply the senators or those he imagined were treasonous or whose money he wanted that died, but now anyone that disappointed or irritated him faced torture and execution. The manager of the gladiatorial shows was beaten with chains for days. Caligula refused to kill him until he began to smell too bad. Writers were burned alive for ambiguity. He was only just waking up to the possibilities offered by absolute power. At a banquet one night, he suddenly burst out laughing and told his guests that he'd just realized he could have their heads removed at a single stroke.

But arbitrary murder was not a sufficient test of his authority, and his gestures became grander, as he strove for a confrontation with Heaven. Thrasyllus the favourite Astrologer of Tiberius had apparently told him that Caligula had as much chance of becoming Emperor as he had of riding on horseback across the Gulf of Baiae. Hearing this, Caligula ordered a bridge over three miles long to be built. Ships were anchored two abreast across the bay, and a road modelled on the Appian Way laid on top of them. So many ships were required that some had to be built, and the withdrawal of others from trade caused a financial catastrophe in Rome. In a two-day festival, Caligula charged pointlessly back and forth across the bridge at the head of a group of cavalry, dressed in the armour of Alexander the Great and crowned with jewels and oak-leaves. He gave a speech in which he praised himself for building this bridge and his troops for their courage in walking on water, and declared that the calmness of the sea indicated that the Gods themselves were now afraid of him.

Invasion and conquest were other ways he could express his Imperial powers. He hadn't quite made himself a God yet, but it was clearly on the cards. He dashed North into Germany, and tried to emulate his father's deeds by taking on the Huns. Unfortunately, he couldn't find any and was forced to send his own German bodyguards across the Rhine, so that the other troops could chase after them and bring them back as enemy captives. He hid Germans who were already prisoners in bushes and trees so that he could personally find and them and force them to surrender. In moments of insecurity, he interrupted the hide-and-seek to call the Legions together and order them to Hail him Emperor.

Having subdued Germany, he now proceeded with the conquest of Britain. His unorthodox and peaceful invasion merits attention. He assembled his entire forces along the French coast, looking out across the Channel, facing the distant cliffs of Dover. Batteries of catapults and siege engines were lined up next to the troops. After an enormous wait, the troops began to embark onto ships, but were no sooner at sea than they were told to turn back. Caligula retreated to a tower, from which he demanded that a charge be sounded, and afterwards that the soldiers use their helmets and clothing to gather up seashells. Wagon-loads of these, which he described as the spoils of his victory, were returned to Rome along with a few Gauls who he dressed up and displayed as Germans and Britons.

There was nothing left for him to achieve as a mortal; he had done all that the public could expect of an Emperor. As everything was now permissible, the only way he could escape the terror of boredom was to elevate himself to Godhead.

He built new quarters on the Capitoline Hill in order to be close to his "brother", Jupiter, whom he challenged to a duel when thunder interrupted a pantomime he was watching. A whole temple was dedicated to him, and he forced his family and senators to pay ten million sesterces each for the privilege of becoming his priests. He had always enjoyed dressing up as a woman; now he dressed himself as whatever deity took his fancy. He couldn't decide which God he was; he tried out all the male ones, and then appeared as Juno, Diana and Venus. Everybody had to prostrate themselves in his presence and the living grovelled among the dead on the floors of his Palace. He made love to the moon. A provincial governor, Lucius Vitellus, encountered Caligula during one of his conversations with the divine planet. Caligula asked him if he, too, had seen the Goddess. The man saved his life by replying that "Only you Gods, Master, can see one another". He was enraged at the refusal of the Jews to worship him, and ordered his image to be placed in the Temple at Jerusalem. This almost plunged Rome into a provincial war, and he reluctantly backed down.

The God dined in splendour with his favourite horse, Incitatus, serving loaves of gold bread to his guests. Incitatus, who had a marble stall and ivory manger, was his most trusted adviser. Caligula recognized the value of his loyalty, and announced that he intended to make the horse a Consul of the Roman people, as a preparatory step to full Senatorial rank and eventual rule over the Empire. He would see how the horse shaped up to the job.

The eventual assassins were Senators, Tribunes and Prefects from the Imperial guard; all close associates of Caligula. One Tribune, Cassius Charea, had a particular grudge against Caligula. Cassius had to obtain the new password from Caligula every day, and Caligula had taken to choosing sexually explicit ones to mock him. Cassius had become a laughing stock.

The 24 January, AD 41 was the last day of the Palatine Games. The night before, Caligula announced he had a dream in which Zeus had kicked him out of Heaven. Some of the conspirators accompanied Caligula to the Games. He got bored, and left after lunch. They cornered him in a narrow, unguarded passage between the Theatre and the Palace. Charea struck the first few blows, putting Caligula on the ground. In the ensuing frenzy, he was stabbed over thirty times.

• chapter three •

IDI AMIN: MONSTER FROM THE ASHES

Years into his disastrous reign, standing knee-deep in blood and with his country in ruins around him, Idi Amin proudly announced: "Uganda is a paradise in Africa. If you have a shirt and trousers you can live in Uganda for years".

Clearly, he was mad. He was speaking of a state in which enforced self-cannibalism was being used as a means of execution. In fact, his doctor John Kibukamusakie revealed before his sudden and violent death that Amin had actually been receiving treatment for a cocktail of hypomania, bringing on rapid and wildly conflicting ideas, syphilis whose sufferers often experience grand paranoia; and schizophrenia with a dash of general paralysis of the insane thrown in. Otherwise, Idi was on fine form and had recently vowed to erect statues of his two idols, Queen Victoria and Adolf Hitler, and was pursuing his plans to recruit a bodyguard of six-foot tall, bagpipe-playing Scots. The West didn't know whether to laugh or cry when Idi Amin spoke. In the end he seemed too much of a fool to be taken seriously, but while the world laughed at his latest ludicrous pronouncement – how he had offered to send a cargo of vegetables to Britain to solve their recession or had refused to attend the Commonwealth Games unless the Queen sent a personal aircraft to fetch him complete with Scottish soldiers and a new pair of his size 13 shoes – Amin was probably indulging one of his favourite vices; crushing the genitals of selected victims with his bare hands. No doubt he was laughing too; he was famous for his sense of humour. The sound of his enormous, body-shaking mirth was the last sound thousands heard through their dying agony, and it was a noise that haunted Britain as well as Africa, the noise of a monster risen from the ashes of their Empire.

Amin's words about Uganda had an uncanny echo in them. It was the young Winston Churchill who had described Uganda as a "fairy-tale". "You climb up a ladder" he said, "and at the top there is a wonderful new world".

It did seem that way. Uganda was the pearl of Africa, the cradle of the Nile, containing the legendary mountains of the moon which rise 17,000 feet to Equatorial snowfields. The country is rich and fertile with forest, rolling plain and gentle hills. The British who arrived there late in the last century found an ancient, intelligent and cruel civilization among whom roasting and burial alive were still popular as punishments. It was also a country riven with historic tribal disputes and enmity which remain a powerful force even today. There are over forty tribes with local and family loyalties that make them far more sympathetic to their own leaders than any overall government. The ruling monarch was the cruel and despotic Kabuka Butesa I, king of the dominant Buganda tribe who, in a pronouncement which Amin would have been proud of, demanded a daughter of English royalty in return for allowing the Christian missionaries freedom to preach. But in general the British experience in Uganda was a happy one. However, when the "Wind Of Change" swept through Africa after World War II and they withdrew, they left a country which was ill-prepared for democracy. Although the hastily arranged elections in 1962 brought a Socialist Government led by Milton Obote to power, there were already allegations of corruption and worse hanging over ministers, and the tribal disputes were as violent as ever. In the uncertainty, men who had acquired great authority as loyal servants of their British rulers benefited from their head-start and tightened their grip on the reins of power. The future Army Chief of Staff, Idi Amin, was one of these. In the words of one contemporary: "He was just the type that the British liked, the type of African that they used to refer to as from the 'warrior tribes': black, big, uncouth, uneducated and willing to obey orders".

Amin's willingness to obey orders had brought him a long way. He was born in the North of Uganda, the furthest province bordering on the wastes of the Sudan, into one of the smallest tribes, the Kakwa, on 1 May 1928. His mother left her husband and fled South from the tiny mud and wattle village. She supported herself and her growing child by supplying love potions and charms, and Amin's childhood was steeped in

In 1913 Charles Dawson, a solicitor and amateur anthropologist, was digging about in a gravel pit in Sussex when he came across the skull fragments and bones of a creature which looked remarkably human. He published his findings in the *Quarterly Journal of the Geological Society of London*, claiming that, at last, here was the incontrovertible evidence for Charles Darwin's theory of evolution – he had discovered the remains of the missing link in the evolutionary chain between ape and man. It was remarkably fortunate for believers in the Empire that the earliest man just happened to be British. The reconstructed skull was named Eoanthropus Dawsoni as a tribute to the man who found it and the whole scientific world was abuzz with the news.

Meanwhile back in Piltdown, the closest village to the site of the gravel pit in which the bones were found, all sorts of things were happening. The town had become a tourist attraction and coachloads of eminent scientists were to be seen wandering around the area and checking out the site. Further evidence was found to support the original claim and the bones were given to the British Museum who were just thrilled at their own importance and sent copies of the bones to museums all over the world. Piltdown Man had a place in history.

Years later, when dating techniques had improved beyond recognition, the bones were re-examined and discovered to be not 500,000 years old, as Charles Dawson had believed, but a mere 50,000. Piltdown Man's teeth were twentieth-century and, rather more drastically, not actually human at all but those of an orang-utan.

superstition and old tribal legends. A decidedly large boy, he became a natural leader among the village children, having discovered, even at this early age, how sensitive the testicles of his play-fellows were.

In 1946 he enlisted in the King's African Rifles. He had developed quite serious military ambitions, and was very attracted by the mystique and traditions of the British Army but it took him seven years of hard graft to make Lance-Corporal even in a regiment where intelligence was not necessarily considered a virtue. Obedience and enthusiasm were preferable, and there he had his admirers. "Not much grey matter, but a splendid chap to have about," said one British officer. People liked him; he made them laugh. The Europeans thought the world of him. He showed pride in his regiment, his boots were always spotless and he excelled on the sports field. Six foot four inches tall and weighing in at his peak at twenty stone, he became heavyweight boxing champion of Uganda. Slowly he inched up the ranks as the British, faced with the problem of which Africans to make officers opted for those who, however illiterate, were at least strong and loyal. Amin was semi-literate, and could speak a little English. In spite of failing to complete military training courses in both England and Israel he was, by 1960, a lieutenant.

There is a story originating from this time which shows how simple he still was. His commanding officer, Major Graham, persuaded Amin to open a bank account. He duly deposited £10, but within a few hours had spent £2000. Swaggering through town in his uniform he had purchased new suits, a car and an indecent amount of food and drink. It was the grand behaviour of a king, a role he obviously relished. There were other stories as well, not so humorous. Rumours of atrocities committed in distant frontier villages by soldiers of the King's African Rifles, of captives trussed up and bayoneted and common to these rumours was the figure of a big, happy, laughing officer with a particular line in sadism. Someone should have seen, but it was the eve of independence and the British had other things on their minds, and besides, Lieutenant Amin seemed to get the job done.

After independence, with the British officers gone, Amin's career took off. True, some mud did stick to him, but it was curiously difficult to find anyone living to back up the allegations of cruelty and illegal gold, ivory and coffee smuggling. He was Deputy Commander of the Army when in 1966, the Prime Minister, Milton Obote, asked him for help.

Obote had tried to resolve the conflict between tribal loyalties and the legal government by appointing the traditional King, still from the large Buganda tribe to the position of President to assure the Buganda that they still exercised authority within a government which was dominated by members of other, smaller tribes. Obote himself was from the minority Langi tribe. Thus the improbably named Edward William Walugembe Luwangula Mutesa III, thirty-fifth Kabuka of Buganda, otherwise known as "King Freddie", assumed what was intended to be a largely ceremonial position. A rift rapidly developed, and when Obote tried to reduce Freddie's powers, the Buganda tribe rebelled.

Amin responded in typical style to Obote's request that he flex some muscle. He assaulted the Presidential Palace with a 122mm gun mounted on his own jeep, knocking great chunks out of the walls. In fighting, 1,500 Buganda died, and King Freddie fled to Britain where he died. Obote came to rely on Amin and his forthright approach to problems.

They say "he who sups with the devil must use a long spoon". Obote supped with Amin until 1971. Growing discontent with the government's increasing bureaucracy and corruption formed a backdrop to this unfortunate marriage, and in 1969 there was an assassination attempt on Obote. It failed and Obote survived, unlike one Brigadier Okoya who was foolish enough to doubt Amin's loyalty during the crisis. Both he and his wife mysteriously died. The relationship between Amin and Obote cooled. Obote had good cause to fear Amin, who, in turn suspected he was being squeezed out and the air was thick with rumours of Amin's impending arrest when in January 1971, Obote flew off to Singapore to attend the Commonwealth Conference. It was to prove one of the longest business trips in history; he would not be able to return for nine years. In his absence, Uganda fell victim to a man whose staggering incompetence ran a close second to his genuine pleasure in murder. Nothing that is said about Idi Amin can be worse than the truth.

The coup Amin launched on 25 January 1971 was a traditional affair. Starting at 3 a.m., the Army stormed the Parliament, the Airport (killing two priests) and the radio station. Telephones and telex lines were cut. Amin watched the proceedings from his luxurious and now heavily fortified mansion situated in Prince Charles drive on one of Kampala's seven imposing hills. It became known as The Command Post. Surrounded by tanks, it bristled with barbed wire and machine-guns.

In the aftermath of the coup, there was a strange, carnival atmosphere. The anti-Obote crowds took to the streets, breaking the curfew and hailing Major General Amin as their saviour. They were principally Buganda tribesmen who resented Obote's expulsion of their King. Amin denounced Obote as a corrupt Communist. He would ensure free elections and then return his troops to barracks, he declared to the outside world as he took to the streets and countryside, stopping looting and dispensing personal cheques to the population, which naturally earned their approval. He also freed some political prisoners and allowed the Buganda to bring the body of the dead King Freddie back for burial. One British observer wrote: "I have never encountered a more benevolent and apparently popular leader than General Amin".

But if Idi Amin was going to prepare the country for elections, he was doing so in a strange way. Within three weeks of his coup, 2,000 Army officers and men died on his orders; within three months, 10,000 civilians were slaughtered. Perhaps he thought the electoral role needed shortening.

The murder began in a systematic and initially secretive way. The prime targets were members of the Acholi and Langi tribes – the tribes of Milton Obote and other potential rivals. Obote's brother-in-law and his family were wiped out. Killer squads fostered by Amin within the Army were unleashed. When in doubt of their next victims, they simply chose names beginning with "O", as this was a common characteristic of Acholi and Langi names. The soldiers had absolute powers of arrest; the names of these new organizations were both chillingly ambiguous and hideously inappropriate: "The Public Safety Unit"; "The State Research Bureau".

Thirty-six senior officers from the unlucky tribes were summoned to Mackindye prison for "training in internal security". They were locked in cells and bayoneted at leisure.

The former Army Chief of Staff, Brigadier Hussein Suleiman, whose appointment Amin had once deeply resented was arrested and beaten slowly to death with rifle butts and wrenches. According to some, his head subsequently disappeared, only to reappear deep frozen, in the hands of a marauding Amin at an infamous dinner party a year later. Suleiman's was possibly the first head in a collection that became so extensive it required its own refrigerator.

At Mbarara and Jinja barracks the officer corps were crushed by tanks as they mustered on the parade grounds to salute Amin. Elsewhere, others were apparently herded into rooms and grenades lobbed through the windows. In the prisons and cells of Mackindye, Naguru and Nakasero limbs were smashed with sledgehammers and car-axles, and prisoners were compelled to kill each other with 16lb sledgehammers in the vain hope that they would be spared. Then the hammers were given to others to whom the same promise was made, and the chain killings went on until the overflowing human jam of eyes, teeth and bone tissue was shovelled onto trucks like garden refuse and dumped in the rivers, lakes and forests outside Kampala. When the lights went out in Kampala, the story goes, the locals knew that forty miles away at the Owen Falls Dam on Lake Victoria, the hydro-electric generators were once again clogged with bodies.

Whilst Amin pursued his genocidal course, his government was officially recognized by Britain amongst others, and Idi launched himself upon the international scene with all the charming naivety of a debutante. He was finally playing the Imperial role he fancied for himself. Dressed in full military attire with a museum's worth of medals pinned to his chest, he visited Israel and England. Israel took Amin seriously. Here was a friendly Moslem leader of an African country; through Uganda, Israel could have access to the strategically important Sudan. The Israelis were a bit perturbed by their conversations with Amin, one of which went something like this:

"I would like twenty-four Phantom Jets."

"Why?"

"I need to bomb Tanzania".

It was that much-admired straight-forwardness again; Amin's ambitions were obviously not limited to his own country. When the military hardware he demanded from Israel was not forthcoming his attitude changed. In 1972, after Palestinian terrorists murdered Israeli athletes at the Olympic Games in Munich he sent an extraordinary telegram to Kurt Waldheim, the United Nations Secretary General, and Golda Meir, the Israeli Prime Minister, in which he informed them:

"Germany is the right place, where, when Hitler was Prime Minister and Supreme Commander, he burnt over six million Jews. This is because Hitler and all the German people know that the Israelis are not people who are working in the interest of the people of the world and that is why they burned the Israelis alive with gas in the soil of Germany . . ."

This was just one of the many shocking and incoherent messages he was liable to dash off to world leaders when the mood took him, sometimes giving advice on their political and personal problems, at others simply taunting them. The Prime Minister and the Queen of Britain were favourite targets. Whilst Amin adored and aped the style of the colonial Empire, he took a special delight in tormenting England. On his inauguration as President he had his huge body carried aloft by Europeans to symbolize "the white man's burden", and announced that he was "the Conqueror of the British Empire".

The highlights of his first official visit to Britain, where he was preferred to the left-wing Obote, included dinners and parties with Conservative Prime Minister Edward Heath and the Queen and Prince Philip. He also went to Scotland, where he acquired his fetish for things Scottish and where the official reception obviously went to his head; a few years later he decided that the Scots wanted him as King, an honour he would be happy to accept. Amin also made a familiar request for arms and Harrier Jets on the pretext that he simply had to bomb South Africa, Tanzania, and Sudan. The British began, too late, to realize what a monster they had helped give birth to.

Back at home the process of good government was made difficult by a shortage of living Cabinet Ministers. Uganda was not an impoverished country, but the incompetence of Amin soon began to triumph. He had no economic policies, apart from extortion, and his speech at the inaugural meeting of the so-called Uganda Development Bank showed his unorthodox approach to finance: "Every one hundred years, God appoints one person to be very powerful in the world to follow what the Prophet directed. When I dream, then things are put into practice . . ."

The dreams were another problem; Amin was in touch with God and Uganda was now being ruled by his visions. "The problem takes on fantastic dimensions", said one Minister. "He cannot concentrate . . . he does not read . . . he cannot write. He has to have recourse to people of his own intelligence and calibre – the illiterate Army officers who rule the country . . ."

Most of the army officers were now former drivers and cooks who had become Majors and Colonels. Military spending went up five hundred per cent. Inflation soared to seven hundred per cent; a bar of soap cost two weeks wages. Amin's solution was to print more money, whilst annexing the foreign reserves for his own use. Special flights to London and Paris took Amin's cronies, their pockets stuffed with Uganda's dwindling cash, on spending sprees for luxury goods. The killing of politicians and civilians continued at a breathtaking pace. The Church was another target. The Archbishop of Uganda died in a "motor accident" along with two Government Ministers, and Amin personally shot Archbishop Luwun, telling his aides that he had "lost his temper". The killer squads had complete control of the country. When not eliminating suspected opponents they were simply killing people for their possessions; they had to be paid somehow. One ingenious method was to take people off the streets, murder them and then charge their relatives for the recovery of their mutilated corpses. So much to do, so little time; it was hardly surprising they fell behind with the work. In one incident a former civil servant, Frank Kalimazo, was attending a wedding when he heard that his "disappearance" had been announced over the radio. He was part of the backlog.

News of this hell-on-earth did reach the outside world, but so staggering was it that it was only slowly believed. It was difficult to confirm. Two young American journalists, Nicholas Stroh and Robert Siedle, who, early in the regime had begun to ask questions about the army massacres were gunned down at Mbarara barracks. Their murderer, Major Juma Aigu, a former taxi driver, reputedly drove about Kampala in Stroh's Volkswagen. Refugees and exiles began to tell terrible stories. Education Minister Edward Rugomayo escaped and detailed a lengthy list of atrocities including slow deaths by bleeding and amputation, genital mutilation, people being fed on their own flesh until they died, reproductive organs being set on fire, electric shocks and the gouging out of eyes. Some of the equipment being used for this was imported from Britain by Amin's close advisor, the "Mephistopheles of Uganda", English exile Bob Astles, Head of the "Anti-Corruption Unit". Astles suffered the fate he had condemned so many to. His decomposing body turning up in the grounds of a hotel after Amin's eventual fall. It was dangerous to take gifts from Amin. Bob McKenzie, another white ally and former Kenyan Minister who quarrelled with Amin flew out of Kampala clutching a kiss-and-make-up gift from him, a lion's head trophy. It exploded mid-air.

Amin's home life was no less remarkable. He had a harem of wives and twenty-five to thirty-five children. It is alleged that when Kay, one of his wives (whom he had recently divorced) died in a botched abortion attempt, he ordered the surgeons to cut her up and reassemble her with her legs on her shoulders and arms on her pelvis as a warning to the others. On the testimony of his housekeeper it is known that he kept the head of Jesse Gitta, the former husband of his wife Sarah in the fridge in his "Botanical Room". She discovered it after her marriage, along with the head of Ruth Kobusinje, a girl he was sleeping with and suspected of infidelity. One nurse describes decapitating six bodies and sending the shaved, preserved heads to Amin. Nobody knows what he wanted them for, which is odd, as he usually left nothing to the imagination. Henry Kyemba, the Ugandan health minister confessed from the safety of foreign exile: "I am ashamed to admit that on several occasions he told me quite proudly that he had eaten the organs or flesh of his human victims".

Back overseas Amin switched his loyalty from Israel to Libya, supporting the anti-Jewish and anti-Western policies of the eccentric Gaddaffi in return for military support and cash most of which he stashed away for his own use, buying three villas outside Libya's capital, Tripoli. Gaddaffi was under the mistaken impression that Uganda was a Moslem country, Amin assured him that eighty per cent of the population were followers of Islam; it was actually nearer fifteen per cent. To please Libya he expelled the Israeli engineers who built his Entebbe airport and who were working on vital dam projects. He now saw himself as the champion of the Third World against the Imperial West. In spite of his risible offers to Britain and America to sort out Northern Ireland and Vietnam for them in his own brutal way, he styled himself the opponent of colonialism, which won him support among Africans even as he murdered them, so eager were they for a champion against the West; at least, they thought, he has their attention. "I consider myself the most powerful figure in the world," he said. "I am the greatest politician in the world. I have shaken the British so much I deserve a degree in philosophy". He confiscated British property, but simultaneously started the "Save Britain Fund", to "help Britain through its economic crisis". He fired off another telegram to Edward Heath saying that Britain's state was a disgrace to the rest of the Commonwealth, but offering to organize a whipround amongst Uganda's friends, "If you will let me know the exact position of the mess". How they must have hated those patronising telegrams.

Amin's neighbours in Tanzania and the Sudan were not spared his sabre-rattling. He made claims on their territory, and it was only with great effort that Tanzania could restrain itself. As usual, Idi would threaten one moment and the next he would fire off a conciliatory telegram. "I love you very much," he wrote to President Julius Nyerere, "And if you were a woman I would consider marrying you". It was Nyerere who was to eventually bring Amin down.

There were two remarkable events which put this grinning Satan in the centre of the international limelight. The first was the expulsion of the Asians, and the second was the Entebbe hijack.

In a move which dealt a death-blow to the economy, Amin expelled the entire Asian population of Uganda, who ran about eighty per cent of the country's small businesses. "Asians came to Uganda to build the railway. The railway is finished. They must leave now," he pronounced, having once again been counselled by the voice of God. The Asians were told they could take their possessions but were habitually stripped of everything, even their bedding and watches. Most of the Asians had to seek asylum in Britain. When Amin thought that the British High Commission were not processing the Asians fast enough, he kidnapped one hundred British Citizens and held them until the Commission worked a twelve hour day and hired more premises and staff. The businesses were handed over to his tribal henchmen. The shelves were soon empty, the shops closed; Uganda became a desert; people were near starvation, but Amin, still dwelling in his fantasy world, offered help simultaneously to thirty-two Third World countries afflicted by drought. As far as he was concerned, he could still write cheques, so there was no problem.

The Entebbe affair began with the hijacking of an Air France airliner carrying three hundred passengers from Tel Aviv to Paris by Palestinian terrorists. Amin had allied himself with the Palestinian Liberation Organization as part of his anti-Jewish, anti-Western bravado, and the airliner was allowed to land at Entebbe Airport, from where the hijackers issued a string of demands. The passengers were to die in forty-eight hours unless fifty-three terrorists imprisoned in Israel and Europe were released. The eyes, and cameras of the world, were turned on Uganda. Amin revelled in it; he was instrumental in holding the West to ransom. An extension of the deadline was negotiated and the non-Jewish passengers released. The hostages were taken to the Airport terminal. Amin passed among them, smiling benevolently. One old lady, Dora Bloch, a joint British and Israeli citizen, choked on her food, and had to be taken to Kampala's Hospital. She missed her chance to live, as while she was away, Israeli commandos staged a spectacular rescue. Landing at the airport, they routed Amin's soldiers and destroyed a flight of Mig Fighters that were lined up. One hour and sixteen minutes later they flew out of Entebbe leaving all seven kidnappers and twenty Ugandan troops dead and taking with them all the hostages. All, that is, except Dora Bloch.

When Amin heard, he was paralysed with fury. His hour of glory had turned into deep humiliation. The first victim of his anger was the little old lady, Dora Bloch. She was taken from the hospital and shot. Her body was dumped on wasteland on the outskirts of Kampala. It was made a capital offence to talk about the affair. Two Kampala girls vanished after joking that their boyfriends were "strong as Israeli Pilots". Amin sent Israel yet another insane telegram threatening to attack them unless compensation was paid for his destroyed aircraft – he was particularly upset about these – as well as "expenses" he had incurred "entertaining" the hostages.

It had to end. People find it astonishing that he lasted so long, but the West was reluctant to intervene in a country that had only recently gained its independence; besides, for the British, he was an embarrassment, and they preferred to try and ignore him in the hope that, like the bogeyman of nightmares, he would just disappear. If they intervened, they would be accused of colonialism and risked turning Amin into a hero. They couldn't win, and he rubbed their noses in it. The other African states were reluctant to become publicly involved in possibly bloody fighting amongst themselves; they too hoped he would vanish. Libya still actively supported him. Within his country, Amin was protected by the tribal henchmen he had elevated and whose lifestyles were dependent on him. He was surrounded by military hardware. He carried a loaded, cocked gun at all times. It was advisable not to make any sudden movements in his presence. That was how he survived; by exploiting the fears of others. He may have been incoherent, clinically mad, illiterate and savage, but he had an animal cunning which told him which parts of a person, in mind as well as body, hurt when he squeezed them. Moreover, there was nothing complicated about his needs, which made them all the easier to supply and protect; he got the same pleasure from murder as from eating and often combined the two for convenience and satisfaction.

In Idi Amin, primitive tribal brutality was mixed with a fixation for the military trappings of Empire to hideously comic effect. The bully-boy qualities that made him so useful to the British rulers of Uganda as a servant came to horrible fruition when he became the master; in serving their interests they had put the means to power in the hands of a man who was an unmitigated disaster for the whole continent of Africa. It was a tragic legacy; it was one of history's worst jokes.

In October 1978, Amin carried out one of his long-standing threats and sent 3,000 troops into Tanzania. They raped and massacred their way through the countryside. Amin announced he had conquered Tanzania. When President Julius Nyerere retaliated and Amin's troops were driven back, Amin frantically suggested that he and Nyerere settle the war with a boxing match refereed by Mohammed Ali. The Tanzanians continued to advance and by the Spring of 1979 they were on the outskirts of Kampala. In vain Amin called for a last stand at Jinja; the troops didn't show up and neither did Amin; he had already fled to hide behind the skirts of his ally, Colonel Gaddafi in Libya. He spent the next few years there until even Gadaffi could take no more and kicked him out. There were rumours of some unpleasant business involving Amin and Gadaffi's fourteen-year-old daughter. He made his way through a series of African states, all of which have spat him out, and was last sighted in the Ivory Coast.

In Uganda, when Tanzanian troops entered the office of the Head of the State Research Bureau, they found a framed epigram. It read:

"No wisdom is greater than kindness. Those who build their success on others' misfortunes are never successful".

It was unlikely that the previous occupant had been able to read. In any case, it was a most inappropriate moral all round.

chapter four

GENGHIS KHAN: SACKER OF CITIES

There can be no greater testament to the enduring terror of Genghis Khan than the title he is still known by among the Muslim writers of Persian nations whose cultured Empire he destroyed seven centuries ago. They call him "The Accursed". Many of the great cities he razed in China, the Middle East and the Caucasus have never recovered their former status; some have never been rebuilt, and their ruins still retain an eerie, desolate silence. It is the kind of oppressive atmosphere that hangs over places where, at one time, all living creatures have been systematically slaughtered.

It was not that he took any pleasure in the business. The Mongols were strictly pragmatic about the slaughter. As they advanced, they simultaneously wished to secure themselves against any uprising behind them. Their army was always outnumbered by the population, so they were simply re-adjusting the odds. There was an obvious psychological spin-off from this, in that the terror the news of these tactics inflicted on the next city understandably reduced the will of the defenders. Frequently they offered to surrender, so long as the population might be spared. Often, the Mongols would agree, and then kill them anyway. They did not regard this as treachery, just good military sense; they shouldn't look a gift-horse in the mouth.

After they took a city, either by siege or subterfuge, there was a fairly standard menu of behaviour. First, they plundered in a very democratic fashion and drove the population outside the city walls, where they would be assembled and men and women divided. Of the men, those with useful skills might be enslaved and returned to Mongolia. Other young men would be taken for

In 1938 Orson Welles, with two colleagues, created a production company for radio plays called Mercury Theatre. They had a regular slot on Sunday evenings on CBS radio but were handicapped in their grasp for media fame and fortune by the fact that no-one listened to it.

Welles therefore decided to pull out all the stops and go for the big one. He would dramatise a version of H.G. Wells' *The War of the Worlds* and the team would endeavour to make it as realistic as possible. It would all be terrifically dramatic and after five days of rehearsals everyone was rearing to go. Assisted by the fact that there was, for a change, nothing good on the other channel, the War of the Worlds had an unusually high tune-in rating. Straight after the weather report, the show was introduced by a linkman stating:

"Ladies and gentlemen, I have a grave announcement to make. The strange object which fell at Grovers Mill, New Jersey, earlier this evening was not a meteorite. Incredible as it seems, it contained strange beings who are believed to be the vanguard of an army from the planet Mars."

The production continued in what the actors considered to be a highly ear-catching way with no straight narrative but a series of up-to-the-minute bulletins about hideous, scaly creatures from Mars running amok all over the exotic surroundings of New Jersey. Another announcer cut in to urge the people of the world not to panic but, as it happened, thousands of citizens all over America were currently being slaughtered by the deathly force of ray guns. The climax of the play was an announcer apparently screaming that Manhattan had been taken over by aliens and then trailing off into an anguished death rattle and then silence.

The actors were not wrong. Their thespian skills were so convincing that by the time the production ended, thousands of people had already fled their homes and were heading for that traditional haven from landing Martians, the hills. In New Jersey, where panic was at its greatest, whole families packed into their station wagons with wet towels over their heads, since they assumed this would save them from the deadly effects of Martian poison gas.

The only people who were unaware of the national State of Emergency were those inside the CBS studio who all, shattered after a hard day's serious acting, went straight home to bed. Orson Welles awoke the next day to find his name spread like mud over the front pages of all the national newspapers. Dozens of people brought cases for shock against CBS but none of them were pursued. Mercury Theatre would never be "that programme on the other channel" again and Orson Welles, who was only twenty-four at the time, was instantaneously a star.

military purposes. The Mongols used these as unarmed cannon-fodder in their assaults, herding several thousand in front of them as they swept down on their enemy, as if stampeding cattle. The remainder would be killed, generally decapitated, and their heads stacked in neat pyramids. The women were, without exception, raped. A few might be taken for slaves or concubines, and the rest also killed. If an example was to be made of a particular city, then no-one would be spared, for any purpose. The inhabitants might be driven out through a gate and decapitated as they walked through it, in a sort of ghastly conveyor belt. Sometimes each Mongol soldier was designated a number of executions to perform, which on occasion was as high as five hundred per man. This could take days to perform, even with the famous stamina of the Mongol troops, particularly if the order was given that no living thing was to escape. Even dogs and cats were then executed and babies in the womb were run through with swords. This was all performed in a highly disciplined fashion. Finally the city would be set on fire and afterwards flooded where conditions permitted. The prospect of all this happening produced some fairly drastic reactions. At Peking, 60,000 women threw themselves off the city walls rather than face tea with the Mongols; when the siege left them starving, the whole population resorted to cannibalism rather than surrender.

The advance of the Mongol hordes is one of the most signifi-cant historical events of the last thousand years. Quite apart from the destruction they wrought, they completely altered the distribution of people, wealth and disease within the known world. But the home life of Genghis Khan, whose name is legendary, is something of a mystery.

He was born plain Temuchin on the banks of the Onon river in 1162. Mongolia, his homeland, is the vast, high, plateau between the forests of Siberia in the North and the wastes of the Gobi desert in the South. At the time of his birth, the Mongols were a collection of nomadic tribes, with occasional, but unreliable alliances. Among them, his father was leader of a sizable group of clans. They lived on the move, in tents, and had no conception of organized town life. In fact, they could see no virtue in society as understood by others, which partly explains their lack of remorse in destroying all those they overran. Temuchin's father, a chieftain of the Borjigid clan named Yesukai, died when he was aged nine. He had been returning from arranging the betrothal of his young son to Borte, an equally young wife, when he was poisoned by some Tartars.

It was a Mongol tradition that a new-born be named after the most important event that occurred immediately before the birth, and hence Temuchin was appropriately named after a chieftain that Yesukai had killed shortly before his son's arrival.

In his new-born baby's hand Yesukai had observed a stone the colour of coagulated blood, a powerful omen of the infant's potential greatness. The Mongols were a superstitious race. They had no organized, public religion, but believed all sorts of shamanism, oracles, magic and images. There was also one overall God, Tengri. The Mongols regarded the tops of mountains and the origins of springs as sacred to these higher powers, and even revered the spirit of water. It was considered sacrilege to wash clothes, cooking utensils or bodies in water, with devastating consequences to personal hygiene, which did not exist. They were a ripe, smelly bunch, capable of enduring the most unimaginable hardships in temperatures as low as −42, where the encrusted dirt helped to provide protection against the deadly cold. In their own myths, they were the offspring of a blue wolf.

The early life of Temuchin was spent in struggle and poverty. His father's death had broken up the clan alliance, with many tribes refusing to swear allegiance to the boy. According to Mongol legend, he began his rise to power with only two arrows to his name. His mother, Ho'elun, a tough and canny woman succeeded in holding some allies together, and he also received protection from a former blood-brother of his father. His mother's council saved his life on a number of occasions. The Mongols were polygamous but women were also regarded as wise companions, who wielded considerable influence through their advice which was frequently sought. For thirty years he waged an unceasing war against the neighbouring tribes and the former allies of his father, until in 1206, he felt strong enough to call himself Ruler of an Empire, a title which was confirmed by his official election by representatives of the now subdued and loyal followers. The many strongholds, hiding places and battle-grounds of these early years became sacred places to the Mongols, who conferred on him the name Genghis Khan, meaning "Perfect Warrior".

After all these years of warring, Genghis Khan had amassed considerable military expertise, and, as early explorers noted, there was a remarkable discipline among his troops. Discipline was a feature of the Mongol world that evolved under him. Although frequent drunkenness on the obligatory fermented mare's milk was a traditional and substantial part of life, there was little serious quarrelling or crime among the Mongols themselves, and they reserved murder for their enemies. Loyalty was much valued, with oaths sealed by the drinking of blood, and the ceremonial slaughter of horses. The vast and impeccably co-ordinated military operations that Genghis Khan now undertook depended upon skills that were perfected in the huge hunting expeditions the clans would make. The Mongols were principally meat-eaters, and happy to chew on anything with a decent calorific value, be it rabbit, rat or wolf. They had a particular penchant for horse, but as all their army was cavalry and their way of life depended on their tough, stocky horses, they only ate them in dire circumstances. The meat from these was so tough, they would stick it under a saddle and ride it until it was tender, marinating it between their thighs.

These huge hunts could take one to three months. The entire Mongol army might be deployed on them. This army, at its greatest strength and including the various auxiliaries, slaves and reserves, was probably never greater than 120,000. The entire population of the region was unlikely to have been more than 500,000. On a great hunt, the army would cordon off an area occupying thousands of miles, and slowly but thoroughly begin to herd every living creature, over hill and through forest, towards a central killing ground no bigger than nine miles. As described by witnesses, the scene was mind-boggling. Lions, wolves, bears, deer, yak, asses and hares were driven together in their hundreds of thousands, killing, mating, panicking, eating and sleeping. An apocalyptic picture, accompanied by the discordant, awful shriek of the frightened animals. No killing whatsoever was allowed until Genghis Khan arrived at the scene with his entourage and wives and took up a good position from which to overlook the entertainment. After he gave permission for the hunting to begin, the chase, slaughter and feeding would go on for days.

The first object of this new military power was the Jurchen Dynasty of China, who considered themselves the masters of the Mongolian Steppes. From 1206–1211, Genghis Khan punched a hole through the neighbouring Tangut territory towards China, about which he accumulated as much military intelligence as possible. He only had one enemy on the Mongolian Steppes to worry about, Kushlek the Naiman Khan, who had fled after a sizable defeat to the Irtysh river, where Genghis routed him again, and from there to the Khitian Tartars, seeking support from neighbouring Persia. Kushlek would remain a thorn in his side. The operation against China was highly successful, with a string of victories encouraging desertion to the Mongolians and the terror that went in advance of them persuading garrisons to surrender without a fight. The army, split into three prongs, moved with phenomenal speed. By 1214, Genghis Khan was able to say to the Jurchen Emperor: "By the decree of heaven you are now as weak as I am strong, but I am willing to retire from my conquests . . . as a condition of my doing so it will be necessary for you to distribute largesse to my officers and men to appease their fierce hostility".

Appease them he did, with 3,000 horses, two royal princesses, five hundred young men and girls, a herd of white camels and as much swag as they could carry. Genghis Khan went back to Mongolia, leaving an army to mop up. However, the Jurchen were not completely subdued, and the war against the Chinese would go on after his death.

Back in Mongolia, Genghis Khan came up against his old friend, Kushlek. He had ingratiated himself with his hosts, the Khitian Tartars and then, with consummate treachery, enlisted the help of the Persian neighbours to usurp the existing ruler, who was forced to abdicate in favour of his former guest. Kushlek then measured up to Genghis Khan once more, who again defeated him, and this time managed to put him to death. As Kushlek counted as nobility, and it was forbidden to shed the blood of nobles, Genghis had him suffocated under a pile of carpets. The Mongols had a number of ingenious ways to circumvent this regulation, and at other times nobles were strangled with a bow-string, or buried alive.

Kushlek's ill-gotten kingdom now became part of the Mongol Empire. A curious consequence of this was that, for a brief time, Genghis Khan became something of an Islamic hero. Kushlek had treated the Moslems of his hijacked realm badly, but Genghis Khan and his Mongol hordes were tolerant in matters of religion, and when the dial was not set to "massacre", the Mongols could be very easy-going generally, preferring parties to pogroms. His position as saviour of the Moslem world did not last long.

His territories now extended up to the border with the Khwarizm Empire of Eastern Iran/Iraq. Genghis was eager to establish trade links with other nations; trade was also another means of diplomatic dialogue. After he had encountered merchants from the Khwarizm Empire, he sent a Mongol delegation back to the Khwarizm ruler, Shah Mohammed, with a message of intended peace couched in evocative terms:

"We have . . . dispatched to your country a group of merchants in order that they may acquire the wondrous wares of those regions; and that henceforth the abscess of evil thoughts may be lanced by the improvement of relations and agreement between us and the pus of sedition and rebellion removed . . ."

If the delegation bearing this message had reached Mohammed, who was keen on peace and trade, the Mongol advance might have stopped right there, instead of coming to the very doors of Europe, and several million people would probably have lived. Unfortunately, then followed one of the more significant mistakes in history.

At the border town of Otrar, the governor was a rather stupid, suspicious and greedy man named Inaljuk. He was ignorant of any proposed dialogue between Mohammed and the Mongols, and didn't bother to check the official position with Mohammed before massacring the delegation on the grounds that they were spies and seizing their goods.

Genghis Khan demanded satisfaction, which Mohammed was too proud to concede, sending the Mongol envoys back minus their beards. What began as a punitive expedition by the Mongols soon turned into a Blitzkrieg invasion which took them through Khwarizm into Armenia and Russia, capturing almost the entire Middle East.

The Mongols attacked with four armies under the command of Genghis Khan's various sons and himself. Mohammed faced them with an army of 400,000, and quickly lost 160,000 of these in a spectacular rout. The Mongol's capacity to co-ordinate vast, tactical troop movements on several simultaneous fronts and proceed according to minutely devised plans was simply too sophisticated for the Moslem forces, who favoured the open, pitched battle. In addition, the Mongols had picked up a whole new range of siege machinery in their Chinese wars, and now put these to good use as city after city fell to them. Otrar fell, then Khojent, Tashkent and Nur. Bokhara, "The City of Science", was utterly destroyed, and Merv, one of the legendary jewels of Moslem civilization and home of the "1001 Nights of Arabia" was burned to the ground. Merv surrendered after making one of those unwise bargains with the Mongols and 700,000 people were killed. These were only some of the cities that were obliterated in the Mongol advance. The populous centre of Herat was spared initially.

Mohammed died of pleurisy, much regretting his earlier pride. His son, the gallant Jelaliddin, took up the fruitless battle against Genghis Khan, who pursued him relentlessly, whilst developing a healthy admiration for his courage. In 1221, Jelaliddin raised enough support to start a serious uprising, but after bitter fighting the Persian forces were defeated and Jelaliddin only escaped by jumping twenty foot into a river on his horse, which impressed Genghis considerably. Jelaliddin escaped to Delhi, out of the Mongol's reach, and Genghis had to console himself with ravaging the Asian provinces of Peshawar and Lahore.

In the meantime, one or two cities which had initially co-operated to avoid destruction, rebelled. Herat was one of these, and it is here that 1,600,000 are recorded as having been killed in methodical executions lasting a week. At Nishapur, where one of his favourite commanders was killed, Genghis Khan decreed: "That the town be laid waste, that the site be ploughed upon and that in the exaction of vengeance not even cats and dogs should be left alive . . ."

By 1222, the Mongols, conquerors of China and the Middle East, had advanced through Astrakhan to the Don River, where the Russians stood, dismayed at this strange, invincible enemy.

The mobility, toughness and discipline of the Mongol army was a new phenomenon. The Mongols were stocky troops, and their army was exclusively cavalry. Each man had at least one spare mount, often three or four of the squat strong horses that roamed the Mongolian steppes. The soldier wore a fur cap with protective ear pieces for casual wear, and a leather and metal helmet for combat. On his horse he carried a vast array of tools and weapons; two bows, and several quivers of arrows, a lance with a hook on it for pulling people off horses, an axe, a lasso, sharpening stone, kettle and a few emergency rations. These consisted of about ten pounds of curdled milk dried in the sun. When required, about half a pound was dissolved with enough water to make a foul smelling, cheesy syrup. The men literally lived on their horses, and could happily sleep in the saddle. The horse also enabled them to cross seemingly impassable rivers, as they would float across on a bundle of possessions, holding onto the tail of their mount. The Mongol cavalryman could go for several days without a cooked meal, and if necessary would open up a vein in the neck of his horse and suck some of the blood, afterwards closing up the wound. His proficiency with bow and arrow was such that he could hit a man at 200–400 metres.

The psychology of inducing terror was an important part of the Mongolian war-plan. In this, the massacres, and rumours of massacres played their part. Although their army was generally smaller than the opposing forces, they deliberately built up the illusion of a vast "horde". The horses helped with this, and they would often mount dummies on their spare horses to give the impression that their army was three or four times its actual size. At night, each soldier lit several torches; from the walls of a besieged city, these myriad, misleading pin-pricks of flame must have been demoralizing evidence of their army's numbers.

They had another secret weapon; their total lack of hygiene. The Mongol hordes stank to high heaven; their approach could be smelled miles away, as they advanced in terrifying, completely, controlled silence. And then, in attack, the stench of the great, unwashed Mongol hordes and their horses was both so potent and alien that defenders became paralysed with nausea and fear.

It was this enemy that the Russians faced. The Mongols sent envoys, and the Russians made the fatal mistake of killing them, thus precipitating a conflict in which the Mongols rampaged throughout Bulgaria, and even penetrated as far North as Novgorod, after which they returned, stuffed with booty to Mongolia. It seems that the basis of the nation's economy was loot from their expeditions.

Having given the Europeans a taste of things to come in future years, Genghis Khan turned his attention once more to China, and particularly its Southern regions which still eluded him. Along with the booty, he had acquired a growing appreciation for the benefits of education from the Chinese, and determined that, illiterate though he was, his sons should be able to read and write. He had splendid sons who all distinguished themselves in the massacres of his military campaigns, but were also noted for wildness and alcoholism even among a nation of serious drinkers. Under Genghis Khan and with the Chinese influence, Mongol society became a closer-knit structure, with a distinct aristocracy, the "Golden Family", and a strict code of laws, the Yasa. Genghis Khan became interested in Chinese mysticism, and heard about a learned Taoist monk, Ch'ang-Ch'un, renowned for his knowledge of Taoist alchemy which pursued the elixir of life. Genghis Khan, mistaking the pursuit of the philosophic idea as indication of the elixir's actual existence, became convinced that this man might know where he could find the philosopher's stone that would confer immortality on him. With this, he intended to subjugate the heavenly powers to his will. He ordered the monk to be fetched. It was a journey of 3,108 miles and well over a year before they actually met. When they did, and Genghis Khan asked the monk where the means to immortality lay, he was forced to reply that "There are many means of prolonging life, but no medicine of immortality". Surprisingly, Genghis Khan although naturally disappointed, thanked the monk courteously for his honesty, and consulted with him about Taoist philosophy for several days. After the monk's departure, they maintained contact until death came for the Perfect Warrior in 1227.

Campaigning in Southern China, he derived from the conjunction of the planets that evil awaited him, and turned homewards. At the Si-Kiang river in Kansuh he fell ill and died. He had named his son Ogatai as his successor, but until he was securely enthroned, news of Genghis Khan's death was savagely suppressed to prevent instability. Any witnesses of the procession of his body back to Mongolia were executed, including many casual travellers. In keeping with Mongolian custom, the location of his tomb was kept secret, and the slaves who carried his body were killed. Horses were stampeded over the place of burial to remove all traces of his interment . . . The Mongolian Emperors have no burial mounds, and no-one will ever disturb the resting place of the "Conqueror of the World".

chapter five

NICOLAE CEAUCESCU: A FAMILY AFFAIR

Rumania is a country where fact and fiction, history and horror-story are freely mixed. The vampires and ghouls of European legend stalk the wilds of Transylvania. Its inhabitants have always been able to describe their present experiences in terms of their mythic past. For many of them, Nicolae Ceaucescu was a reincarnation of that other great Romanian tyrant, Vlad Dracul, called "The Impaler", popularly thought to be one of the sources for Bram Stoker's "Dracula".

Nicolae Ceaucescu was born on 26 January 1918 in a two-room peasants cottage in Scornicesti, an unspectacular village a hundred miles or so from Bucharest. He was one of ten children. His mother was a resolute Christian and illiterate, his father a celebrated drunk and bully. The young Nicolae was distinguished by an appalling stutter. An early convert to Communism, it is said that he learned to regurgitate vast amount of Party dogma by heart to prove his conquest of this impediment. Unfortunately, the stutter remained conspicuous and was secretly much mocked to the end.

The subsequent re-writing of history for propaganda purposes has drawn a risible picture of his early years, full of idealized rosy-cheeked and barefoot peasants, oppressed but cheerfully socialist. Rebuilt, retimbered, whitewashed and spread with suitably working-class straw, his birthplace was opened to the public as a shrine after his ascension to power. There is scarcely a document relating to Ceaucescu's life which has not been altered or simply faked and inserted into the files years afterwards. This mania for tampering with the past extended to the most petty incidents. Photographs of Ceaucescu had to be re-touched to remove any unsightly wrinkles before they were used in publications. The work was dreadfully done, giving the impression that his face had been sand-blasted. In a photograph that appeared in the official newspaper Scienteia in 1989, Ceaucescu was seen posing happily with Zhikov the Bulgarian leader, obviously unaware that he had grown a third hand. In the original photograph, Zhikov was holding a hat. It was thought necessary that Ceaucescu should also have a hat, so one was painted in, and a hand added to hold it. The official artist had forgotten to amputate one of the original limbs.

During World War II under the effective rule of the fascist General Ion Ionescu, Rumania actively supported Germany, particularly after the invasion of Russia. Ceaucescu, who had met the future leader of the Rumanian Communist party, Gheorghiu-Dej, in jail, worked his way up through the junior ranks of the outlawed Party. In 1944 in a coup that was afterwards portrayed as a great Communist uprising, King Michael ousted Ion Antonescu, restored democracy and pulled Rumania out of the war. A coalition government of which the Communists were part, gave them a back door to power. Ceaucescu, recently made Secretary General of the Communist Youth Movement, was off romancing with his bride Elena and took no part in these dramatic proceedings.

Unknown to the Rumanians, their fate was being simultaneously decided at Yalta, where Churchill and Stalin sat down to carve up the wreckage of post-war Europe. With a legendary stroke of the pen, the Russians were given a large chunk of the civilized world, including ninety per cent influence in Rumania, and virtual occupation rapidly followed. Now the Communists became the ruling party.

In the years that followed the fascists were replaced by the Securitate and Russian troops. Opposition was savagely suppressed with liberal use of the cosh and the lie. Democrats were branded as nazis, condemned by their own confessions extracted under torture. In the General Election of 1946 the Rumanians overwhelmingly rejected their Communist rulers. Suppressing the results, Gheorghiu-Dej branded the opposition "fascist traitors" and put their leaders on trial. He abolished the popular Nation Peasants Party and King Michael was forced to abdicate at gunpoint, under the threat that if he didn't go, the Communists would start a civil war. Open season was now declared on the opposition. Between 1945–1955, 280,000 members of the National Peasants Party were arrested, and jailed for a total of 900,000 years. In prison seventy-two per cent of them died of principally unnatural causes.

Ceaucescu did very well out of all this. In 1945, there was a slight set-back when he was fired because he fell out with Moscow's Communist representative, who thought him backward and dim. He bounced back as a dubiously elected deputy to the Rumanian Parliament after the fraudulent 1946 elections and by 1948 he had reached the dizzy heights of Deputy Minister for Agriculture. He took to wearing a badly fitting general's uniform. His passionate nationalism made him popular with the other Rumanian Communists, who were growing increasingly distant from Moscow. In a classically Stalinist piece of career-Communism, he used his promotion to "Secretary to the Central Committee in charge of Party Organization" to ensure that everybody appointed to the endless committees owed their positions to him and knew it. All applications for these positions passed across his desk. He controlled the access to privileges and power in a society where luxuries were desperately sought after. Like Stalin, Ceaucescu's road to power lay in mastering the arts of bureaucracy and graft. He did not move until he felt secure of his support.

The gap between Rumania and Russia continued to widen. There was a strong nationalist streak in the Rumanian Communists and a traditional hatred of Russians among the people. Even after Stalin's death and fall from grace, the Rumanians remained firm believers in his methods. Russia wanted Rumania to be a supplier of grain in the Eastern Bloc's common market. The Rumanian Communists wanted to copy Stalin's industrialization of the Soviet economy. They resented being cast in the role of an agricultural society; they wanted big, stinking factories like the Russians. The upshot was that when Georghiu-Dej died in 1965, his body riddled with cancer, the Rumanian Communists looked to quickly elect a leader who would maintain Rumania's relative independence from the Soviet Union; indecision might encourage the Russians to intervene. In this way at the age of forty-seven, Nicolae Ceaucescu, with his strong Stalinist and patriotic views became the Secretary General of the Rumanian Communist Party, and hence the ruler of his country. There were other, better qualified candidates, but they declined to stand against him, knowing that if they opposed and failed they probably wouldn't live. Ceaucescu had arrived at the position of leader without ever having to have an original thought.

Ceaucescu proceeded to implement a frenzy of diplomatic visits and large, heavily staged speeches and public appearances.

This ostentatious style became known as "The Frenzy", and it marked the beginnings of his grotesque personality cult. The visits and speeches became increasingly stage-managed and artificial, with motorcades, flower-draped cars, long, dull speeches and balcony appearances in front of orchestrated crowds. He was casting about for a bigger role, both as Communist leader and fervent Rumanian patriot. Something on the world stage, perhaps.

Then he had a huge stroke of luck. In Czechoslovakia, Communism was undergoing a remarkable thaw in the warmth of the "Prague Spring". In 1968 the Russians, who had crushed similar resistance in Hungary, sent the tanks in. This was Ceaucescu's big break. Voicing Rumania's terror of Russian interference he passionately declared:

"There is no justification whatsoever for military intervention in the affairs of a fraternal socialist state . . . the entire Rumanian people will never allow anybody to violate our homeland".

This stirring piece of nationalism miraculously transformed his position. Overnight, the lad from Scornicesti became a national hero and an international sensation.

So delighted were the Western powers to discover an Eastern ally against the Soviet Union, they happily misinterpreted his patriotic rhetoric as progressive thinking worth cultivating. A Communist leader who was anti-Soviet was a prize attraction, and from that moment on they flocked to meet him. De Gaulle, Nixon, and Margaret Thatcher all met the great Nicolae. He could do no wrong. He had become, in Richard Nixon's words, "One of the great leaders of the world". Nixon knew one when he saw one.

It all went to his head. With Western leaders generously manuring his growing personality cult, his ego went spinning dizzily out of control. The "Frenzy" sprouted. Public appearances became completely artificial, with the Securitatae leading the applause by the use of tape-recorded clapping. A visit to North Korea, where the demented Kim Il Sung compelled the whole population to wear badges with his face on them, and where every road had a separate lane for his sole use finally showed Ceaucescu the way forward for Communism.

He was very impressed with the total regimentation of that hideous totalitarian state, as was Elena, who was very concerned her husband should get the respect due to him. After the visit to Korea she became a bossy, demanding career wife, egging the already over-bearing Ceaucescu on. Her favourite words to the champion of the Rumanian people were "They don't deserve you; you are too great for them".

They quickly acquired an entourage of toadies and sycophants only too happy to preserve Ceaucescu from the realities of life in exchange for power and privilege. In common with other similar despots, Ceaucescu rapidly began to believe in his own publicity, the sole content of which was that he was a hero and people loved him.

Lots of things started to disappear and shift mysteriously. It was impossible to trust one's memory or senses. Ceaucescu's old father, drinking as usual in a bar in Bucharest, had told his cronies not to take any notice of his son: "he tells nothing but lies". By daylight, the whole pub had vanished, to be replaced by a long established dairy-outlet. It was not advisable to remark on this. Psychiatric treatment was the favoured punishment for those who saw things differently. At institutions like the Doctor Petra Groza hospital in Bucharest, patients were referred for treatment suffering from odd diseases like "political paranoia". Priests were treated when they complained about corruption; journalists and writers were diagnosed as suffering from "senile dementia" when they wrote about human rights abuses. The political prisoners were locked up with the genuinely disturbed. One case was described as "suffering from": "Persecution complex, neurotic behaviour, delusions, self-preservation drive, discordant character structure; a paranoic, he claims that his flat has been confiscated, and writes numerous complaints . . .".

Finally, when they were genuinely crazed and sick, prisoners were made to build their own coffins and disposed of with drug-overdoses. Relatives were lucky if they were informed within a year.

> The bureaucracy devoted vast efforts to satisfying Ceaucescu's whims. On one occasion he decided that he fancied making a welcome speech to the new students at the polytechnic institute in Bucharest. The only rallying point was currently taken up by a vast, 12,000 cubic meter access hole for the new Bucharest Metro. The morning after his decision, the engineers arriving to work went hay-wire. They had lost their hole. The great, thirty-meter long gash had disappeared. Instead, there were mature trees, grass, flowers; a very pleasant park, perfect for a rally. No-one could bring themselves to tell Ceaucescu that his plans to make the speech were inconvenient, so they were obliged to change reality to conform to his desires. His fantasy now became the only permissible truth.

> General Ion Pacepa describes the drunken Nicu at the height of his powers ordering oysters in a party restaurant, and liberally seasoning them with his own urine before assaulting the waitress over the packed table.

Ceaucescu marched triumphantly on. In 1974, he made himself President of Rumania and awarded himself a regal sceptre. The rampant nepotism and family control of Ceaucescu's reign is astonishing. The horrible Elena, who acquired a string of titles to go with her fake degrees and qualifications became a member of the Central Committee and effectively deputy in charge of the country. His brother Ilie leapt up the ladder of power to take control of the armed forces. His brother Floria was the leading journalist on the official newspaper *Scienteia*. His brother Ioan, also a member of the Central Committee, was Vice President of State Planning. His sisters did similarly well in politics, business and the health service. Nicu, Ceaucescu's son, was in charge of the Communist Youth Organization. He also preserved the family's reputation for alcoholism, and is still slowly dying of cirrhosis of the liver in prison. Nicu had a reputation as a rapist from the age of fourteen. Ceaucescu's daughter, Zoia, became a melancholy nymphomaniac. Corruption and prostitution reigned at the highest levels.

Ceaucescu decided that Rumania should repay its national debt. There was no reason for this other than it was one of his few ideas and it also was part of his simplistic nationalism that Rumania should not owe anybody any money. It was another idea he had picked up from Kim Il Sung. It meant that there was even less for the Rumanian people to eat, as it all had to be exported. In international dealings he was unsophisticated, mean and untrustworthy. Elena, who loved being received like a queen overseas, pressed Ceaucescu into obtaining an invitation to stay at Buckingham palace. Ceaucescu dangled the carrot of a £300 million aircraft deal with the British to obtain this coveted photo-opportunity for the family collection and subsequently tried to pay for it not in cash as agreed, but with cloth and steel of dreadful quality from his polluting factories. When this was refused he offered ice cream, yoghurt and strawberries for the aircraft.

The Queen found the whole experience highly distasteful. Ceaucescu had grown obsessed with health and hygiene and arrived with a personal food taster and several bottles of alcohol with which he constantly sterilized his hands after shaking them with anybody. Ever since it was rumoured that Georghiu-Dej's cancer had been caused by radiation beamed at him by the Russians, Ceaucescu had ordered every room swept by Geiger counters before he set foot in them. Both he and Elena were terrified of germs and disease. If they had to shake hands with or, God forbid, kiss a child on a public appearance, the Securitate would select, disinfect and lock them up weeks beforehand. They drenched themselves in alcohol after the slightest human contact. After Fidel Castro had told Ceaucescu that he had uncovered a CIA plot to smear the inside of his clothes with poison that would make his hair fall out, Nicolae decided that it was unsafe to wear any of his clothes more than once. They became a priority State matter. The Securitate designed and made them all, keeping a year's hermetically sealed supply in a climate-controlled warehouse outside Bucharest. He took his own bed linen and basic foods everywhere. The Queen's staff were most surprised to find Ceaucescu and his vast entourage holding a conference in the Palace grounds at 6 a.m. Ceaucescu had naturally assumed that his rooms would be bugged.

Ceaucescu had a passion for eavesdropping, which he undertook with religious zeal, claiming that fear was the only way of creating an "honest population". Behind his office he had a personal monitoring room where he could select households like TV channels. A new telephone was created capable of doubling up as a microphone. It became the only one available in Rumania. Televisions came with built in transmitters. By 1980, every restaurant was equipped with ceramic ashtrays and vases stuffed full of listening devices. As the dissident Carol Kiraly said in 1984:

> On official visits, Elena devoted herself to acquiring free gifts, honorary titles and diamonds. She even opened a "National Museum of Gifts to the Ceaucescus". Neither she nor Nicolae ever set foot in a shop or store, and officially were paid nothing. They simply accepted gifts from the State. Moreover, according to Pacepa, there was a slush fund with over $400 million in cash from Securitate operations. These included the selling of the Jewish population back to Israel at up to $50,000 a head and money from arms and, notoriously, drug smuggling. When they ran out of Jews, Ceaucescu tried to sell ethnic Germans back to their own country

"The atmosphere of terror is beyond description. It permeates every aspect of everyday life. Distrust is so prevalent that no-one dares to communicate to anyone else . . ."

In spite of all this, the West still regarded him as an ally and sanctioned his absurd behaviour. As late as 1988, President Bush paid him an affectionate visit. Many leaders went hunting with him. He adored hunting, although he was a terrible shot and Securitate snipers were responsible for most of his hits.

His dogs were his other passion and he was very kind to them, taking good care that they weren't poisoned and generously giving them their own luxury villa complete with telephone and television. The motorcades of police-cars and bullet-proofed limousines that thundered through Bucharest often contained no-one other than Corbu, his favourite black labrador, riding in splendid isolation to the country.

The country was in an awful state. Animal feed was used in bread instead of flour. Petrol queues were two or three miles long. With no fuel people froze solid in temperatures of up to −30. The erratic gas supplies meant that fires would go off and come back on again, lethally unlit as people slept and then died by them. The whole population was suffering from acute depression; the suicide rate soared. Ceaucescu had banned contraception and abortion to increase the population. The birth rate rose by ninety-two per cent; the infant mortality rate by one hundred and forty-six per cent. There were no hospitals, doctors, nurses, milk and clothes to cope with the children. It was a cruel and ghastly blunder in social engineering. Still he persisted; women had to undergo monthly checks to ensure that they were not using contraceptive devices. AIDS, spread by contaminated blood and re-used needles, went unrecognized. The mentally handicapped, the unwanted children and the children of unwanted parents were dumped in remote hospitals to die of hepatitis and cholera. The industries that Ceaucescu established were appalingly inefficient. Huge expense and time was devoted solely to managing his endless speeches and rallies. There were more absurd aspects to the horror. The regime had 20,000 Bibles sent to Rumania by a Christian organization secretly pulped into toilet paper which appeared with strange words like "Esau" "Jeremiah" and "God" still legible on it. A parrot, formerly a pet at one of the Ceaucescu households, was arrested by the Securitate after it was overheard saying "stupid Nicu", in reference to Ceaucescu's son. It was reputedly interrogated and throttled when it refused to disclose who had taught it the insult.

The final acts of megalomania were the "systematization" of the ancient, rural communities and his wanton destruction of old Bucharest to make his monolithic "House Of the People", one of the world's most boring buildings, a huge grey slab of concrete designed as a tribute to his own achievements. One of the largest buildings ever, this horror is now empty and decaying. It has no practical use at all. Icicles form in its hundreds of vast staterooms. The lighting and heating alone would take more power than all Bucharest's domestic users have at their disposal.

The "systematization" programme involved obliterating thousands of villages and moving the populations into "urban collectives" or "agro industrial complexes" where they would have to rent tiny flats on godless concrete estates. Sheer enslavement and vandalism, it was all part of Ceaucescu's distrust of the peasants and desire to put people where they could more easily be spied upon by himself and inform on each other. Elena thought that the new buildings would look much more tidy and clean than the old picturesque villages.

It was a Priest who eventually started the uprising in Rumania, in an incident unrelated to the upheavals elsewhere. Pastor Laszlos Tokes, who had been sent to remote Timisoara in disgrace for preaching sermons denouncing Ceaucescu found himself continually harassed by the Securitate, who were frustrated in their desire to simply murder him by the international attention he had gained. In December 1989, the Securitate tried to evict him. His congregation, and then the whole town resisted. The unrest spread. "You do not quieten your enemy by talking to him, but by burying him," screamed Ceaucescu at an emergency meeting. "Some few hooligans want to destroy Socialism and you make it child's play for them!".

Securitate were despatched to Timisoara with orders to kill. In the ensuing carnage and confusion there were reports of up to 60,000 dead, although after the revolution it was reduced to about one hundred with several hundred injured. Ceaucescu, still believing in his own god-like status as national saviour and genius called for a huge rally to woo the people as he had done in 1968. He could not believe he was hated, and began to show signs of confusion and strain. His court sycophants humoured him and arranged a 100,000 strong rally on 21 December. It was a disaster. In front of the World's press his own people began to boo him, and he retreated in disbelief.

Several of the army commanders, sensing which way the wind blew and with an eye on their future prospects switched sides.

Javiar Ortiz, aged twenty-five, of Badajoz, Spain was a higher grade of criminal altogether. For one thing, he realised that the last place to go after a bank raid was home. For sophisticated technical reasons which are not entirely clear to the non-criminal mind, he decided that it would be a great idea to run into the nearest convent and dress up as a nun.

His first mistake was that he became hungry and stole down to the kitchen where he stole a leg of ham which he stuck up his habit. The Mother Superior walked past at this moment and was fairly sure that her convent did not contain any pregnant nuns. His second mistake was that although he was wearing full religious regalia he had not bothered to change out of his size ten Wellington boots. This convinced the Mother Superior of his fake identity. She blew her whistle and twenty eager nuns suddenly surrounded him, separated him from his unsightly habit and turned him over to an astonished local police force.

Most importantly Generals Ilescu and Stanculescu, who had actually initiated the killing in Timisoara, suddenly transformed themselves into revolutionaries. General Milea was shot before he could defect, for failing to disperse the crowds. Ceaucescu went into hiding.

That night, as demonstrations finally erupted in the capital, the Securitate started shooting anything that moved. Using their huge web of tunnels under Bucharest to move about, they fought a bloody battle with the people and the army whilst other countries were celebrating Christmas. It only ended after the capture and execution of Ceaucescu, who incoherent and babbling with rage and disbelief had fled with Elena and their bodyguard by helicopter. Hearing news of proceedings in Bucharest, their pilot cheerfully abandoned them on a lonely country road. Reduced to hitch-hiking, but with no idea of where they should go, they flagged down a local doctor who was driving past. In a bizarre last act, Elena held a gun to the man's head as he drove them aimlessly around, until he finally stopped in front of a police station. Their bodyguard disappeared. Resigned, but still refusing to believe that anything could happen to them, Nicolae and Elena gave themselves up.

They were wrong. A kangaroo court was quickly assembled
and in a cynical trial worthy of his own regime they were
condemned to death and shot. There were good reasons for
wanting to dispose of them; it was felt that whilst they were ·
alive the Securitate would not surrender, but more sinisterly,
there were many army officers who were keen that Ceaucescu
should not have the public opportunity to implicate them in his
atrocities, not now the revolution had fallen into their hands. The
Rumanians would still have to battle with Ceaucescu's former
henchmen for their freedom.

There is an old Rumanian saying: "kiss the hand you cannot
bite". It reflects a history of painful subservience to cruel masters.
It was not only Ceaucescu's ego that created his hallucinatory
bureaucracy of fear, but those who hoped to benefit from it,
and even the people who submitted so completely for so long
have some responsibility. Where strong rulers are favoured
irrespective of their humanity, and wherever patriotism is a
substitute for policies, democracy is a rapid casualty. Finally,
that Nicolae Ceaucescu was admired and assisted by so many
reputable leaders of the West may have been to their immediate
political advantage; but it will endure to their eternal shame.

chapter six

IVAN THE TERRIBLE: SACRIFICES TO CRONUS

There are few stories in all history to compare with that of Ivan IVth, The Terrible. Pious and depraved, majestic and bestial, Ivan is a tragic figure. He embodied the contradictory impulses of his society; a devout Christianity in which Russia was to be the last, and greatest Rome, and a terrible, dark, worship of destruction.

Cronus is the ancient, pagan father of the Gods. He is Time itself, and devours his own children. Late in his life, Ivan confessed to secretly worshipping this shadowy deity. Referring to his beloved wife, Anastasia, who died of suspected poisoning before his abdication, he wrote to the aristocrats; "If you had not taken her from me, there would have been no sacrifices to Cronus".

This self-portrait of a dark God-of-Wrath, consuming his subjects in revenge and anger, echoes the words of a prophecy said to have been made on his birth. Far away from Moscow, in the Tartar stronghold of Kazan, which was to be the scene of his greatest triumph, the wife of the ruling Khan had a strange premonition. She called the Russian envoy to her and said; "A Tsar is born among you; two teeth has he. With one he shall devour us; but with the other, you".

Ivan was crowned Prince in the Cathedral of the Assumption at the age of three and a half. His father Vasily III died on 3 December. Earlier in the year, an inconspicuous purple mark had appeared on Vasily's thigh. This refused to go away, and turned into a boil. In September, the boil suppurated,

Ivan IV, Czar of Russia – "The Terrible". *Hulton-Deutsch*

swelling up with oozing pus. Vasily was barely able to walk, and rapidly moved to secure the throne for his tiny son. He set up a Regency Council to rule during Ivan's childhood, and obliged the Boyars, Russia's aristocrats, to swear allegiance to Ivan.

The boil became a huge abscess; the pus "filled a basin". A core, one and a half inches wide, came out. Vasily recovered briefly, but when gangrene followed along with a putrefying stench, he died of blood poisoning.

Ivan inherited a country equivalent to France, Spain, Britain and Italy in size. In spite of its enormity, it hardly appeared on a map. Explorers firmly expected to find China battened onto the Eastern side of Europe. The huge plains and wastes of Russia had only ten to twelve million inhabitants in total, less than the number that died under Stalin in the 1930s. Most were peasants, many in conditions of serfdom that was little more than slavery. The peasants were further crushed by taxes.

The Russians were a tough, stocky race, with fashionable beards and big bellies, a passion for alcohol and celebration, and a reputation for sodomy. The prevalence of the latter amazed foreigners, who reported that they do it "not only with boys but with men and horses". A popular Russian curse was "may a dog defile your mother". Women were habitually beaten by their husbands, as the saying went: "if a woman be not beaten with the whip once a week, she will not be good . . ." Torture was legal. Women convicted of killing their husbands were buried alive; counterfeiters had molten lead poured down their throats. Only spoken evidence was necessary for conviction, but as this was above all, a religious society, witnesses first kissed the Cross. This was the most serious action this people could perform; their souls were in peril if they lied.

The Russian Orthodox Church saw itself as the last bastion of true Christianity. All other Churches and faiths were heretical. Foreigners, particularly Catholics and Jews, were regarded with acute suspicion, as potential carriers of some other doctrine which might sweep through the country like a disease. All movements of the population were restricted, and foreign travel without permission was punishable by death ". . . so that the people may learn nothing about foreign lands . . ." It was a situation similar to Stalin's Russia, with the Church in the place of the Communist Party. It was a vast, wealthy and powerful organization, with a Messianic mission as successor to the Christian Empires of Rome and Constantinople. A monk had prophesied to Ivan's father: ". . . the ruler of the present

Orthodox Empire is on Earth the sole Emperor of the Christians
. . . two Romes have fallen, but the third stands and a fourth
there shall not be . . ."

According to Ivan's fabricated family tree he was descended
from the Roman Emperor Augustus himself. The symbolic
importance of his position placed a suffocating burden on the
young Ivan.

Acclaimed publicly as a virtual God, and privately abused and
ignored by his ministers, Ivan's childhood was spent in shadows
and fear. Later he wrote that no-one gave him ". . . any loving
care . . . everything I experienced was unbefitting my tender
years . . ." When not trussed up in the stifling uniform of a
Prince, he was treated like a beggar. He flitted through the inky,
labyrinthine corridors and chambers of the Kremlin, a frightened
creature, nursing distrust and revenge in his blackening heart.

Ivan's mother, Elena, made her own bid for the throne. The
Regency Council disintegrated as its members were imprisoned
and exiled. Elena was not a bad ruler, but not a good mother.
In 1538, four years after she took power, she was poisoned.
Ivan was left utterly alone in the world. The Boyars, and their
governing body, the Duma, who had sworn to his father to
protect and support him, quarrelled and fought over power
they now considered theirs. The Tartars took advantage of
bitter in-fighting to invade, burning monasteries, raping and
dismembering nuns and monks. Meanwhile Ivan, aged twelve
and developing a savage and morbid temperament, had taken
to throwing dogs off the Kremlin battlements "to observe their
pain and convulsions".

There was clearly something violent in the air. At the age
of fourteen, he gathered together a teenage gang and roamed
the streets of Moscow, exorcizing his anger and frustration by
mugging innocent pedestrians. Increasingly, he confided in the
Metropolitan Makary, the leader of the Orthodox Church, and
Ivan Voronstov, a member of the old Moscow gentry. After
Prince Andrey Shuisky, a member of the dominant Boyar family,
broke in on a meeting of the three and tried to kill Vorontsov in
front of him, he asserted his position and had Shuisky thrown
to the dogs.

At sixteen he told the Duma that he intended to marry, and
that furthermore, he would take the title of Tsar, equivalent to
Emperor, or Caesar. It also resembled the Tartar title of Khan,
meaning "A king that giveth not tribute to any man". His mother
had Tartar ancestors; in Ivan the blood of both Christian Russian
autocrats and their bitter enemies, the pagan Mongol Emperors,

flowed together. The Duma were astonished at the maturity of his speech. His budding cruelty was matched by unsurpassed intelligence. In January 1547, he was crowned Tsar and Autocrat of All Russia.

He married Anastasia Romanovna, who came from an untitled but loyal Boyar family. The older aristocracy felt snubbed by this, regarding her as an upstart commoner. Her descendants, the Romanovs were still ruling three hundred and fifty years later, when the Revolution came and the Bolsheviks wiped them out. After his wedding, Ivan made the first of many penitential pilgrimages, covering over forty miles on foot in the bitter Winter cold.

The country was in a troubled state. The aristocratic Glinsky family had now become the lords of misrule. The population resorted to arson to express their despair. They appealed to Ivan in vain; he toyed with them, singing the beards of petitioners and splashing them with boiling wine. In June, a fire gutted the heart of Moscow, killing thousands. The mob confronted Ivan, who woke up to his awesome responsibility, and began to govern.

He had a reputation for intellectual brilliance, but by his own admission was also wild and cruel. He was aware that he needed good advice, and surrounded himself with a "Chosen Council".

Priestly figures often exerted great influence at the Russian Court. The Rasputin of Ivan's day was a monk named Sylvester, who dazzled Ivan with his stories of ghosts and miracles, "scaring me with bogies", as Ivan later described it. Significantly Ivan was also influenced by the theories of a pamphleteer called Peresvetov. This man was a much travelled mercenary, who referred in his writing to the occult wisdom contained in a book he called the "Secreta Secretorum". This book, which Ivan had in his Palace Library, supposedly contained the secret advice given by Aristotle to Alexander the Great. The Turkish Emperor Mehmet had learned a philosophy of terror from it, and swept away all who opposed his reforms. The book urged rulers to inspire awe in their subjects; to be remote and distrustful and to test the loyalty of nobles by seeing "what each will suffer on your account". Those who wished to be absolute rulers should not be afraid of shedding blood; it was the only reputation worth having.

Ivan started off trying to reform the land-laws, and proposing reforms in taxation and the system of justice to benefit the peasants. He cursed the Boyars for their treatment of him as a child. "Usurious bloodsuckers", he called them. They looked down at their feet, nervously apologizing. His reforms soon ran up against their interests, however. Ivan desperately needed to have land that he could reward people with for loyalty. But thirty per cent of all arable land was owned by the Church, the Russian real-estate moguls, who were opposed to any reforms which might affect their vast wealth. The Church was a notoriously tough bank and building society, always eager to re-possess property. Life in the cloisters had become opulent and corrupt; the Church had little time for charity, and took badly to Ivan's attempts to make it liable for tax or to make it set up poor-houses.

His other policy was to wage war. In 1552, at the age of twenty-two his army took the fortified Tartar city of Kazan and massacred the cream of the Tartar nobility. This was an historic victory over Russia's old enemies, and afterwards the Russian people gave him the title of "Terrible", to indicate the awesome stature he had acquired.

Ivan fell ill after Kazan. His fever was not thought to be pure coincidence; his reforms had not been popular with the Boyars. Now, as he lay on what many thought was his deathbed, he asked the Boyars to swear allegiance to his infant son, Dimitry, just as his own father had done. In spite of his stature, they would not "serve a babe". Hailed as a hero one minute, Ivan discovered how little he could trust even his closest allies. Rallying his strength, he manipulated his loyal forces from his sickbed and succeeded in crushing the rebellion.

In the ten years that followed, Russia became the region's greatest power, but afterwards became locked into an endless, draining and failed war to conquer the Baltic. English traders, looking for China, found their way to Russia, and an erratic relationship began between the two monarchs, Ivan and Elizabeth.

The English merchants saw Ivan at the height of his reign, enthroned in splendour, encrusted with jewels and crossing himself before each of his frequent mouthfuls of food and drink; "He setteth his whole delight upon two things. First to serve God, as undoubtedly he is very devout in his religion, and the second, how to subdue and conquer his enemies."

Despite riding high on conquest and initiating reforms which improved the peasants lot, Ivan was increasingly cynical and debauched. He drank furiously and having decided that no-one was trustworthy surrounded himself with sycophants, from whom he expected nothing but shallowness. They kissed his hands and feet, flattering and soothing him. He developed an addiction to masked balls and theatrical executions. He was promiscuous with both sexes. Criticism was unwelcome. Dmitry Obolensky, a Prince, reproached the son of one of Ivan's generals for his homosexual relationship with Ivan. Dmitry was invited down into Ivan's cellars to select a favourite vintage and hacked to death among the casks.

The stalemate of the Baltic Wars angered Ivan, who detected a plot. He slew one of his princes with a mace, and accused his prize general, Kurbsky, of treason. Kurbsky saw the shadow of Ivan reaching out to touch him and deserted, denouncing Ivan for "torturing his subjects with red-hot pincers and needles driven under the nails . . .". Ivan compelled the messenger who brought Kurbsky's letter to read it aloud whilst Ivan drove the iron point of his staff through his foot into the floor. It was the first instalment of a bizarre correspondence these two entered into. In long angry letters to Kurbsky, who in exile became an unwilling confidant, Ivan revealed an exceptional literary talent, and the soul of a man who resented the position his fate had thrust upon him.

His personality was driven and obsessive, eating up the world around him. But the full potential of his latent cruelty and bitterness was restrained by his wife, Anastasia. They had already shared in the tragedy of his first son's death. Dimitry had drowned when his nurse accidentally dropped him in a river. Since then she had borne him another five children, but only a couple, Ivan Ivanovna and his brother, the imbecilic Theodore, survived beyond the age of two. Ivan called his wife his "little heifer", and she was regarded with universal love by the Russian people. She was beautiful, wise and graceful, and ". . . bore no malice towards anyone". Her decline and death in 1560, when Ivan was still not quite thirty years old brought about a distinct change in his personality. Impatience became anger, suspicion deepened into paranoia. Casual cruelty grew into a need for daily sadism. Ivan distanced himself from his former advisers, and in the words of one contemporary "lived in great danger and fear of treason which he daily discovered, and spent much time in the examination, torturing and execution of his subjects . . ."

Amidst growing dissent, he began to toy with the idea of abdication. At the end of 1564, hundreds of sleds began to cart off tons of treasure and icons from the Palace and treasury to Sloboda, a hunting lodge sixty miles from Moscow. This was transformed into a fortified camp. Nobody had the faintest idea what Ivan was up to. They watched, mystified. Then, without disclosing his intentions to anybody, and designating no heir, he slipped out of Moscow and left the nation leaderless. In a letter read out to the Boyars by a messenger on 3 January 1565, he bitterly accused the Church and Government of corruption, treason and responsibility for all his personal troubles, past and present and wallowed in melodramatic self-pity: "Wherefore the Tsar and Grand Prince not wishing to endure these many acts of treachery, has abandoned the Tsardom with a heavy heart and now travels wheresoever God may lead him . . ."

The peasants feared they might have lost a champion. A popular uprising was on the cards; anarchy loomed. The foreign powers on the borders licked their lips.

The Duma humbled itself, and despatched the Archbishop of Novgorod to plead with Ivan. Without Ivan, they were "poor and inconsolable sheep . . . without a shepherd, and the wolves, our enemies surround us . . ." If he returned, he could "punish traitors at his own discretion". Ivan categorically refused to resume his position. He wanted more than that.

When he returned to Moscow in February, still only thirty-five years old, most of his hair had fallen out; his eyes were curiously glazed. After four weeks of negotiation, he had been granted absolute power over the life and property of any disobedient subject. A part of the nation was to be set aside for him, existing only to further his will, staffed and run by his hand-picked personnel. This part of Muscovy was to be called the "Oprichina" – the "widow's portion", reflecting his continuing self-pity. The Oprichina initially consisted of twenty towns and their surroundings. Ivan expanded it to include over a third of the entire Empire. His intention was plain; to undermine and destroy the hereditary aristocracy he so feared and blamed for his childhood misery and the obstruction of his authority. The rest of Russia was left to the former administration, with Ivan presiding over everything.

He now possessed power the Pharaohs would have envied. Those he employed to staff and run his personal Empire had only one thing in common; they had to swear complete and unquestioning obedience to Ivan in all things: "He that loveth father or mother more than me is not worthy of me; and he that loveth son or daughter more is not worthy of me . . ."

Ivan's revenge began immediately. No specific charges were necessary for the deaths that followed, though generally a vague accusation would be made that so-and-so had done, or plotted, or thought "all manner of evil things". Ivan showed no gratitude for past services; the hero of Kazan, Prince Gorbaty, along with his adolescent son were executed, as well as countless lesser nobles. Some faced death bravely, protesting their innocence. One Dmitri Sheyev "sang all day from memory the canon to our Lord Jesus Christ" as he was slowly impaled on a stake. An English merchant arrived in Moscow in 1566, just in time to catch the fall-out; "This Emperor of Moscovia hath used lately great cruelty towards his nobility and gentlemen, by putting to death, whipping and banishing above 400 . . . one worried with bears, of another he cut off his nose, tongue, his ears and his lips, the third he set upon a pole . . ."

When Ivan discovered a real plot a year later, the carnage extended beyond the immediate suspects and their families. The Oprichniki rode around Moscow for days armed with axes, chopping down whosever they chanced upon. One Boyar, discovered hiding in a monastery, had needles driven under his nails before he was roasted alive in a large pan. Moscow was not the place to be. The English ambassador, negotiating between Ivan and Elizabeth wrote anxiously to his Queen: "Of late the Tsar hath beheaded no small number of his nobility . . . causing their heads to be laid in the streets to see who dares to mourn them . . . I intend to see him so soon as I can . . . the sooner to be out of his country where heads go so fast to the pot".

Ivan, who had annexed a whole suburb of Moscow for his personal use, spent most of his time at the fortress town of Sloboda, indulging simultaneously in his twin pleasures of religion and depravity. One brought on a craving for the other. It was a strict regime. There were several church services each day, commencing at 3 a.m., and after each he would make frequent excursions to the dungeons to gratify the desire for torture that worship aroused in him. Here he was described as "never so happy in countenance and speech": "Blood often splashes in his face, but he does not mind; indeed he is delighted, and to indicate his joy, he shouts 'Hoyda! Hoyda!'"

Occasionally there were large-scale entertainments, as when he had several hundred beggars drowned in a lake, or fed

Ivan's servants, from all social classes, including aristocrats, were called the Oprichniki. They looked and behaved like the Devil's own slaves. Dressed in black, riding black horses, with a strange, ever-present insignia of a dog and broom, they were forbidden any contact with the normal citizens and developed their own customs and religious rites. They were the model in eeriness and brutality for Hitler's SS.

rebellious friars to wild animals, or sewed enemies up in bearskins and threw them to the dogs. At other times, Ivan would beat himself, pounding his own forehead on the ground until it turned black with bruises and ran red with blood.

Russia's now disastrous wars in the Baltic laid an enormous burden of taxation on the people. Ivan, who had managed to maintain a trading agreement with England, looked to Elizabeth for weapons and a possible alliance and refuge in case unrest should force him to flee. Elizabeth would not be drawn into Ivan's wars, and although she offered Ivan refuge, she declined his reciprocal offer of shielding her from her own subjects, which offended Ivan. She did supply him with weapons, to the consternation of the Polish King, Sigismund, who told her that Ivan was the ". . . hereditary foe of all free nations . . . he maketh himself strong to vanquish all others". She also obstructed his efforts to marry into the English Royal family; Ivan had become inflamed with passion at the thought of some youthful English flesh; he already claimed to have deflowered a thousand Russian virgins.

After Anastasia's death he had made a political marriage to a Tartar princess, Maria who had a reputation for cruelty. When she was poisoned by a nasty fish supper in 1569, Prince Staritsky, one of the Boyars who ran what little was left of Russia, was convicted on the evidence of a cook. Ivan compelled Staritsky to drink poison, and murdered his entire family; even his mother was strangled. The cook, the cook's sons, the fishmonger who sold the offending fish, and even the fisherman who caught it were all executed along with their families. Two years later, Ivan's third wife, Marfa also died of poisoning.

It was in this year, 1569, that Ivan staged his most spectacular massacres, at Novgorod and Pskov. Novgorod was virtually on the border with warring Lithuania, and a prime target for Ivan's paranoia. When a disreputable source suggested that these cities were planning treason, Ivan moved an army of 15,000 Oprichniki northwards, in great secrecy. In order to maintain surprise they killed anyone who crossed their path, and by 2 January 1571, they reached the outskirts of Novgorod. The Oprichniki ominously sealed up all exits and refuges. Having denounced the Archbishop as "a thief, traitor, murderer and a wolf", Ivan went to Church to get himself in the right frame of mind for the ensuing sport, praying with particular intensity during the service. Afterwards, he repaired to the Archbishop's residence for a spot of supper. As he began to eat, the massacre began.

Just when death seemed certain for everybody, Ivan decided

The old accounts of the slaughter give the number of victims as 60,000, with the killing continuing for five weeks. The occupants, irrespective of age or sex, were hanged, flayed, beheaded, impaled or thrown off the bridge. Ivan built a chute into the Volkhov River, and slid the still-breathing remains of his torture-victims down in to the shallows. There the Oprichniki waded in their boots, hacking and stabbing and gouging. The river turned red.

to pardon the survivors, and requesting them to wish him a long and happy reign, he moved on to Pskov. There the population suffered a similar fate, and were only spared extinction by the intervention of a "Holy Fool", who foresaw Ivan's death if the killing continued. Ivan remained susceptible to prophecies.

That Winter, Russia suffered a terrible famine, with the peasants resorting to cannibalism to stave off starvation. Many of Ivan's victims were put to practical use. After the famine came plague. To cap Russia's misery, in Summer the Tartars invaded from the South and swept into Moscow.

Ivan had been preoccupied with torturing a couple of old enemies when the Tartars attacked. He had devised an ingenious death for one suspected opponent, Nikita Funikov who the Oprichniki had doused with alternately boiling and freezing water until his skin literally peeled off. It made an interesting change from flaying. Learning of the invasion, he made for Novgorod, where he planned to take a ship for England along with four hundred and fifty tons of treasure he had dragged along with him. Having been deprived of what he felt to be rightfully his in his youth, he had now become an insatiable plunderer.

The Tartars set fire to Moscow, and then surrounded and cut down any trying to escape the flames. Half the population died, as many as half a million people.

The English observers were rather smug about this latest catastrophe, calling it the "just punishment of God on such a wicked nation", and concluding that the Russians had been destroyed because of their fondness for sodomy. They also observed that what with his own cruelty and the famines, plagues and Tartars, "the Tsar hath but few people left".

The Tartars were defeated at the battle of Molodi, after which, the Oprichina was slowly re-integrated back into the state, and the thugs disbanded. The organization disintegrated through

Tiberius was a bad-tempered, withdrawn, introverted man who was fifty-six when he became emperor, and whose early life had been soured when he was forced to divorce a wife whom he adored, to marry Julia, the nymphomaniac daughter of the emperor Augustus. He was an excellent but strict general who was disliked by his soldiers. He once said, "Let them hate me so long as they obey me". And this also seems to have been his attitude towards the people of Rome. Yet there- is also evidence that he was a kindly and fair-minded man. The historian Suetonius tells how, in his days as a tribune, he visited the island of Rhodes, and expressed a wish to visit the local sick. His staff misunderstood him and all the patients were carried to a public cloister. Tiberius was shocked, and went among them apologising for the inconvenience, "even to the humblest".

After a dozen years as emperor, he retreated to the island of Capri where, according to Suetonius, "No longer feeling himself under public scrutiny, he rapidly succumbed to all the vicious passions which he had for a long time tried but not very successfully, to disguise." He was a voyeur, who organised a private brothel in which he could watch young men and women engaging in "unnatural practices". "Some aspects of his criminal obscenity", says Suetonius with obvious relish, "are almost too vile to discuss, much less believe. Imagine training little boys, whom he called his 'minnows', to chase him while he went swimming and get between his legs to lick and nibble him. Or letting babies not yet weaned from their mother's breast, suck at him - such a filthy old man he had become. The story goes that once, while sacrificing, he took an erotic fancy to the acolyte who carried the incense casket, and could hardly wait for the ceremony to end before hurrying him and his brother, the sacred trumpeter, out of the temple and indecently assaulting them both. When they protested at this dastardly crime he had their legs broken." One Roman lady whom he summoned to his bed showed such a distaste for the things he wanted her to do that he persecuted her until she committed suicide.

sheer exhaustion. Moreover, there was little left in Russia worth fighting over.

Ivan survived for another decade, presiding over the collapse of the Russian Empire he had taken to such heights. His cruelty did not abate, though the scale diminished. His experiments with terror and debauchery left him shattered. His attempt to create a new class based on loyalty alone failed. He was feared, hated, but could not command loyalty without purchasing it. Russia was demoralized and poor, plunged into pagan medieval gloom. While the rest of Europe basked in the light of the Renaissance, the figure of Cronus still ruled in the shadows of Russia. Out of 34,000 settlements recorded in Russia at the end of his reign, eighty-three per cent were deserted. On 14 November, 1581, Ivan upbraided his daughter in law Elena who was pregnant, about her clothes. Ivanovitch intervened, and Ivan drove the spike on his iron-tipped staff into his son's head. The wound festered and he died a few days later. He had been the one surviving hope of the people, although he shared in many of Ivan's vices.

Ivan went insane with grief, tearing his hair and crying for nights without end. He began to dispense his hoarded wealth to the monasteries, ordering that they pray for his son every day. He also drew up a list of the victims of his terror whom he wished the clergy to pray for, displaying an amazing memory for names. From Novgorod alone he listed 1,500 men and their wives and families. The countless unknown were to be acknowledged by the constant, sad refrain: "as to their names, O Lord, you know them . . ."

In 1583 he started suffering acutely from a condition rather like arthritis, which resulted in the rapid deterioration of his joints. Horribly, the vertebrae of his very spine fused solid. He was bent nearly double. In January 1584 he began to rot on his feet; in the words of an English merchant: "The Emperor began to swell grievously in his coddes, with which he had much offended above fifty years, boasting of a thousand virgins he had deflowered . . ."

His body putrified internally. Ivan sat, playing chess and doting on his treasure, regretting that he would have to leave it. Sixty Lapland witches were imported to predict the precise moment of death. After consultation they came up with 18 March.

Ivan improved. He even took guests on an extraordinary tour of his treasury, where he lectured them on the occult properties of his jewels and used them in front of his amazed audience to confirm his impending demise.

On 18 March, to general consternation, Ivan rose up healthy and cheerful. The witches remained confident. Later Ivan leapt out of a relaxing bath, sat down for a game of chess and at last fell over dead.

Russia was left to his idiot son Theodore, civil war and destruction at the hands of the Polish and Tartar armies.

chapter seven

EMPEROR BOKASSA I: THE NAPOLEON OF BANGUI

Jean Bedel Bokassa, President and self-styled Emperor of the Central African Republic, had an expensive obsession with French history. The former French colony that he ruled is one of the poorest countries in the world. Its total budget in 1977 was $70 million, about the annual turnover of the largest branch of a major supermarket. Bokassa contrived to spend a third of this on his coronation as Emperor Bokassa I. It was a memorable forty-eight hours.

The ceremony faithfully replicated the coronation of his favourite historical figure, Napoleon Bonaparte, and the attention paid to detail in this orgy of spending is staggering. The short, squat, ugly Emperor wore an ankle length tunic of velvet and shoes of pearls. The Imperial mantle was embroidered with gold bees, precisely like Napoleon's. Everywhere, two golden laurel fronds bracketed the gold initial "B" for Bokassa, replacing the "N" of Napoleon. He trailed behind him a thirty-foot, crimson velvet, gold embroidered and ermine trimmed mantle weighing over seventy pounds. He was weighed down by a jewel encrusted, gold-hilted sword and ebony staff of office. The heavy crown was also an exact replica of Napoleon's, fronted with the golden French Imperial eagle. The throne, covered with more red velvet, trimmed with gold, was backed by another, vast gold eagle, whose outspread wings threw an appropriate shadow over the Emperor and his Empress Catherine, formerly plain

A century after the death of Ezzelino, another "haematomaniac" spread terror from India to southern Russia. His name was Timur Lenk, Timur the Lame - better known in the west as Tamerlane - and he was a descendant of the Mongol conqueror Genghis Khan, who had spread terror from China to the Mediterranean a century earlier. From 1362 to 1380, Tamerlane made himself master of what is now Russian Turkestan, fighting invading nomads. Then he spent another seven years conquering Persia. Unfortunately for the people he conquered, he was an obsessive killer, who felt that a conqueror's chief business was to murder on a massive scale. His violence was pointlessly sadistic; when he took Sabwazar in 1383 he had 2,000 prisoners built into a living mound, then bricked in. Later the same year, he had 5,000 captives beheaded at Zirih, and their heads made into an enormous pyramid. In 1386 he had all his prisoners at Luri hurled over a cliff. In Delhi, he massacred 100,000 prisoners. This extraordinary man invaded Anatolia (Turkey) in 1400, took the garrison of Sivas, and had its 4,000 Christian defenders buried alive. Yet since he lacked political good sense, and was more interested in conquest and murder than in consolidating his gain his empire collapsed within half a century of his death in 1405.

The cannibalism stories that emerged during and after his overthrow received a boost from the discoveries made at his Royal Palace, where it seems he had been butchering children and allegedly feeding the bits he couldn't manage to his four pet crocodiles. In some lurid, accounts the bodies of up to forty of them were found at the bottom of his swimming pool, with another dozen in the cold-storage room, left over from the feasting of the previous night. There is one question that springs to mind in reading these extraordinary claims: if he ate them, who cooked them? Who was Bokassa's chef? Was he French?

Mrs Bokassa, a peasant girl from the same mud-hut village as the Emperor.

The Emperor was conveyed through the dusty tracks of the capital, Bangui, to his coronation in a gilded coach drawn by eight white, imported Normandy horses. Fourteen had been sent from France but the rest had died in the heat. His raggle-taggle army lined the route, cheering fitfully. Bokassa, who had warmed up by spending several days watching films of Queen Elizabeth's Coronation, gave a much practised Royal wave with his white-gloved hand. Even the church had been re-titled Notre Dame de Bangui for the occasion.

Over 2,500 guests attended from all over the world. Many more had been invited, including every European leader and monarch. Most had politely returned their gold edged invitations. The British were rude, the Americans cut off aid. Of those international dignitaries who came, six hundred had been lodged for several days in the best hotels or in specially constructed housing, fed and watered in Imperial style at the country's expense. The French had provided Bokassa with $2.5 million worth of credit to purchase a fleet of Mercedes limousines to ferry his guests about in, and to provide a ceremonial escort of two hundred BMW motorcycles.

After the ceremony, at which Bokassa solemnly promised to continue "the democratic evolution of the Empire", 4,000 guests sat down to a full, French style banquet at the Renaissance Palace in Bangui. There, to the strains of a French Naval Band, the Emperor and Empress waltzed the night away, clad in elegant Parisian evening dress.

When Bokassa's regime blossomed from tyranny and bad taste into open horror a couple of years later, an appalling but compelling sub-plot to this parody was rumoured. As part of his coronation celebrations, Bokassa had ordered that conditions for a number of political prisoners be made more lenient. They were taken out of chains, and given decent food and exercise. They were told that after the ceremony they would receive an Imperial pardon. In fact, having been suitably fed up, it is claimed, they were expertly diced and served to the guests in coronation sauce of Parisian richness.

The story, however speculative, has distinct echoes of classical tragedy; a false Emperor begins his reign with an accursed banquet at which, in eating his victims, the guests symbolically share in his crimes. It would be convenient to simply consider the Bokassas of history as evil incarnate, occurring in spite of the best efforts of others, but their stories show nothing so straightforward. Their creation involves a mechanism as complex and far-reaching as the stock market; responsibility – and guilt – for the final debacle is shared by all who expected to profit.

Like Idi Amin in Uganda, Jean Bedel Bokassa was the worst possible publicity for an African nation struggling to be taken seriously; an unfortunate mutant prodigy of the colonial past. The Imperial ceremony was both a way of flattering the French, and a means of announcing that he had inherited their mantle of absolute rule and was above the rest of his nation.

The rest of his Empire consisted of a central portion of Equatorial Africa which, though nearly as large as France itself, has a tiny population of around two and a half million, forty per cent of whom are under the age of fifteen. In some areas there is less than one person per seven hundred and forty-one acres. The population is largely tribal, and frequently nomadic, which contributes to the lack of a single national identity. Westerners trying to connect the Central African Republic with anything other than the excesses of Bokassa will probably come up with the image of naked pygmies with huge lip plugs being pursued through steaming jungle by roaring lions. It is Bongo Bongo land of Western prejudice, the homeland of African stereotypes, showing not only our own ignorance, but also what an artificial, haphazard creation the country is.

When the French moved into the area it was known as Ubangi-Shari, and from 1920, it was a full scale colony. The French leased fifty per cent of the country to a mere seventeen French companies, who were given free rein to exploit the labour and natural products. These used enforced labour, torture and

There was no Central African Republic before the French came into Equatorial Africa at the turn of the century. The area, remote and unexplored had been the location of a number of mythical kingdoms, including that of Prester John, the legendary Christian Emperor of Ethiopia. In the sixteenth century, the Portuguese had invaded, lured by these fabulous stories and looking for gold, without success. In the next century, the Arabs, sweeping down from the North found it, in the shape of "black gold" as slaves were known. The African tribes, originally quite populous, were decimated by the slave trade and the smallpox, measles and syphilis that came with it. Slaves were Africa's major wealth, and were rapaciously mined like a precious ore.

hostage – forcing the population to collect the increasingly rare but precious natural rubber vine. In 1927, a local leader, Chief Mindogon, was whipped to death by the territorial guards of one French company, because he had failed to supply enough rubber-collectors. He was the father of Jean Bedel Bokassa, then aged six.

After World War II, in which many Africans served their French masters courageously, President De Gaulle sought to retain a more subtle grip over the African colonies. They were offered two choices: remain willingly as extensions of France, subject to French rule but also French assistance, or take complete independence. The fear of Barthelmy Boganda, then French-appointed ruler of Ubangi-Shari, was that now the colonial powers had divided Equatorial Africa up into a system of small states, if they took independence, Ubangi-Shari would definitely be drawing the short straw. It was now, by comparison with its neighbours, a small and insignificant province which could expect to be trampled on. And while the French could withdraw their troops and administrators, their businessmen still had a firm grip on the sources of the country's meagre wealth. This state was not yet a nation. It had never had a central authority, such as an independent government; it had always been a loose collection of tribes. It needed help to make the transition.

There were no compromises available, and in 1960, the Central African Republic was born. It was a reluctant independence, a nation that was forced into being. Barthelmy, the only man with sufficient wisdom and stature to solve the nation's dilemmas, died in an unexplained aircraft crash. He was succeeded by David Dacko, and five years of increasing corruption and chaos followed, before on 31 December 1965, Bokassa seized power.

Bokassa was raised in a French, Catholic Mission and joined the French army at the earliest possible opportunity. By 1965, then forty-four years old, he had served in French Indochina, and risen to the rank of Lieutenant, impressing with his loyalty and obvious fascination for French military history. He claimed to be the nephew of Barthelmy Boganda, thus giving him a vague, tribal right to the position of national leader. He became a member of Dacko's Government after leaving the French army, and used his French contacts and influence to acquire the position of Chief of Staff at the Ministry of Defence.

His coup was a surprise for the French. Although the country was officially independent, they reserved the right to interfere when necessary. The unrest of Dacko's regime had made them fear for their business and strategic interests in the country; they were worried about the possibility of a Marxist-led, popular uprising. They had been planning their own coup, and were out-manoeuvred by Bokassa, who learned about their intentions and arrested the chosen replacement to Dacko on New Year's Eve. A few hours later, troops loyal to Bokassa, many of whom had served with him in the French army, overran Bangui. Dacko handed over the combination of the safe to Bokassa, and went into exile in Paris.

Until that extraordinary coronation twelve years later, there was little to distinguish Bokassa's government from any other confused, violent and corrupt post-colonial regime. It was run on the simple maxim of "to the victors, the spoils". Bokassa abolished any vestiges of democracy, making himself President and head of the Armed Forces, the Ministry of Information and Minister for Justice. Like Amin, he appointed people from his own tribal background to ministerial positions, and, like Amin, he regularly shot them. The army officers who had supported him were rewarded with vast salary increases and promotions. Towards the public, he behaved initially like a benign tribal chieftain, making extravagant public gestures to compensate for his inability to govern. He donated his first month's salary towards the building of a hospital, and even paid in cash one or two of the country's outstanding bills. Work was started on a public transport system; a central market was built. To a population thoroughly accustomed to mere exploitation, these were definite signs of improvement, which predictably, were not sustained.

France didn't care for military leaders who took charge without first obtaining permission from them. However, Bokassa's regime was preferable to the communism they dreaded, and the man was such a Francophile, it was touching. He never renounced his French citizenship and idolized De Gaulle. The death of his father as a result of French colonialism only seemed to have filled him with superstitious admiration for their power, and gratitude to the French Church and Army for taking the position of surrogate parent. He regarded De Gaulle's successor, Giscard D'Estang, as his "cousin". The country was still financially dependent on France, which was the outlet for half its exports and from whom it received vast amounts of aid, up to $20 million a year. However, nearly ninety per cent of that aid was "bi-lateral", that is, it involved some return concession from the Central African Republic; the more aid it provided, the bigger France's financial interest in the country, and effectively in Bokassa became. The country was better off as an outright colony. Within a few years of taking power, Bokassa persuaded the French to send a small contingent of paratroopers to guarantee the stability of his regime. The original group of eighty quickly swelled until by 1969, twenty per cent of the armed forces were French. Bokassa was not particular about where his money came from, however, and at various times the United States, the Soviet Union, Yugoslavia, Rumania and South Africa were all involved in "projects".

The thin line that existed between Bokassa's private bank account and that of the Government was removed when his Minister of Finance, Colonel Alexandra Banza was arrested, tortured and executed in 1969. Banza, something of a anomaly, had foolishly attempted to restrict the tide of personal enrichment. From then on, Bokassa began a process of what he termed "privatization" of state assets and revenue. This meant that the diamond and uranium mining interests which were the most desirable of the country's assets became the property of a handful of closely related people, with French companies owning the mining concessions. These accounted for fifty per cent of the country's exports. Bokassa had shares in every national business, and a complete monopoly on internal trade. By bribery and fear he completely subjugated the whole civil service to his will. There were 4,000 Government officials, but few bothered to do any work, and even fewer had any power. They lived in the old colonial villas and clubs, desperately aping their former French rulers. The country was only saved from bankruptcy because its currency was still the French franc, and France protected its value. It was a profoundly sad situation.

Bokassa made himself President for life in 1972. There was always a plot in the offing somewhere, but they became a regular, bi-annual event in the following years, generally launched by those who were jealous of the success of Bokassa's "privatization" and wanted a piece of the action. He was desperately attached to even the most meagre portion of the fortune he had amassed. In 1973, after an attempted robbery at his palace he became crazed with anger at the idea of being stolen from and personally beat to death three convicted thieves being held in a nearby prison. They had absolutely nothing to do with the failed burglary, but he had long before ceased to regard the populace as individuals, rather than a squirming mass of limbs to be hacked at. The following day he passed a decree sanctifying property, with ears and limbs to be cut off for the most minor theft.

He now had annexed the major portion of his country's

wealth, and showered it on visiting diplomats. Giscard D'Estang made a trip in 1975, and was greeted by a handful of diamonds and taken on hunting trips to Bokassa's personal game reserve, which took up most of the Eastern half of the country.

Bokassa, now an established alcoholic, announced his intention to become Emperor in 1976, and started building himself a palace at Berengo. This was not yet finished at the time of his coronation. It was to have landscaped lawns, swimming pools, fountains, bullet-proof glass and fortress-like defences. The cost of this, added to his absurd coronation, devastated the nation's finances. No one could curb him, and a year later he announced yet more publicly financed celebrations to commemorate the anniversary of his coronation. The government ran out of money, and was unable to pay any of its civil servant salaries or any student grants. In January 1979, Bokassa decreed that all school children had to purchase and wear ludicrous, French-style uniforms, the sole manufacturer of which was an establishment owned by his wife. As most of the schoolchildren of Bangui had no books, and many went barefoot, it was not a practical or popular decision. Bokassa was being quite serious, and students found themselves turned away from school for being incorrectly dressed. General unrest spread, and a certain amount of looting began in the town centre. The army were sent in and gunned down one hundred and fifty to two hundred disruptive students and children. Bokassa blamed it all on the Russians and denounced the "stupid" government decree about school uniforms; as Emperor, he would overrule it and make sure that whoever was responsible was punished. The French bailed out the country, and civil service salaries were raised by fifty per cent to keep them quiet.

In April, Bokassa arrested a number of students and teachers for circulating leaflets denouncing his wealth. Strikes and "sit-ins" began. Between 18 and 20 April, the "Imperial Guard" rounded up one hundred students and children and took them to Ngaragbo prison. In the days that followed they were systematically beaten to death in the presence of, and with the active participation of Bokassa. Their bodies were then secretly buried. This was in the International Year of the Child.

The French were now horribly embarrassed by the stories coming out of Bangui. Stalling for time, they set up an African Mission Of Inquiry with representative from five other African States to investigate the allegations. In the meantime, they tried desperately to get rid of Bokassa before the inquiry could find him guilty, and put them in the position of being the principle sponsors of a mass-murderer. Their efforts were in vain, Bokassa refused all their invitations to take trips outside his own country, and stayed in his fortified palace.

The inquiry found him guilty in August 1979. In September, because of the sanctions his barbarous behaviour had earned for his country, Bokassa was forced to take his begging bowl to that banker to the criminally insane, Colonel Gadaffi of Libya. Whilst he was out of the country, the French launched "Operation Barracuda", and in a bloodless coup dragged David Dacko out of bed in Paris and thrust him, still half-asleep back into the Presidential Palace in Bangui. Bokassa found himself stranded in Libya, which is a kind of rest-home for people nobody wants. The French refused him an entry visa when he tried to move to his beloved Paris, and he ended up selling tropical swim-wear on the Ivory Coast. In 1983, he managed to obtain entry to France, and took a villa outside Paris. Miraculously, he ended up flat broke, and suffered the indignity of having his water, telephone and electricity cut off. His three children were arrested for shoplifting and he was unable to bail them out. In 1986, he drifted back to Bangui, where, in his absence he had been sentenced to death. This was commuted to life in solitary confinement. And there the Ogre of Berengo sits; the only head of state to have been tried for cannibalism.

chapter eight

ADOLF HITLER: THE REVENGE OF A FAILED ARTIST

Night, inside the Bunker, April 1945. The clocks say that day is approaching, but here, deep underground among the suffocating labyrinth of concrete corridors and in the stale offices and conference rooms, the only light is that cast by the sallow coloured bulbs hanging from the ceilings. These tremble and sway gently, registering the fact that above, high-explosive shells are pouring down on what remains of Berlin. In one of the corridors, trying to stay out of public view, an orderly and another soldier with flashes on his collar, indicating his membership of the SS, are haggling grimly over something in a box tied with delicate ribbon. The SS man is adamant about the value of what he has to sell. The orderly doesn't have the time to argue. Reluctantly, he gives in, only asking that he be allowed to view the merchandise. The soldier opens the lid of the box gingerly, and together they both gawp in astonishment. It is a beauty. In the midst of this apocalypse, someone has made an immaculate, vast Black Forest gateau.

Among the ruins, the light of dawn is obscured by a thick pall of oily smoke; an inextinguishable fire burns the city. On the outskirts, old men and children are waiting to fight the Russians. At their backs stand the remaining ranks of the Waffen SS, urging them on with boots and guns. Russian tanks come clanking across the rubble; behind them, the shadows of men flow swiftly from doorway to doorway. All is horror, confusion and inevitable, hopeless defeat.

The inhabitants of the underworld have lost track of time or purpose. In contrast to the inferno above, there is a curious, numb quiet. Some are sleeping, others, in the conference rooms, listen to the panic-stricken reports that indicate the scale of the catastrophe. The typists are still tapping out reams of directives to non-existent armies, reprimands to dead men and execution orders for those who have failed, but this is a charade. There is nothing anyone can do; most have no idea why they are still here. A telephone begins to ring. No-one answers it, and after a while it goes dead forever. A few hours ago, they were issued with cyanide capsules and rehearsed a mass suicide as choreographed by Heinrich Himmler, head of the SS, but they don't want to die. Under their subdued tones, there is a dreadful hysteria. Occasional violent squabbles break out. One or two are visibly snivelling, their noses and eyes streaming. All have appalling migraines, and are suffering from acute claustrophobia. Many are only held together by the stretched, narcotic threads of amphetamines and morphine. The sour air smells of fear and sweat. They want to smoke, but Adolf Hitler has strictly forbidden this. For the last month he has screamed ceaselessly at them, in monologues of hatred up to three hours long. They do have one purpose left, to keep him quiet.

Adolf Hitler has been awake all night and is looking forward to his breakfast at 6, after which he will sleep until late in the day. Sitting in the corner of an upright sofa in his office, he has just finished dictating an eighty page memorandum, giving his generals precise instructions on how to win the war, whilst simultaneously blaming them for Germany's defeat. On his lap is a golden labrador puppy, which he is rhythmically stroking and occasionally whispering endearments to. His hair is lank and his pebbly eyes dull, and between the corners of his mouth and his chin there is a drying beard of spittle.

The hand he is stroking the dog with has a spasmodic tremor. Every so often his left leg picks up this twitch and begins to shake. He struggles to contain this by wrapping his foot tightly round the leg of the sofa. At these times, his body shrinks and goes tense with furious concentration. The memorandum is utterly incoherent.

The exhausted young secretary, who has finished taking dictation, rises and makes for the door. As she opens it Hitler indicates the clock, which now reads 6 in the morning. "Chocolate," he says, appealing with a smile radiating self-pity. It is pleading, greedy and childish, the petulant ghost of his charm. Outside the door, she nearly crashes into the triumphant orderly, who is carrying a tray into the Fuhrer; on it is hot chocolate and a plate piled high with thick slabs of Black Forest gateau smothered under cream and cherries. The procurement of this under the current circumstances is nothing short of miraculous. Impending destruction has vastly increased Hitler's consumption of sickly pastries.

Hitler tries to stand, but there is something uncertain about his balance, and frantically clutching the dog, he collapses back onto the sofa. "Just two pieces," he lies, in response to the orderly's inquiry as to how much cake the Fuhrer would like, "But leave the tray". And then he adds, excusing his appetite, "I didn't eat much supper last night". The orderly fusses ingratiatingly about his health and hands him the heavy plate. "Ah!" Hitler exclaims in anticipation, addressing the dog, "my darling little Wolf. Can you understand people who do not crave sweets? Art requires nourishment as well as fanaticism." Then he picks up a wedge of gateau and, feigning delicacy for a moment, hesitates, before suddenly pelicaning it. Cream, crumbs of chocolate and a glace cherry fall onto his revolting, soup-stained suit. He rubs them in and licks more goo off his moustache, absorbed, pausing with pleasure before the next mouthful. Outside, in fields, cities and concentration camps, lie the bodies of fifty million dead.

Adolf Hitler was born on 20 April 1889 in Braunnau, Austria, then a part of the vast Austro-Hungarian Empire which was to fall apart in World War I. His father Alois was a customs official, a noted drunkard and rapacious lecher, who married Adolf Hitler's mother, his own second cousin, when he was old enough to be her father. It was his third wedding. He had driven his first wife away when he took up with her maid, who had died within a few years. Klara, young and pretty, had been sent into his care when only sixteen, and he had been violating her for some years. She was already pregnant when they married, though the son that was born died within a few days. Hitler was the fourth of five children of this unhappy union, but only he and a half-witted sister Paula survived infancy. His half-sister, Angela Raubal had a child, Geli Raubal who was to be one of the strange loves of his life.

Alois was violent towards both the children and his wife. His death when Adolf was fourteen liberated his mother, who set about spoiling her darling son rotten. Adolf was not an unintelligent pupil at school, but was described as arrogant, argumentative, evasive, sly and above all, lazy. He had a tendency for self-dramatization and assumed the position of misunderstood and persecuted outcast from an early age. He failed to gain a school-leaving certificate, dropping out through illness, and his favourite pastimes were playing war-games and reading endless adventure stories about the North American Indians.

After leaving school, Hitler spent two crucial years in Linz between the ages of sixteen and eighteen. He had decided his vocation was art and his intention was to enter the Vienna Academy of Arts, but he repeatedly put off taking the entrance examination, preferring to fantasize about the extent of his undiscovered talent than put it to the test.

Supported by his indulgent mother, he posed around Linz, growing extremely dandified, sketching and painting and drawing up grandiose designs for the complete reconstruction of the city. He dressed like an elegant, wealthy student, and was thrilled to be mistaken for the genuine article. In his conceit he was unsure upon which branch of art to bestow the prodigious gifts he credited himself as possessing. Literature, architecture, music and painting all attracted him; to his dying day, Hitler was vexed by the thought of his neglected talent, exclaiming, "What an artist dies with me!".

In Vienna, Hitler displayed an avid interest in sex without ever having a girlfriend. It is during this period that some theorists maintain that Hitler contracted syphilis from a Jewish prostitute. Quite apart from the final madness this would bring, it would explain his inability to have a normal sex life, and his reliance on a series of extreme perversions to obtain sexual gratification. It was a team of American psychologists, compiling a war-time, mental profile of the "Fuhrer" who concluded that, as consequence of his early experiences, which may have included syphilis, he required young women to urinate and defecate upon him, a fact that was supported by several sadly unidentified partners and his niece Geli Raubal. Certainly, he had developed an obsession with disease, dirt and putrefaction, and the term "shithead" remained one of his favourite and most frequent epithets.

Probably the only syphilitic disease he picked up during these years was his anti-Semitism, his pathological hatred of all things Jewish. No matter how he sought to rationalize this, it remained an irrational, infantile obsession. Just as his laziness was excused by calling himself an "artist", so his failures were explained as the work of the Jews. At the time of his stint in Vienna, it was a city with a large and prosperous Jewish population, who dominated artistic and cultural life. Jealousy of their material or intellectual accomplishments was common. Anti-semitic pamphlets were cheap and plentiful, and they took pride of place on his shelf, next to his collections of pornography, mythology and that other favourite subject of the idle and envious mind, the occult.

To compound Hitler's self-imposed isolation, his mother died of cancer. Much has been made of the fact that the doctor who could not save her life was Jewish, which Hitler was later fond of pointing out. He was stricken by her death. During the period of her treatment, Hitler authorized the use of painful and futile chemical treatments, saying that "sometimes one must use a poison to drive out a greater poison". The same chlorine-based chemicals were later used to murder millions of Jews in the concentration camps.

Hitler tried again to gain entrance into the Vienna Academy of the Arts, and this time was refused permission to take the examination. At the end of 1908, consumed with self-pity, he disappeared from his lodgings, and without telling anyone of his whereabouts, vanished into the underbelly of Vienna.

Hitler claimed that during the following years he experienced hardship, poverty, unemployment; in short, real life. But he initially still had a good supply of money from private sources and added to this a small but useful income from the sale of dull postcards and sketches of Vienna. He also claimed that he read voraciously, when he merely continued his anti-Semitic "studies".

In 1909, Hitler hit rock bottom, ending up on the streets, hungry and homeless, surviving on handouts of soup and living in a shelter for the destitute. His pretensions to be an artist were now blown away; the spoiled and snobbish young man was now a tramp. From 1910-13 he found a place in a charitable Home for Men. Hitler became one of the established residents in the Home. Without ever forming any close relationships, it gave him an easy forum in which to begin lecturing a captive audience in the reading-room. He did not discuss, he spouted; he had no time for democracy, despising the debates of Parliamentary institutions. He scraped a living selling postcards of Vienna copied from photographs.

In 1913, Hitler moved to Munich in the German heartland of Bavaria. He told friends that he intended to enter the Munich Art Academy. He did nothing about this, but fell in love with the city: "A German city! So different from Vienna, that Babylon of races!" He styled himself "painter and writer" and became even more isolated, speaking to no-one apart from the family he lodged with and those he quarrelled with in cafés. Unfortunately, he had forgotten, or avoided, registering for military service in Vienna, and was arrested in Munich. He wrote a desperate, pitiable plea for mercy to the authorities, on the basis of his poverty and ignorance of the law. He was excused both his misdemeanour and, after examination. military service on the grounds of "physical weakness".

A year later, the Great War erupted, and Germany and Austria declared war on Russia and Serbia. Internal differences and unrest were forgotten; national unity broke out along with an ecstatic sense of patriotism. The German Kaiser declared everyone to be "German brothers", and to millions of them the war signalled an end to everyday monotony and a clear, simple direction in their lives; to fight. To Hitler, rescued from his aimless existence, the sense of purpose was a blessing: "For me these hours came as a deliverance . . . I sank down on my knees to thank Heaven for the favour of having been permitted to live in such a time".

He volunteered for the army, and to his delight was accepted. After a couple of months training he was sent to the front as a regimental runner. This position suited him ideally; it was with difficulty that he was persuaded to take leave. It was a lonely, dangerous job conveying messages between regiments, and he remained aloof from his fellow soldiers who quickly lost their enthusiasm for the war, for which he furiously and persistently accused them of being traitors. He, of course, was the super-patriot, thrilled to be involved in what he perceived as a racial conflict. He was living out his heroic, mythological fantasies, which nourished his courage.

Without exception, other soldiers and officers found him dreary and odd, and although his devotion to duty resulted in decoration (he was awarded the Iron Cross), he was never promoted beyond the rank of corporal. He never showed any discomfort with the horrors and destruction of the trenches. On the contrary, he enjoyed it all, recounting his experiences with relish. He regarded this complete lack of compassion as proof of his manhood; "War" he would say, in a pronouncement reeking of Wagnerian gloom "is for a man what childbirth is for a woman"; he could not distinguish between the values of life and death.

Hitler was lying in hospital, suffering from the after effect of a gas attack when news came of the Armistice, by which Germany surrendered. By the treaty of Versailles, Germany was required to make vast payments to its former enemies in compensation. In addition, thirteen per cent of its territory was taken away, and it was disarmed. For Hitler, and other right-wing nationalists, it was a moment of complete humiliation; those who signed the treaty were regarded as traitors.

Hitler, failed school-pupil, failed artist, social misfit, successful

soldier on the losing side and leader-in-waiting, first went to a
meeting of the German Workers' Party on 12 September 1919. He
was disappointed with the Workers' Party at his first encounter,
but went again with the encouragement of the founder, who had
been impressed by Hitler's fluency in a tirade he had launched
at the meeting. Hitler, after some hesitation, joined the Party as
member responsible for recruitment and propaganda. A career
in politics had to start somewhere; none of the big parties would
offer an opportunity to a nobody. On 16 October 1919, he made
his first public speech, and a great career as an actor was
launched. "I talked for thirty minutes, and what I had always
felt deep down in my heart was . . . was here proved true; I
could make a good speech".

Hitler soon had the name of the party changed to the "National
Socialist German Workers' Party" – the Nazis – and by 1921 he
had become its "Fuhrer".

Hitler's skill as an orator and actor grew to a peak at the
huge, staged rallies of the 1930s, when there was a distinctly
sexual relationship between him and his massed audiences.
His technique had a particular effect on women, who not
infrequently experienced orgasm listening to his rhetoric. It
was said that "Hitler!" was a popular exclamation for German
housewives to utter at the moment of ecstasy. Homosexual
listeners experienced a similar excitement. His attitude to the
crowd was not to persuade, but appeal to their feelings, to
do what God refused to – liberate them from reason and
responsibility.

Beneath the barely coherent language of his speeches lurked
a sado-masochistic relationship, in which he alternately beat and
flattered the crowd, controlling the relationship as he whipped
it towards a peak of ecstatic emotional excitement. He gained
as much from this as the crowds, and, like a lover, would
thank them after the climax. This was the closest human
relationship he possessed. As Otto Strasser, one of the original
Nazis who later deserted Hitler, said: "Hitler responds to the
vibrations of the human heart with the delicacy of a seismograph
. . . or perhaps of a wireless set . . . enabling him to act as

---

**Hitler was an animated, passionate speech maker, who appealed
to the emotions of his audience rather than their reason, and fed
off their excitement, fears and hopes. It was to prove a vital
discovery.**

a loudspeaker proclaiming the most secret desires, the least admissible instincts, the suffering and personal grievances of a whole nation . . . he sniffs the air . . . he gropes . . . he feels his way . . . senses the atmosphere. Suddenly he bursts forth. His words go like an arrow to their target . . . telling it what it most wants to hear . . ."

When his performance was combined with the vast stage spectacles of the Nuremburg rallies, the Germans willingly fell under his spell, and freely put themselves in the hands of the failed artist and former tramp from Braunnau. In spite of his passion, he never lost sight of his objectives in a speech; the whole experience remained remarkably calculating. He would practice his facial expressions in the mirror for hours, and take a long time to warm up, to sense the mood of his audience, before moving into gear, with a series of simple, repeated statements and questions to which the audience could only answer "yes" or "no". There were no complexities to be found in his speeches and he wanted no thought from an audience. A speech lasted two or more hours. Leaving them, in a style that Hollywood would admire, with an up-beat, optimistic ending, they always wanted more. In the crucial elections of the 1930s, he would make several speeches a night, dashing around the country by aeroplane.

To back up propaganda was violence. The Nazis formed a paramilitary wing called the SA, or "Brownshirts". These thugs, made up of disillusioned ex-soldiers carried out whatever intimidation and brutality was necessary against political rivals, particularly the Communists. The head of the SA was Ernst Rohm, a fat ex-soldier, who had a team of pimps scouring the school-yards of Munich to keep him supplied with the boys that were his pleasure. Hitler was hanging around with an unsavoury crew in those Munich days; a collection of misfits, sexual bandits, seedy ex-convicts, decadent aristocrats and occult weirdos. A less qualified collection of hopeful ministers was never seen.

The conditions were ideal for the Nazis. In the wake of the Great War, Germany was a humiliated, poor, and turbulent country. There was an awful vacuum where there should gave been leadership; the Kaiser had been forced to abdicate, and Germany had highly unstable governments, cobbled together from endlessly quarrelling coalitions of parties, which toppled monthly. Depression and astonishing inflation added to the chaos. In November 1923, a thousand billion marks had the same spending power as one solitary mark had in 1914. The

Nongqawuse was only fourteen years old but she was a very persuasive teenager. In 1856 she sat staring into the Gxara river and considered that she had received the call of her forebears.

On returning to her village in a semi-ecstatic state, she declared herself to be the liberator of her people whose ancestors had told her that they were just about ready to rise up from the dead and lead their descendants into an undeniably victorious war against the colonial Europeans who were taking over everywhere.

The Gcaleka Xhosa leaders were very pleased to hear this news and asked Nongqawuse what they should do to assist the planned rebellion. Well, she said, they would have to prove their devotion to the cause by burning all their crops, slaughtering all their livestock and destroying any worldly possessions that might remain lying around. The Xhosas couldn't really win on this one since they were also informed that, were they not to do this, they would be destroyed by a plague of man-eating locusts.

The Xhosas spent the entire year getting ready for their big day and on 18 February 1857, they stood out in the fields waiting for the miracle to happen. Nongqawuse told them that, for the first time in the history of mankind, the sun would turn on its tail at midday and return to set in the east, thus heralding the dawn of the new age. The tribesmen stared and stared, and they didn't have sunglasses in those days, but the sun just carried on its normal arc and, finally, sank down over the horizon in the west. This was rather a blow for Nongqawuse who realised immediately that, having burnt all their goods and having nothing left to eat for their supper that night, this was very likely to be her. She ran away and sought refuge with the very people she had been keen to annihilate a few hours earlier and the British placed her, for her own safety, on Robben Island where she assumed a new identity and became a farmer, dying peaceably in 1898.

The Xhosa tribe were not so fortunate. Twenty-five thousand died of hunger.

final crippling blow were the immense sums Germany still had to pay in compensation to her war-time enemies. The country was a black hole, in which any monster might arise. In Italy too the fascists were in the ascendancy.

Hitler's new party, devoid of policies which might confuse the voters, and with simple explanations for Germany's ills, was successful enough for him to attempt to mount a violent takeover of the State of Bavaria in November 1923. Starting with a meeting at a beer cellar in Munich, the Nazis planned to eventually march on Berlin itself. Hitler was uneasy about the whole event, but was persuaded that there would be support from the army and police. The plan was a fiasco, in which he was notably distinguished by his lack of heroism. The Bavarian Police opened fire, killing sixteen, and Hitler ended up in prison. He was sentenced to five years, but only served nine months. During this time he wrote "Mein Kampf" with its 164,000 grammatical and syntactical mistakes, enjoyed considerable comfort and received as many visitors as he pleased. When he came out, he was a hero.

Hitler was the Nazis' greatest asset; as far as he was concerned, he was the party. Hitler, so long an outcast, had now become a celebrity. His company was sought at the houses of the rich and famous. He dined with industrialists, and spent weekends at the home of Winifred Wagner, granddaughter of his idol the composer; his pride and pleasure knew no bounds. He remained lazy, having little time for the day to day running of affairs. Being a genius, he needed time to think, and was frequently in retreat at his country hideaway at Berchtesgarten.

Nevertheless, he had a very clear idea of what he wanted. After the failure of the attempt to seize power by use of force, he was determined that he should ascend the throne legally. It is common for dictators to desire their terror to be sanctioned by law; they are forever holding elections at which they are the only candidate. He drove the Nazi party on over ten years and countless disappointments. By 1932, it was the largest single Party, with over fourteen million votes but could not win an outright majority over the ruling conservative and nationalist coalition. What Hitler could do was force election after election to continually de-stabilize the authorities, to gnaw away at their support until they were at last forced to do a deal with him, and invite him to join the coalition.

Of the seven women known to have had relationships of some sort with Hitler, no less than six committed or attempted to commit suicide. Suicide, we are told, is often a reaction induced by shame in the wake of enforced sexual deviancy. Some of these deaths are deeply suspicious giving the impression that women who came to know Hitler's intimate habits rather too well were disposed of if they threatened to reveal them. One of the more dramatic is the death of Renate Mueller, a well known film actress, whom Hitler invited back to his quarters one evening. She confided in tears to her director that after graphically describing the process of Gestapo torture to her, Hitler, who had become increasingly animated, fell on the floor in front of her and begged to be beaten. Pleading that he was unworthy, he demanded that she kick him. The scene became unbearable, and she finally gave in to his wishes. The more she kicked him, the more excited he became. Shortly after relating this, she mysteriously flew out of the window of a Berlin hotel. This was in 1937, with the Nazis firmly in power and her death was ruled a suicide.

Before this there was Geli Raubal, daughter of his half sister, Angela. After Hitler's holiday in prison, he summoned Angela and her daughter to work as his housekeepers. Geli, in her late teens had become something of a beauty. Hitler's interest went well beyond that of a friendly uncle. She was blonde and youthful, the Nazis dream of an Aryan maiden. Straight out of Wagner, she went straight to Hitler's heart.

The incestuous overtones made it more appealing. Before long, the seventeen-year-old had been set up in a Munich apatment, and was being escorted around town by "Uncle Alf". He even paid for her singing lessons with the best available teachers to complete the fantasy by turning her into a Wagnerian opera singer. Hitler was infatuated, which did not go unnoticed by those around him. Complaints were made that Hitler was "excessively diverted from his political duties by the constant company of his niece".

In 1929, Hitler bought a luxurious apartment in Munich, exiled Geli's mother to his weekend house, and moved Geli in with him. They had separate bedrooms, but on the same floor. Hitler was extremely possessive about her, and having initially enjoyed the power and celebrity that was hers through her relationship with the rising star of German politics, she was increasingly cooped in and suffocated by Hitler's jealousy. She was frightened of what she had found inside him.

She had been plotting to escape for several months when, on 18 September, 1931, she died. It was another "suicide". Geli shot herself in the chest after an argument with Hitler. The true circumstances surrounding her death are a continuing controversy. It is thought that she was murdered, either on Hitler's orders, or by Nazis who feared her influence on Hitler. Certainly her death was rapidly covered up and the body hastily buried with the co-operation of the right-wing authorities.

Fritz Gerlich, a journalist who claimed to have conclusive evidence of Hitler's involvement with her murder was killed before he could print his evidence. All his documents were burned and his secret died with him, but before her death, Geli had confided to Strasser the nature of Hitler's sexual requirements – that she was obliged to urinate on him. Revelations of this sort would have been most damaging to his career.

By this time, he was already having an affair with Eva Braun, which continued until their mutual suicide in 1945. Being Hitler's girlfriend was no fun. He never called, showed her little or no affection, never told her his whereabouts and flirted incessantly with other women, who found this reptile quite charming and fascinating, though physically he was not impressive, being short and flabby with spindly limbs and rotting teeth. He preferred women who were petite and blonde like his mother. He might flatter the others, but he knew what he liked: "A woman must be a cute, cuddly, naive little thing – tender, sweet and stupid . . ."

Against a background of growing racial violence and outright murder engineered by his own brownshirts, Hitler broke into the government in 1933 as part of a coalition, personally taking the position of Chancellor. The politicians who had done deals with the Nazis in order to keep a measure of power for their own parties were now gobbled up. They had assumed that he would simply shoot the Communists, which showed how little they understood Hitler. Von Papen, the Vice-Chancellor, had boasted that Hitler was not to be taken seriously. "No danger at all," he said; "We've hired him for our act". Overseas, few could take Hitler seriously on a personal level and failed to see how the Germans could do so on a national scale. The British firmly believed the Nazis had peaked and no longer presented a threat.

A stage-managed fire at the seat of Government allowed Hitler to declare a state of emergency. Under threat of using his legal powers to dissolve the government and throw the country in chaos once more, he obtained an Enabling Act which gave him dictatorial powers and banned all other political parties. Unbelievably, still without a practical policy to their name, the Nazis had triumphed. The failed artist was about to have his revenge.

The Nazi manifesto had been simple. Faced with a country in a severe economic crisis, they promised to solve everything by restoring German pride. This meant tearing up the Treaty of Versailles. They would refuse to pay compensation; they would re-arm; they would reclaim Germany's lost lands and extend these to provide "Lebensraum" or living room for the great German race, and they would solve the Jewish problem, which naturally included the Communists. In other words, Hitler's policy was to wage war and spill blood.

Whilst his nation geared up for war, Hitler began to suffer physical problems to accompany his mental sickness. He had long been principally vegetarian because of bowel problems. After Geli's death he never touched meat again, complaining that it was like eating corpses. The bowel problems of abdominal pains, constipation and vast flatulence increased. He began to see a quack doctor, Theo Morrel, who became his constant companion. By the end of the war, Hitler was taking up to thirty drugs and vitamin compounds for his real and imagined complaints.

Morrel's favourite treatment, which Hitler took huge quantities of was called "Mutaflor". In keeping with his paranoid theories about the Jews, Hitler saw himself being persecuted by "noxious bacteria" which had "invaded" his colon. Mutaflor, claimed Morrel, would replace the evil bacteria with a pure Aryan strain cultured from the faeces of "a Bulgarian peasant of the most vigorous stock".

Morrel also started giving Hitler pain killing injections for his bowel pains. These contained amphetamines, and it is medically thought that Hitler became addicted to the drugs, which perked him up.

Driven by a policy of huge deficit spending, Germany rearmed, flaunting the Versailles treaty, building the autobahns that would carry its troops to war. By 1938, Germany faced something of a financial crisis. There was nothing left in the kitty. The war which Hitler planned had to begin.

First to go was Austria, which was annexed as part of Germany without a fight. Hitler could now claim that he was German by birth; the Rhineland, under French occupation since the end of the Great War had already been infiltrated by his soldiers. Czechoslovakia and then Poland were attacked under the pretext that he was acting to protect German minorities within them. He treated Czechoslovakia like cake, claiming he only wanted a little piece of it, then wolfing the whole country. He called it a "ridiculous state", rightfully German property. Chamberlain, the British Prime Minister, flew to meet him, and came back clutching a worthless agreement to "peace in our time". Hitler signed a non-aggression treaty with Stalin, in which they agreed to help themselves to Poland, and on 31 August, 1939, the Germans launched a Blitzkrieg which swept the million strong but antiquated Polish army away within hours.

There was no way back. In Hitler's words: "I go the way that providence guides me, with the assurance of a sleepwalker".

Britain and France declared war. After twenty-nine postponements, the Invasion of France took place in Spring 1940. It was a daring and completely successful plan created by General Erich von Marsten. So rapidly did the Germans advance that Hitler lost his nerve several times, afraid that his tanks were too far ahead of the rest of his army. The troops were equally matched on both sides, but the Germans had an overwhelming superiority in terms of hardware. The screaming dive-bombers, fitted with Wagnerian sirens on Hitler's orders, smashed a path for the massive panzer tank divisions. After them poured the troops. Within six weeks they had the French army in tatters and the British on the beach at Dunkirk. It was here that Hitler decided to halt the advance, frightened by his success. Goering promised that the Airforce would finish off the British troops. They failed, and the British managed the remarkable evacuation.

Hitler was now master of greater Europe. His forces were in Norway, Africa and Greece. Italy was an ally, and Spain neutral but friendly. He was now sure of his military genius, took less advice and shouted more. His quarelling Generals began to simply agree with him. The planned invasion of England was to be preceded by massive air-strikes against military and civilian targets. On "Eagle Day", 13 August 1940, Goering's Air force began to bomb Britain. By 17 September, the raids had stopped in the face of huge losses. On one day, seventy-one aircraft were downed. Hitler could not afford to sustain these losses indefinitely. Germany had a limited supply of oil and raw materials. To build the Third Reich they would have to conquer Russia.

Stalin, although he knew that war with Germany was inevitable, was buying time, and picking up any territorial scraps that Hitler overlooked. Hitler had plans for Russia, when he had subjugated the inferior Slavs to their correct position as slaves of the German master-race: "This Russian desert . . . we shall populate it. We'll take away its character of an Asiatic steppe, we'll Europeanize it. With this object in mind we have undertaken the construction of roads. Studded along their whole length will be German towns and around these towns our colonists will settle . . ."

Everything outside Germany was a wasteland inhabited by sub-humans to be enslaved, part turned into one enormous, Nazi holiday camp, the remainder reserved for slave-labour and extermination. The "Final Solution" began in 1941. Poland was turned into an abattoir. Of the eighteen million victims of Nazi brutality in Europe, eleven million died on Polish soil. Of that eleven million, five million were Jews. The names of these places in which, without compassion, young and old of both sexes, were systematically gassed, shot, tortured, starved and worked to death with complete indifference on the part of their German captors will never be forgotten; Dachau, Buchenwald, Belzec, Chelmno, Treblinka, Mauthausen and the model of hell-on-earth, the heart of the Third Reich, the inside of Hitler's head and the summit of his art, Auschwitz.

In June, 1941, operation "Barbarossa", the invasion of Russia, began. Behind the three separate armies that smashed their way into Russia went the "Einsatzgruppen", the extermination squads sent to liquidate the "Jewish-Bolshevik ruling class". Over 300,000 civilians were killed in the first six months. Of the 5,700,000 Russian prisoners taken, barely one million survived the war. Instead of casting themselves as an army come to liberate the Russians from the repression of the Stalinist regime, they continued their policy of racist genocide, thus motivating the Russians to fight tooth and nail.

In Africa, Rommel began his campaign victoriously. For a time, it looked as if the Nazis might, unbelievably, prevail.

A year later, in November 1942, the tide turned. Although the war would go on for another two and a half years, the Germans could no longer emerge victorious. In Africa, Rommel was defeated at El Alamein. America had joined the war. The Allies were bombing Germany. And crucially, in Russia, the Germans came to a grinding halt in the carnage of the Eastern Front.

Hitler began increasingly to isolate himself, rarely emerging from his rural hideaway, the "Wolf's Lair", a depressing complex in the midst of a thick and gloomy forest in Prussia. He aged rapidly, and his consumption of drugs rocketed. He refused to read reports about the military situation and bomb damage to Germany, like a petulant actor who will not read the bad reviews. He ate with his secretaries who were forbidden to mention the war. After 1943, he made only two speeches.

Rather than seek practical ways to increase Germany's military hopes, Hitler looked for miracle weapons to bring him victory.

This was a consequence of his love of mythology; he believed in magic more than people and science only when it supported his preconceptions; above all, like most dabblers in the occult, he wanted instant results. It is due to his impatience that he gave little serious attention to the Atomic bomb; he preferred to send his VI and V2 rockets over the English Channel. Though they killed nearly 10,000 civilians, they were hopelessly inaccurate and militarily insignificant. He had no interest in defensive weapons as the possibility of retreat and defeat had not occurred to him. He threw his armies forwards into hopeless battle and inglorious death. In 1943, the Allies declared that they would not seek a peace settlement; they would accept only "unconditional surrender".

In June 1944, the Allies landed in France. Rommel, who was in charge of coastal defences was on his way to see Hitler when the news broke, Hitler was asleep, and no-one dared disturb him. By the time he woke up in the afternoon and ordered, with a typical lack of realism, that "the enemy must be annihilated at the bridgehead by the evening of 6 June", the Allies were well ensconced. Within ten days, 600,000 troops were ashore. By the end of a month, nearly a million. Hitler could not accept it. He was convinced that the Allies could not hold together, that their alliance would collapse, that the British would fight the Russians, that his miracle weapons would destroy their spirit. In the East, the Russians expelled the Germans from their territory. They were only four hundred miles from Berlin.

There were heroes inside the Church, and the Army, who understood the nature of the evil the Nazis had created, and others who now realized the suicide that Hitler intended for Germany. They realized Hitler had to die. Henning von Tresckow, one of a small number of high ranking Army officers who were involved with the bomb-plot to kill Hitler that Summer, wrote to his fellow conspirator Klaus von Stauffenberg: "The assassination must be attempted at all costs . . . Even should it fail . . . we must prove to the world and to future generations that the men of the German Resistance dared to take this step and hazard their lives upon it . . ."

Many of these men were highly decorated, gallant and intelligent soldiers from old German families. Von Stauffenberg, crippled and blind in one eye with war-wounds, planted a brief-case with a bomb in it under a table in the conference room on 20 July. They had made earlier attempts on his life, but the bombs had refused to go off. After his death, they planned to use the army to take Berlin and sweep the

Nazis away. The bomb did explode, but by a freak Hitler survived.

In the resulting purge, the principal conspirators, who had gathered together in expectation of Hitler's death, were shot or committed suicide. Planned rebellions by the army in Germany and France stuttered and faltered when they heard Hitler was alive. Himmler and the Gestapo went to work. Field Marshal von Witzleben, Generals Hoepner, von Hase and Stieff, together with four others were hanged by piano wires from meat-hooks, a means of death by slow throttling which is prolonged and agonizing. Hitler had a film made of the execution, and watched and re-watched it with delight. The men, who had been tortured for days, showed considerable dignity.

The failure of the bomb plot rejuvenated the will of the deranged Fuhrer. Now he was convinced Heaven had spared him. It also reassured him that all the defeats he had suffered were due entirely to treachery on the part of his generals. For the little that remained of his life, he excluded from power anyone he did not feel was personally loyal to him. Goebbels, Himmler and Bormann, all fanatical Nazis, wielded the power. Each strove to establish a personal Empire amidst the ruins.

On 25 August, Paris was liberated. On 11 September, an American patrol crossed the German frontier. The war had come home to Hitler, five years after his assault on Poland.

He moved into the bunker permanently. From above ground, it looked like an Egyptian tomb. Its concrete walls, sixteen feet thick, further insulated Hitler from the outside world. In December, the Germans launched a desperate bid to break the allied lines in the Ardennes with the object of taking Antwerp. It was Hitler's last encore, and an entirely futile military gesture, which sacrificed the last of the German reserves. The offensive was opposed by most of the surviving army officers, whom Hitler shouted down. This was the "Battle of the Bulge". After an initial success, which Hitler trumpeted as the greatest victory of the war, they suffered terrible losses – 100,000 men, six hundred tanks, 1,600 aircraft – and were compelled to withdraw. A month after the attack, they were once again in full retreat. People began to hide from Hitler, who was seeking consolation in a vast, illuminated model of the rebuilding he planned for his home town of Linz. He was returning in his mind to those far-off days when, posing as a student, he had sketched and dreamed of the great, though undefined, destiny that lay in store for him.

As his own suicide drew nearer, he ordered a scorched earth policy, and the destruction of anything which might be used to

26 April, 1945. The Bunker is shaking as the Chancellery above is shelled and collapses. The Russians are now only a mile away. Hitler cannot understand why nothing has been done to launch a counter attack. He is hysterical with rage; all who hear him are shaken and exhausted; "I expect the relief of Berlin! Where is Heinrici's army? Where is Wenck's army? I expect them!"

Eva Braun and Goebbels have announced their intention of seeking death among the ruins with him. They too have moved into the Bunker. In the words of Hitler's architect, Speer, who secretly calls the Bunker the "Isle of the Departed", so far away from life are its inhabitants: ". . . he had reached the last station of his flight from reality, a reality which he had refused to acknowledge since youth".

re-build Germany after the war: "If the war is lost, the people will be lost also . . . In any case only those who are inferior will remain after this struggle . . ."

He showed no concern for the fate of his people; he took no responsibility for the defeat. He thought only of himself.

Hitler will not consider surrender. His speech has become an invariable string of meaningless phrases: "no retreat; only with permission; accepting the risk; concentrated bold and determined attack; fanatical will". Even the most faithful rats are baling out. Himmler is off trying to do a deal with the Allies. Goering has already tried. Neither will succeed. When Hitler finds out they too have betrayed him, he orders their arrest and shoots those connected with them. Speer is refusing to follow his orders to blow up the world. His armies are rushing West to surrender to the British and Americans; anything to avoid the Russians. When not shouting, he dribbles and talks incessantly about his two Golden Labradors, Blondi, and the little puppy, Wolf. He will not let anybody touch Wolf. He has a stock of dog stories and repeats them over and over again. He eats only vegetable soup, cake and drugs.

A few insufferable days later, on the evening of the 29th, with the enemy only streets away, he marries Eva Braun. Since she has volunteered to die with him, he has been affectionate with her. They drink champagne, and talk about the old days. Hitler, armed with cake, retires to dictate his Last Political Will and Testament. In this he again disclaims all responsibility for all that has happened, and claims that: "I myself, as founder and creator of the movement have preferred death to cowardly abdication or even capitulation".

Hitler is finally going to kill himself. He has washed his hands of those he has led to their destruction, in whom he invoked the power of old myths to encourage acts of unspeakable evil, to enact his fantasies for him.

It is now the afternoon of the 30th. Outside the door of Hitler's suite, they are tense, waiting for the moment when this nightmare will end. Hitler and his wife have said their goodbyes. Someone murmurs the news that Mussolini has been caught and shot by Italian partisans, his body hung up to public ridicule in Milan. Hitler's chauffeur thinks momentarily about the two hundred litres of petrol he has acquired on Hitler's orders. He wonders if it will be enough to obliterate the bodies. Will they be safe, burning them above, while the shells come raining down?

At last, a shot. After a brief struggle with the door, they enter. At either end of an upright sofa are Mr and Mrs Adolf Hitler. He has shot himself in the temple, she is dead from poison. The spell begins to drop from the followers immediately. There is a strange lifting, a sense of release. Adolf Hitler is dead. In a few days Germany will surrender. But the World, thank God, has not been destroyed by the failed artist from Braunnau.

chapter nine

VLAD DRACUL: THE IMPALER STRIKES BACK

The rehabilitation of dead dictators by their successors in tyranny is common; the new always looks to the old to justify itself. If the image of the old is grubby, the official historians are sent to clean it up.

Nicolae Ceaucescu, the late, despised President of Rumania, often drew comparison with the legendary Rumanian tyrant, Vlad Dracul or Dracula, better known as Vlad the Impaler, who was three times king of Wallachia between 1448 and 1476. Wallachia is one of the three main provinces of modern Rumania, and is considered to be the symbolic heartland of the country. As his name suggests, Vlad was well-known for punishing his enemies by impaling them, which earned him a fearsome reputation even in an age where being burned alive was the equivalent of receiving a parking-fine. Bram Stoker, whose novel "Dracula" was much inspired by Rumanian folk-tales, gave Vlad's other name to his blood-sucking Count Dracula, who was proud to claim descent from the ferocious Wallachian Prince. The Americans felt that "Dracula" was such a good representation of the Communist menace that they made the novel recommended reading for their troops. It was not an image that Ceaucescu enjoyed, and his historians were unleashed in an attempt to prove that Vlad had been slandered, that he should be remembered as a great patriot, who never kebabbed a man without good reason.

Impaling is a very old form of execution. It is described by the Greeks, and was much practised by the ancient Turkish regimes. It was the Turks who first gave Vlad the title of "Kazakli", meaning Impaler, which in Rumanian is "Tepes".

In Vlad's time, impalement was also practised in Transylvania, then part of neighbouring Hungary.

It was not a short, swift death. The stakes on which people were impaled were carefully rounded at the end and bathed in oil, so that the entrails of the victims should not be pierced by a wound too immediately fatal. The legs of the victim were stretched apart by horses and attendants held the stake steady while the body was dragged onto it. The stake was then hoisted upright, and the victim was slowly impaled by the force of their own weight. Not everybody was impaled from the buttocks upwards, but sometimes through the heart, stomach and chest. It is estimated that Vlad disposed of over 100,000 unwanted opponents in this manner over a six-year period. There are many German woodcuts from the period showing graphic representations of these atrocities. A bishop visiting the court of Mathhias Corvinus, King of neighbouring Hungary at the time was told: "That 40,000 men and women of the opposite faction had been put to death shortly beforehand upon Vlad Tepes' order subject to the most devilish torments. He killed some by breaking them under the wheels of carts; others stripped of their clothes were skinned alive up to their entrails; others placed upon stakes, or roasted upon red hot coals placed under them; others punctured with stakes piercing their head, their breast, their buttocks, and the middle of their entrails with the stake emerging from their mouths; and in order that no form of cruelty shall be missing he stuck stakes in both the mothers breasts and thrust their babies unto them. Finally he killed them in various ferocious ways, torturing them with many kinds of instruments such as the atrocious cruelties of the most frightful tyrant could devise . . ."

Even in his own times, the reputation of Vlad Dracul exerted a profound grip on the imagination. The modern Rumanians would attempt to show that these incidents, although they undeniably happened, were exaggerated by the fifteenth-century Germans, who took to writing propaganda pamphlets about Vlad, with titles like "About the bad Tyrant, Dracula", and "About a great tyrant named Dracula". Ceaucescu's historians claimed that Vlad had punished German merchants for their greed, and these had retaliated by blackening the name of the "Defender of the Christian World".

The date of Vlad the Impaler's birth is uncertain. He was probably born and bought up in Sighishoara, a Transylvanian town. Confusingly, his father, Vlad II, also had the title of Dracul. This translates as "Devil", which may be in reference to his cruelty, but may also have something to do with his coat of arms given to him by the Hungarian ruler, Sigismund. This featured a dragon, from which "Dracul" can be traced. Hence, Dracula means son of the devil, or dragon. Some Rumanians tried to argue that the title "devil" shows affection, as in "he's a devil of a fellow", but this seems somewhat hopeful, although the Turks definitely did admire the Impaler's handiwork. One Rumanian historian even advanced the argument that Dracul is derived from "Drago", meaning "dear one". Ho ho.

At the time of Vlad Dracula's childhood in the first half of the fifteenth century, Wallachia was just emerging as an important strategic province, forming a valuable buffer between Christian Hungary and Moslem Turkey. Whilst realizing the mutual benefit they enjoyed from having such a punch-bag, these two great powers were forever seeking to establish a hold over it, and made sure it was governed by someone loyal to their respective rulers. Vlad II maintained a difficult balancing act between these two, falling off the swing several times. After being dethroned by the Hungarians for allowing the Turks to use Wallachia as a military base to attack them, he was re-installed by the Turks in 1444. As security for his future conduct, they took his sons Vlad Dracula and Radu The Handsome into Turkey, as hostages. This period in Turkish captivity probably provided Vlad with a unique opportunity to study their applied use of terror. He must also have feared for his life, as meanwhile Vlad Senior had teamed up with the Hungarians and rashly started a Christian Crusade against the Turks, which failed. In the aftermath of defeat, the Christian Allies started quarrelling as to whose fault it was. Vlad lost this battle too, and was killed by the Hungarians. His eldest son, Mircea who had stayed with him, was tortured and buried alive. The Hungarians took over Wallachia.

Dracula claimed his inheritance with Turkish help in 1448, but was booted out by the Hungarians a month later, who put a man called Vladislav on the throne. Dracula spent the next eight years worming his way back into favour with the Hungarians, who finally decided in 1456, that they no longer cared for Vladislav, and Dracula got his kingdom back. On 6 September 1456 he took an oath of allegiance to the Hungarian King, and a few days later he pledged obedience to the Turks. It was a tricky situation.

In the following six years, the Impaler struck back, ruling with a ruthlessness and full-blooded commitment to cruelty previously unseen in Europe. Ceaucescu's historians argued that his principle targets were the potentially traitorous and wealthy aristocratic or "Boyar" class, the German merchants and the non-Christian Turks, plus those that he thought to be "idle" or "dishonest", with the result that the people were so terrified, crime, or any form of dissent, was unknown, making Wallachia a paradise for the poor but loyal, hard-working and honest peasant. This is merely justifying Ceaucescu's own extremes. There are folk-stories and histories that see Dracula as "just", but his behaviour in them has nothing to do with our idea of justice, and everything to do with inspiring blind obedience through sheer terror. The sixteenth century historian, Sebastian Munster wrote:

"It is recalled that Dracula was unimaginably cruel, and just. When the Turkish envoys refused to honour him and take their caps off, because that was their old age custom, he is said to have strengthened their custom by ordering their caps to be fixed with three nails to their heads so that they could never take them off again; and he had numberless Turks impaled while he was feasting amidst them with his friends. Besides, he had all the beggars and idlers, the sick, the poor, the old and the destitute; all the miserable people gathered to a feast and when they had eaten everything up and were dizzy with wine he had the house burnt down to ashes. He was said to have had the feet of Turkish prisoners skinned and rubbed with salt and while they were moaning with pain, goats were admitted to lick their soles and make their suffering greater . . ."

"Just" merely indicates a perverted notion of equality. Vlad displayed considerable imagination in devising suitable, grisly punishments to fit the crime. The poor and sick could sleep easily, assured that they would be accorded the same ghastly treatment as the healthy and wealthy.

In one folk story, Dracula comes across a peasant wearing badly fitting clothes, which he takes as a sure sign that the man's wife is lazy. In spite of the man's protestations that he is very happy with his wife, who works too hard to worry about his clothes, Vlad has her impaled and marries the peasant to another woman. She is so terrified of meeting the same fate that she doesn't even stop to eat, and works with her bread on one shoulder and salt on the other, nibbling on the move. In a Russian story, Vlad so hated dishonesty or evil that if anyone so much as told a lie they faced impalement. The legend says he put a gold cup by a remote fountain for the use of travellers, and though it was unguarded, no-one dare steal it. In other folk-tales, Dracula has a fetish for tidiness and a reputation as an impatient master: "Woe to any soldier he saw improperly attired, he rarely escaped with his life . . . he could not tolerate anyone who was slow in his work". The modern Rumanian historians, choosing slyly to present these legends as literal history, saw in them evidence of a man of morality, upright, demanding, severe perhaps, but always with a purpose – to create good, well-behaved citizens; an insidious attempt to justify the Stalinist terror of Ceaucescu by invoking a re-vamped Dracula as his noble precedent. These old tales show nothing of the sort; they show that so deep was the fear Dracula inspired that he endures in folk-stories as a bogeyman used to frighten children into behaving themselves. When adults used to tell children to say their prayers or they would go to Hell, they surely did not mean to suggest that the Devil approved of prayer.

Meanwhile, back in fifteenth century Wallachia, Vlad set out to exterminate potential opponents and to restrict the trade the Saxon merchants carried out. The towns of Sibiu and Brasov were the scenes of major impalements in 1457–8. He believed he might find his half-brother and rival, Vlad the Monk at Sibiu, and raided it, impaling and burning women and children. At Brasov, other claimants to the throne were thought to be hiding, besides its being a Saxon stronghold. This old, fortified town is overlooked by St Jacob's Hill, 1,200 feet high. The many he chose to impale here rather than kill immediately must have made an awesome sight, planted in droves up the rocky slopes. It is claimed that up to 30,000 died, though this is certainly exaggerated. The German prints that began to circulate recording this massacre, show him happily sitting amongst this forest, munching on human remains. Understandably, it is from this point that his reputation rapidly declined. A noble who was unable to bear the stench and complained was impaled on an extra large stake with the words; "You live up there, where the smell cannot reach you!".

Dracula was obsessed with eliminating possible pretenders to his throne, and caught up with another, Danciel III in 1460. Having literally been forced to dig his grave, Danciel was obliged to deliver his own obituary before being decapitated. Only seven of his supporters escaped. The remainder were impaled with their families for company.

At this point in his history we find the story of the Turkish envoys, whose turbans, which they were forbidden by their religion to remove, were nailed to their heads. It has been written that this shows Dracula's sense of dignity; everyone had to take off their hats in his presence, but he was simply spoiling for a fight with the Turks. He should have been paying them 10,000 ducats a year and sending them five hundred boys for their army. Instead of this he put their bills and reminders on the fire and chased any stray envoys out of the country. Those whom he caught were skewered in the usual manner.

The old boyar, or aristocratic class, who might have been a threat to his authority, were exterminated en masse in one highly successful evening. He invited them, and their families, to dinner at his castle at Tirgoviste. Surprisingly, they fell for it, and five hundred men, women and children joined the growing plantation of human lollipops outside the city walls. A few, principally young men, were spared in order to work as slave labour on the construction of another castle at Poenar.

Predictably, the Turks wanted to have a word with him. Dracula was evasive. He refused to leave the country for talks on the grounds that he feared a revolt in his absence, a not altogether unlikely scenario. A meeting was arranged in neighbouring Bulgaria. This was still Turkish territory, but at least Dracula was not obliged to travel to Constantinople, a long and dangerous trip. Dracula, however, suspected a trap, and pre-empted any Turkish move by ambushing the Turks' envoy, Hamza Pasha. Then, masquerading as the Turkish party, Dracula's troops entered the Turkish border stronghold of Giurgiu, which they utterly destroyed and set on fire. Dracula beheaded the envoys, and took the captives back to the comfort of Tirgoviste where he added their impaled bodies to his thriving, maggoty collection. Having enraged the Turks, he then courted the Hungarians for support in his escalating dispute, sending the Hungarian King, Matthias Corvinus a consignment of Turkish delight; two bags full of noses, ears and heads to show he was serious.

Dracula was not a believer in the free market. The German traders were again massacred at the port of Braila. Four hundred Saxon apprentices and older merchants were burned alive and impaled. Most of them were only boys who were there to learn the language. Ceaucescu's historians decided that they were almost certainly "spies". Ceaucescu himself feared the Hungarian and German minorities living in Rumania. It was Hungarians who initiated the revolution against him. When they revolted, he ordered a Dracula-like response, sending gunmen in to mow down the crowds.

Over five hundred years later, Ceaucescu would cast himself as the defender of his country and the true Stalinist faith. He considered it vital that Dracula should appear in the history books as a Christian Crusader, and his campaigns against the Turks were therefore blown up in importance, though they achieved little. Dracula plunged into war for his own reasons and then could not persuade the rest of Europe to join him in what he tried to portray as a Holy Crusade. Perhaps he was just not their cup of tea.

Dracula ravaged the countryside along the Danube to the Black Sea, killing, in his own words an estimated 24,000 "without counting those who we burned in their homes or whose heads we did not take". As his figure was based on the number of heads he took home with him, the estimate is reliable. The Turkish Sultan Mohammed II invaded with a force of 60,000, twice the size of Dracula's army, with the intention of putting the less blood-thirsty Prince Radu on the throne. In spite of bitter fighting and a scorched-earth policy, Dracula was forced to retreat towards Tirgoviste. The Turks followed him. Dracula prepared a suitable spectacle for them.

The country the Turks marched through on their way to Tirgoviste was burned, desolate and unusually quiet. It was an uneasy experience. Just outside the city, they came across a sight that halted them in dismay and horror. In a narrow gulley a mile long, were the impaled bodies of 20,000 Turks, boyars, women and children. In some accounts the amount is even greater, with the forest of pales extending for three kilometres. Crows and vultures had made their nests in the chests of the corpses, which had, to all intents and purposes, become unholy trees. The Sultan was shocked and impressed by this display of torture and carnage, and, it is claimed, admitted that he could not take the land from a man who was capable of such things to his own people.

In the event, the Sultan was wrong. Dracula retreated, and his army and nobles deserted him before he could impale them for losing. Terror he inspired, but not loyalty. This was angrily dismissed by Ceaucescu's historians as "treachery". There was nothing wrong with the leader; it was his people who were not up to scratch.

Dracula fled into Hungarian Transylvania, where he expected to be received as a Christian hero, but found himself promptly locked up by the Hungarians for the next ten years. He was a diplomatic embarrassment; Europe could only take him in small doses. He was an unlovable figure, described in a contemporary account as: "Short and stocky, with a cold and terrible appearance. A strong and aquiline nose, swollen nostrils, a thin and reddish face in which very long eyelashes framed large wide open green eyes; the bushy black eyebrows made them appear threatening. His face and chin were shaven, but for a moustache. Swollen temples . . . a bulls neck . . . and black curly locks."

But in 1476, when Wallachia had, in their view, become too pro-Turkish, the Hungarians unleashed their pet Devil-dog once more, and on 26 November, Vlad Dracula III, The Impaler, bounded back onto the throne. The Turks only retreated momentarily and on 26 December, Dracula was killed in battle outside Bucharest. His army of 4,000 was also wiped out. It is strongly rumoured that he was killed by his own officers, or even relatives. His old enemy Mohammed II had the great pleasure of receiving his head, which he displayed proudly on a pole. It was third time lucky for the Sultan. Perhaps this is the origin of the belief that you have to cut off a vampire's head to be properly rid of it.

The rest of Dracula's body was buried outside a church door so that everybody should have the chance to walk on him. Not so, say the Rumanian historians. He was much mourned; it was in fact because he'd married a Roman Catholic and therefore couldn't be buried inside an Orthodox church. A likely story. They claimed to have found his grave at Snagov, Ceaucescu's favourite watering hole. It was by an ironic coincidence that Nicolae Ceaucescu, who had tried so hard to enhance Dracula's reputation, should have met his death at the same time of the year as his hero, at Christmas, and also at the hands of his own officers; the kind of happy coincidence historians can't prevent.

There was clearly a political and military purpose behind some of Dracula's extraordinary behaviour, but it was not ultimately a success. As he devoted his life to cruelty, we must presume that is how he wished to be remembered; to separate the man from his deeds is opening the way for those who argue that Hitler had nothing to do with the Final Solution.

A typical Rumanian verdict on him in Ceaucescu's time was ". . . a harsh if just man; a brave defender of the independence of his homeland", or "a great hero of the common man. A fighter against wealthy corruption and foreign imperialism . . ." These descriptions are virtually interchangeable with the endless praise the official press heaped upon the head of Ceaucescu. Whatever justification is made for the actions of either of them, their philosophy was one of terror, an obstinately sterile soil in which to cultivate fond memories of oneself.

• chapter ten •

SADDAM HUSSEIN: STILL CRAZY AFTER ALL THESE YEARS

The 28 April, 1992 is President Saddam Hussein's fifty-fifth birthday. It is over a year since the "Mother of all Battles" and the spectacular rout of the Iraqui forces in Kuwait. Contrary to hopes, Saddam Hussein is firmly back in power. In his home town of Takrit, north of Baghdad, columns of carefully organized demonstrators chant "We all love Saddam", and "Our blood, our soul, we sacrifice to Saddam!". The eighty mile road from Baghdad is clogged with lorries bussing in more demonstrators, under the supervision of officials of the ruling Baath party. They are herded into the football stadium to watch colourfully dressed folk dancers perform a piece entitled "The village hears of the birth of Saddam". Various government dignitaries watch, mostly relatives of Saddam Hussein. There is only one significant absence; the birthday boy himself. He is notoriously elusive, and like a God, can only be worshipped via his many priests and images. It is not divine inscrutability that makes him so aloof, but fear of assassination. As compensation for his physical absence the impression is given that he is everywhere and everybody. His portrait, dressed as sober statesman, military genius, historic conqueror or even telephone engineer is plastered all over Baghdad. His name is mentioned on the radio every minute of the day. He is constantly on television, but cannot give live interviews or an off-the-cuff response to events as his speeches are filmed hours or days beforehand in secret locations, for fear of betraying his whereabouts to the agents and aircraft of his enemies. The Israelis have sworn to be revenged for the random rocket attacks on their country during the war, and they generally keep their promises. Inside Iraq, the Kurdish and Shia populations hate him; the enthusiasm that surrounds his personality cult is orchestrated. Iraq is a police state.

By still clinging to power after a decade of disastrous warfare, worsening social conditions, internal repression and the systematic murder of minorities, Saddam Hussein has qualified as one of the world's great dictators. As slippery and tough as a cockroach, and entirely without shame, he exhibits the callous lack of emotion and preference for solving problems with violence that one would expect of an ambitious mobster.

The historian John Addington Symonds was so puzzled by the cruelty of tyrants that he invented his own word- haematomania, meaning "blood-madness" to describe it. He devotes an appendix in his work *The Renaissance in Italy* to the subject, taking as an example the Dark Age tyrant Ibrahim ibn Ahmed, prince of Africa and Sicily in the second half of the ninth century. "This man, besides displaying peculiar ferocity in his treatment of enemies and prisoners of war, delighted in the execution of horrible butcheries within the walls of his own palace. His astrologers having once predicted that he should die by the hands of a "small assassin", he killed off the whole retinue of his pages, and filled up their place with a suite of negroes whom he proceeded to treat after the same fashion. On another occasion, when one of his three hundred eunuchs had by chance been witness of the tyrant's drunkenness, Ibrahim slaughtered the whole band. Again, he is said to have put an end to sixty youths, originally selected for his pleasures, burning them by gangs of five or six in the furnace, or suffocating them in the hot chambers of his baths. Eight of his brothers were murdered in his presence; and when one, who was so diseased that he could scarcely stir, implored to be allowed to end his days in peace, Ibrahim answered: "I make no exceptions". His own son Abu l-Aghlab was beheaded by his orders before his eyes; and the execution of chamberlains, secretaries, ministers and courtiers was of common occurrence.

Which is how he started out, and where he cultivated his instinct to survive at any cost; hell would be playing Monopoly with Saddam Hussein. So erratic and unrealistic is his behaviour, that in an effort to understand what zany clock makes him tick, one Western security service came up with the theory that the drugs he takes for angina have the side effect of making him feel invulnerable.

He was born in 1937, in Al Ouja, a village outside Takrit. He remains proud of his humble origin in a mud hut, in the midst of a poor, water-melon growing, Sunni community. Iraq is an overwhelmingly Moslem society, but within it there are innumerable religious and tribal groups. Sunni Moslems, the majority orthodox doctrine of Islam generally, form only a fifth of Iraq's population. Saddam himself, nominally Sunni, uses religion only as a political tool, posing hypocritically as an Islamic hero in his efforts to present his opposition to the West as a Holy War. His weakness for cigars, scotch and adultery is too well known for the sight of him kneeling in prayer to be taken seriously.

His father died before he was born. The gossip was that he was illegitimate. As Saddam developed his later obsession with history, he claimed that he was the illegitimate child of the Iraqui Hashemite King, through which he traced his direct descent from the Prophet Mohammed himself.

His mother re-married, and Saddam was raised in the house of his stepfather, Ibrahim al Hassan, who delighted in beating the boy remorselessly. With the shadow of his rumoured illegitimacy hanging over him, Saddam was an outcast in the impoverished but custom-bound society. As he walked to school in Takrit, he carried a steel bar to protect himself from the other boys. His only allies were his cousin, Adnan Khairallah, rewarded for his kindness by a future position as Defence Minister, and his uncle, Khairallah Tulfah, who became Governor of Baghdad. Tulfah was a monstrous bigot, who wrote a tract proposing that there are "three who God should not have created; Persians, Jews and flies". Adnan eventually went the way of all flesh, when, after complaining about Saddam's blatant infidelity to his wife, who was Adnan's sister, he died in a helicopter crash.

They were small-time gangsters, feared as local brigands. In his search for acceptance and prestige, Saddam was inevitably drawn into their web of corruption, crime and murder. At the age of ten, Saddam's cousins gave him his first real possession; a revolver. In his young teens, he committed his first killings on Tulfah's behalf. By the time he moved to Baghdad in the late 1950s, he had a considerable reputation as a thug and assassin.

He enrolled in law school, but crime kept him too busy to attend. In 1957, at the age of twenty-one, he joined the Baath Party, a tiny fledgling movement espousing the creation of a single Arab state. Anti-Western, anti-Persian and anti-Jewish, it was a synthesis of Arab nationalism and socialism founded by a Syrian secondary school teacher, Michel Alfaq. Saddam became highly useful as a hit-man and tough enforcer in the Baath Party's violent opposition to the Hashemite monarchy. Having backed the military overthrow of the King, the Baath then sought to subvert the new government by assassinating the President, Brigadier Qassem.

Saddam Hussein was one of an eight-man hit squad selected for the task. They planned to shoot up Qassem's car as he drove between his house and his office at the Defence Ministry. When the plan finally went into operation on 7 October 1959, it was a total farce. One of the assassins was supposed to use his car to block the street and force Qassem's car to a halt, Unfortunately, he lost his keys, and while the would-be killers fell to arguing about whose fault it was, Qassem arrived at the destined spot. They managed to shoot the driver, but in the cross-fire, the successful marksman was then shot dead by his comrades. Several others, including Saddam, also wounded each other. The assassins hobbled off, convinced that some of the mass of flying lead must have hit Qassem. The debacle was re-written when Saddam came to power as a mass-battle against overwhelming odds, in which Saddam, although grievously wounded, was the hero, pulling cannon-shell out of his leg with a pair of scissors. The doctor who actually treated him remembers a tiny superficial wound. Needless to say, the doctor later fled Iraq when he discovered a huge bomb under his car.

Whilst his fellow assassins were rounded up, Saddam escaped to Syria and then moved to Egypt where he spent the next few years, manoeuvring his way into the inner circles of the exiled Baath movement. The Egyptians were generally sympathetic towards the Baath, but distrusted the naked ambition of Saddam.

In 1963, the Baath took power in Iraq in a bloody coup, and Saddam returned as a gun-toting bodyguard on the right of the Party. He won favour and fear by his willingness to dispose of opponents by the most direct methods. He even offered to blow away the leader of the Party's left faction, then Deputy

Premier. His offer was politely refused by Hassan-al Bakr, his boss, who didn't want to set a precedent he guessed he might fall victim to.

The Baath were turfed out of power by the army, disgusted at the violence and chaotic in-fighting. Going underground suited Saddam Hussein. This was the kind of electioneering he understood, proceeding via violence and intrigue. Saddam was never without a machine-gun and at least one revolver. In this environment he flourished. Michel Alfaq thought his limited skills particularly appropriate to the Baath's need for violence rather than diplomacy, and supported his claim to the position of Secretary and Leader. The job was to be shared. His co-appointee, Abdel al Shaikhili, was later purged and murdered. It was an unprecedented appointment, as he had no credentials and no experience, and was not accepted by the rest of the Party. Saddam would have to resort to his customary methods to achieve power.

In 1966, Saddam seized the post of Deputy Secretary General at gunpoint, and began to build up a net-work of intimates dependent upon him for favour. These were usually his relatives, or failing that, from his home town of Takrit. He was known to the public only as a lowly gunman, entirely uncultured, vulgar and with a complete absence of moral values. He had a growing fascination for history, particularly the great figures of the mythic Arab past, and began to see himself as a man of destiny, following in the footsteps of Nebuchadnezzar, the enslaver of Israel and Emperor of Babylon.

In 1968, the Baath returned to power in another coup. Saddam's forthright abilities earned him the position of Deputy President. Hassan-al-Bakr, the President, needed his sheer ruthlessness to create a Baathist State. He was the power behind the throne, instrumental in implementing the policies of repression and terror that evolved. He established a "Department of Internal Security", the official state torture-service, run by Nadlum Kazar, a notorious psychopath who ran the central interrogation unit at Qasr al Nihayyah in Baghdad. It was there, in 1973, that a survivor saw Saddam Hussein, Deputy President of Iraq, bodily pick up a still struggling prisoner and toss him into a vat of acid, watching fascinated as the wriggling man dissolved.

The Baath State that Saddam inevitably inherited on 16 July 1979 was well on the way to being run on the only emotional lines he understood, those of terror. He had systematically eradicated everyone who posed a threat, real or imagined, to him, often with his own hands. He was quite happy to take part in torture. It is unlikely that he takes any pleasure in killing; it is simply business for him, as natural as breathing. During the war with Iran, with Iraq in pieces, Saddam, feeling insecure, suggested to his ministers that he might step down. Most took the hint, disagreed and began to flatter him as required. His health minister, Riaz Hussein foolishly took him at his word and said he would be happy to accept Saddam's resignation. Saddam promptly dragged him into the next room, shot him, and had his dismembered body returned to his wife in a carrier bag. As one former official says:

"You quickly realize that he trusts absolutely no-one. Everyone is a potential enemy. Sometimes you see him with children, and he is smiling and stroking their hair. That's because they are no threat to him."

Under Saddam, torture became a customary experience, used not to extract information, but to re-model the very thoughts of the populace. Thus, torturers saw themselves as creative artists, engineers of the human soul. Exacting confessions to non-existent crimes is a means of compelling victims to surrender their individuality, to accept without question the truth as presented by the state. In order to heighten the impression of an organization as omniscient and divine as its leader and to cultivate the necessary sense of sin and guilt within the people, the security services are anonymous and select victims at random. No explanations are offered; the event is efficiently calculated to suggest unimaginable horrors. As Samir al Khalil, Iraqui dissident and author writes: "The pattern is for agents to pick someone up from work, or at night from his house . . . what one assumes to be the corpse is brought back weeks or maybe months later and delivered to the head of the family in a sealed box. A death certificate is produced for signature to the effect that the person has died of fire, swimming or other such accidents. Someone is allowed to accompany the police and box for a ceremony, but at no time are they allowed to see the corpse. The cost of proceedings is demanded in advance . . ."

Acid baths are commonly used to make thousands of corpses disappear. Amnesty International has detailed thirty methods of torture used in Iraq, from beating to mutilation, from rape to electrocution, including the gouging out of eyes, the cutting off of noses, breasts, penises and limbs. Heavy-metal poisoning is a favoured means of killing off undesirables. Lead and thallium are administered to prisoners in soft drinks during uneventful but deliberately prolonged interrogation. Children are routinely tortured to extract confessions from their parents. In 1985, three hundred children were held at Fusailiyya Prison, where they were whipped, sexually abused and given electric shocks. In order to assist their work, the security forces have become master players of the rumour machine. They use it to create the enemy within, which they must flush out, and then use it again to spread rumours of the horrendous punishments that traitors face. A constant stream of videos showing confessions, trials and executions are released to the public. Baath officials are required to take part in executions and filmed doing so, thus binding themselves together in responsibility with "blood cement".

It was with the application of this mafia-style ideology of shared guilt that Saddam Hussein opened his account as President. A couple of nights after taking office, he hosted a dinner party for senior Baath officials. After the meal, he casually suggested that they all jot down details of any meetings they might have had with two of their colleagues, Muhie Abdel Hussein and Mohamed Ayesh. He gave no explanation. The following day he informed the Baath Revolutionary council that the two named officials were the ringleaders of a plot to overthrow the regime. Fortunately, he added, he was in possession of a complete list of their fellow conspirators. With crocodile tears streaming down his face, he read out a list compiled from among his dinner party guests. It included several of the highest ranking officials and a quarter of the Revolutionary Council. The Baath leadership was subsequently invited to accompany Saddam to where their former colleagues were now held. There, they were issued with guns, and along with Saddam formed the firing squad. The Secret Police stood behind them, to provide an added spur to their loyalty.

Iraq is potentially a prosperous country. It has vast oil reserves and healthy agricultural resources. Like many of the Middle Eastern nations its size, borders and very existence are a consequence of colonial influence and World War. The Baath Movement, which has never exerted much influence outside Iraq and for a brief time Syria, has its roots in the desire for the collective Arab nation, so long kicked about by the colonial superpowers, to assert themselves as a force on the world stage. Since President Nasser of Egypt, the Arabs have looked for a strong representative and spokesman for all, not just the small, incredibly rich and pro-Western oil states, whose wealth is often bitterly resented among the poorer nations. It is this vacancy that Saddam Hussein had his eye on.

In 1979, the Shah of Iran was overthrown and Iran became a strictly Muslim and violently anti-Western country. The conflict between the Arabs and Persians is historic, and there has been a long-standing dispute over territory between Iran and Iraq. Saddam thought he would be able to take advantage of the instability in Iran to launch a swift smash and grab as a prelude to Imperial expansion. Saddam was confident the war would be over in a fortnight. He was certain Iraq had the hardware. It had been shopping worldwide for the best the arms trade could offer. Throughout the following conflict, the West began to favour and actively support Iraq with arms and finance. America, finding itself in bitter opposition to the Iranian regime, thought Saddam an attractive prospect. It has recently been revealed that the Bush administration were still supplying economic aid, intelligence and advanced weapons technology to "The Butcher of Baghdad" two months before he invaded Kuwait. The mind boggles at the self-interested and self-defeating idiocy of American foreign policy.

Iran had a seemingly endless supply of eager Muslim heroes. Ayatollah Khomeini promised anyone who died for Iran would be perishing as a Muslim martyr. Large numbers of young Iranians seemed to be happy to commit suicide in the cause, jogging up to the frontline carrying their own coffins. The Ayatollah called for an army of twenty million. The Iranians were indifferent to the loss of life. In two attacks in the Basra region alone they lost 100,000 men and boys. The War became a hideous, life-consuming stalemate, and a jamboree for the arms trade.

By the third week of the War, Saddam was turning on Iranian civilian targets. Military spending rocketed. The hardware was inefficiently used, with Iraqi gunners frequently shooting down their own aircraft. In the first six years of this awful, pointless conflict, France alone sold $15–17 billion of military hardware to the Iraquis. Saddam had to find ways of killing more Iranians faster. By 1984 Iraq was using mustard and nerve gas against the Iranians. Reporters could not believe the scale of the carnage. On the battlefield, soldiers no older than children tore at each other with their bare hands. The rivers and swamps were clogged with bodies.

When he became leader of Iraq, Saddam had no military experience whatsoever. His gangland, bar-room, bottle-in-the-face tactics in both his disastrous wars displayed his failure to grasp any military tactics. He compensated by portraying himself to the public as a great military leader to demonstrate he was in charge. Huge portraits showed him in permanent uniform, armed to the teeth. His whole cabinet dressed as soldiers. This backfired when it became apparent that the war was a complete cock-up.

As a gangster, Saddam had fought personal battles with his opponents, using whatever means came to hand to survive, be it broken bottle or gun. He has no notion of the "last resort". He used gas, not because it was a last ditch effort, but because it was an effective weapon to kill his enemies. If he had possessed nuclear weapons, either then or during the subsequent war in Kuwait, he would have used them without compunction. During the war with Iran, Iraq developed military applications for typhoid, cholera, anthrax, and equine encephalitis. Much of the research was underwritten by Western banks. Gas was used on his own deserters. In spite of this chamber of horrors, the war dragged on until September 1988.

When it finished, with nearly two million dead, Iraq was at least $80 billion in the red. Furthermore, it ended without victory and with the Iranians in the ascendant. This didn't stop Saddam declaring himself the victor, and raising monuments and awarding himself an endless string of titles to prove it.

Towards the end of the war he had rounded on the Kurdish minority in the North of Iraq. At Halabja, in March 1988, 5,000 civilians were killed, in what was the first documented use of nerve gas in history. His intention was to depopulate Kurdistan, a traditional bastion of resistance, whilst attention was still on the fighting at the front. By mid-1989, he had destroyed 4,000 Kurdish settlements. A British documentary film-maker managed to smuggle out conclusive evidence of the atrocities; bodies lay piled high in desolate villages, a film over their eyes and a horrible slime pouring out of their noses and mouths, their skin peeling and bubbling. An American Senator tried to introduce the "Prevention of Genocide Act", but Reagan's government squashed it, still thinking its interests lay in keeping Saddam sweet.

Having, as he saw it, beaten Iran, all Saddam needed now was to turf Israel out of Palestine to make himself the great Arabian hero that, in believing his own publicity, he imagined himself destined to be. Here was an irony; whilst killing the Kurds, he compared himself to the greatest of Kurdish heroes and scourge of the Crusaders, Saladin. He began to rebuild Babylon, having each brick stamped with his mark, as Nebuchadnezzar had done. Around the country, there were over eighty palaces for his personal use. The rumour spread that he was in fact, the illegitimate offspring of the Hashemite King Ghazi. It was thought he might declare himself a monarch, an incongruous decision for a once revolutionary, socialist, rabid anti-monarchist to take. It was all part of making the people somehow think that if he was a hero, they must have won.

In reality, having fought a losing, costly draw, social unrest began to spread, and with a tide of several million idle soldiers slopping around the country, Saddam needed another national cause fast to preserve his position. He needed a real victory.

In order to further his plans against Israel, which he openly threatened to burn to destruction, he required money to buy conventional weapons and develop nuclear and biological ones. The need became greater after the Israelis, who have learned to take seriously what other countries dismiss as mere rhetoric, bombed his nuclear facilities. Saddam's theory for removing Israel was indicative of how little he values human life. Israel's precious resource is its people. It could not afford to fight a long, corpse laden war, such as Saddam is fond of. With such a war draining Israel of human life, immigration would dry up and the nation vanish. It didn't matter how many Iraqi's it took.

He needed money, but with these huge debts, his country would be paying off its loans for years. To cap Saddam's problems, but also to provide him with the excuse he needed, the price of oil slumped and with it Iraq's income. He rounded on the Gulf oil producing states, in particular, Kuwait, which had given and lent him millions of dollars to fight Iran. He accused the small states of keeping the oil price low by overproducing, and hence "harming even the milk our children drink". He demanded that Iraq's debts be written off. As Saddam saw it, he had seen off the Persian threat on their behalf. In Kuwait's case, he unearthed an old territorial dispute over two islands in the Gulf.

The scene was set for the Mother of all Battles. On August, 1990, Saddam invaded Kuwait. To the moment the first bombs started falling on Baghdad, he never believed that the Allies would go to war. He told the US Ambassador: "Yours is a society which cannot accept 10,000 dead in one battle".

The West, forever in a terrible tangle over its relations in the Middle East and what to make of Saddam, breathed a sigh of relief. At last they knew what he was: a good, old-fashioned imperialist dictator with genocidal tendencies.

Saddam had been obliged to fall in love with himself so much, he firmly believed that the Arab coalition which formed against him would fall apart, that its people would rise to acclaim him as the leader of the Arab world and overthrow their governments. Hence he turned to firing missiles at Israeli cities, to turn what was, for both sides, a war about politics and oil into one about race. It failed. Israel stayed out and the Allies stayed cemented together by cash and a common purpose. Saddam's behaviour, using hostages and prisoners for human shields and propaganda purposes, was a big mistake. Far from frightening people, it gave impetus to what was an initially shaky cause. It was, yet again, the misapplication of small-time mob tactics in the big arena. It looked awful.

Saddam's army of a million men was humiliated in a ground war lasting a mere four days. His hardware was destroyed. After a year of haggling and threats, his nuclear facilities are being destroyed. But the Kurds and Shia Muslims who rebelled against him at the end of the war have been suppressed; they received no support from the Allies. It is typical of the confused attitude of West and East towards Iraq that they want Saddam Hussein replaced, but only so long as it is by someone they find amenable; that definition changes daily. They still have not posted a job description. As dictators go, the Emirs of Kuwait, now back in control, figure decently in the world ranking. Meanwhile, Saddam licks his wounds and re-establishes his control within the country. There really have been few dictators so obstinate and bloody-minded in this century. He is not a new Hitler, because that comparison would diminish the scale and intent of the evil that was Hitler. Saddam has no ideology other than personal survival and personal ambition; this instinct is unquenchable. It is what keeps him crazy after all these years.

• *World Famous* •

SERIAL KILLERS

COLIN WILSON
with
Damon and Rowan Wilson

· chapter one ·

AN ADDICTION TO MURDER

*T*he *term serial killer was invented in the early 1980s by FBI agent Robert Ressler, to describe someone who kills repeatedly and obsessively.*

In the past we called anyone who killed several people a "mass murderer". But then, the mass murderer may be someone like the unknown killer who slaughtered the Evangelista family in Detroit on 2 July, 1929, chopping off the heads of all six. Or like Charles Whitman, the sniper who shot eighteen people from a tower on the campus of the University of Texas in August 1966. These were clearly not serial killers – which means one after another – because the murders all happened on the same occasion. Neither was the French "Bluebeard" Landru, because although he killed eleven women between 1914 and 1918, his crimes were coldly and carefully planned, and the motive was purely financial. For, as we shall see, the modern serial killer tends to choose his victims at random, and the motive is usually sexual. Even more important is the fact that he (or she) becomes addicted to murder, exactly as if it were a drug.

Eighteenth and Nineteenth Century Crimes

Now oddly enough, sex crime is a relatively modern phenomenon. In the eighteenth century, the usual motive for most crime was money, and throughout most of the nineteenth century, the majority of murders were committed in the course of robbery – with a few during domestic quarrels. It was only towards the end of the century that "sex crime", in our modern sense of the word (that is, murder for rape) began to appear. In the eighteen and nineteenth centuries, prostitutes were so cheap – and almost any lower class girl could be had for a few pence – that sex crime would have been pointless. But Victorian prudery gradually created a new attitude towards sex – as something rather wicked and forbidden. This was first reflected in the rise of pornography ("dirty books" were also an invention of the nineteenth century) which was often about rape or child-sex. And, inevitably, a time came when dreams of "the forbidden" turned into the real thing. In July 1867, a clerk named Frederick Baker persuaded eight year old Fanny Adams to go with him for a walk in the fields near Alton, Hampshire. Her dismembered body was found a few hours later in a hop garden. Baker had written in his diary: "Killed a young girl today. It was fine and hot." Baker was hanged at Winchester.

Two years later, in Boston, a bellringer named Thomas Piper began attacking and raping girls, battering them unconscious; in May 1875 he lured five year old Mabel Young into the belfry knocked her unconscious with a cricket bat, but was interrupted. The girl died in hospital and Piper was hanged after confessing to five sex murders and several rapes of children. Piper had some claim to be regarded as the first serial killer.

On the other hand, that dubious distinction might be claimd by a German murderess named Anna Zwanziger, a domestic servant who, in the first decade of the nineteenth century, developed a strange obsession with poisoning with arsenic. The wife of a judge named Glaser seems to have been her first victim in August 1808; the judge himself followed, probably because he resisted Anna's hints about marriage. Another judge named Grohmann died in May 1809. Weeks later she poisoned the wife of her latest employer, a magistrate named Gebhardt. When he dismissed her, most people in the house became violently ill, and it was discovered that someone had put arsenic in the salt cellars. Tests for arsenic had just been invented, and Anna was arrested in September 1809. Frau Glaser's body was exhumed and found to be full of arsenic. After being sentenced to death by beheading, Anna Zwanziger admitted that she frequently administered poison simply for her own entertainment. She is quoted as saying that "poison was her truest friend", and the German judge Feuerbach says that she trembled with rapture when she looked upon arsenic. This casual attitude towards her victims certainly entitles her to be labelled a serial killer rather than someone who murdered for profit.

Gesina Gottfried, another German, began by poisoning a brutal husband who beat her, then killed her second husband and his parents. In the course of her subsequent travels as a domestic servant she killed at least another half a dozen people. Her last intended victim, a man called Rumf, wondered about the white powder she had sprinkled on the leg of pork, and went to the police to get it analysed. When it was identified as arsenic, she confessed to her murders with a certain pride, and was executed in 1828. Like Anna Zwanziger, she had somehow become addicted to administering poison.

This is even more true of a Frenchwoman named Helene Jegado, a Breton peasant woman who went on a poisoning spree over a twenty year period, beginning around 1830. In one house where she worked, seven people died in agony, including her own sister; by 1851 the number of her victims had swelled to at least twenty-three, although a more probable estimate is sixty. Arrested for poisoning a fellow servant of whom she was jealous, she was executed in 1852.

A Dutch nurse named van der Linden – of whom, unfortunately, little is known – surpassed all three women by poisoning more than a hundred.

Here, then, we can see the true characteristics of the serial killer – a kind of obsessive *repetitiveness* that resembles a hiccup. What causes it? Some religiously-inclined people suggested that a demon had got into them (and many serial killers have, in fact, declared that they were possessed by the Devil). Whatever the answer, there seems to be no doubt that murder can become an addiction, and that most serial killers are, in some sense, "driven by a demon".

One of the oddest cases of "murder addiction" on record took place in the Lyon area of France in the mid-nineteenth century. In May 1861, an attractive twenty-seven year old servant girl named Marie Pichon was accosted by a peasant with a deformed upper lip, who asked her the way to the registry-office for servants. When the man learned that Marie was looking for work, he offered her a good job at a country house near Montlul. The girl agreed to accompany him there, and they travelled to Montlul by train. The peasant, who seemed a stolid but decent sort of man, told her that he was the gardener of a certain Madame Girard, and that another servant who was due to arrive the day before had fallen ill, so that Madame was in urgent need of a replacement.

At Montlul, the peasant took her box on his shoulder, and told her they would take a short cut across the fields. As night closed in, he stopped to take breath, and suggested that they should abandon her trunk until morning. Without waiting for her agreement, he dropped it in a ditch, then he plodded on into the darkness. The girl became increasingly nervous at his odd behaviour, and when they came to a hilltop, and there was still no sign of lights, she declared her unwillingness to go any further. The man then rounded on her suddenly and threw a noose round her neck. She pushed him and they both fell down. Marie was first on her feet, running into the darkness. She crashed through hedges, scratching herself and tearing her clothes, and frequently fell over. But eventually, the footsteps of her pursuer died away, and she almost collapsed with relief when she came to a house. Its owner, who was still unharnessing his horse after a journey, was startled by this bloodstained apparition, but he let her in, and sent for the local constable. Then she was taken to the police station, where she repeated her story. In spite of her exhaustion, she was taken back over the route she had traced with the murderous peasant. They eventually found the ditch where the man had dropped her trunk – but it had vanished.

The news caused a sensation in the Trevoux district – particularly when it was recollected that Marie Pichon was not the first girl to place her trust in a peasant with a deformed lip. Six years earlier, in 1855, a servant girl named Josephine Charloty had become suspicious as she plodded across the fields behind the squarely-built man who was carrying her trunk, and had finally fled and taken refuge in a farmhouse. Another girl, Victorine Perrin, had simply lost her trunk when the man had run off into the trees. In all, five girls had escape alive. But others had vanished and never been seen again. In February 1855, a few months before the escape of Josephine Charloty, hunters had found the battered corpse of a young woman hidden in a thicket; she was naked except for her bloodstained shoes and a piece of ribbon. The body was later identified as that of Marie Buday, who had left Lyon with a "countryman" a few days before she was found. Another girl, Marie Curt, had turned down the offer of a job from the man with the twisted lip, but recommended a friend named Olympe Alabert; Olympe had then vanished.

Now although the police had been aware that a peasant posing as a gardener was abducting and murdering girls, no one seems to have made a determined effort to find him. (The French police force was still in its infancy.) But the case of Marie Pichon was discussed all over the district. And three men in an inn at nearby Dayneux decided that the peasant with the deformed lip sounded like a local gardener known as Raymund, who lived nearby. Raymund kept himself to himself, spent a great deal of time in Lyon – where he was supposed to work as a porter – and had a lump on his upper lip. His real name, it seemed, was Martin Dumollard.

A local Justice of the Peace agreed that Dumollard certainly sounded as if he might be the wanted man, and issued a search warrant. This search was conducted by the magistrate himself, and it left no doubt that Dumollard was a major suspect. The house was found to contain many women's garments, and some of them were bloodstained. Dumollard was immediately arrested. He strenuously denied knowing anything about missing women, and went on denying it even when confronted by Marie Pichon herself, who identified him as her attacker.

Meanwhile, Dumollard's wife had decided to save her own neck by confessing. She admitted that her husband had brought home Marie Pichon's box, and that he had burned much of its contents in a wood – obviously concerned that if the police tracked him down the box would conclusively prove his guilt. The investigators went to the spot she indicated, and found buried ashes and fragments of books and clothes, which Marie Pichon identified.

Martin Dumollard continued to insist stolidly that he knew nothing about any crimes. But his wife Anne admitted that a woman's watch found in their house had been brought home one night four years earlier, with a quantity of bloodstained clothes. Dumollard had told her he had killed a girl in a wood at Mont Main, and was now going to bury her. He left the house with a spade . . .

A careful search of the wood revealed a depression that might be a grave. Two feet below the surface, the diggers found a female skeleton. The skull showed she had died from a violent blow on the head.

Dumollard continued to deny all knowledge of the crime. But his wife went on to describe another occasion when he had returned home and told her he had killed a girl. This body was also discovered buried in a wood, the Bois de Communes. The dry earth had preserved the flesh, and the position of the body made it clear that the girl had been buried alive and had suffocated while trying to claw her way out of the grave. She was identified as Marie Eulalie Bursod.

In the seven months that followed, it became clear that Martin Dumollard had killed at least six girls (clothes of ten were found in his home), and had unsuccessfully tried to lure another nine to their deaths. On 20 January, 1862, he and his wife were tried at the Assizes at Bourg (Ain), and he was found guilty and sentenced to death. Anne Dumollard was sentenced to twenty years imprisonment. He was guillotined on 20 March, 1862, and his head sent to be examined by phrenologists, who declared that, according to the shape of his skull, Dumollard should have been a man of the finest character.

Why did Dumollard kill? We do not know whether sex played any part in the crimes. But the notion that he murdered purely for profit seemed unlikely. The possessions of a servant girl would fetch very little money on the second-hand market, and it seems relatively certain that such girls would have very little money. So Dumollard's relative prosperity (his house was larger than that of most peasants) can hardly be explained by his crimes.

We know little of Dumollard's background except that his parents were tramps who wandered around Italy, and that his father was a murderer who was broken on the wheel. He was undoubtedly miserly, obsessed by money – his last words to his wife were to remind her that someone had failed to repay a debt – and it seems just possible that he killed the girls for their meagre possessions. But the likeliest explanation is that Dumollard became a "murder addict", and went on killing because it gave him pleasure to lure girls to their death. He has all the characteristics of the modern "serial killer".

Jack the Ripper

Early in the morning of 31 August 1888, a carter named George Cross was walking along Bucks Row, Whitechapel – in London's East End – when he saw what he thought was a bundle of tarpaulin lying on the pavement. It proved to be a woman with her skirt above her waist. In the local mortuary, it was discovered that she had been disembowelled. Mary Ann Nicholls was almost certainly the first victim of the sadistic killer who became known as Jack the Ripper. (He provided himself with the nickname in a series of letters that he wrote to the Central News Agency.) Just over a week later, he killed and disembowelled a prostitute named Annie Chapman in a Whitechapel backyard. On the morning of 30 September, he was interrupted soon after he had cut the throat of a third victim – a woman called Elizabeth Stride – and immediately went and killed and then disembowelled another woman, Catherine Eddowes. On the morning of 9 November, he committed his last murder indoors, and spent hours dissecting the body of Mary Kelly by the light of a pile of rags burning in the grate. By this time Londoners were in a

---

The Marquis de Sade, who gave his name to sadism, never actually killed anyone. He had a taste for whipping prostitutes on their bare behinds – for which he paid them well – but only harmed one of them inadvertently when he gave her an aphrodisiac called Spanish Fly which made her ill. It was his atheism and anticlerical views that first landed him in jail, and he was later imprisoned in an asylum for writing dirty books. Nowadays, in the company of Jean Genet and William Burroughs, he would simply be a respected writer.

state of hysteria, and the Chief of Police was forced to resign. But the Whitechapel murders were at an end.

All theories suggesting that the Ripper was a "gentleman" – an insane doctor, a cricket-playing lawyer, a member of the royal family – are almost certainly wide of the mark. The kind of frustration that produced the Ripper murders is characteristic of someone who lacks other means of self-expression, someone who is illiterate or only semi-literate. Such a suspect came to the attention of Daniel Farson after he had directed a television programme about Jack the Ripper.

He received a letter (signed G.W.B.) from a seventy-seven-year-old man in Melbourne, Australia, who claimed that his father had confessed to being the Ripper.

> My father was a terrible drunkard and night after night he would come home and kick my mother and us kids about, something cruelly. About the year 1902 I was taught boxing and after feeling proficient to hold my own I threatened my father that if he laid a hand on my mother or brothers I would thrash him. He never did after that, but we lived in the same house and never spoke to each other. Later, I emigrated to Australia . . . and my mother asked me to say goodbye to my father. It was then he told me his foul history and why he did these terrible murders, and advised me to change my name because he would confess before he died.

He goes on to explain: "He did not know what he was doing but his ambition was to get drunk and an urge to kill every prostitute that accosted him." Whether or not G.W.B.'s father – whose job was collecting horse-manure – was Jack the Ripper, he is certainly a far more likely suspect than a member of "Walter's" social class.

To us, it seems obvious that Jack the Ripper's murders were sex crimes (for example, the impulse that drove him to seek out another victim when he was interrupted while killing Elizabeth Stride). But it was by no means obvious to the Victorians, who preferred to think in terms of religious mania and "moral insanity". Sexual murders were a new phenomenon in the 1880s, and the average Victorian still found it puzzling that anyone should want to kill for the sake of sexual satisfaction.

The Whitechapel murders changed all this: they produced a deep disquiet, a morbid thrill of horror that made the name of Jack the Ripper a byword all over the world. It was an instinctive recognition that some strange and frightening change had taken place. In retrospect, we can see that the Ripper murders were a kind of watershed between the century of Victorian values and the age of violence that was to come.

Jack the Ripper, as depicted in a drawing in the "Illustrated Police News" of 1889.

• chapter two •

SERIAL MURDER IN EUROPE

*T*he age of sex crime began slowly. Until after World War I, sexual murder remained a rarity, an exception. In 1901, a carpenter named Ludwig Tessnow was arrested on the island of Rugen, off the Baltic coast, on suspicion of killing and mutilating two small boys; three years earlier he had escaped being charged with murdering two little girls by insisting that stains on his clothes were of wood dye, not blood. But by 1901, new techniques of forensic medicine were able to prove that the stains on his clothes were human blood, and that others were of sheep he had slaughtered and mutilated. Tessnow was executed.

The Gatting Mystery

Near Brisbane, Australia, in 1898, two girls named Norah and Ellen Murphy, together with their brother Michael, set out for a dance on Boxing Day, and failed to return home. Their bodies were found the next day in a paddock near Gatton; both girls had been raped and battered to death. Convicts were suspected of the crime but it was never solved.

Two years earlier, in 1896, another rape case had made headlines, but the girl had survived. Sixteen-year-old Mary Jane Hicks made the mistake of accepting a lift from a Sydney cabman, who tried to "take liberties" with her. A group of youths interrupted the attempted seduction and persuaded her to go with them. Three of them also tried to assault her, and her screams brought two would-be rescuers. But they were overwhelmed by a gang of eighteen hooligans – known as the "Waterloo Push" – who soon overpowered them. One of the rescuers ran to the nearest police station. But by the time mounted policemen arrived, the girl had been forcibly raped by a dozen gang members. Six hours later, several members of the gang were in custody. In New South Wales at that time, the penalty for rape was death. Eleven gang members and the cab driver, Charles Sweetman, were charged. Public indignation was tremendous, and nine of the eleven were found guilty and sentenced to death. Eventually, only four were hanged. The cabman Sweetman was sentenced to two floggings and fourteen years hard labour. The savagery of the sentences is an indication of the Victorian horror of sex crime – the feeling that it was something that had to be stopped at all costs. Even the later revelation that Mary had not been a virgin, and had not protested when the cabman tried to "take liberties", made no difference. "Victorian morality" took the sternest possible view of such matters.

H. H. Holmes

The Chicago murderer H. H. Holmes – real name Herman Webster Mudgett – has some claim to be America's first serial killer. The son of a postmaster, Holmes became a doctor, then a swindler. After a chequered career as a con man, Mudgett moved to Chicago in 1886 – when he was twenty-six – and became the partner of a certain Mrs Holten, who needed an assistant in her drugstore. Mrs Holten mysteriously vanished, and Holmes – as he now called himself – took over the store. He did so well that he built himself a large house – it was later to become known as "Murder Castle" – full of hidden passageways and secret rooms; its innovations included chutes down to the basement, whose purpose – it was later realized – was to facilitate the conveyance of bodies to the furnace. During the World Fair of

1893, many out-of-town guests who came to stay in Holmes's "castle" disappeared. So did a whole succession of attractive secretaries and mistresses. Holmes was finally betrayed by the train robber Marion Hedgepeth, whom he had met in jail and promised a share in the loot – from a dishonest insurance scheme – in exchange for an introduction to a crooked lawyer. Holmes failed to keep his part of the bargain; Hedgepeth contacted the insurance company, and revealed that the "accidental" death of a man called Pitezel was actually murder. Holmes's insurance scheme also included killing off Pitezel's wife and five children to cover his tracks, and by the time the police had caught up with him, three of the children were dead, buried under the floorboards of houses rented by Holmes or incinerated in their stoves. The subsequent investigation revealed that Holmes had committed at least twenty-seven murders. He was hanged in May 1895.

Bela Kiss

Holmes differs from more recent serial killers in that his motives were partly financial – although it seems clear that an intense sexual obsession also played its part in the murders. This is also true of Hungary's most notorious mass murderer, Bela Kiss.

In 1916, the Hungarian tax authorities noted that it had been a long time since rates had been paid on a house at 17 Rákóczi Street in the village of Cinkota, ten miles northwest of Budapest. It had been empty for two years, and since it seemed impossible to trace the owner, or the man who rented it, the district court of Pest-Pilis decided to sell it. A blacksmith named Istvan Molnar purchased it for a modest sum, and moved in with his wife and family. When tidying-up the workshop, Molnar came upon a number of sealed oildrums behind a mess of rusty pipes and corrugated iron. They had been solidly welded, and for a few days the blacksmith left them alone. Then his wife asked him what was in the drums – it might, for example, be petrol – and he settled down to removing the top of one of them with various tools. And when Molnar finally raised the lid, he clutched his stomach and rushed to the garden privy. His wife came in to see what had upset him; when she peered into the drum she screamed and fainted. It contained the naked body of a woman, in a crouching position; the practically airless drum had preserved it like canned meat.

Six more drums also proved to contain female corpses. Most of the women were middle-aged; none had ever been beautiful. And the police soon realized they had no way of identifying them. They did not even know the name of the man who placed them there. The previous tenant had gone off to the war in 1914; he had spent little time in the house, and had kept himself to himself, so nobody knew who he was. The police found it difficult even to get a description. They merely had seven unknown victims of an unknown murderer.

Professor Balazs Kenyeres, of the Police Medical Laboratory, was of the opinion that the women had been dead for more than two years. But at least he was able to take fingerprints; by 1916, fingerprinting had percolated even to the highly conservative Austro-Hungarian Empire. However, at this stage, fingerprinting was unhelpful, since it only told them that the women had no criminal records.

Some three weeks after the discovery, Detective Geza Bialokurszky was placed in charge of the investigation; he was one of the foremost investigators of the Budapest police. He was, in fact, Sir Geza (*lovag*), for he was a nobleman whose family had lost their estates. Now he settled down to the task of identifying the female corpses. If Professor Kenyeres was correct about time of death – and he might easily have been wrong, since few pathologists are asked to determine the age of a canned corpse – the women must have vanished in 1913 or thereabouts. The Missing Persons' Bureau provided him with a list of about 400 women who had vanished between 1912 and 1914. Eventually, Bialokurszky narrowed these down to fifteen. But these women seemed to have no traceable relatives. Eventually, Bialokurszky found the last employer of a thirty-six-year-old cook named Anna Novak, who had left her job abruptly in 1911. Her employer was the widow of a Hussar colonel, and she still had Anna's "servant's book", a kind of identity card that contained a photograph, personal details, and a list of previous employers, as well as their personal comments. The widow assumed that she had simply found a better job or had got married. She still had the woman's trunk in the attic.

This offered Bialokurszky the clue he needed so urgently: a sheet from a newspaper, *Pesti Hirlap*, with an advertisement marked in red pencil:

> Widower urgently seeks acquaintance of mature, warm-hearted spinster or widow to help assuage loneliness mutually. Send photo and details, Poste Restante Central P.O.Box 717. Marriage possible and even desirable.

Now, at last, fingerprinting came into its own. Back at headquarters, the trunk was examined, and a number of prints were found; these matched those of one of the victims. The post office was able to tell Bialokurszky that Box 717 had been rented by a man who had signed for his key in the name of Elemer Nagy, of 14 Kossuth Street, Pestszenterzsebet, a suburb of Budapest. This proved to be an empty plot. Next, the detective and his team studied the agony column of *Pesti Hirlap* for 1912 and 1913. They found more than twenty requests for "warm-hearted spinsters" which gave the address of Box 717. This was obviously how the unknown killer of Cinkota had contacted his victims. On one occasion he had paid for the advertisement by postal order, and the post office was able to trace it. (The Austro-Hungarian Empire at least had a super-efficient bureaucracy.) Elemer Nagy had given an address in Cinkota, where the bodies had been found, but it was not of the house in Rákóczi Street; in fact, it proved to be the address of the undertaker. The killer had a sense of humour.

Bialokurszky gave a press conference, and asked the newspapers to publish the signature of "Elemer Nagy". This quickly brought a letter from a domestic servant named Rosa Diosi, who was twenty-seven, and admitted that she had been the mistress of the man in question. His real name was Bela Kiss, and she had last heard from him in 1914, when he had written to her from a Serbian prisoner of war camp. Bialokurszky had not divulged that he was looking for the Cinkota mass murderer, and Rosa Diosi was shocked and incredulous when he told her. She had met Kiss in 1914; he had beautiful brown eyes, a silky moustache, and a deep, manly voice. Sexually, he had apparently been insatiable . . .

Other women contacted the police, and they had identical

stories to tell: answering the advertisement, meeting the hand-some Kiss, and being quickly invited to become his mistress, with promises of marriage. They were also expected to hand over their life savings, and all had been invited to Cinkota. Some had not gone, some had declined to offer their savings – or had none to offer – and a few had disliked being rushed into sex. Kiss had wasted no further time on them, and simply vanished from their lives.

In July 1914, two years before the discovery of the bodies, Kiss had been conscripted into the Second Regiment of the Third Hungarian Infantry Battalion, and had taken part in the long offensive that led to the fall of Valjevo; but before that city had fallen in November, Kiss had been captured by the Serbs. No one was certain what had become of him after that. But the regiment was able to provide a photograph that showed the soldiers being inspected by the Archduke Joseph; Kiss's face was enlarged, and the detectives at last knew what their quarry looked like. They had also heard that his sexual appetite was awe-inspiring, and this led them to show the photograph in the red-light district around Conti and Magyar Street. Many prostitutes recognized him as a regular customer; all spoke warmly of his generosity and mentioned his sexual prowess. But a waiter who had often served Kiss noticed that the lady with whom he was dining usually paid the bill . . .

Now, at last, Bialokurszky was beginning to piece the story together. Pawn tickets found in the Cinkota house revealed that the motive behind the murders was the cash of the victims. But the ultimate motive had been sex, for Kiss promptly spent the cash in the brothels of Budapest and Vienna. The evidence showed that he was, quite literally, a satyr – a man with a raging and boundless appetite for sex. His profession – of plumber and tinsmith – did not enable him to indulge this appetite so he took to murder. He had received two legacies when he was twenty-three (about 1903) but soon spent them. After this, he had taken to seducing middle-aged women and "borrowing" their savings. One of these, a cook name Maria Toth, had become a nuisance, and he killed her. After this – like his French contemporary Landru – he had decided that killing women was the easiest way to make a living as well as indulge his sexual appetites. His favourite reading was true-crime books about con men and adventurers.

Bialokurszky's investigations suggested that there had been more then seven victims, and just before Christmas 1916, the garden in the house at Cinkota was dug up; it revealed five more bodies, all of middle-aged women, all naked.

But where was Kiss? The War Office thought that he had died of fever in Serbia. He had been in a field hospital, but when Bialokurszky tracked down one of its nurses, she remembered the deceased as a "nice boy" with fair hair and blue eyes, which seemed to suggest that Kiss had changed identity with another soldier, possibly someone called Mackavee; but the new "Mackavee" proved untraceable. And although sightings of Kiss were reported from Budapest in 1919 – and even New York as late as 1932 – he was never found.

Fritz Haarmann

Where sex crime is concerned, World War I seems to have been a kind of watershed. Now, suddenly, the twentieth century entered the "age of sex crime". And – perhaps predictably – the country in which this first became apparent was Germany where, after 1918, the miseries and deprivations of inflation and food shortage made a maximum impact. Hanover in Saxony was one of the cities that was most badly hit. It was in Hanover that Haarmann committed one of the most amazing series of crimes in modern times.

Necrophile Ed Gein, on whom Thomas Harris based "Buffalo Bill" in *Silence of the Lambs*, used the skin of corpses to make himself waistcoats. This was not the first use of human skin for practical purposes. Concentration camp guard Irma Grese is said to have made lampshades of human skin. The skin of a victim of the guillotine was used to bind the second edition of Rousseau's *Social Contact* – the book that, more than any other, was responsible for the French Revolution. The skin of William Corder, who murdered Maria Marten in the Red Barn in 1827, was used for book binding in the following year.

Haarmann was born in Hanover on 25 October 1879; he was the sixth child of an ill-assorted couple; a morose locomotive stoker known as "Sulky Olle" and his invalid wife, seven years his senior. Fritz was his mother's pet and hated his father. He liked playing with dolls, and disliked games. At sixteen he was sent to a military school (for NCOs) at New Breisach, but soon released when he showed signs of epileptic fits. He went to work in his father's cigar factory but was lazy and inefficient. He was soon accused of indecent behaviour with small children and sent to an asylum for observation; he escaped after six months. He then took to petty crime, as well as indecent assaults on minors. He also had a brief sexually normal period about 1900, when he seduced a girl to whom he was engaged and then deserted her to join the Jäger regiment. The baby was still-born. He served satisfactorily until 1903, then returned to Hanover, where his father tried to have him certified insane again – without success. He served several sentences in jail for burglary, pocket-picking and confidence trickery. His father tried getting him to do respectable work, setting him up as the keeper of a fish-and-chip shop. Fritz promptly stole all the money he could lay his hands on. In 1914 he was sentenced to five years in jail for theft from a warehouse. Released in 1918, he joined a smuggling ring, and soon became prosperous. With his headquarters at 27 Cellarstrasse, he conducted business as a smuggler, thief and police spy. (This latter activity guaranteed that his smuggling should not be too closely scrutinized.)

Many refugee trains came into Hanover; Haarmann picked up youths and offered them a night's lodging. One of the first of these was seventeen-year-old Friedel Rothe. The lad's worried parents found that he had been friendly with "detective" Haarmann; the police searched his room, but found nothing. (Haarmann later admitted that the boy's head lay wrapped in a newspaper behind his stove at the time.) But they caught Haarmann *in flagrante delicto* with another boy, and he received nine months in jail for indecency. Back in Hanover in September 1919, he changed his lodging to the Neuestrasse. He met another homosexual, Hans Grans, a pimp and petty thief, and the two formed an alliance. They used to meet in a café that catered for all kinds of perverts, the Café Kröpcke. Their method was always the same; the enticed a youth from the railway station back to Haarmann's room; Haarmann killed him (according to his own account, by biting his throat), and the boy's body was dismembered and sold as meat through Haarmann's usual channels for smuggled meat. His clothes were sold, and the useless (i.e. uneatable) portions were thrown into the Leine. At the trial, a list of twenty-eight victims was offered, their ages ranging between thirteen and twenty. One boy was killed only because Grans took a fancy to his trousers. Only one victim, a lad named Keimes, was found, strangled in the canal. There was a curious incident in connexion with this case; Haarmann called on the missing youth's parents as a "detective" and assured them he would restore their son in three days; he then went to the police and denounced Grans as the murderer! Grans was in prison at the time, so nothing came of the charge.

Haarmann had some narrow escapes; some of his meat was taken to the police because the buyer thought it was human flesh; the police analyst pronounced it pork! On another occasion, a neighbour stopped to talk to him on the stairs when some paper blew off the bucket he was carrying; it was revealed to contain blood. But Haarmann's trade as a meat smuggler kept him from suspicion.

In May 1924, a skull was discovered on the banks of the river, and some weeks later, another one. People continued to report the disappearance of their sons, and Haarmann was definitely suspected; but months went by, and Haarmann continued to kill. Two detectives from Berlin watched him, and he was arrested for indecency. His lodgings were searched and many articles of clothing taken away. His landlady's son was found to be wearing a coat belonging to one of the missing boys. And boys playing near the river discovered more bones, including a sack stuffed with them. A police pathologist declared they represented the remains of at least twenty-seven bodies.

Haarmann decided to confess. His trial began at the Hanover Assizes on 4 December 1924. It lasted fourteen days and 130 witnesses were called. The public prosecutor was Oberstaatsanwalt Dr Wilde, assisted by Dr Wagenschiefer; the defence was conducted by Justizrat Philipp Benfey and Rechtsanwalt Oz Lotzen. Haarmann was allowed remarkable freedom; he was usually gay and irresponsible, frequently interrupting the proceedings. At one point he demanded indignantly why there were so many women in court; the judge answered apologetically that he had no power to keep them out. When a woman witness was too distraught to give her evidence about her son with clarity, Haarmann got bored and asked to be allowed to smoke a cigar; permission was immediately granted.

He persisted to the end in his explanation of how he had killed his victims – biting them through the throat. Some boys he denied killing – for example, a boy named Hermann Wolf, whose photograph showed an ugly and ill-dressed youth; like Oscar Wilde, Haarmann declared that the boy was far too ugly to interest him.

Haarmann was sentenced to death by decapitation; Grans to twelve years in jail.

During the same period Karl Denke, landlord of a house in Münsterberg, killed more than a dozen vagrants – male and female – who called at his door, and ate portions of their bodies, which he kept pickled in brine. Georg Grossmann, a sadistic sexual degenerate, lived from 1914 to 1921 on the flesh of victims he lured to his room in Berlin; police investigating sounds of a struggle found the trussed-up carcase of a girl on the bed, the cords tightened as if for butchering into neat sections.

Peter Kurten, the "Dusseldorf Vampire"

In the year 1913 another notorious sex killer committed his first murder. On a summer morning, a ten-year-old girl named Christine Klein was found murdered in her bed in a tavern in Köln-Mülheim, on the Rhine. The tavern was kept by her father, Peter Klein, and suspicion immediately fell on his brother Otto. On the previous evening, Otto Klein had asked his brother for a loan and been refused; in a violent rage, he had threatened to do something his brother "would remember all his life". In the room in which the child had been killed, the police found a handkerchief with the initials "P.K.", and it seemed conceivable that Otto Klein had borrowed it from his brother Peter. Suspicion of Otto was deepened by the fact that the murder seemed otherwise motiveless; the child had been throttled unconscious, then her throat had been cut with a sharp knife. There were signs of some sexual molestation, but not of rape, and again, it seemed possible that Otto Klein had penetrated the child's genitals with his fingers in order to provide an apparent motive. He was charged with Christine Klein's murder, but the jury, although partly convinced of his guilt, felt that the evidence was not sufficiently strong, and he was acquitted.

Sixteen years later, in Düsseldorf, a series of murders and sexual atrocities made the police aware that an extremely dangerous sexual pervert was roaming the streets. These began on 9 February 1929, when the body of an eight-year-old girl, Rosa Ohliger was found under a hedge. She had been stabbed thirteen times, and an attempt had been made to burn the body with petrol. The murderer had also stabbed her in the vagina – the weapon was later identified as a pair of scissors – and seminal stains on the knickers indicated that he had experienced emission.

Six days earlier, a woman named Kuhn had been overtaken by a man who grabbed her by the lapels and stabbed her repeatedly and rapidly. She fell down and screamed, and the man ran away. Frau Kuhn survived the attack with twenty-four stab wounds, but was in hospital for many months.

Five days after the murder of Rosa Ohliger, a forty-five-year-old mechanic named Scheer was found stabbed to death on a road in Flingern; he had twenty stab wounds, including several in the head.

Soon after this, two women were attacked by a man with a noose, and described the man as an idiot with a hare lip. An idiot named Stausberg was arrested, and confessed not only to the attacks but to the murders. He was confined in a mental home, and for the next six months, there were no more attacks. But in August, they began again. Two women and a man were stabbed as they walked home at night, none of them fatally. But on 24 August, two children were found dead on an allotment in Düsseldorf; both had been strangled, then had their throats cut. Gertrude Hamacher was five, Louise Lenzen fourteen. That same afternoon, a servant girl named Gertrude Schulte was accosted by a man who tried to persuade her to have sexual intercourse; when she said "I'd rather die", he answered: "Die then", and stabbed her. But she survived, and was able to give a good description of her assailant, who proved to be a pleasant-looking, nondescript man of about forty.

The murders and attacks went on, throwing the whole area into a panic comparable to that caused by Jack the Ripper. A servant girl named Ida Reuter was battered to death with a hammer and raped in September; in October, another servant, Elizabeth Dorrier, was battered to death. A woman out for a walk was asked by a man whether she was not afraid to be out alone, and knocked unconscious with a hammer; later the same evening, a prostitute was attacked with a hammer. On 7 November, five-year-old Gertrude Albermann disappeared; two days later, the Communist newspaper *Freedom* received a letter stating that the child's body would be found near a factory wall, and enclosing a map. It also described the whereabouts of another body in the Pappendelle meadows.

Albert Anastasia, the Mafia's "King of Brooklyn", was also known as "The Mad Hatter" or "The Executioner". A homicidal maniac with a violent temper, he liked killing for the sake of killing and ordered deaths on the slightest pretext. After reading in the newspaper that a local citizen had recognized the famous bank robber Willie Smith and turned him in to the police, Anastasia ordered that this conscientious citizen be immediately killed. "I hate a rat," he said, "no matter who he is." He liked to have murder victims hideously tortured before their death and when unable to participate himself he insisted that every detail of the torture be later recounted to him; he particularly relished it when they begged for mercy. He lived like an emperor near New York Harbour in New Jersey, in a vast house surrounded by a seven-foot barbed-wire fence, a pack of Dobermans and a permanent bodyguard. His money came from the waterfront rackets: extortion, theft, gambling, loan-sharking and kick-backs. The 40,000 longshoremen who worked in the port were all under his thumb. Also, his brother "Tough Tony" was president of the biggest union and he was thought to have the entire roll-call of local police and politicians on his payroll.

Gertrude Albermann's body was found where the letter had described, amidst bricks and rubble; she had been strangled and stabbed thirty-five times. A large party of men digging on the Rhine meadows eventually discovered the naked body of a servant girl, Maria Hahn, who had disappeared in the previous August; she had also been stabbed.

By the end of 1929, the "Düsseldorf murderer" was known all over the world, and the manhunt had reached enormous proportions. But the attacks had ceased.

The capture of the killer happened almost by chance. On 19 May 1930, a certain Frau Brugmann opened a letter that had been delivered to her accidentally; it was actually addressed to a Frau Bruckner, whose name had been misspelled. It was from a twenty-year-old domestic servant named Maria Budlick (or Butlies), and she described an alarming adventure she had met with two days earlier. Maria had travelled from Cologne to Düsseldorf in search of work, and on the train had fallen into conversation with Frau Bruckner, who had given the girl her address and offered to help her find accommodation. That same evening, Maria Budlick had been waiting at the Düsseldorf railway station, hoping to meet Frau Bruckner, when she was accosted by a man who offered to help her find a bed for the night. He led her through the crowded streets and into a park. The girl was becoming alarmed, and was relieved when a kindly-looking man intervened and asked her companion where he was taking her. Within a few moments, her former companion had slunk off, and the kindly man offered to take the girl back to his room in the Mettmänner Strasse. There she decided his intentions were also dishonourable, and asked to be taken to a hostel. The man agreed; but when they reached a lonely spot, he kissed her roughly and asked for sex. The frightened girl agreed; the man tugged down her knickers, and they had sex standing up. After this, the man led her back to the tram stop, and left her. She eventually found a lodging for the night with some other nuns, and the next day, wrote about her encounter to Frau Bruckner.

Frau Brugmann, who opened the letter, decided to take it to the police. And Chief Inspector Gennat, who was in charge of the murder case, sought out Maria Budlick, and asked her if she thought she could lead him to the address where the man had taken her. It seemed a remote chance that the man was the Düsseldorf murderer, but Gennat was desperate. Maria remembered that the street was called Mettmänner Strasse, but had no idea of the address. It took her a long time and considerable hesitation before she led Gennat into the hallway of No. 71, and said she thought this was the place. The landlady let her into the room, which was empty, and she recognized it as the one she had been in a week earlier. As they were going downstairs, she met the man who had raped her. He went pale when he saw her, and walked out of the house. But the landlady was able to tell her his name. It was Peter Kürten.

Kürten, it seemed, lived with his wife in a top room in the house. He was known to be frequently unfaithful to her. But neighbours seemed to feel that he was a pleasant, likeable man. Children took to him instinctively.

On 24 May 1930, a raw-boned middle-aged woman went to the police station and told them that her husband was the Düsseldorf murderer. Frau Kürten had been fetched home from work by detectives on the day Maria Budlick had been to the room in Mettmänner Strasse, but her husband was nowhere to be found. Frau Kürten knew that he had been in jail on many occasions, usually for burglary, sometimes for sexual offences. Now, she felt, he was likely to be imprisoned for a long time. The thought of a lonely and penniless old age made her desperate, and when her husband finally reappeared, she asked him frantically what he had been doing. When he told her that he was the Düsseldorf killer, she thought he was joking. But finally he convinced her. Her reaction was to suggest a suicide pact. But Kürten had a better idea. There was a large reward offered for the capture of the sadist; if his wife could claim that, she could have a comfortable old age. They argued for many hours; she still wanted to kill herself. But eventually, she was persuaded. And on the afternoon of the 24th, Kürten met his wife outside the St Rochus church, and four policemen rushed at him waving revolvers. Kürten smiled reassuringly and told them not to be afraid. Then he was taken into police custody.

In prison, Kürten spoke frankly about his career of murder with the police psychiatrist, Professor Karl Berg. He had been born in Köln-Mülheim in 1883, son of a drunkard who often forced his wife to have sexual intercourse in the same bedroom as the children; after an attempt to rape one of his daughters, the father was imprisoned, and Frau Kürten obtained a separation and married again. Even as a child Kürten was oversexed, and tried to have intercourse with the sister his father had attacked. At the age of eight he became friendly with a local dog-catcher, who taught him how to masturbate the dogs; the dog-catcher also ill-treated them in the child's presence. At the age of nine, Kürten pushed a schoolfellow off a raft, and when another boy dived in, managed to push his head under, so that both were drowned. At the age of thirteen he began to practise bestiality with sheep, pigs, and goats, but discovered that he had his most powerful sensation when he stabbed a sheep as he had intercourse, and began to do it with increasing frequency. At sixteen he stole money and ran away from home; soon after, he received the first of seventeen prison sentences that occupied twenty-four years of his life. And during long periods of solitary confinement for insubordination, he indulged in endless sadistic day-dreams, which "fixed" his tendency to associate sexual excitement with blood. In 1913, he had entered the tavern in Köln-Mülheim and murdered the ten-year-old girl as she lay in bed; he had experienced orgasm as he cut her throat. The handkerchief with initials P.K. belonged, of course, to Peter Kürten.

And so Kürten's career continued – periods in jail, and brief periods of freedom during which he committed sexual attacks on women, sometimes stabbing them, sometimes strangling them. If he experienced orgasm as he squeezed a girl's throat, he immediately became courteous and apologetic, explaining "That's what love's about." The psychiatrist Karl Berg was impressed by his intelligence and frankness, and later wrote a classic book on the case. Kürten told him candidly that he looked with longing at the white throat of the stenographer who took down his confession, and longed to strangle it. He also confided to Berg that his greatest wish was to hear his own blood gushing into the basket as his head was cut off. He ate an enormous last meal before he was guillotined on 2 July 1931.

chapter three

THE PSYCHOPATHIC KILLER

*I*n 1970, an American publisher brought out a volume called Killer, A Journal of Murder, and made the world suddenly aware of one of the most dangerous serial killers of the first half of the twentieth century. His name was Carl Panzram, and the book was his autobiography, written more than forty years earlier. It was regarded as too horrifying to publish at the time, but when it finally appeared, it was hailed as a revelation of the inner workings of the mind of a serial killer. However, Panzram belongs to a rare species that criminologists label "the resentment killer". Far more common – particularly in the last decades of the twentieth century – is the travelling serial killer, the man who moves restlessly from place to place. In a country as large as America, this makes him particularly difficult to catch, since communication between police forces in different states is often less efficient than it should be. Earle Nelson, the "Gorilla Murderer", is generally regarded as the first example of the "travelling serial killer".

Carl Panzram

Panzram was born in June 1891, on a small farm in Minnesota, in the American midwest. His father had deserted the family when Carl was a child, leaving his mother to care for a family of six. When Carl came home from school in the afternoon he was immediately put to working in the fields. "My portion of pay consisted of plenty of work and a sound beating every time I done anything that displeased anyone who was older and stronger . . ."

When he was eleven, Carl burgled the house of a well-to-do neighbour and was sent to reform school. He was a rebellious boy, and was often violently beaten. Because he was a highly "dominant" personality, the beatings only deepened the desire to avenge the injustice on "society". He would have agreed with the painter Gauguin who said: "Life being what it is, one dreams of revenge."

Travelling around the country on freight trains, the young Panzram was sexually violated by four hoboes. The experience suggested a new method of expressing his aggression. ". . . whenever I met [a hobo] who wasn't too rusty looking I would make him raise his hands and drop his pants. I wasn't very particular either. I rode them old and young, tall and short, white and black." When a brakesman caught Panzram and two other hoboes in a railway truck Panzram drew his revolver and raped the man, then forced the other two hoboes to do the same at gunpoint. It was his way of telling "authority" what he thought of it.

Panzram lived by burglary, mugging and robbing churches. He spent a great deal of time in prison, but became a skilled escapist. But he had his own peculiar sense of loyalty. After breaking jail in Salem, Oregon, he broke in again to try to rescue a safe blower named Cal Jordan; he was caught and got thirty days. "The thanks I got from old Cal was that he thought I was in love with him and he tried to mount me, but I wasn't broke to ride and he was, so I rode him. At that time he was about fifty years old and I was twenty or twenty-one, but I was strong and he was weak."

In various prisons, he became known as one of the toughest

troublemakers ever encountered. What drove him to his most violent frenzies was a sense of injustice. In Oregon he was offered a minimal sentence if he would reveal the whereabouts of the stolen goods; Panzram kept his side of the bargain but was sentenced to seven years. He managed to escape from his cell and wreck the jail, burning furniture and mattresses. They beat him up and sent him to the toughest prison in the state. There he promptly threw the contents of a chamberpot in a guard's face; he was beaten unconscious and chained to the door of a dark cell for thirty days, where he screamed defiance. He aided another prisoner to escape, and in the hunt the warden was shot dead. The new warden was tougher than ever. Panzram burned down the prison workshop and later a flax mill. Given a job in the kitchen, he went berserk with an axe. He incited the other prisoners to revolt, and the atmosphere became so tense that guards would not venture into the yard. Finally, the warden was dismissed.

The new warden, a man named Murphy, was an idealist who believed that prisoners would respond to kindness. When Panzram was caught trying to escape, Murphy sent for him and told him that, according to reports, he was "the meanest and most cowardly degenerate that they had ever seen." When Panzram agreed, Murphy astonished him by telling him that he would let him walk out of the jail if he would swear to return in time for supper. Panzram agreed – with no intention of keeping his word; but when supper time came, something made him go back. Gradually, Murphy increased his freedom, and that of the other prisoners. But one night Panzram got drunk with a pretty nurse and decided to abscond. Recaptured after a gun battle, he was thrown into the punishment cell, and Murphy's humanitarian regime came to an abrupt end.

This experience seems to have been something of a turning point. So far, Panzram had been against the world, but not against himself. His betrayal of Murphy's trust seems to have set up a reaction of self-hatred. He escaped from prison again, stole a yacht, and began his career of murder. He would offer sailors a job and take them to the stolen yacht; there he would rob them, commit sodomy, and throw their bodies into the sea. "They are there yet, ten of 'em." Then he went to West Africa to work for an oil company, where he soon lost his job for committing sodomy on the table waiter. The US Consul declined to help him and he sat down in a park "to think things over". "While I was sitting there, a little nigger boy about eleven or twelve years came bumming around. He was looking for something. He found it too. I took him out to a gravel pit a quarter of a mile from the main camp . . . I left him there, but first I committed sodomy on him and then killed him. His brains were coming out of his ears when I left him and he will never be any deader . . .

"Then I went to town, bought a ticket on the Belgian steamer to Lobito Bay down the coast. There I hired a canoe and six niggers and went out hunting in the bay and backwaters. I was looking for crocodiles. I found them, plenty. They were all hungry. I fed them. I shot all six of those niggers and dumped 'em in. The crocks done the rest. I stole their canoe and went back to town, tied the canoe to a dock, and that night someone stole the canoe from me."

Back in America he raped and killed three more boys, bringing his murders up to twenty. After five years of rape, robbery and arson, Panzram was caught as he robbed the express office in Larchmont, New York and sent to one of America's toughest prisons, Dannemora. "I hated everybody I saw." And again more defiance, more beatings. Like a stubborn child, he had decided to turn his life into a competition to see whether he could take more beatings than society could hand out. In Dannemora he leapt from a high gallery, fracturing a leg, and walked for the rest of his life with a limp. He spent his days brooding on schemes of revenge against the whole human race: how to blow up a railway tunnel with a train in it, how to poison a whole city by putting arsenic into the water supply, even how to cause a war between England and America by blowing up a British battleship in American waters.

It was during this period in jail that Panzram met a young Jewish guard named Henry Lesser. Lesser was a shy man who enjoyed prison work because it conferred automatic status, which eased his inferiority complex. Lesser was struck by Panzram's curious immobility, a quality of cold detachment. When he asked him: "What's your racket?" Panzram replied with a curious smile: "What I do is reform people." After brooding on this, Lesser went back to ask him how he did it; Panzram replied that the only way to reform people is to kill them. He described himself as "the man who goes around doing good". He meant that life is so vile that to kill someone is to do him a favour.

When a loosened bar was discovered in his cell, Panzram received yet another brutal beating – perhaps the hundredth of his life. In the basement of the jail he was subjected to a torture that in medieval times was known as the strappado. His hands were tied behind his back; then a rope was passed over a beam and he was heaved up by the wrists so that his shoulder sockets bore the full weight of his body. Twelve hours later, when the doctor checked his heart, Panzram shrieked and blasphemed, cursing his mother for bringing him into the world and declaring that he would kill every human being. He was allowed to lie on the floor of his cell all day, but when he cursed a guard, four guards knocked him unconscious with a blackjack and again suspended him from a beam. Lesser was so shocked by this treatment that he sent Panzram a dollar by a "trusty". At first, Panzram thought it was a joke. When he realized that it was a gesture of sympathy, his eyes filled with tears. He told Lesser that if he could get him paper and a pencil, he would write him his life story. This is how Panzram's autobiography came to be written.

When Lesser read the opening pages, he was struck by the remarkable literacy and keen intelligence. Panzram made no excuses for himself:

> If any man was a habitual criminal, I am one. In my life time I have broken every law that was ever made by God and man. If either had made any more, I should very cheerfully have broken them also. The mere fact that I have done these things is quite sufficient for the average person. Very few people even consider it worthwhile to wonder why I am what I am and do what I do. All that they think is necessary to do is to catch me, try me, convict me and send me to prison for a few years, make life miserable for me while in prison and turn me loose again . . . If someone had a young tiger cub in a cage and then mistreated it until it got savage and bloodthirsty and then turned it loose to prey on the rest of the world . . . there would be a hell of a roar . . . But if some people do the same thing to other people, then the world is

surprised, shocked and offended because they get robbed, raped and killed. They done it to me and then don't like it when I give them the same dose they gave me.

(From *Killer, a Journal of Murder*, edited by Thomas E. Gaddis and James O. Long, Macmillan, 1970.)

Panzram's confession is an attempt to justify himself to one other human being. Where others were concerned, he remained as savagely intractable as ever. At his trial he told the jury: "While you were trying me here, I was trying all of you too. I've found you guilty. Some of you, I've already executed. If I live, I'll execute some more of you. I hate the whole human race." The judge sentenced him to twenty-five years.

Transferred to Leavenworth penitentiary, Panzram murdered the foreman of the working party with an iron bar and was sentenced to death. Meanwhile, Lesser had been showing the autobiography to various literary men, including H. L. Mencken, who were impressed. But when Panzram heard there was a movement to get him reprieved, he protested violently: "I would not reform if the front gate was opened right now and I was given a million dollars when I stepped out. I have no desire to do good or become good." And in a letter to Henry Lesser he showed a wry self-knowledge: "I could not reform if I wanted to. It has taken me all my life so far, thirty-eight years of it, to reach my present state of mind. In that time I have acquired some habits. It took me a lifetime to form these habits, and I believe it would take more than another lifetime to break myself of these same habits even if I wanted to . . ." ". . . what gets me is how in the heck any man of your intelligence and ability, knowing as much about me as you do, can still be friendly towards a thing like me when I even despise and detest my own self." When he stepped onto the scaffold on the morning of 11 September 1930, the hangman asked him if he had anything to say. "Yes, hurry it up, you hoosier bastard. I could hang a dozen men while you're fooling around."

Earle Nelson

On 24 February 1926, a man named Richard Newman went to call on his aunt, who advertised rooms to let in San Francisco; he found the naked body of the sixty-year-old woman in an upstairs toilet. She had been strangled with her pearl necklace, then repeatedly raped. Clara Newman was the first of twenty-two victims of a man who became known as "the Gorilla Murderer". The killer made a habit of calling at houses with a "Room to Let" notice in the window; if the landlady was alone, he strangled and raped her. His victims included a fourteen-year-old girl and an eight-month-old baby. And as he travelled around from San Francisco to San Jose, from Portland, Oregon to Council Bluffs, Iowa, from Philadelphia to Buffalo, from Detroit to Chicago, the police found him as elusive as the French police had found Joseph Vacher thirty years earlier. Their problem was simply that the women who could identify "the Dark Strangler" (as the newspapers had christened him) were dead, and they had no idea of what he looked like. But when the Portland police had the idea of asking newspapers to publish descriptions of jewellery that had been stolen from some of the strangler's victims, three old ladies in a South Portland lodging-house recalled that they had bought a few items of jewellery from a pleasant young man who had stayed with them for a few days. They decided – purely as a precaution – to take it to the police. It proved to belong to a Seattle landlady, Mrs Florence Monks, who had been strangled and raped on 24 November 1926. And the old ladies were able to tell the police that the Dark Strangler was a short, blue-eyed young man with a round face and slightly simian mouth and jaw. He was quietly spoken, and claimed to be deeply religious.

When the problem of serial murder was first publicized in the United States, various experts estimated that the number of victims amounted to between 3,000 and 5,000 a year. In the late 1980s, a more careful estimate by the National Center for the Analysis of Violent Crime (NCAVC) revealed that the actual figure was probably between 300 and 500 a year – frightening enough, but hardly on the same scale as the earlier "expert" estimate.

On 8 June 1927, the strangler crossed the Canadian border, and rented a room in Winnipeg from a Mrs Catherine Hill. He stayed for three nights. But on 9 June, a couple named Cowan, who lived in the house, reported that their fourteen-year-old daughter Lola had vanished. That same evening, a man named William Patterson returned home to find his wife absent. After making supper and putting the children to bed, he rang the police. Then he dropped on his knees beside the bed to pray; as he did so, he saw his wife's hand sticking out. Her naked body lay under the bed.

The Winnipeg police recognized the *modus operandi* of the Gorilla Murderer. A check on boarding-house landladies brought them to Mrs Hill's establishment. She assured them that she had taken in no suspicious characters recently – her last lodger had been a Roger Wilson, who had been carrying a Bible and been highly religious. When she told them that Roger Wilson was short, with piercing blue eyes and a dark complexion, they asked to see the room he had stayed in. They were greeted by the stench of decay. The body of Lola Cowan lay under the bed, mutilated as if by Jack the Ripper. The murderer had slept with it in his room for three days.

From the Patterson household, the strangler had taken some of the husband's clothes, leaving his own behind. But he changed these at a second-hand shop, leaving behind a fountain pen belonging to Patterson, and paying in $10 bills stolen from his house. So the police now not only had a good description of the killer, but the clothes he was wearing, including corduroy trousers and a plaid shirt.

The next sighting came from Regina, two hundred miles west; a landlady heard the screams of a pretty girl who worked for the telephone company, and interrupted the man who had been trying to throttle her; he ran away. The police guessed that he might be heading back towards the American border, which would take him across prairie country with few towns; there was a good chance that a lone hitch-hiker would be noticed. Descriptions of the wanted man were sent out to all police stations and post offices. Five days later, two constables saw a man wearing corduroys and a plaid shirt walking down a road near Killarney, twelve miles from the border. He gave his name as Virgil Wilson and said he was a farm-worker; he seemed quite unperturbed when the police told him they were looking for a mass murderer, and would have to take him in on suspicion. His behaviour was so unalarmed they were convinced he was innocent. But when they telephoned the Winnipeg chief of police, and described Virgil Wilson; he told them that the man was undoubtedly "Roger Wilson", the Dark Strangler. They hurried back to the jail – to find that their prisoner had picked the lock of his handcuffs and escaped.

Detectives were rushed to the town by aeroplane, and posses spread out over the area. "Wilson" had slept in a barn close to the jail, and the next morning broke into a house and stole a change of clothing. The first man he spoke to that morning noticed his dishevelled appearance and asked if he had spent the night in the open; the man admitted that he had. When told that police were on their way to Killarney by train to look for the strangler, he ran away towards the railway. At that moment, a police car appeared; after a short chase, the fugitive was captured.

He was identified as Earle Leonard Nelson, born in Philadelphia in 1897; his mother had died of venereal disease contracted from his father. At the age of ten, Nelson was knocked down by a streetcar and was unconscious with concussion for six days. From then on, he experienced violent periodic headaches. He began to make a habit of peering through the keyhole of his cousin Rachel's bedroom when she was getting undressed. At twenty-one, he was arrested for trying to rape a girl in a basement. Sent to a penal farm, he soon escaped, and was recaptured peering in through the window of his cousin as she undressed for bed. A marriage was unsuccessful; when his wife had a nervous breakdown, Nelson visited her in hospital and tried to rape her in bed. Nothing is known of Nelson's whereabouts for the next three years, until the evening in February 1926, when he knocked on the door of Mrs Clara . Newman in San Francisco, and asked if he could see the room she had to let . . .

Gordon Cummins, the "Blackout Ripper"

Sex crimes invariably increase during wartime. This is partly because the anarchic social atmosphere produces a loss of inhibition, partly because so many soldiers have been deprived of their usual sexual outlet. Nevertheless, the rate of sex crime in England during World War II remained low, while the murder rate actually fell. One of the few cases to excite widespread attention occurred during the "blackouts" of 1942. Between 9 and 15 February, four women were murdered in London. Evelyn Hamilton, a forty-year-old schoolteacher, was found strangled in an air raid shelter; Evelyn Oatley, an ex-revue actress, was found naked on her bed, her throat cut and her belly mutilated with a tin-opener; Margaret Lower was strangled with a silk stocking and mutilated with a razor blade, and Doris Jouannet was killed in an identical manner. The killer's bloody fingerprints were found on the tin-opener and on a mirror in Evelyn Oatley's flat. A few days later, a young airman dragged a woman into a doorway near Piccadilly and throttled her into unconsciousness, but a passer-by overheard the scuffle and went to investigate. The airman ran away, dropping his gas-mask case with his service number stencilled on it. Immediately afterwards, he accompanied a prostitute to her flat in Paddington and began to throttle her; her screams and struggles again frightened him away. From the gas-mask case the man was identified as twenty-eight-year-old Gordon Cummins, from north London, and he was arrested as soon as he returned to his billet. The fingerprint evidence identified him as the "blackout ripper", and he was hanged in June 1942. Sir Bernard Spilsbury, who had performed the post-mortem on Evelyn Oatley, also performed one on Cummins.

Christie, the "Monster of Notting Hill"

John Reginald Halliday Christie, whose crimes created a sensation in post-war London, belonged to another typical class of serial killer: the necrophile. (Henry Lee Lucas and Jeffrey Dahmer are later examples.)

On 24 March 1953, a Jamaican tenant of 10 Rillington Place was sounding the walls in the kitchen on the ground floor, previously occupied by Christie. One wall sounded hollow and the Jamaican pulled off a corner of wallpaper. He discovered that the paper covered a cupboard, one corner of which was missing. He was able to peer into the cupboard with the help of a torch and saw the naked back of a woman. Hastily summoned policemen discovered that the cupboard contained three female bodies. The first was naked except for a brassière and suspender belt; the other two were wrapped in blankets and secured with electric wire. There was very little smell, which was due to atmospheric conditions causing dehydration. (Some of the more sensational accounts of the case state inaccurately that the tenant was led to the discovery by the smell of decomposition.) Floorboards in the front room appeared to have been disturbed, and they were taken up to reveal a fourth body, also wrapped in a blanket.

Christie had left on 20 March, sub-letting to a Mr and Mrs Reilly, who had paid him £7, 13s. in advance. The Reillys had been turned out almost immediately by the owner, a Jamaican, Charles Brown, since Christie had no right to sub-let, and had, in fact, left owing rent.

The back garden was dug up, and revealed human bones – the skeletons of two more bodies. A human femur was being used to prop up the fence.

It was now remembered that in 1949, two other bodies – those of Mrs Evans and her baby daughter Geraldine – had been discovered at the same address. Both had been strangled, and the husband, Timothy Evans, was hanged for the double murder. Evans was a near-mental defective, and it seemed conceivable that the murders for which he was hanged were the work of the man who had killed the women in the downstairs flat.

On 31 March, Christie was recognized by PC Ledger on the embankment near Putney Bridge and was taken to Putney Bridge Police Station. In the week since the discovery of the bodies, the hue and cry had been extraordinary, and newspapers ran pictures of the back garden of 10 Rillington Place and endless speculations about the murders and whether the murderer would commit another sex crime before his arrest. (Mr Alexie Surkov, the secretary of the Soviet league of writers, happened

---

The three doctors called in to pronounce upon Henri Desire Landru's mental condition were agreed upon one thing: the man, despite the ten women he was said to have murdered, was not mad. The first medical expert, Dr. Vallon, faced the crowded court at the lady-killer's trial and stated:

'I already had to examine the accused in 1904, when he was being charged with obtaining money by false pretences. I found him then in a state bordering on the psychopathic, but he was not mad. Perhaps he was on the borderline, but not beyond it. I find now that Landru is perfectly lucid, perfectly conscious of what he is doing. He is quick and alert in his mind. He is easy and facile in repartee. In short, he must be considered responsible for the acts of which he is accused.'

Landru - whose criminal and sexual career had been under police surveillance for some twenty years - was jubilant when he heard this. 'The crimes of which I am accused could only be explained by the most pronounced insanity.' he asserted. 'The doctors say I am sane - therefore I am innocent.'

Said to be 'completely lacking in moral responsibility', Landru displayed an ambivalent attitude towards women, whom he courted like any other men and later killed with a brutal lack of feeling that branded him as a monster without humanity or heart.

'Bluebeards' ? The original Bluebeard, the 15th century Marshal of France, Giffe de Rais, who fought beside Joan of Arc, was not a killer of women, but of children. Noted because of his glossy blue-black beard, he was a sexual pervert, and also thought he could use the children's blood in the making of gold. But it was the French writer of fairy stories, Charles Perrault, who created the popular version of Bluebeard the lady-killer in the late seventeenth century. One of his more macabre stories tells how a young girl, Fatima, marries the rich landowner Bluebeard, and one day looks into a secret room - to find there the bodies of his previous wives. Although Perrault wrote the tale from the Gallic viewpoint, many countries have similar legends of wife-killers - Cornwall has a story of a giant called Bolster who killed his wives each year by throwing rocks at them. The folk- imagination understands these dark male compulsions to destroy women and also the woman's half-frightened, half-fascinated- attitude towards it.

to be in England at the time, and later commented with irony on the press furore.)

Christie made a statement admitting to the murders of the four women in the house. In it he claimed that his wife had been getting into an increasingly nervous condition because of attacks from the coloured people in the house, and that on the morning of 14 December 1952, he had been awakened by his wife's convulsive movements; she was having some kind of a fit; Christie "could not bear to see her", and strangled her with a stocking. His account of the other three murders – Rita Nelson, aged twenty-five, Kathleen Maloney, aged twenty-six, Hectorina McLennan, aged twenty-six, described quarrels with the women (who were prostitutes) during the course of which Christie strangled them. Later, he also confessed to the murders of the two women in the garden. One was an Austrian girl, Ruth Fuerst, whom Christie claimed he had murdered during sexual intercourse; and Muriel Eady, a fellow employee at the Ultra Radio factory in Park Royal where Christie had worked in late 1944.

A tobacco tin containing four lots of pubic hair was also found in the house.

There were many curious features in the murders. Carbon monoxide was found in the blood of the three women in the cupboard, although not in Mrs Christie's. The three had semen in the vagina; none was wearing knickers, but all had a piece of white material between the legs in the form of a diaper. This has never been satisfactorily explained.

Christie admitted at his trial that his method of murder had been to invite women to his house and to get them partly drunk. They were persuaded to sit in a deck-chair with a canopy, and a gas pipe was placed near the floor and turned on. When the girl lost consciousness from coal-gas poisoning, Christie would strangle her and then rape her. But since the women were prostitutes, it would hardly seem necessary to render them unconscious to have sexual intercourse. One theory to explain this has been advanced by Dr Francis Camps, the pathologist who examined the bodies. He suggests that Christie had reached a stage of sexual incapability where the woman needed to be unconscious before he could possess her. (In Halifax, as a young man, Christie had earned from some girl the derogatory nicknames, "Can't Do It Christie" and "Reggie-No-Dick".)

The body of Rita Nelson was found to be six months' pregnant.

Christie was tried only for the murder of his wife; his trial opened at the Central Committee Court on Monday 22 June 1953, before Mr Justice Finnemore; the Attorney-General, Sir Lionel Heald, led for the Crown; Mr Derek Curtis Bennett, QC defended.

Christie's case history, as it emerged at his trial, was as follows: He was fifty-five years-old at the time of his arrest. He was born in Chester Street, Boothstown, Yorkshire, in April 1898, son of Ernest Christie, a carpet designer. The father was a harsh man who treated his seven children with Victorian sternness and offered no affection. Christie was a weak child, myopic, introverted, and jeered at by his fellow pupils as a "cissy". He had many minor illnesses in his childhood – possibly to compensate for lack of attention. He was in trouble with the police for trivial offences, and was beaten by his father whenever this occurred.

At the age of fifteen (this would be in about 1913) he left school and got a post as a clerk to the Halifax Borough Police. Petty pilfering lost him the job. He then worked in his father's carpet factory; when he was dismissed from there for petty theft, his father threw him out of the house.

Christie was a chronic hypochondriac, a man who enjoyed being ill and talking about his past illnesses. (His first confession starts with an account of his poor health.) In 1915 he suffered from pneumonia. He then went to war, and was mustard-gassed and blown up. He claimed that he was blind for five months and lost his voice for three and a half years. The loss of voice was the psychological effect of hysteria, for there was no physical abnormality to account for it. His voice returned spontaneously at a time of emotional excitement.

Christie claimed that one of the most important events in his childhood was seeing his grandfather's body when he was eight.

In 1920, Christie met his wife Ethel, and they were married in the same year. They had no children. Christie claimed he had no sexual relations with his wife for about two years – which, if true, supports the view of his sexual inadequacy and the inferiority neurosis that afflicted his relations with women. In 1923, he quarrelled with his wife and they separated; he also lost his voice for three months. Details of the life of the Christies between the two wars are not available, except that he was knocked down by a car which did not stop, in 1934, and sustained injuries to the head, the knee and collar-bone. (Christie seems to have been one of those unfortunate people who are born unlucky.) And when he worked for the post office, it was found that he was stealing money and postal orders from letters; for this he received seven months in prison. His longest term of employment was with a transport firm; this lasted for five years.

Duncan Webb, who was not the most reliable of crime-writers, declared that Christie claimed to be a rich man when he married his wife, and that he joined the Conservative Association (presumably in Halifax) and tried to play the man about town. On separating from his wife in 1923, (after a second term in prison for false pretences), he came to London, and lodged in Brixton and Battersea. He struck a woman over the head with a cricket bat, and went to jail again. His wife was induced to visit him, and started to live with him again when he came out.

Jerry Thompson was a rapist. His one and only murder victim was found on the morning of June 17, 1935, in a ditch in the cemetery at Peoria, Illinois. She was a pretty girl, and her white dress had been pulled up under her armpits; her torn underwear lay nearby. The medical report revealed that she had been raped and strangled. She was identified as 19-year-old Mildred Hallmark, a waitress, who had vanished the evening before, shortly after leaving the cafeteria where she worked. When the police appealed for information, several girls came forward, and disclosed that they had also been raped. The attacker was a good-looking young man who had offered them a lift, then driven them to a quiet place and forced them to submit.

The police decided to make a general appeal through the newspapers, asking for all women who had been attacked to come forward, with a promise of complete anonymity. They hoped that one of these women might be able to give them some due to the identity of the rapist. The response startled them. More than 50 women came forward, and it became clear that the police were looking for a serial rapist.

In many cases he had stopped beside a girl walking along a lonely street and dragged her into the car. If she resisted or - screamed, he silenced her with a violent punch dn the jaw or in the stomach. He would drive to a lonely place, undress the girl, and commit rape. Then he would take out a camera, and take photographs of her naked, sprawled in obscene positions. He would tell the girl that if she told the police her name would appear in the newspapers, and everyone would know what had happened to her. There are few girls who do not prefer privacy to revenge.

In 1939, Christie joined the War Reserve Police, and became known as an officious constable who enjoyed showing his authority and "running in" people for minor blackout offences. His wife often went to visit her family in Sheffield, and it was during one of her visits there that Christie brought Ruth Fuerst back to the house and strangled her. Although in his second confession he mentions strangling her during the act of intercourse, it is almost certain that he somehow persuaded her to inhale gas – perhaps from the square jar of Friar's Balsam, which he covered with a towel, claiming that it was a cure for nose and throat infections; while the victim's head was hidden under the towel, Christie inserted a tube leading from the gas tap. It may be that he only wanted to render the girl unconscious in order to have sexual intercourse, and decided to kill her later to cover up the assault. In his confession he told of hiding Ruth Fuerst's body under the floorboards when his wife returned with her brother. The next day, when they were out, he moved the body to the wash-house and later buried it in the back garden under cover of darkness.

At his trial, Christie declared that he was not sure whether Ruth Fuerst was his first victim. However, unless he had some other place in which to dispose of bodies, it seems probable that his "vagueness" was intended to impress the jury that his mind was wandering.

In December 1943, Christie was released from the War Reserve and went to work at Ultra Radio. Here he became friendly with Muriel Eady, who often came to visit the Christies. On one occasion she came alone when Christie's wife was on holiday, and complained of catarrh. She buried her face in Christie's jar of Friar's Balsam, and later ended, like Ruth Fuerst, buried in the tiny garden.

Whether the Evans Murders were committed by Christie or by Timothy Evans will now never be known, but it seems almost certain that Christie committed them. In his third confession from Brixton prison, he declares that in August 1949, Timothy Evans and his young wife (who lived above the Christies) quarrelled violently about a blonde woman. Christie claimed that he found Mrs Evans lying on the floor in front of the gas fire, having attempted suicide, and that he gave her a cup of tea. The next day he found her there once again, and she asked his help in killing herself, offering to let him have sexual intercourse. He strangled her with a stocking, and (in view of the later cases) probably had intercourse with her. When Timothy Evans came home, Christie told him that his wife had gassed herself and that no doubt Evans would be suspected of her murder. What happened then is not certain. It is possible that Evans then murdered the baby, Geraldine, who was later found with her mother in the wash house. Within a few days he sold his furniture and disappeared. But he then walked into the Merthyr Tydfil police station and claimed that he had killed his wife and put her body down a drain. The bodies were discovered in the wash house, and Evans was charged with murder. At one point, he claimed that Christie was the murderer, but when told that the child's body had also been found, he withdrew this allegation. Evans was of low mentality and illiterate; it is impossible to know what went on in his mind before his execution, or whether he murdered his daughter. What is most surprising is that he did not inform on Christie when he found that his wife was strangled; this makes it seem possible that he had murdered his daughter, and saw no point in involving Christie too.

In December 1952 came the murder of his wife. The motive for this is not clear, although it may well have been a desire to have the house to himself for further murders. Whether or not this was his intention, Christie killed again a few weeks later. Rita Nelson had last been seen alive on 2 January 1953. Hers was the second body in the cupboard. Christie claimed she had accosted him and demanded money, finally forcing herself into his house and starting a fight. What seems more likely is that she came back to the house by his invitation and was gassed as she sat in the deck-chair.

The next victim was Kathleen Maloney, last seen alive on 12 January 1953. Again, Christie claims she started a fight, but this seems unlikely.

Christie had no money at this time, and sold his furniture for £11 and his wife's wedding ring. He had written to his wife's bank in Sheffield, forging her signature, and asked for her money to be sent. (He had also sent a postcard to his wife's sister before Christmas claiming that she had rheumatism in her fingers and could not write.)

Some time in February, Christie claims that he met a couple who told him they had nowhere to stay. The man was out of

ON 2 JUNE 1985, a security guard at South City Lumber in San Francisco observed a young Asian walking out with a vice without stopping at the check-out desk. The guard alerted a policeman, who caught up with the man just as he was putting the vice into the boot of a car. As soon as he saw the policeman, the Asian ran away, and disappeared among the parked cars. An older, bearded man who was bending over the open boot explained that it was all a mistake, and offered to pay for the vice. The policeman insisted on making a routine search of the car, and in a green holdall, discovered a hand gun with a silencer. Since this was against the gun laws of California, the policeman told the bearded man that he would have to accompany him to the station. There, the man handed over his documentation, which gave his name as Robin Stapley, and then asked for a glass of water. When it was handed to him, he popped a small capsule into his mouth, and swallowed it down with the water. A moment later, he slumped forward dead. A check with the fingerprint records revealed that the name of the dead man was, in fact, Leonard Lake, and that he had a criminal record for burglary. Papers found in his wallet led the police to a small ranch at Wilseyville, Calaveras County, a hundred and fifty miles north east of San Francisco. There they discovered a bedroom equipped with chains, shackles, and hooks in the ceiling - it looked ominously like a torture chamber. And in an underground bunker with prison cells, they discovered video tapes that showed young women being sexually abused by Leonard Lake and by his partner, a young Chinaman called Charles Ng. In a trench nearby, police unearthed the remains of eight victims. Eventually, fragments of bone found on the property and photographed in the ranchhouse brought the total to twenty-four, including two small children. It eventually became clear that Lake and Ng had made a habit of luring men and women to the bungalow, and then murdering them work. They came and stayed with Christie for a few days, and then left. Later, the woman – Hectorina McLennan – returned alone, and was murdered by Christie around 3 March. After this, Christie claims he lost his memory and wandered around London (subsequent to 20 March, when he left Rillington Place) sleeping in a Rowton House part of the time. When caught, he was unshaven and shabby, with no money.

The defence was of insanity, but the jury rejected it, following several medical opinions that Christie was sane, and he was sentenced to death and executed on 15 July 1953.

Henry Lee Lucas, the American serial killer, confessed to three hundred and sixty murders, but doubts have been expressed about this figure – although it is certain that his victims ran into dozens. But no one has doubted the record of another killer, Pedro Alonzo Lopez, the "Monster of the Andes", who confessed in 1980 to raping and murdering three hundred and sixty young girls, most of whom were under the age of twelve, in Columbia and Ecuador. He was sentenced to sixteen years in prison, the maximum under Ecuadorian law.

chapter four

THE HIGH IQ KILLER

*F*rom Martin Dumollard onward, most serial killers have been curiously stupid – Carl Panzram was one of the few exceptions. But in the second half of the twentieth century, criminologists became aware of a new phenomenon – the "high IQ" killer. Dumollard killed for money; Earle Nelson and Christie killed for sex. But the "high IQ" killer cannot be classified so simply. He has often read books on criminology and psychology, and he may argue lucidly in favour of a life of crime. The "Moors murderer" Ian Brady was of this type; so was the Muswell Hill murderer Dennis Nilsen and the "Hillside Strangler" Kenneth Bianchi.

The emergence of the "high IQ" killer dates from the 1960s. But Brady and Manson were pre-dated by an American case that dates from the late 1950s.

Melvin Rees

On Sunday, 11 January 1959 an old blue Chevrolet forced another car off a lonely country road in Virginia, and a tall, thin young man with staring eyes advanced on it waving a revolver. He ordered the Jackson family – consisting of Carrol

Jackson, his wife Mildred, and their two children, Susan, aged five, and a baby, Janet – into the boot of his car, and sped off. Carrol Jackson was later found dead in a ditch; underneath him lay Janet, who had also been shot. Two months later, the bodies of Mildred Jackson and Susan were uncovered in Maryland; Mildred Jackson had been strangled with a stocking and Susan battered to death.

Two years earlier, in June 1957, a man with staring eyes had approached a courting couple in a car – an army sergeant and a woman named Margaret Harold – and asked for a lift. On the way he pulled out a gun and demanded money; when Margaret Harold said: "Don't give it to him", he shot her in the back of the head. The sergeant flung open the door and ran. When police found the car, they also found the body of Margaret Harold lying across the front seat without her dress; a police spokesman described the killer as "a sexual degenerate". Near the scene of the crime the police discovered a deserted shack full of pornographic pictures.

Five months after the murders of the Jackson family, in May 1959, the police received an anonymous tip-off that the murderer was a jazz musician named Melvin Rees; but police were unable to trace Rees. Early the following year, a salesman named Glenn Moser went to the police, acknowledged that he was the author of the anonymous tip-off, and told them that he now had the suspect's address: Melvin Rees was working in a music shop in Memphis, Arkansas. Rees was arrested there, and soon after he was identified by the army sergeant as the man who had shot Margaret Harold. A search of the home of Rees's parents uncovered the revolver with which Carrol Jackson had been shot, and a diary describing the abduction of the Jacksons and their murder. "Caught on a lonely road . . . Drove to a select area and killed the husband and baby. Now the mother and daughter were all mine." He described forcing Mildred Jackson to perform oral sex, and then raping her repeatedly; the child was also apparently raped. (Full details have never been released.) He concluded: "I was her master." The diary also described the sex murders of four more girls in Maryland. Rees was executed in 1961.

Violent sex murders were common enough by the late 1950s. What makes this one unique for its period was Rees's "Sadeian" attitude of self-justification. On the night before the Jackson killings, Rees had been on a "benzedrine kick", and in the course of a rambling argument had told Moser: "You can't say it's wrong to kill. Only individual standards make it right or wrong." He had also explained that he wanted to experience everything: love, hate, life, death . . . When, after the murders, Moser asked him outright whether he was the killer, Rees disdained to lie; he simply refused to answer, leaving Moser to draw the self-evident conclusion. Rees was an "intellectual" who, like Moors murderer Ian Brady in the following decade, made the decision to rape and kill on the grounds that "everything is lawful". He may therefore be regarded as one of the first examples of the curious modern phenomenon, the "high IQ killer". His sexual fantasies involved sadism (Mildred Jackson's death had been long and agonising) and power. In that sense, his crimes anticipate those of the serial killer who was to emerge two decades later.

Unfortunately we know nothing of Rees's background, or what turned him into a serial killer. Yet on the basis of other cases, we can state with a fair degree of confidence that parental affection was lacking in childhood, and that he was a lonely introverted child who was not much liked by his schoolmates. It is difficult, if not impossible, to find a case of a serial killer of whom this is not true.

Werner Boost, the Düsseldorf "Doubles Killer"

7 January, 1953 was a cold, snowy night in Düsseldorf, West Germany. Shortly before midnight, a fair-haired young man, who was bleeding from a head wound staggered into the police station and said that his friend had just been murdered. The "friend", it seemed, was a distinguished lawyer named Dr Lothar Servé. The officer on duty immediately telephoned Kriminal Hauptcommissar Mattias Eynck, chief of the North Rhineland murder squad, who hurried down to the station. The young man had identified himself as Adolf Hullecremer, a

nineteen-year-old student, and explained that he and Dr Servé had been sitting in the car "discussing business", and looking at the lights on the river, when both doors of the car had been jerked open by two men in handkerchief masks. One of the men began to swear, then shot Servé in the head. As Hullecremer begged for his life, the second man whispered that if he wished to stay alive, he should "sham dead". He then hit Hullecremer on the head with a pistol. As he lost consciousness, Hullecremer heard him say: "He won't wake again." When the men had gone, he made off as fast as he could.

After Hullecremer's head had been bandaged, he said he felt well enough to take the police and the doctor back to the car. It was parked in a grove of trees on the edge of the river, its engine still running. Across the rear seat lay the body of a man of about fifty, bleeding from a wound in the temple. The doctor pronounced him dead.

The motive was clearly robbery – the dead man's wallet was missing. Eynck concluded that the robbers were "stick-up men" who had chosen this spot because it was known as a "lovers' lane". The fact that the two men had been in the rear seat when attacked suggested a homosexual relationship.

Forensic examination revealed no fingerprints on the car, and falling snow had obliterated any footprints or other tyre tracks. The murder enquiry had reached an impasse when, a few weeks later, a tramp found a .32 calibre pistol – of Belgian make – in the woods, and forensic tests showed it to be the murder weapon. Photographs of its bullets were sent to all police stations, and the Magdeburg police – in former East Germany – contacted Eynck to say that the same gun had been used in a murder a few years earlier in a town called Hadersleben. Two East Germans attempting to flee to the former West had been shot with the same weapon. This seemed to suggest that the murderer was himself an East German refugee who had moved to Düsseldorf. But there the trail went cold – thousands of East Germans had fled the Communist regime to the large cities of West Germany since the war.

Almost three years later, in October 1955, Eynck found himself wondering whether the double killers had struck again. A young couple had vanished after an evening date. The man was twenty-six-year-old Friedhelm Behre, a baker, and his fiancée was twenty-three-year-old Thea Kurmann. They had spent the evening of 31 October in a "bohemian" restaurant called the Cafe Czikos, in the old quarter of Düsseldorf, and had driven off soon after midnight in Behre's blue Ford. The next day, worried relatives reported them missing. But there was no sign of the couple or of the blue car. Four weeks later, a contractor standing by a half-dredged gravel pit near Düsseldorf was throwing stones at a metal object when he realized that it was the top of a blue car. He called some of his men, and they heaved it ashore. In the back seat lay two decomposing corpses. They proved to be those of the missing couple, the girl still dressed in her red satin evening dress, which had been torn and pulled up.

The medical report revealed that Friedhelm Behre had been shot through the head at close range. The girl had been garrotted, possibly by a man's tie, after being raped. It looked as if the killer had wrenched open the rear door as the couple were petting, shot the man, then dragged the girl out. After rape, her body was thrown into the back seat, and the car driven to the gravel pit, where it was pushed into the water.

To Eynck, this sounded ominously like the Servé murder. Again, there were no fingerprints – suggesting that the killer had worn gloves. The bullet had disappeared. It had gone right through the victim's skull, but it should have been somewhere in the car. Its absence suggested that the murderer had removed it to prevent the identification of the gun.

The murder caused panic among Düsseldorf's young lovers, and over the Christmas period, the usual lay-bys were deserted. Meanwhile, Chief-Inspector Botte, in charge of the investigation, quickly found that he had run out of clues.

Three months later, on the morning of 8 February, 1956, a businessman named Julius Dreyfuss reported that his Mercedes car was missing – together with its chauffeur, a young man named Peter Falkenberg. The chauffeur had failed to arrive to pick up his employer. It seemed possible that Falkenberg had driven away to sell the expensive car. But an hour or so later, a woman reported that a black car was parked in front of her house with its headlights on. It proved to be the missing Mercedes. And there was a great deal of blood inside – both in the front and the rear seats.

At about the same time, a woman had reported that her daughter, twenty-three year old Hildegard Wassing, had failed to return home after a date. A few days before, Hildegard and a friend had met a young man named Peter at a dance; he had told them he was a chauffeur. Hildegard had agreed to go out with him the following Tuesday, 7 February, and her brother had noticed that he was driving a black Mercedes. To Eynck, it sounded as if Peter Falkenberg and Hildegard Wassing had fallen victim to the "car murderer".

The next morning, a gardener was cycling to work near the small village of Lank-Ilverich, near Düsseldorf, when he saw the remains of a burning haystack some distance from the path. He strolled over to look – and then rushed for the nearest telephone as he saw the remains of two corpses among the burnt hay.

Eynck arrived soon after, and noticed the smell of petrol. Both bodies were badly charred, but rain had prevented the fire from totally incinerating them. Forensic examination revealed that the man – identified from dental charts as Peter Falkenberg – had been shot through the head. Hildegard Wassing had been raped and then strangled – the rope was still sunk in the burnt flesh.

Thousands of Düsseldorf residents were questioned, but once again, there were no obvious leads. The car killer was evidently a man who took great care to leave no clues. Then a detective named Bohm came upon a possible suspect. In the small town of Buderich, not far from the burnt haystack, he was told of a young man named Erich von der Leyen, who had once attacked some children with a manure fork, and was regarded as a "loner" by his neighbours. He was originally from East Germany, and now lived in lodgings in a place called Veert. Von der Leyen worked as a travelling salesman for agricultural machinery, so his log-book should have shown precisely where he was when the couple were murdered. But the entry for 7 February had been made later, and the travelling times for drives seemed implausible. Moreover, there were red spots on the front seat-covers. These were sent for forensic examination, and were reported to be human bloodstains. Erich von der Leyen was placed under arrest. Stains on his trousers also proved to be blood.

Von der Leyen insisted that he had no idea where the stains came from – the only way he could account for them was to recall that his girlfriend's dachsund had been in his car when it was on heat. That sounded unlikely. The police asked another forensic expert to examine the bloodstains on the trousers, and see if he could determine their age. Under the microscope, he saw epithelial cells – evidence that it *was* menstrual blood. The stains on the car seat were re-tested, and the laboratory admitted with embarrassment that these were also of menstrual blood – and, moreover, from a dog. The police had to release von der Leyen, and to apologize for the intense interrogations he had endured.

Soon after this, on the evening of 6 June, 1956, a forest ranger named Erich Spath was walking through woods near Meererbusch, not far from the burnt haystack site, when he saw a man lurking in the undergrowth, and peering from behind a tree at a car in which a courting couple were petting. The man was so absorbed that he did not hear the ranger. Then Spath saw him draw a revolver from his pocket, and creep towards the car.

Spath placed his rifle to his shoulder and crept up behind the young man. "Drop it!" The man turned round, then threw away his gun and ran. Spath chased him and soon caught up with him, crouching in a hollow.

Half an hour later, the car with the courting couple – and also containing the ranger and his captive – pulled up in front of Düsseldorf's main police station. The suspect – who was dark and good-looking – had accompanied them without protest and without apparent concern, as if his conscience was clear. And when they stood in the office of Kriminal Hauptkommissar Mattias Eynck, Spath understood why. The young man – who gave his name as Werner Boost – explained that he had merely been doing a little target practice in the woods, and had thought *he* was being attacked. He obviously felt that no one could disprove his story and that therefore the police would be unable to hold him.

"Is your gun licensed?" asked Eynck.

"Well . . . no. It's a war trophy . . ."

"In that case, I am charging you with possessing an illegal weapon."

The gun was found in the undergrowth where Boost had thrown it. Nearby was a motor cycle, which proved to have been stolen. Boost was also charged with its theft. A magistrate promptly sentenced him to six months in jail, which gave Eynck the time he needed to investigate the suspect.

At first the trail seemed to be leading nowhere. The pistol had not been used in any known crime; Boost was, as he said, an electrical engineer who worked in a factory, and who was regarded as a highly intelligent and efficient worker; he had been married for six years, had two children, and was a good husband and provider. His wife, Hanna, told Eynck that he spent most of his evenings at home, working in his own laboratory or reading – he was an obsessive reader. Occasionally, she admitted, he became restless and went out until the early hours of the morning.

She led Eynck down to the basement laboratory. There he discovered various ingredients for explosives, as well as some deadly poison. He also found a quantity of morphine.

Back in the flat, Eynck noticed a letter postmarked Hadersleben. He recalled that the Belgian pistol, which had been found within a few hundred yards of Boost's flat, had been used in a double murder in Hadersleben, near Magdeburg. "Do you know someone in Hadersleben?" he asked. Hanna Boost told him that it was her home town, and that she had married her husband there.

"How did you both escape from East Germany?"

"Werner knew a safe route through the woods."

But she insisted that, as far as she knew, her husband had never owned a gun.

Now, at last, the case was beginning to look more promising. Back in his office, Eynck looked through the latest batch of information about Boost, which had come from a town called Helmstedt, which had been taken over by the Russians in 1945. And at about this period, there had been a great many murders – about fifty in all – of people trying to escape from the Russian to the British zone. Werner Boost had been in Helmstedt at the time. Then he had moved to Hadersleben, and the murders had ceased. But the two would-be emigrés had been shot in Hadersleben while trying to escape . . .

There was another interesting item – a notebook which had been found in the saddle of Boost's stolen motorcycle. And it contained an entry: "Sunday, 3 June. Lorbach in need of another shot. Must attend to it."

Eynck sent for Boost and questioned him about the item. Boost said smoothly:

"Frank Lorbach is a friend of mine, and we go shooting

together. On that day, he just couldn't hit the bull's eye, so I made a note to give him another shot."

Eynck did not believe a word of it. He asked Boost about his days in Helmstedt, and whether he had ever helped refugees to escape. Boost admitted that he had, and said he was proud of it. "And did you ever shoot them?" Boost looked horrified. "Of course not!"

Eynck now sent out one of his detectives to try to locate Franz Lorbach. This was not difficult. Lorbach proved to be a man of twenty-three with dark curly hair, whose good looking face lacked the strength of Werner Boost's. He was a locksmith, and insisted that he only had the most casual acquaintance with Boost. Eynck knew that he was lying. He also noticed Lorbach's dilated pupils, and surmised that he was a drug addict, and that Boost was his supplier. He was certain that, when his craving became strong enough, Lorbach would talk. He held him in custody for questioning.

Meanwhile, Boost and Lorbach were placed in a police line-up, wearing handkerchief masks over the lower half of their faces. Adolf Hullecremer, the student who had been with Dr Servé when he was shot, was able to identify Boost as Serve's assailant. He said he recognized the eyes. But he failed to identify Lorbach.

After a day or two in custody, Lorbach began to show symptoms of withdrawal from drugs. And one day, as Eynck was questioning Boost again – and getting nowhere – he received a phone call saying that Lorbach wanted to talk to him.

Lorbach was pale, his eyes were watery, and his nose twitched like a rabbit's.

"I want to tell you the truth. Werner Boost is a monster. It *was* he who killed Dr Servé, and I was his accomplice . . ."

Lorbach admitted that it was a love of poaching that had drawn the two of them together in 1952. They often went shooting in the woods. But Boost seemed to have a maniacal hatred of courting couples. "These sex horrors are the curse of Germany." So they would often creep up on couples who were making love in cars and rob them. Then, he said, Boost had an idea for rendering them unconscious. He had concocted some mixture which he forced them to drink. Then he and Lorbach would rape the unconscious girls. "Some of them were very lovely. I feel ashamed – my wife is going to have a baby. But it was Boost who made me do it. I had to do it. He kept me supplied with morphine, which he obtained from the chemist who sold him chemicals."

He insisted that he had taken part only in the attack on Servé and Hullecremer. Boost had been indignant to see two men in a car together, and had ordered him to kill the young man. But Lorbach had not the stomach for it. Instead, he had whispered to him to pretend to be dead. Lorbach's failure to shoot Hullecremer enraged Boost – he made Lorbach kneel in the snow, and said: "I ought to kill you too . . ."

Lorbach led the police to a place at the edge of the forest, where Boost kept his loot concealed. In a buried chest, they found watches, rings and jewellery. There were also bottles of poison, some knives, and a roll of cord which proved to be identical to that which had been used to strangle Hildegard Wassing.

Lorbach also disclosed that Boost had ordered Lorbach to kill his wife, Hanna Boost, if he was arrested. There was a phial of cyanide hidden behind a pipe in his flat, and Lorbach was to slip it into her drink, so that she could not incriminate her husband. Eynck found the phial exactly where Lorbach had said it was.

Lorbach also confirmed that he and Boost had been involved in an earlier attempt at crime, a year before the murder of Dr Servé. The two men had placed a heavy plank studded with long nails across the road, to force motorists to stop. But the first car to come along had contained four men – too many for them to tackle – and it had driven on to the verge and around the plank. Two more cars also contained too many passengers. Then a security van came, and a man with a gun removed the plank. After that, police arrived – evidently alerted by one of the cars – and Boost and Lorbach had to flee. In fact, as long ago as 1953, Eynck had suspected that Dr Servé's murderer' was responsible for this earlier attempt.

Lorbach also detailed Boost's plans to rob a post office by knocking everyone unconscious with poison gas, and to kidnap and murder a child of a rich industrialist for ransom.

On 11 December, 1956, Boost was charged with the murders of Dr Servé, Friedhelm Behre, Thea Kurmann, Peter Falkenberg and Hildegard Wassing. But when Lorbach, the main prosecution witness, suffered a nervous breakdown due to drug problems, the trial had to be postponed. Meanwhile,

Boost was extradited to Magdeburg for questioning about the murder of the couple at Hadersleben. But he stonewalled his questioners as he had tried to stonewall the Düsseldorf police, and was finally returned to Eynck's jurisdiction with no additional charges against him.

Boost's trial began in the courthouse at Düsseldorf on 3 November, 1961, before Judge Hans Naecke, two associate magistrates, Dr Warda and Dr Schmidt, and a six man jury. Boost maintained his total innocence, and his lawyer, Dr Koehler, lost no time in pointing out that the testimony of a drug addict like Franz Lorbach was hardly reliable. Lorbach himself was a poor witness, who mumbled and became confused. But he was able to tell one story that strengthened the case against Boost. Lorbach confessed that Boost had blackmailed him – by threatening withdrawal of his drug supply – into taking part in another attack on a couple. They had held up two lovers in the woods. Boost had tried to kill the man, but the gun had misfired. The girl had run away screaming, and Boost had ordered Lorbach to catch her. Lorbach had done so – but then whispered to her to lie low for a while. When he returned, Boost had knocked the man unconscious – but Lorbach had warned him there was a car coming, and they had roared away on Boost's motorbike.

Eynck told the court that he had traced this couple, and that they had confirmed the story in every detail. They were not married – at least not to one another – which is why they had failed to report the incident. But Eynck was able to offer their deposition in evidence.

Boost's lawyer counter-attacked by pointing out that there had recently been a murder of a couple in a car near Cologne, and that Boost was obviously not guilty of this crime.

After a month of listening to this and similar evidence, the six jurors decided that the evidence that Boost had murdered the two couples was insufficient. But they found him guilty of murdering Dr Servé. He was sentenced to life imprisonment, and Lorbach to three years, as his accomplice – much of which he had already served. Boost's sentence was exactly the same as if he had been found guilty on all charges.

Lucian Staniak, the "Red Spider"

For criminologists, one of the most frustrating things about the Iron Curtain was that it was virtually impossible to learn whether its police were facing the same types of crimes as in the west. But in the late 1960s, accounts of the "Red Spider" case made it clear that communist regimes also spawned serial killers.

In July 1964, the communist regime in Poland was getting prepared to celebrate the twentieth anniversary of the liberation of Warsaw by Russian troops; a great parade was due to take place in Warsaw on the 22nd. On the 4 July the editor of *Przeglad Polityczny*, the Polish equivalent of *Pravda*, received an anonymous letter in spidery red handwriting: "There is no happiness without tears, no life without death. Beware! I am going to make you cry." Marian Starzynski thought the anonymous writer had him in mind, and requested police protection. But on the day of the big parade, a seventeen-year-old blonde, Danka Maciejowitz, failed to arrive home from a parade organized by the School of Choreography and Folklore in Olsztyn, one hundred and sixty miles north of Warsaw. The next day, a gardener in the Olsztyn Park of Polish Heroes discovered the girl's body in some shrubbery. She had been stripped naked and raped, and the lower part of her body was covered with Jack-the-Ripper-type mutilations. And the following day, the 24th, another red-ink letter was delivered to *Kulisy*, a Warsaw newspaper: "I picked a juicy flower in Olsztyn and I shall do it again somewhere else, for there is no holiday without a funeral."

The first group of organized serial killers in history were the Hindu "thugs" (pronounced "tugs"), from whom we derive our modern word "thug". When the British annexed India in the late eighteenth century the conquerors noted that the roads were infested with bands of robbers who strangled their victims. It became slowly apparent that the killing was, in fact, a religious ceremony, and that the Thugs killed people – often a whole caravan-load consisting of dozens – as a sacrifice to the black goddess Kali. The bodies were mutilated, then buried. In 1829, a British army captain, William Sleeman, organized the suppression of Thuggee, so that within twenty years it had virtually ceased to exist.

Analysis of the ink showed that it had been made by dissolving red art paint in turpentine.

On 16 January 1965, the Warsaw newspaper *Zycie Warsawy* published the picture of a pretty sixteen-year-old girl, Aniuta Kaliniak, who had been chosen to lead a parade of students in another celebration rally the following day. She left her home in Praga, an eastern suburb of Warsaw, and crossed the river Vistula to reach the parade. Later, she thumbed a lift from a lorry driver, who dropped her close to her home at a crossroads. (The fact that a sixteen-year-old girl would thumb a lift like this indicates that the level of sex crime in Poland must be a great deal lower than in England or the US.) The day after the parade, her body was found in a basement in a leather factory opposite her home. The killer had removed a grating to get in. The crime had obviously been carefully planned. He had waited in the shadows of the wall, and cut off her cry with a wire noose drooped over her head. In the basement, he had raped her, and left a six-inch spike sticking in her sexual organs (an echo of the Boston Strangler). While the search went on another red-ink letter advised the police where to look for her body.

Olsztyn and Warsaw are one hundred and sixty miles apart; this modern Ripper differed from his predecessor in not sticking to the same area. Moreover, like Klaus Gosmann, he was a man with a strong dramatic sense: the selection of national holidays for his crimes, the letter philosophising about life and death.

The Red Spider – as he had come to be known, from his spidery writing – chose All Saints day, 1 November, for his next murder, and Poznan, one hundred and twenty-four miles west of Warsaw, as the site. A young, blonde hotel receptionist Janka Popielski, was on her way to look for a lift to a nearby village, where she meant to meet her boyfriend. Since it was her holiday, the freight terminal was almost deserted. Her killer pressed a chloroform-soaked bandage over her nose and mouth. Then he removed her skirt, stockings and panties, and raped her behind a packing shed. After this, he killed her with a screwdriver. The mutilations were so thorough and revolting that the authorities suppressed all details. The Red Spider differed from many sex killers in apparently being totally uninterested in the upper half of his victims. Janka was stuffed into a packing case, where she was discovered an hour later. The police swooped on all trains and buses leaving Poznan, looking for a man with bloodstained clothes; but they failed to find one. The next day, the Poznan newspaper *Courier Zachodni* received one of the now-notorious letters in red ink, containing a quotation from Stefan Zeromsky's national epic *Popioly* (1928): "Only tears of sorrow can wash out the stain of shame; only pangs of suffering can blot out the fires of lust."

May Day, 1966, was both a communist and a national holiday. Marysia Galazka, seventeen, went out to look for her cat in the quiet suburb of Zoliborz, in northern Warsaw. When she did not return, her father went out to look for her. He found her lying in the typical rape position, with her entrails forming an abstract pattern over her thighs, in a tool shed behind the house. Medical evidence revealed that the killer had raped her before disembowelling her.

Major Ciznek, of the Warsaw Homicide Squad, was in charge of the case, and he made a series of deductions. The first was that the Red Spider was unlikely to confine himself to his well-publicized murders on national holidays. Such killers seek victims when their sexual desire is at maximum tension, not according to some preconceived timetable. Ciznek examined evidence of some fourteen other murders that had taken place since the first one in April 1964, one each in Lublin, Radom, Kielce, Lodz, Bialystock, Lomza, two in Bydgoszcz, five in the Poznan district. All places were easily reached by railway; the *modus operandi* was always the same. Every major district of Poland within two hundred and forty-eight miles of Warsaw was covered. Ciznek stuck pins in a map and examined the result. It looked as if Warsaw might be the home of the killer, since the murders took place all round it. But one thing was noticeable. The murders extended much farther south than north, and there were also more of them to the south. It rather looked as if the killer had gone to Bialystock, Lomza and Olsztyn as a token gesture of extending his boundaries. Assuming, then, that the killer lived somewhere south of Warsaw, where would this be most likely to be? There were five murders in the Poznan district, to the west of Warsaw. Poznan is, of course, easily reached from Warsaw. But where in the south could it be reached from just as easily? Cracow was an obvious choice. So was Katowice, twenty miles or so from Cracow. This town was also at the centre of a network of railway lines.

On Christmas Eve, 1966, Cracow was suddenly ruled out as a

possibility. Three service men getting on a train between Cracow and Warsaw looked into a reserved compartment and found the half naked and mutilated corpse of a girl on the floor. The leather miniskirt had been slashed to pieces; so had her abdomen and thighs. The servicemen notified the guard, and a message was quickly sent to Warsaw, who instructed the traindriver to go straight through to Warsaw, non-stop, in case the killer managed to escape at one of the intervening stations. A careful check of passengers at Warsaw revealed no one stained with blood or in any way suspicious. But the police were able to locate the latest letter from the killer, dropped into the post slot of the mail van on top of all the others. It merely said: "I have done it again," and was addressed to *Zycie Warsawy*. It looked as if the Red Spider had got off the train in Cracow, after killing the girl, and dropped the letter into the slot.

The girl was identified as Janina Kozielska, of Cracow. And the police recalled something else: another girl named Kozielska had been murdered in Warsaw in 1964. This proved to be Janina's sister Aniela. For Ciznek, this ruled out Cracow as the possible home of the killer. For he would be likely to avoid his home territory. Moreover, there surely had to be some connection between the murders of two sisters . . . The compartment on the Cracow-Warsaw train had been booked over the telephone by a man who said his name was Stanislav Kozielski, and that his wife would pick up the tickets. Janina had paid 1,422 zloty for them – about twenty-five pounds. Janina had come to the train alone and been shown to her compartment by the ticket inspector. She said that her husband would be joining her shortly. The inspector had also checked a man's ticket a few moments later, but could not recall the man. It was fairly clear, then, that the Red Spider knew the girl well enough to persuade her to travel with him as his wife, and had probably paid for the ticket. He had murdered her in ten minutes or so, and then hurried off the train.

Ciznek questioned the dead girl's family. They could not suggest who might have killed their daughter, but they mentioned that she sometimes worked as a model – as her sister had. She worked at the School of Plastic Arts and at a club called The Art Lovers Club.

Ciznek recollected that the red ink was made of artist's paint dissolved in turpentine and water; this looked like a lead.

The Art Lovers Club proved to have one hundred and eighteen members. For an Iron Curtain country, its principles were remarkably liberal; many of its members painted abstract, tachiste and pop-art pictures. Most of them were respectable professional men – doctors, dentists, officials, newspapermen. And one of them came from Katowice. His name was Lucian Staniak, and he was a twenty-six-year-old translator who worked for the official Polish publishing house. Staniak's business caused him to travel a great deal – in fact, he had bought an *ulgowy bilet*, a train ticket that enabled him to travel anywhere in Poland.

Ciznek asked if he could see Staniak's locker. It confirmed his increasing hope that he had found the killer. It was full of knives – used for painting, the club manager explained. Staniak daubed the paint on with a knife blade. He liked to use red paint. And one of his paintings, called "The Circle of Life", showed a flower being eaten by a cow, the cow being eaten by a wolf, the wolf being shot by a hunter, the hunter being killed by a car driven by a woman, and the woman lying with her stomach ripped open in a field, with flowers sprouting from her body.

Ciznek now knew he had his man, and he telephoned the Katowice police. They went to Staniak's address at 117 Aleje Wyzwolenia, but found no one at home. In fact, Staniak was out committing another murder – his last. It was a mere month after the train murder – 31 January 1967 – but he was impatient at the total lack of publicity given to the previous murder. So he took Bozhena Raczkiewicz, an eighteen-year-old student from the Lodz Institute of Cinematographic Arts, to a shelter built at the railway station for the use of stranded overnight travellers, and there stunned her with a vodka bottle. In accordance with his method when in a hurry, he cut off her skirt and panties with his knife. He had killed her in a few minutes between 6 o'clock and 6.25. The neck of the broken bottle had a clear fingerprint on it.

Staniak was picked up at dawn the next day; he had spent the night getting drunk. His fingerprints matched those on the bottle. He was a good-looking young man of twenty-six. And when he realized that there was no chance of escape, he confessed fully to twenty murders. He told the police that his parents and sister had been crossing an icy road when they were hit by a skidding car, being driven too fast by the young wife of a Polish Air Force pilot. The girl had been acquitted of careless driving. Staniak had seen the picture of his first victim in a newspaper, and thought she looked like the wife of the pilot; this was his motive in killing her. He had decided against killing the wife of the pilot because it would be traced back to him.

Sentenced to death for six of the murders – the six described here – Staniak was later reprieved and sent to the Katowice asylum for the criminally insane.

The Soviet Union always played down its crime figures, insisting that crime was largely a problem for the wicked Capitalist west, although in the mid-1980s, the Tass News Agency admitted that a man would go on trial in the city of Vitebsk for the murder of thirty-three women. But in April 1992, in the new Russia, Andrei Chikatilo, a fifty-six-year-old teacher of literature, went on trial in Moscow for murdering fifty-three children – eleven boys and forty-two girls – at Rostov over a twelve-year period. Chikatilo admitted that he lured his victims into the woods, tied them to trees and stabbed them between the eyes, after which he sliced up the bodies and ate the flesh. After three months in prison in 1984 for theft of State property, he made up for lost time by killing eight people in one month. A convicted rapist was mistakenly executed for one of Chikatilo's crimes.

chapter five

THREE BRITISH CASES

*C*ompared to America, or even Germany, France and Italy, Great Britain has had few cases of serial murder. In fact, compared to America, England's murder rate is absurdly low. Until well into the 1960s it was a mere 150 a year, compared to America's 10,000. (America's population is about three times that of England.) By the 1990s, England's murder rate has risen to around 700 a year; America's was 23,000. (Los Angeles alone has more murders per year than the whole of Great Britain.)

It seems odd, then, that in spite of its low murder rate, Britain has produced three of the most horrific cases of serial murder of the twentieth century.

The first of these has become known simply as the Moors Murder Case.

The Moors Murder Case

Between July 1963 and October 1965, Ian Brady and his mistress Myra Hindley collaborated on five child murders. They were finally arrested because they tried to involve Myra's brother-in-law, David Smith, in one of the murders, and he went to the police.

In 1922 America produced a classic triangle case, with comic variations. On the night of August 22nd neighbours of the Oesterreich family in Los Angeles heard gunshots and screams. The police found Mrs. Walburga Oesterreich in hysterics, and her husband dead upon the floor. Questioned, she said they had returned from an evening out to find an intruder in the house. Her husband had grappled with him, and been shot.

Fred, a 60-year-old sewing-machine factory owner, proved to be a millionaire. While his wife was winding up his business affairs, the police became increasing sceptical of her story; finally, they arrested her on suspicion. Mrs. Oesterreich sent for her lawyer, and told him that her ne'er-do-well 'half brother' was living in the attic at her home; would he go along and legally evict him?

The lawyer duly went to the house, climbed the stairs, and tapped on a trapdoor in Walburga's bedroom ceiling. There was a short wait, then out stepped a small, shy-looking man, who identified himself as Otto Sanhuber. Inspired by the lawyer's friendly manner, Sanhuber poured out the true version of Fred Oesterreich's death and the incredible account of a 19-year-old love affair, in which he had lived in the attic of the Oesterreich's house, emerging to raid the icebox and make love to Walburga.

The story began in 1903, when Walburga was 36. Her 41-year-old husband was a drunk, and unpleasant with it. One day Otto - then a 17-year-old mechanic - called at the Oesterreich home to repair Walburga's sewing machine. They were attracted to each other, and he soon became her lover. Fred suspected that his wife was 'seeing someone', and had her followed by a private detective. Mrs. Oesterreich found out about this, and in a fury threatened to leave her husband - who quickly gave way and apologized. However, Walburga knew that her lover would have to stop his visits altogether. Either that, or he must move into the house for good.

The psychology of women who kill is one of the most fascinating subjects in the whole field of criminology, for, on the whole, women are not inclined to crimes of violence. At present, women form a negligible percentage of all criminals - well under 10%.

It *is* true that crimes of violence among adolescent girls - mostly from slum areas - more than doubled in the first three years of the 1970s, but there is no sign of a general rise. And, in spite of overcrowding in the big cities which always produces a rise in the crime rate - it seems unlikely that female crime will ever become a serious social problem.

The reason is obvious; woman's basic instinct is for a home and security, and someone who values security will think twice about doing anything to jeopardize it. Man, with his more restless desires, his wider sense of purpose, is more likely to take risks, including crime.

What about the women who do commit crimes - particularly the most serious crime of all, murder? The first noticeable thing in considering a cross-section of such women is that so many of them are sexually unattractive, often downright ugly. There *are* cases of pretty criminals - Marie de Brinvilliers, Ruth Ellis, Sharon Kinne - but they are rarities. Most murderesses are physically unattractive, highly dominant, and highly sexed. And this immediately explains why they take to crime, for *all* crime springs out of frustration - from the drunken husband who batters the baby to the company director who embezzles millions.

Ian Brady, who was twenty-seven at the time of his arrest, was a typical social misfit. The illegitimate son of a Glasgow waitress, he was brought up in a slum area of Clydeside. Until the age of eleven he seems to have been a good student; then he was sent to a "posh" school, together with a number of other re-housed slum boys, and began to develop a resentment towards the better-off pupils. From then on he took to petty crime; his first appearance in court was at the age of thirteen, on a charge of housebreaking. He had served four years on probation for more burglaries when he moved to Manchester to live with his mother and a new stepfather in 1954. As a result of another theft he was sentenced to a year in Borstal. Back in Manchester, he went back on the dole. It was a dull life in a small house, and he seems to have been glad to get a job as a stock clerk at Millwards, a chemical firm, when he was twenty-one.

It was at this point that he became fascinated by the Nazis and began collecting books about them. They fed his fantasies of power. So did his discovery of the ideas of the Marquis de Sade, with his philosophy of total selfishness and his daydreams of torture. It becomes clear in retrospect that Brady always had a streak of sadism. A childhood friend later described how he had dropped a cat into a deep hole in a graveyard and sealed it up with a stone. When the friend moved the stone to check on his story, the cat escaped.

For Brady, the Nazis represented salvation from mediocrity and boredom, while de Sade justified his feeling that most people are contemptible. Brady particularly liked the idea that society is corrupt, and that God is a lie invented by priests to keep the poor in a state of subjugation. Stifled by ennui, seething with resentment, Brady was like a bomb that is ready to explode by the time he was twenty-three.

It was at this time that a new typist came to work in the office. Eighteen-year-old Myra Hindley was a normal girl from a normal family background, a Catholic convert who loved animals and children, and favoured blonde hair-styles and bright lipstick. She had been engaged, but broken it off because she found the boy immature. Brady had the sullen look of a delinquent Elvis Presley, and within weeks, Myra was in love. Brady ignored her, probably regarding her as a typical working-class moron. Her diary records: "I hope he loves me and will marry me some day." When he burst into profanity after losing a bet she was deeply shocked. It was almost a year later, at the firm's Christmas party in 1961, that he offered to walk her home, and asked her out that evening. When he took her home, she declined to allow him into the house – she lived with her grandmother – but a week later, after another evening out, she surrendered her virginity on her gran's settee. After that, he spent every Saturday night with her.

Myra found her lover marvellously exciting and sophisticated. He wore black shirts, read "intellectual" books, and was learning German. He introduced her to German wine, and she travelled as a pillion passenger on his motorbike. He talked to her about the Nazis, and liked to call her Myra Hess (a combination of a famous pianist and Hitler's deputy). He also introduced her to the ideas of the Marquis de Sade, and set out converting her to atheism, pointing out the discrepancies in the gospels – it did not take long to demolish her faith. He also talked to her a great deal about his favourite novel, *Compulsion* by Meyer Levin, a fictionalized account of the Leopold and Loeb murder case.

It was in July 1963 – according to her later confession – that he first began to talk to her about committing "the perfect murder", and suggesting that she should help him. In her "confession" (to Chief Superintendent Peter Topping) she alleges that Brady blackmailed her by threatening to harm her grandmother, and by showing her some pornographic photographs of her that he had taken on an occasion when he had slipped a drug into her wine. The photographs certainly exist – thirty of them – some showing them engaged in sexual intercourse and wearing hoods. (These were taken with a time-lapse camera.) Emlyn Williams, who saw them, states that some show keen pleasure on their faces, which would seem to dispose of Myra's claim that they were taken when she was unconscious. Whether or not she was telling the truth about blackmail, it seems clear that Brady could have persuaded her to do anything anyway.

In her confession to Chief Inspector Peter Topping (published in 1989 in his book *Topping*), she described how, on 12 July 1963, she and Brady set out on their first "murder hunt". By now Myra Hindley owned a broken-down van. She was sent ahead in the van, with Brady following behind on his motorbike. Her job was to pick up a girl and offer her a lift. The first child they saw was Myra's next-door neighbour, so she drove past her. The second was sixteen-year-old Pauline Reade, who was on her way to a dance. Myra offered her a lift, and she accepted. In the van, Myra explained that she was on her way to Saddleworth Moor to look for a glove she had lost at a picnic. If Pauline would like to come and help her search, she would give her a pile of records in the back of the van. Pauline was delighted to accept.

Once on the moor, Brady arrived on his motorbike, and was introduced as Myra's boyfriend. Then Brady and Pauline went off to look for the glove. (Since it was July it was still daylight.) By the time Brady returned to the car, it was dark. He led Myra to the spot where Pauline Reade's body was lying. Her throat had been cut, and her clothes were in disarray; Myra accepted that Brady had raped her. That, after all, had been the whole point of the murder. Together they buried the body, using a spade they had brought with them. Brady told her that at one point Pauline was struggling so much that he had thought of calling for her to hold the girl's hands – clearly, he had no doubt that she would co-operate. On the way home, they passed Pauline's mother and brother, apparently searching for her. Back at home, Brady burned his bloodstained shoes and trousers.

In an open letter to the press in January 1990, Brady was to contradict Myra Hindley's account; he insisted that injuries to the nose and forehead of Pauline Reade had been inflicted by her, and that she had also committed some form of lesbian assault on Pauline Reade. According to Brady, Myra participated actively and willingly in the murders.

Five months later, Brady was ready for another murder. On Saturday 23 November, 1963 they hired a car – the van had been sold – and drove to nearby Ashton market. There, according to Myra, Brady got into conversation with a twelve-year-old boy, John Kilbride, and told him that, "If Jack would help them look for a missing glove, he would give him a bottle of sherry he had won in the raffle". Because Myra was present, John Kilbride accompanied them without suspicion. They drove up to Saddleworth Moor, and the boy unsuspectingly accompanied Brady into the darkness. Myra Hindley claims that she drove around for a while, and that when she came back and flashed her lights, Brady came out of the darkness and told her that he had already buried the body. He also mentioned taking the boy's trousers down and giving him a slap on the buttocks. In fact, Myra said, she was fairly certain that he had raped John Kilbride. He had explained that he had strangled him because the knife he had was too blunt to cut his throat.

In June the following year – in 1964 – Brady told her he was "ready to do another one". (Like all serial killers he had a "cooling-off period" – in this case about six months.) According to Myra, he told her that committing a murder gave him a feeling of power. By now they had their own car, a Mini. On 16 June, 1964 she stopped her car and asked a twelve-year-old boy, Keith Bennett, if he would help her load some boxes from an off-licence; like John Kilbride, Keith Bennett climbed in unsuspectingly. The murder was almost a carbon copy of the previous one; Keith Bennett was strangled and buried on Saddleworth Moor. Brady admitted this time that he had raped him, and added: "What does it matter?" Keith Bennett's body has never been found.

On Boxing Day, 1965, Brady and Hindley picked up a ten-year-old girl, Lesley Ann Downey, at a fairground at Ancoats. Myra Hindley had taken her grandmother to visit an uncle. They took the child back to the house, and Brady switched on a tape recorder. Myra claims she was in the kitchen with the dogs when she heard the child screaming. Brady was ordering her to take

No criminologist has so far succeeded in explaining why so many serial killers have emerged in the second half of the twentieth century. One thing seems clear: that in the past, such crimes were almost invariably committed by tyrants like Ivan the Terrible, or wealthy perverts like the French child murderer Gilles de Rais. The explanation that suggests itself is that the advance of civilisation has raised the general level of comfort so that large numbers of people have a security that was almost-unknown in the ancient world. Millions of people are now able to enjoy the kind of leisure that would have been envied by Greek tyrants or Roman emperors. The trouble is that leisure and comfort also produce boredom, a desire for sensation, and this seems to explain why an increasing number of criminals have come to behave like Ivan the Terrible or Gilles de Rais.

off her coat and squeezing her by the back of the neck. Then Lesley's hands were tied with a handkerchief and Brady set up the camera and a bright light. The child was ordered to undress, and Brady then made her assume various pornographic poses while he filmed her. At this point, Myra claims she was ordered to go and run a bath; she stayed in the bathroom until the water became cold. When she went back into the bedroom, Lesley had been strangled, and there was blood on her thighs – from which Myra realized that she had been raped. At 8 o'clock that evening they took the body up to Saddleworth Moor and buried it.

In his open letter to the press in January 1990, Ian Brady denied that Myra had played no active part in the murder of Lesley Ann Downey. "She insisted upon killing Lesley Ann Downey with her own hands, using a two-foot length of silk cord, which she later used to enjoy toying with in public, in the secret knowledge of what it had been used for."

In October 1965, Brady decided it was time for another murder. He had also decided that he needed another partner in crime, and that Myra's seventeen-year-old brother-in-law, David Smith, was the obvious choice. Smith had already been in trouble with the law. He seemed unable to hold down a job. His wife was pregnant for the second time, and they had just been given an eviction notice. So Smith listened with interest when Brady suggested a hold-up at an Electricity Board showroom. On 6 October Smith came to the house hoping to borrow some money, but they were all broke. Brady suggested: "We'll have to roll a queer." An hour later, Brady picked up a seventeen-year-old homosexual, Edward Evans, and invited him back to the house in Hattersley. Back at the flat, Myra went off to fetch David Smith. They had only just returned when there was a crash from the living room. Brady was rolling on the floor, grappling with Evans. Then he seized an axe and struck him repeatedly: "Everywhere was one complete pool of blood." When Evans lay still, Brady strangled him. Then he handed the bloodstained hatchet to Smith, saying "Feel the weight of that". His motive was obviously to get Smith's fingerprints on the haft. Together, they mopped up the blood and wrapped up the body in polythene. Then Smith went home, promising to return the next day to help dispose of the body. But Brady had miscalculated. Smith might feel in theory that "people are like maggots, small, blind and worthless", but the fact of murder was too much for him. When he arrived home he was violently sick and told his wife what had happened. Together they decided to phone the police, creeping downstairs armed with a screwdriver and carving-knife in case Brady was waiting for them. The following morning, a man dressed as a baker's roundsman knocked at Brady's door, and when Myra opened it, identified himself as a police officer. Evans's body was found in the spare bedroom. Forensic examination revealed dog hair on his underclothes – the hair of Myra Hindley's dog – indicating that he and Brady had engaged in sex, probably while Myra was fetching David Smith.

Hidden in the spine of a prayer book police found a cloakroom ticket, which led them to Manchester Central Station. In two suitcases they discovered pornographic photos, tapes and books on sex and torture; the photographs included those of Lesley Ann Downey, with a tape recording of her voice pleading for mercy. A twelve-year-old girl, Patricia Hodges, who had occasionally accompanied Brady and Hindley to the moors, took the police to Hollin Brown Knoll, and there the body of Lesley Ann Downey was dug up. John Kilbride's grave was located through a photograph that showed Hindley crouching on it with a dog. Pauline Reade's body was not found until 1987, as a result of Myra Hindley's confession to Topping. Brady helped in the search on the moor and as we know, the body of Keith Bennett has never been recovered.

Brady's defence was that Evans had been killed unintentionally, in the course of a struggle, when he and Smith tried to rob him. Lesley Ann Downey, he claimed, had been brought to the house by Smith to pose for pornographic pictures, for which she had been paid ten shillings. (His original story was that she had been brought to the house by two men.) After the session, she left the house with Smith. He flatly denied knowing anything about any of the other murders, but the tape recording of Lesley Ann Downey's screams and pleas for mercy made it clear that Brady and Hindley

---

When Moors Murdered Myra Hindley – who participated with Ian Brady in murdering children – heard that her dog had died in police custody, she remarked: "They're just a lot of bloody murderers".

were responsible for her death. Both were sentenced to life imprisonment.

The Yorkshire Ripper

During the second half of the 1970s, the killer who became known as the Yorkshire Ripper caused the same kind of fear among prostitutes in the north of England as his namesake in the Whitechapel of 1888.

His reign of terror began in Leeds on a freezing October morning in 1975, when a milkman discovered the corpse of a woman on a recreation ground; her trousers had been pulled down below her knees, and her bra was around her throat. The whole of the front of the body was covered with blood; pathologists later established that she had been stabbed fourteen times. Before that, she had been knocked unconscious by a tremendous blow that had shattered the back of her skull. She was identified as a twenty-eight-year-old prostitute, Wilma McCann, who had left her four children alone to go on a pub crawl. Her killer seemed to have stabbed and slashed her in a frenzy.

Three months later, on 20 January, 1976, a man on his way to work noticed a prostrate figure lying in a narrow alleyway in Leeds, covered with a coat. Like Wilma McCann, Emily Jackson had been half-stripped, and stabbed repeatedly in the stomach and breasts. She had also been knocked unconscious by a tremendous blow from behind. When the police established that the forty-two year old woman was the wife of a roofing con-tractor, and that she lived in the respectable suburb of Churwell, they assumed that the killer had selected her at random and crept up behind her with some blunt instrument. Further investigation revealed the surprising fact that this apparently normal housewife supplemented her income with prostitution, and that she had had sexual intercourse shortly before death – not necessarily with her killer. The pattern that was emerging was like that of the Jack the Ripper case: a sadistic maniac who preyed on prostitutes.

Just as in Whitechapel in 1888, there was panic among the prostitutes of Leeds, particularly in Chapeltown, the red light area where Emily Jackson had been picked up. But as no further "Ripper" murders occurred in 1976, the panic subsided. It began all over again more than a year later, on 5 February, 1977, when a twenty-eight year old woman named Irene Richardson left her room in Chapeltown looking for customers, and encountered a man who carried a concealed hammer and a knife. Irene Richardson had been struck down from behind within half an hour of leaving her room; then her attacker had pulled off her skirt and tights, and stabbed her repeatedly. The wounds indicated that, like Jack the Ripper, he seemed to be gripped by some awful compulsion to expose the victim's intestines.

Now the murders followed with a grim repetitiveness that indicated that the serial killer was totally in the grip of his obsession. During the next three and a half years, the man whom the press christened the Yorkshire Ripper, murdered ten more women, bringing his total to thirteen, and severely injured three more. Most of the victims were prostitutes, but two were young girls walking home late at night, and one of them a civil servant. With one exception, the method was always the same – several violent blows to the skull, which often had the effect of shattering it into many pieces, then stab wounds in the breast and stomach. In many cases, the victim's intestines spilled out. The exception was a civil servant named Marguerite Walls, who was strangled with a piece of rope on 20 August, 1979, after being knocked unconscious from behind.

One victim who recovered – forty-two-year-old Maureen Long – was able to describe her attacker. On 27 July, 1977, she had been walking home through central Bradford after an evening of heavy drinking when a man in a white car offered her a lift. As she stepped out of the car near her front door, the man struck her a savage blow on the head, then stabbed her several times. But before he could be certain she was dead, a light went on in a nearby gypsy caravan, and he drove away. She recovered after a brain operation, and described her attacker as a young man with long blond hair – a detail that later proved to be inaccurate.

Her mistake may have saved the Ripper from arrest three months later. A prostitute named Jean Jordan was killed near some allotments in Manchester on 1 October, 1977. When the body was found nine days later – with twenty-four stab wounds

– the police discovered a new £5 note in her handbag. Since it had been issued on the other side of the Pennines, in Yorkshire, it was obviously a vital clue. The police checked with the banks, and located twenty-three firms in the Leeds area who had paid their workers with £5 notes in the same sequence. Among the workers who were interviewed was a thirty-one-year-old lorry driver named Peter Sutcliffe, who worked at T and W. H. Clark (Holdings) Ltd, and lived in a small detached house at 6 Garden Lane in Bradford. But Sutcliffe had dark curly hair and a beard, and his wife Sonia was able to provide him with an alibi. The police apologized and left, and the Yorkshire Ripper was able to go on murdering for three more years.

As the murders continued – four in 1977, three in 1978, three in 1979 – the police launched the largest operation that had ever been mounted in the north of England, and thousands of people were interviewed. Police received three letters signed "Jack the Ripper", threatening more murders, and a cassette on which a man with a "Geordie" accent taunted George Oldfield, the officer in charge of the case; these later proved to be false leads. The cassette caused the police to direct enormous efforts to the Wearside area, and increased the murderer's sense of invulnerability.

The final murder took place more than a year later. Twenty-year-old Jacqueline Hill, a Leeds University student, had attended a meeting of voluntary probation officers on 17 November 1980, and caught a bus back to her lodgings soon after 9 p.m. An hour later, her handbag was found near some waste ground by an Iraqi student, and he called the police. It was a windy and rainy night and they found nothing. Jacqueline Hill's body was found the next morning on the waste ground. She had been battered unconscious with a hammer, then undressed and stabbed repeatedly. One wound was in the eye – Sutcliffe later said she seemed to be looking at him reproachfully, so he drove the blade into her eye.

This was the Ripper's last attack. On 2 January, 1981 a black prostitute named Olive Reivers had just finished with a client in the centre of Sheffield when a Rover car drove up, and a bearded man asked her how much she charged; she said it would be £10 for sex in the car, and climbed in the front. He seemed tense and asked if she would object if he talked for a while about his family problems. When he asked her to get in

In June 1983, a serial killer named Gerald Gallego was sentenced to death in California for ten murders. Gallego, with the help of his common-law wife Charlene Williams, daughter of a wealthy Sacramento businessman, had committed the murders because he had an obsessional desire to find "the perfect sex slave". (He had been practising incest with his daughter since she was eight.) Charlene, a spoilt only child, had already been married twice when, at the age of twenty-one, she met the ex-convict Gallego, whose father had been executed in 1954 for three murders. Fascinated by his macho brutality, she finally agreed to help him in his search for the "perfect sex slave". In 1978; she approached two teenage girls in a supermarket and asked them if they would like to smoke some pot. When they got back to the van, Gallego was waiting for them with a gun. He raped them both on a mattress in the back before killing them with bullets in the head. Two years - and six murders - later, they kidnapped a young couple who were leaving a dance in Sacramento. The man was 'executed" and the woman raped and subsequently shot. A friend of the kidnapped couple had seen their abduction and taken the license number of the car. The Gallegos fled, but were captured a few weeks later. In exchange for testifying against her "husband", Charlene was allowed to plead guilty to a lesser charge, and received a sixteen-year jail sentence. Gallego was sentenced to die by lethal injection.

Gallego had told a social worker in prison: "My only interest is in killing God" It echoes a comment made by Ian Brady to Chief Superintendent Topping. Although Brady declared that it was nonsense to believe in God, he admitted that after murdering John Kilbride, he had shaken his fist and the sky and shouted: "Take that, you bastard". Nothing could more clearly demonstrate the "magical thinking" of the serial killer.

the back of the car, she said she would prefer to have sex in the front; this may have saved her life – Sutcliffe had stunned at least one of his victims as she climbed into the back of the car. He moved on top of her, but was unable to maintain an erection. He moved off her again, and at this point, a police car pulled up in front. Sutcliffe hastily told the woman to say she was his girlfriend. The police asked his name, and he told them it was Peter Williams. Sergeant Robert Ring and PC Robert Hydes were on patrol duty, and they were carrying out a standard check. Ring noted the number-plate then went off to check it with the computer; while he radioed, he told PC Hydes to get into the back of the Rover. Sutcliffe asked if he could get out to urinate and Hydes gave permission: Sutcliffe stood by an oil storage tank a few feet away, then got back into the car. Meanwhile, the sergeant had discovered that the number-plates did not belong to the Rover, and told Sutcliffe he would have to return to the police station. In the station, Sutcliffe again asked to go to the lavatory and was given permission. It was when the police made him empty his pockets and found a length of clothes-line that they began to suspect that they might have trapped Britain's most wanted man.

To begin with, Sutcliffe lied fluently about why he was carrying the rope and why he was in the car with a prostitute. It was the following day that Sergeant Ring learned about Sutcliffe's brief absence from the car to relieve himself, and went to look near the oil storage tank. In the leaves, he found a ball-headed hammer and a knife. Then he recalled Sutcliffe's trip to the lavatory at the police station. In the cistern he found a second knife. When Sutcliffe was told that he was in serious trouble, he suddenly admitted that he was the Ripper, and confessed to eleven murders. (It seems odd that he got the number wrong – he was later charged with thirteen – but it is possible that he genuinely lost count. He was originally suspected of fourteen murders, but the police later decided that the killing of another prostitute, Jean Harrison – whose body was found in Preston, Lancashire – was not one of the series. She had been raped and the semen was not of Sutcliffe's blood group.)

A card written by Sutcliffe and displayed in his lorry read: "In this truck is a man whose latent genius, if unleashed, would rock the nation, whose dynamic energy would overpower those around him. Better let him sleep?"

The story that began to emerge was of a lonely and shy individual, brooding and introverted, who was morbidly fascinated by prostitutes and red-light areas. He was born on 2 June 1946, the eldest of five children and his mother's favourite. His school career was undistinguished and he left at fifteen. He drifted aimlessly from job to job, including one as a grave-digger in the Bingley cemetery, from which he was dismissed for bad timekeeping. (His later attempt at a defence of insanity rested on a claim that a voice had spoken to him from a cross in the cemetery telling him he had a God-given mission to kill prostitutes.)

In 1967, when he was twenty-one, he met a sixteen-year-old Czech girl, Sonia Szurma, in a pub, and they began going out together. It would be another seven years before they married. The relationship seems to have been stormy; at one point, she was going out with an ice-cream salesman, and Sutcliffe picked up a prostitute "to get even". He was unable to have intercourse, and the woman went off with a £10 note and failed to return with his £5 change. When he saw her in a pub two weeks later and asked for the money, she jeered at him and left him with a sense of helpless fury and humiliation. This, he claimed, was the source of his hatred of prostitutes. In 1969 he made his first attack on a prostitute, hitting her on the head with a sock full of gravel. In October of that year, he was caught carrying a hammer and charged with being equipped for theft; he was fined £25. In 1971 he went for a drive with a friend, Trevor Birdsall, and left the car in the red-light area of Bradford. When he returned ten minutes later he said, "Drive off quickly," and admitted that he had hit a woman with a brick in a sock. Sutcliffe was again driving with Birdsall in 1975 on the evening that Olive Smelt was struck down with a hammer.

In 1972 Sonia Szurma went to London for a teacher's training course and had a nervous breakdown; she was diagnosed as schizophrenic. Two years later, she and Sutcliffe married, but the marriage was punctuated by violent rows – Sutcliffe said he became embarrassed in case the neighbours heard the shouts, implying that it was she who was shouting rather than he. He also told the prostitute Olive Reivers that he had been arguing with his wife "about not being able to go with her", which Olive Reivers took to mean that they were having sexual problems. Certainly, this combination of two introverted people can hardly have improved Sutcliffe's mental condition.

Sutcliffe's first murder – of Wilma McCann – took place in the year after he married Sonia. He admitted: "I developed and played up a hatred for prostitutes . . ." Unlike the Düsseldorf sadist of the 1920s, Peter Kürten, Sutcliffe never admitted to having orgasms as he stabbed his victims; but anyone acquainted with the psychology of sexual criminals would take it for granted that this occurred, and that in most of the cases where the victim was not stabbed, or was left alive, he achieved orgasm at an earlier stage than usual. The parallels are remarkable. Kürten, like Sutcliffe, used a variety of weapons, including a hammer. On one occasion when a corpse remained undiscovered, Kürten also returned to inflict fresh indignities on it. Sutcliffe had returned to the body of Jean Jordan and attempted to cut off the head with a hacksaw.

It was when he pulled up Wilma McCann's clothes and stabbed her in the breast and abdomen that Sutcliffe realized that he had discovered a new sexual thrill. With the second victim, Emily Jackson, he pulled off her bra and briefs, then stabbed her repeatedly – he was, in effect, committing rape with a knife, Sutcliffe was caught in the basic trap of the sex criminal: the realization that he had found a way of inducing a far, more powerful sexual satisfaction than he was able to obtain in normal intercourse, and that he was pushing himself into the position of a social outcast. He admitted sobbing in his car after one of the murders, and being upset to discover that Jayne MacDonald had not been a prostitute (and later, that her father had died of a broken heart). But the compulsion to kill was becoming a fever, so that he no longer cared that the later victims were not prostitutes. He said, probably with sincerity, "The devil drove me."

Sutcliffe's trial began on 5 May 1981. He had pleaded not guilty to murder on grounds of diminished responsibility, and told the story of his "mission" from God. But a warder had overheard him tell his wife that if he could convince the jury that he was mad, he would only spend ten years in a "loony bin". The Attorney-General, Sir Michael Havers, also pointed out that Sutcliffe had at first behaved perfectly normally, laughing at the idea that he might be mentally abnormal, and had introduced the talk of "voices" fairly late in his admissions to the police.

On 22 May Sutcliffe was found guilty of murder, and jailed for life, with a recommendation that he should serve at least thirty years.

Dennis Nilsen

On the evening of 8 February 1983, a drains maintenance engineer named Michael Cattran was asked to call at 23 Cranley Gardens, in Muswell Hill, north London, to find out why tenants had been unable to flush their toilets since the previous Saturday. Although Muswell Hill is known as a highly respectable area of London – it was once too expensive for anyone but the upper middle classes – No. 23 proved to be a rather shabby house, divided into flats. A tenant showed Cattran the manhole cover that led to the drainage system. When he removed it, he staggered back and came close to vomiting; the smell was unmistakably decaying flesh. And when he had climbed down the rungs into the cistern, Cattran discovered what was blocking the drain: masses of rotting meat, much of it white, like chicken flesh. Convinced this was human flesh, Cattran rang his supervisor, who decided to come and inspect it in the morning. When they arrived the following day, the drain had been cleared. And a female tenant told them she had heard footsteps going up and down the stairs for much of the night. The footsteps seemed to go up to the top flat, which was rented by a thirty-seven-year-old civil servant named Dennis Nilsen.

Closer search revealed that the drain was still not quite clear; there was a piece of flesh, six inches square, and some bones that resembled fingers. Detective Chief Inspector Peter Jay, of Hornsey CID, was waiting in the hallway of the house that evening when Dennis Nilsen walked in from his day at the office – a Jobcentre in Kentish Town. He told Nilsen he wanted to talk to him about the drains. Nilsen invited the policeman into his flat, and Jay's face wrinkled as he smelt the odour of decaying flesh. He told Nilsen that they had found human remains in the drain, and asked what had happened to the rest of the body.

"It's in there, in two plastic bags," said Nilsen, pointing to a wardrobe.

In the police car, the Chief Inspector asked Nilsen whether the remains came from one body or two. Calmly, without emotion, Nilsen said: "There have been fifteen or sixteen altogether."

At the police station, Nilsen – a tall man with metal rimmed glasses – seemed eager to talk. (In fact, he proved to be something of a compulsive talker, and his talk overflowed into a series of school exercise books in which he later wrote his story for the use of Brian Masters, a young writer who contacted him in prison.) He told police that he had murdered three men in the Cranley Gardens house – into which he moved in the autumn of 1981 – and twelve or thirteen at his previous address, 195 Melrose Avenue, Cricklewood.

The plastic bags from the Muswell Hill flat contained two severed heads, and a skull from which the flesh had been stripped – forensic examinaation revealed that it had been boiled. The bathroom contained the whole lower half of a torso, from the waist down, intact. The rest was in bags in the wardrobe and in the tea chest. At Melrose Avenue, thirteen days and nights of digging revealed many human bones, as well as a cheque book and pieces of clothing.

The self-confessed mass murderer – he seemed to take a certain pride in being "Britain's biggest mass murderer" – was a Scot, born at Fraserburgh on 23 November 1945. His mother, born Betty Whyte, married a Norwegian soldier named Olav Nilsen in 1942. It was not a happy marriage; Olav was seldom at home, and was drunk a great deal; they were divorced seven years after their marriage. In 1954, Mrs Nilsen married again and became Betty Scott. Dennis grew up in the house of his grandmother and grandfather, and was immensely attached to his grandfather, Andrew Whyte, who became a father substitute. When Nilsen was seven, his grandfather died and his mother took Dennis in to see the corpse. This seems to have been a traumatic experience; in his prison notes he declares "My troubles started there." The death of his grandfather was such a blow that it caused his own emotional death, according to Nilsen. Not long after this, someone killed the two pigeons he kept in an air raid shelter, another severe shock. His mother's remarriage when he was nine had the effect of making him even more of a loner.

In 1961, Nilsen enlisted in the army, and became a cook. It was during this period tht he began to get drunk regularly, although he remained a loner, avoiding close relationships. In 1972 he changed the life of a soldier for that of a London policeman, but disliked the relative lack of freedom – compared to the army – and resigned after only eleven months. He became a security guard for a brief period, then a job-interviewer for the Manpower Services Commission.

In November 1975, Nilsen began to share a north London flat – in Melrose Avenue – with a young man named David Gallichan, ten years his junior. Gallachan was later to insist that there was no homosexual relationship, and this is believable. Many heterosexual young men would later accept Nilsen's offer of a bed for the night, and he would make no advances, or accept a simple "No" without resentment. But in May 1977, Gallichan decided he could bear London no longer, and accepted a job in the country. Nilsen was furious; he felt rejected and deserted. The break-up of the relationship with Gallichan – whom he had always dominated – seems to have triggered the homicidal violence that would claim fifteen lives.

The killings began more than a year later, in December 1978. Around Christmas, Nilsen picked up a young Irish labourer in the Cricklewood Arms, and they went back to his flat to continue drinking. Nilsen wanted him to stay over the New Year but the Irishman had other plans. In a note he later wrote for his biographer Brian Masters, Nilsen gives as his motive for this first killing that he was lonely and wanted to spare himself the pain of separation. In another confession he also implies that he has no memory of the actual killing. Nilsen strangled the unnamed Irishman in his sleep with a tie. Then he undressed the body and carefully washed it, a ritual he observed in all his killings. After that he placed the body under the floorboards where – as incredible as it seems – he kept it until the following August. He eventually burned it on a bonfire at the bottom of the garden, burning some rubber at the same time to cover the smell.

In November 1979, Nilsen attempted to strangle a young Chinaman who had accepted his offer to return to the flat; the Chinaman escaped and reported the attack to the police. But the police believed Nilsen's explanation that the Chinaman was trying to "rip him off" and decided not to pursue the matter.

The next murder victim was a twenty-three-year-old Canadian

called Kenneth James Ockendon, who had completed a technical training course and was taking a holiday before starting his career. He had been staying with an uncle and aunt in Carshalton after touring the Lake District. He was not a homosexual, and it was pure bad luck that he got into conversation with Nilsen in the Princess Louise in High Holborn around 3 December 1979. They went back to Nilsen's flat, ate ham, eggs and chips, and bought £20 worth of alcohol. Ockendon watched television, then listened to rock music on Nilsen's hi-fi system. Then he sat listening to music wearing earphones, watching television at the same time. This may have been what cost him his life; Nilsen liked to talk, and probably felt "rejected". "I thought bloody good guest this . . ." And sometime after midnight, while Ockendon was still wearing the headphones, he strangled him with a flex. Ockendon was so drunk that he put up no struggle. And Nilsen was also so drunk that after the murder, he sat down, put on the headphones, and went on playing music for hours. When he tried to put the body under the floorboards the next day, rigor mortis had set in and it was impossible. He had to wait until the rigor had passed. Later, he dissected the body. Ockendon had large quantities of Canadian money in his moneybelt, but Nilsen tore this up. The rigorous Scottish upbringing would not have allowed him to steal.

Nilsen's accounts of the murders are repetitive, and make them sound mechanical and almost identical. The third victim in May 1980, was a sixteen-year-old butcher named Martyn Duffey, who was also strangled and placed under the floorboards. Number four was a twenty-six year old Scot named Billy Sutherland – again strangled in his sleep with a tie and placed under the floorboards. Number five was an unnamed Mexican or Philipino, killed a few months later. Number six was an Irish building worker. Number seven was an undernourished down-and-out picked up in a doorway. (He was burned on the bonfire all in one piece.) The next five victims, all unnamed, were killed equally casually between late 1980 and late 1981. Nilsen later insisted that all the murders had been without sexual motivation – a plea that led Brian Masters to entitle his book on the case *Killing for Company*. There are moments in Nilsen's confessions when it sounds as if, like so many serial killers, he felt as if he was being taken over by a Mr Hyde personality or possessed by some demonic force.

In October 1981, Nilsen moved into an upstairs flat in Cranley Gardens, Muswell Hill. On 25 November, he took a homosexual student named Paul Nobbs back with him, and they got drunk. The next day, Nobbs went into University College Hospital for a check-up, and was told that bruises on his throat indicated that someone had tried to strangle him. Nilsen apparently changed his mind at the last moment.

The next victim, John Howlett, was less lucky. He woke up as Nilsen tried to strangle him and fought back hard; Nilsen had to bang his head against the headrest of the bed to subdue him. When he realized Howlett was still breathing, Nilsen drowned him in the bath. He hacked up the body in the bath, then boiled chunks in a large pot to make them easier to dispose of. (He also left parts of the body out in plastic bags for the dustbin men to take away.)

In May 1982, another intended victim escaped – a drag-artiste called Carl Stottor. After trying to strangle him, Nilsen placed him in a bath of water, but changed his mind and allowed him to live. When he left the flat, Stottor even agreed to meet Nilsen again – but decided not to keep the appointment. He decided not to go to the police.

The last two victims were both unnamed, one a drunk and one a drug-addict. In both cases, Nilsen claims to be unable to remember the actual killing. Both were dissected, boiled and flushed down the toilet. It was after this second murder – the fifteenth in all – that the tenants complained about blocked drains, and Nilsen was arrested.

The trial began on 24 October 1983, in the same court where Peter Sutcliffe had been tried two years earlier. Nilsen was charged with six murders and two attempted murders, although he had confessed to fifteen murders and seven attempted murders. He gave the impression that he was enjoying his moment of glory. The defence pleaded diminished responsibility, and argued that the charge should be reduced to manslaughter. The jury declined to accept this, and on 4 November 1983, Nilsen was found guilty by a vote of 10 to 2, and sentenced to life imprisonment.

chapter six

AMERICA'S SERIAL EPIDEMIC

*D*uring *the 1970s, it became increasingly clear that America's law enforcement agencies were facing a new problem: the killer who murdered repeatedly and compulsively — not just half a dozen times, like Jack the Ripper, or even a dozen, like the Boston Strangler, but twenty, thirty, forty, even a hundred times. In Houston, Texas, a homosexual with a taste for boys, Dean Corll, murdered about thirty teenagers — the precise number has never been established — and buried most of the bodies in a hired boatshed; Corll was shot to death by his lover and accomplice, Wayne Henley, in August 1973. In 1979, Chicago builder John Gacy lured thirty-three boys to his home and buried most of the bodies in a crawl space under his house. In 1983, a drifter named Henry Lee Lucas experienced some kind of religious conversion, and confessed to three hundred and sixty murders, mostly of women, killed and raped as he wandered around the country with his homosexual companion Ottis Toole. In 1986, in Ecuador, another drifter named Pedro Lopez confessed to killing and raping three hundred and sixty young girls. Lopez has so far claimed the highest number of victims — Lucas is believed to have exaggerated, although his victims undoubtedly run to more than a hundred.*

Ted Bundy

During the Seventies, the killer who was most responsible for making Americans aware of this new type of criminal was a personable young law student named Theodore Robert Bundy.

On 31 January 1974, a student at the University of Washington, in Seattle, Lynda Ann Healy, vanished from her room; the bedsheets were bloodstained, suggesting that she had been struck violently on the head. During the following March, April, and May, three more girl students vanished; in June, two more. In July, two girls vanished on the same day. It happened at a popular picnic spot, Lake Sammanish; a number of people saw a good-looking young man, with his arm in a sling, accost a girl named Janice Ott and ask her to help him lift a boat onto the roof of his car; she walked away with him and did not return. Later, a girl named Denise Naslund was accosted by the same young man; she also vanished. He had been heard to introduce himself as "Ted".

In October 1974 the killings shifted to Salt Lake City; three girls disappeared in one month. In November, the police had their first break in the case: a girl named Carol DaRonch was accosted in a shopping centre by a young man who identified himself as a detective, and told her that there had been an attempt to break into her car; she agreed to accompany him to headquarters to view a suspect. In the car he snapped a handcuff on her wrist and pointed a gun at her head; she fought and screamed, and managed to jump from the car. That evening, a girl student vanished on her way to meet her brother. A handcuff key was found near the place from which she had been taken.

Meanwhile, the Seattle police had fixed on a young man named Ted Bundy as a main suspect. For the past six years, he had been involved in a close relationship with a divorcee named Meg Anders, but she had called off the marriage when she realized he was a habitual thief. After the Lake Sammanish disappearances, she had seen a photofit drawing of the wanted "Ted" in the *Seattle Times* and thought it looked like Bundy; moreover, "Ted" drove a Volkswagen like Bundy's. She had seen crutches and plaster of Paris in Bundy's room, and the coincidence seemed too great; with immense misgivings, she telephoned the police. They told her that they had already checked on Bundy; but at the suggestion of the Seattle police, Carol DaRonch was shown Bundy's photograph. She tentatively identified it as resembling the man who had tried to abduct her, but was obviously far from sure. (Bundy had been wearing a beard at the time.)

In January, March, April, July, and August 1975, more girls vanished in Colorado. (Their bodies – or skeletons – were found later in remote spots.) On 16 August 1975, Bundy was arrested for the first time. As a police car was driving along a dark street in Salt Lake City, a parked Volkswagen launched into motion; the policeman followed, and it accelerated. He caught up with the car at a service station, and found in the car a pantyhose mask, a crow-bar, an icepick and various other tools; there was also a pair of handcuffs.

Bundy, twenty-nine years old, seemed an unlikely burglar. He was a graduate of the University of Washington, and was in Utah to study law; he had worked as a political campaigner, and for the Crime Commission in Seattle. In his room there was nothing suspicious – except maps and brochures of Colorado, from which five girls had vanished that year. But strands of hair were found in the car, and they proved to be identical with those of Melissa Smith, daughter of the Midvale police chief, who had vanished in the previous October. Carol DaRonch had meanwhile identified Bundy in a police line-up as the fake policeman, and bloodspots on her clothes – where she had scratched her assailant – were of Bundy's group. Credit card receipts showed that Bundy had been close to various places from which girls had vanished in Colorado.

In theory, this should have been the end of the case – and if it had been, it would have been regarded as a typical triumph of scientific detection, beginning with the photofit drawing and concluding with the hair and blood evidence. The evidence was, admittedly, circumstantial, but taken all together, it formed a powerful case. The central objection to it became apparent as soon as Bundy walked into court. He looked so obviously decent and clean-cut that most people felt there must be some mistake. He was polite, well-spoken, articulate, charming, the kind of man who could have found himself a girlfriend for each night of the week. Why *should* such a man be a sex killer? In spite of which, the impression he made was of brilliance and plausibility rather than innocence. For example, he insisted that he had driven away from the police car because he was smoking marijuana, and that he had thrown the joint out of the window.

The case seemed to be balanced on a knife-edge – until the judge pronounced a sentence of guilty of kidnapping. Bundy sobbed and pleaded not to be sent to prison; but the judge sentenced him to a period between one and fifteen years.

The Colorado authorities now charged him with the murder of a girl called Caryn Campbell, who had been abducted from a ski resort where Bundy had been seen by a witness. After a morning courtroom session in Aspen, Bundy succeeded in wandering into the library during the lunch recess, and jumping out of the window. He was recaptured eight days later, tired and hungry, and driving a stolen car.

Legal arguments dragged on for another six months – what evidence was admissible and what was not. And on 30 December 1977, Bundy escaped again, using a hacksaw blade to cut through an imperfectly welded steel plate above the light fixture in his cell. He made his way to Chicago, then south to Florida; there, near the Florida State University in Tallahassee, he took a room. A few days later, a man broke into a nearby sorority house and attacked four girls with a club, knocking them unconscious; one was strangled with her pantyhose and raped; another died on her way to hospital. One of the strangled girl's nipples had been almost bitten off, and she had a bite mark on her left buttock. An hour and a half later, a student woke up in another sorority house when she heard bangs next door, and a girl whimpering. She dialled the number of the room, and as the telephone rang, someone could be heard running out. Cheryl Thomas was found lying in bed, her skull fractured but still alive.

Three weeks later, on 6 February 1978, Bundy – who was calling himself Chris Hagen – stole a white Dodge van and left Tallahassee; he stayed in the Holiday Inn, using a stolen credit card. The following day a twelve-year-old girl named Kimberly Leach walked out of her classroom in Lake City, Florida, and vanished. Bundy returned to Tallahassee to take a girl out for an expensive meal – paid for with a stolen credit card – then absconded via the fire escape, owing large arrears of rent. At 4 a.m. on 15 February, a police patrolman noticed an orange Volkswagen driving suspiciously slowly, and radioed for a check on its number; it proved to be stolen from Tallahassee. After a struggle and a chase, during which he tried to kill the policeman, Bundy was captured yet again. When the police learned his real name, and that he had just left a town in which five girls had been attacked, they suddenly understood the importance of their capture. Bundy seemed glad to be in custody, and began to unburden himself. He explained that "his problem" had begun when he had seen a girl on a bicycle in Seattle, and "had to have her". He had followed her, but she escaped. "Sometimes", he admitted, "I feel like a vampire."

On 7 April, a party of searchers along the Suwanee river found the body of Kimberly Leach in an abandoned hut; she had been strangled and sexually violated. Three weeks later, surrounded by hefty guards, Bundy allowed impressions of his teeth to be taken, for comparison with the marks on the buttocks of the dead student, Lisa Levy.

Bundy's lawyers persuaded him to enter into "plea bargaining": in exchange for a guarantee of life imprisonment – rather than a death sentence – he would confess to the murders of Lisa Levy, Margaret Bowman, and Kimberly Leach. But Bundy changed his mind at the last moment and decided to sack his lawyers.

Bundy's trial began on 25 June 1979, and the evidence against him was damning; a witness who had seen him leaving the sorority house after the attacks; a pantyhose mask found in the room of Cheryl Thomas, which resembled the one found in Bundy's car; but above all, the fact that Bundy's teeth matched the marks on Lisa Levy's buttocks. The highly compromising taped interview with the Pensacola police was judged inadmissible in court because his lawyer had not been present. Bundy again dismissed his defence and took it over himself; the general impression was that he was trying to be too clever. The jury took only six hours to find him guilty on all counts. Judge Ed Cowart pronounced sentence of death by electrocution, but evidently felt some sympathy for the good-looking young defendant. "It's a tragedy for this court to see such a total waste of humanity. You're a bright young man. You'd have made a good lawyer . . . But you went the wrong way, partner. Take care of yourself . . ."

Bundy was taken to Raiford prison, Florida, where he was

placed on Death Row. On 2 July 1986, when he was due to die
a few hours before Gerald Stano, both were granted a stay of
execution.

The Bundy case illustrates the immense problems faced by
investigators of serial murders. When Meg Anders – Bundy's
mistress – telephoned the police after the double murder near
Lake Sammanish, Bundy's name had already been suggested
by three people. But he was only one of 3,500 suspects. Later
Bundy was added to the list of one hundred "best suspects"
which investigators constructed on grounds of age, occupation,
and past record. Two hundred thousand items were fed into
computers, including the names of 41,000 Volkswagen owners,
5,000 men with a record of mental illness, every student who
had taken classes with the dead girls, and all transfers from
other colleges they had attended. All this was programmed
into thirty-seven categories, each using a different criterion to
isolate the suspect. Asked to name anyone who came up on
any three of these programs, the computer produced 16,000
names. When the number was raised to four, it was reduced
to 600. Only when it was raised to twenty-five was it reduced
to ten suspects, with Bundy seventh on the list. The police were
still investigating number six when Bundy was detained in Salt
Lake City with burgling tools in his car. Only after that did
Bundy become suspect number one. And by that time, he had
already committed a minimum of seventeen murders. (There
seems to be some doubt about the total, estimates varying
between twenty and forty; Bundy himself told the Pensacola
investigators that it ran into double figures.) Detective Robert
Keppel, who worked on the case, is certain that Bundy would
have been revealed as suspect number one even if he had not
been arrested. But in 1982, Keppel and his team were presented
with another mass killer in the Seattle area, the so-called Green
River Killer, whose victims were mostly prostitutes picked up
on the "strip" in Seattle. Seven years later, in 1989, he has killed
at least forty-nine women, and the computer has still failed to
identify an obvious suspect number one.

The Bundy case is doubly baffling because he seems to
contradict the basic assertions of every major criminologist
from Lombroso to Yochelson. Bundy is not an obvious born
criminal, with degenerate physical characteristics; there is (as
far as is known) no history of insanity in his family; he was

not a social derelict or a failure. In her book *The Stranger Beside Me*, his friend Ann Rule describes him as "a man of unusual accomplishment". How could the most subtle "psychological profiling" target such a man as a serial killer?

The answer to the riddle emerged fairly late in the day, four years after Bundy had been sentenced to death. Before his conviction, Bundy had indicated his willingness to co-operate on a book about himself, and two journalists, Stephen G. Michaud and Hugh Aynesworth, went to interview him in prison. They discovered that Bundy had no wish to discuss guilt, except to deny it, and he actively discouraged them from investigating the case against him. He wanted them to produce a gossipy book focusing squarely on himself, like best-selling biographies of celebrities such as Frank Sinatra. Michaud and Aynesworth would have been happy to write a book demonstrating his innocence, but as they looked into the case, they found it impossible to accept this; instead, they concluded that he had killed at least twenty-one girls. When they began to probe, Bundy revealed the characteristics that Yochelson and Samenow had found to be so typical of criminals: hedging, lying, pleas of faulty memory, and self-justification: "Intellectually, Ted seemed profoundly dissociative, a compartmentalizer, and thus a superb rationalizer." Emotionally, he struck them as a severe case of arrested development: "he might as well have been a twelve year old, and a precocious and bratty one at that. So extreme was his childishness that his pleas of innocence were of a character very similar to that of the little boy who'll deny wrongdoing in the face of overwhelming evidence to the contrary." So Michaud had the ingenious idea of suggesting that Bundy should "speculate on the nature of a person capable of doing what Ted had been accused (and convicted) of doing". Bundy embraced this idea with enthusiasm, and talked for hours into a tape recorder. Soon Michaud became aware that there were, in effect, two "Teds" – the analytical human being, and an entity inside him that Michaud came to call the "hunchback". (We have encountered this "other person" – Mr Hyde – syndrome in many killers, including Peter Sutcliffe.)

After generalizing for some time about violence in modern society, the disintegration of the home, and so on, Bundy got down to specifics, and began to discuss his own development.

He had been an illegitimate child, born to a respectable young girl in Philadelphia. She moved to Seattle to escape the stigma, and married a cook in the Veterans' Hospital. Ted was an oversensitive and self-conscious child who had all the usual day-dreams of fame and wealth. And at an early stage he became a thief and something of a habitual liar – as many imaginative children do. But he seems to have been deeply upset by the discovery of his illegitimacy.

Bundy was not, in fact, a brilliant student. Although he struck his fellow students as witty and cultivated, his grades were usually Bs. In his late teens he became heavily infatuated with a fellow student, Stephanie Brooks, who was beautiful, sophisticated, and came of a wealthy family. Oddly enough, she responded and they became "engaged". To impress her he went to Stanford University to study Chinese; but he felt lonely away from home and his grades were poor. "I found myself thinking about standards of success that I just didn't seem to be living up to." Stephanie wearied of his immaturity, and threw him over – the severest blow so far. He became intensely moody. "Dogged by feelings of wothlessness and failure", he took a job as a busboy in a hotel dining-room. And at this point, he began the drift that eventually turned him into a serial killer. He became friendly with a drug addict. One night, they entered a cliffside house that had been partly destroyed by a landslide, and stole whatever they could find. "It was really thrilling." He began shoplifting and stealing "for thrills", once walking openly into someone's greenhouse, taking an eight-foot tree in a pot, and putting it in his car with the top sticking out of the sunroof.

He also became a full-time volunteer worker for Art Fletcher, the black Republican candidate for Lieutenant-Governor. He enjoyed the sense of being a "somebody" and mixing with interesting people. But Fletcher lost, and Bundy became a salesman in a department store. He met Meg Anders in a college beer joint, and they became lovers – she had a gentle, easy-going nature, which brought out Bundy's protective side. But she was shocked by his kleptomania.

In fact, the criminal side – the "hunchback" – was now developing fast. He acquired a taste for violent pornography – easy to buy openly in American shops. Once, walking round the university district, he saw a girl undressing in a lighted room. This was the turning point in his life. He began to devote hours to walking around, hoping to see more girls undressing.

He was back at university, studying psychology, but his night prowling prevented him from making full use of his undoubted intellectual capacities. He obtained his degree in due course – this may tell us more about American university standards than about Bundy's abilities – and tried to find a law school that would take him. He failed all the aptitude tests and was repeatedly turned down. A year later, he was finally accepted – he worked for the Crime Commission for a month, as an assistant, and for the Office of Justice Planning. His self-confidence increased by leaps and bounds. When he flew to San Francisco to see Stephanie Brooks, the girl who had jilted him, she was deeply impressed, and willing to renew their affair. He was still having an affair with Meg Anders, and entered on this new career as a Don Juan with his usual enthusiasm. He and Stephanie spent Christmas together and became "engaged". Then he dumped her as she had dumped him.

By this time, he had committed his first murder. For years, he had been a pornography addict and a peeping tom. ("He approached it almost like a project, throwing himself into it, lit-erally, for years.") Then the "hunchback" had started to demand "more active kinds of gratification". He tried disabling women's cars, but the girls always had help on hand. He felt the need to indulge in this kind of behaviour after drinking had reduced his inhibitions. One evening, he stalked a girl from a bar, found a piece of heavy wood, and managed to get ahead of her and lie in wait. Before she reached the place where he was hiding, she stopped at her front door and went in. But the experience was like "making a hole in a dam". A few evenings later, as a woman was fumbling for her keys at her front door, he struck her on the head with a piece of wood. She collapsed, screaming, and he ran away. He was filled with remorse, and swore he would never do such a thing again. But six months later, he followed a woman home and peeped in as she undressed. He began to do this again and again. One day, when he knew the door was unlocked, he sneaked in, entered her bedroom, and jumped on her. She screamed and he ran away. Once again, there was a period of self-disgust and revulsion.

This was in the autumn of 1973. On 4 January 1974, he found a door that admitted him to the basement room of eighteen-year-old Sharon Clarke. Now, for the first time, he employed the technique he later used repeatedly, attacking her with a crow-bar until she was unconscious. Then he thrust a speculum, or vaginal probe, inside her, causing internal injuries. But he left her alive.

On the morning of 1 February 1974, he found an unlocked front door in a students' rooming-house and went in. He entered a bedroom at random; twenty-one-year-old Lynda Healy was asleep in bed. He battered her unconscious, then carried the body out to his car. He drove to Taylor Mountain, twenty miles east of Seattle, made her remove her pyjamas, and raped her. When Bundy was later "speculating" about this crime for Stephen Michaud's benefit, the interviewer asked: "Was there any conversation?" Bundy replied: "There'd be some. Since this girl in front of him represented not a person, but again the image of something desirable, the last thing we would expect him to want to do would be to personalize this person."

So Lynda Healy was bludgeoned to death; Bundy always insisted that he took no pleasure in violence, but that his chief desire was "possession" of another person.

Now the "hunchback" was in full control, and there were five more victims over the next five months. Three of the girls were taken to the same spot on Taylor Mountain and there raped and murdered – Bundy acknowledged that his sexual gratification would sometimes take hours. The four bodies were found together in the following year. On the day he abducted the two girls from Lake Sammanish, Bundy "speculated" that he had taken the first, Janice Ott, to a nearby house and raped her, then returned to abduct the second girl, Denise Naslund, who was taken back to the same house and raped in view of the other girl; both were then killed, and taken to a remote spot four miles northeast of the park, where the bodies were dumped.

By the time he had reached this point in his "confession", Bundy had no further secrets to reveal; everything was obvious. Rape had become a compulsion that dominated his life. When he moved to Salt Lake City and entered the law school there – he was a failure from the beginning as a law student – he must have known that if he began to rape and kill young girls there, he would be establishing himself as suspect number one. This made no difference; he had to continue. Even the unsuccessful kidnapping of Carol DaRonch, and the knowledge that someone could now identify him, made no difference. He merely switched his activities to Colorado. Following his arrest, conviction, and escape, he moved to Florida, and the compulsive attacks continued, although by now he must have known that another series of murders in a town to which he had recently moved must reduce his habitual plea of "coincidence" to an absurdity. It seems obvious that by this time he had lost the power of choice. In his last weeks of freedom, Bundy showed all the signs of weariness and self-disgust that had driven Carl Panzram to contrive his own execution.

Time finally ran out for Bundy on 24 January 1989. Long before this, he had recognized that his fatal mistake was to decline to enter into plea bargaining at his trial; the result was a death sentence instead of life imprisonment. In January 1989, his final appeal was turned down and the date of execution fixed. Bundy then made a last-minute attempt to save his life by offering to bargain murder confessions for a reprieve – against the advice of his attorney James Coleman, who warned him that this attempt to "trade over victims' bodies" would only create hostility that would militate against further stays of execution. In fact, Bundy went on to confess to eight Washington murders, and then to a dozen others. Detective Bob Keppel, who had led the investigation in Seattle, commented: "The game-playing stuff cost him his life." Instead of making a full confession, Bundy doled out information bit by bit. "The whole thing was orchestrated", said Keppel, "We were held hostage for three days." And finally, when it was clear that there was no chance of further delay, Bundy confessed to the Chi Omega Sorority killings, admitting that he had been peeping through the window at girls undressing until he was carried away by desire and entered the building. He also mentioned pornography as being one of the factors that led him to murder. Newspaper columnists showed an inclination to doubt this, but Bundy's earlier confessions to Michaud leave no doubt that he was telling the truth.

At 7 a.m., Bundy was led into the execution chamber at Starke State prison, Florida; behind Plexiglass, an invited audience of forty-eight people sat waiting. As two warders attached his hands to the arms of the electric chair, Bundy recognized his attorney among the crowd; he smiled and nodded. Then straps were placed around his chest and over his mouth; the metal cap with electrodes was fastened onto his head with screws and the face was covered with a black hood. At 7.07 a.m. the executioner threw the switch; Bundy's body went stiff and rose fractionally from the chair. One minute later, as the power was switched off, the body slammed back into the chair. A doctor felt his pulse and pronounced him dead. Outside the prison, a mob carrying "Fry Bundy!" banners cheered as the execution was announced.

The Hillside Stranglers

Between 18 October 1977 and 17 February 1978, the naked bodies of ten girls were dumped on hillsides in the Los Angeles area; all had been raped, and medical examination of sperm samples indicated that two men were involved. The police kept this information secret, and the press nicknamed the unknown killer the Hillside Strangler.

In January 1979, the bodies of two girl students were found in the back seat of a car in the small town of Bellingham, in Washington state. A security guard named Kenneth Bianchi was known to have offered the girls a "house sitting" job (looking after the house while the tenant was away), and he was arrested. Forensic evidence indicated Bianchi as the killer, and when it was learned that Bianchi had been in Los Angeles during the "strangler" murders, he was also questioned about these crimes, and eventually confessed. For a while, Bianchi succeeded in convincing psychiatrists that he was a "dual personality", a "Dr Jekyll and Mr Hyde", and that his "Hyde" personality had committed the murders in association with his cousin, an older man named Angelo Buono. A police psychiatrist was able to

---

One third of all murderers commit suicide. But this is because most murders are committed within the family, in a state of jealousy or rage, and the killer is overwhelmed with remorse or despair. Unfortunately, few serial killers commit suicide – although it has been argued that the incredible carelessness that often leads to their capture is a kind of psychological suicide.

prove that Bianchi was faking dual personality, and his detailed confessions to the rape-murders – the girls were usually lured or forced to go to Buono's house – finally led to sentences of life imprisonment for both cousins.

Richard Ramirez

Throughout 1985 handgun sales in Los Angeles soared. Many suburbanites slept with a loaded pistol by their beds. A series of violent attacks upon citizens in their own homes had shattered the comfortably normality of middle class life. Formerly safe neighbourhoods seemed to be the killer's favourite targets. The whole city was terrified.

The attacks were unprecedented in many ways. Neither murder nor robbery seemed to be the obvious motive, although both frequently took place. The killer would break into a house, creep into the main bedroom and shoot the male partner through the head with a .22. He would then rape and beat the wife or girlfriend, suppressing resistance with threats of violence to her or her children. Male children were sometimes sodomized, the rape victims sometimes shot. On occasion he would ransack the house looking for valuables while at other times he would leave empty-handed without searching. During the attacks he would force victims to declare their love for Satan. Survivors described a tall, slim Hispanic male with black, greasy hair and severely decayed teeth. The pattern of crimes seemed to be based less upon a need to murder or rape but a desire to terrify and render helpless. More than most serial killers the motive seemed to be exercising power.

The killer also had unusual methods of victim selection. He seemed to be murdering outside his own racial group, preferring Caucasians and specifically Asians. He also seemed to prefer to break into yellow houses.

In the spring and summer of 1985 there were more than twenty attacks, most of which involved both rape and murder. By the end of March the press had picked up the pattern and splashed stories connecting the series of crimes. After several abortive nicknames, such as "The Walk-In Killer" or "The Valley Invader", the *Herald Examiner* came up with "The Night Stalker", a name sensational enough to stick.

Thus all through the hot summer of 1985 Californians slept with their windows closed. One policeman commented to a reporter: "People are armed and staying up late. Burglars want this guy caught like everyone else. He's making it bad for their business." The police themselves circulated sketches and stopped anyone who looked remotely like The Night Stalker. One innocent man was stopped five times.

Despite these efforts and thorough forensic analysis of crime scenes there was little progress in the search for the killer's identity.

Things were obviously getting difficult for The Night Stalker as well. The next murder that fitted the pattern occurred in San Francisco, showing perhaps that public awareness in Los Angeles had made it too taxing a location. This shift also gave police a chance to search San Francisco hotels for records of a man of The Night Stalker's description. Sure enough, while checking the downmarket Tenderloin district police learned that a thin Hispanic with bad teeth had been staying at a cheap hotel there periodically over the past year. On the last occasion he had checked out the night of the San Francisco attack. The manager commented that his room "smelled like a skunk" each time he vacated it and it took three days for the smell to clear.

Though this evidence merely confirmed the police's earlier description, The Night Stalker's next shift of location was to prove more revealing. A young couple in Mission Viejo were attacked in their home. The Night Stalker shot the man through the head while he slept, then raped his partner on the bed next to the body. He then tied her up while he ransacked the house for money and jewellery. Before leaving he raped her a second time and force her to fellate him with a gun pressed against her head. Unfortunately for the killer, however, his victim caught a glimpse of him escaping in a battered orange Toyota and memorized the license plate. She immediately alerted the police. LAPD files showed that the car had been stolen in Los Angeles' Chinatown district while the owner was eating in a restaurant. An all-points bulletin was put out for the vehicle, and officers were instructed not to try and arrest the driver, merely to observe him. However, the car was not found. In fact,

The Night Stalker had dumped the car soon after the attack, and it was located two days later in a car park in Los Angeles' Rampart district. After plain clothes officers had kept the car under surveillance for twenty-four hours, the police moved in and took the car away for forensic testing. A set of fingerprints was successfully lifted.

Searching police fingerprint files for a match manually can take many days and even then it is possible to miss correlations. However, the Los Angeles police had recently installed a fingerprint database computer system, designed by the FBI, and it was through this that they checked the set of fingerprints from the orange Toyota. The system works by storing information about the relative distance between different features of a print, and comparing them with a digitized image of the suspect's fingerprint. The search provided a positive match and a photograph. The Night Stalker was a petty thief and burglar. His name was Ricardo Leyva Ramirez.

The positive identification was described by the forensic division as "a near miracle". The computer system had only just been installed, this was one of its first trials. Furthermore, the system only contained the fingerprints of criminals born after 1 January, 1960. Richard Ramirez was born in February 1960.

The police circulated the photograph to newspapers, and it was shown on the late evening news. At the time, Ramirez was in Phoenix, buying cocaine with the money he had stolen in Mission Viejo. On the morning that the papers splashed his name and photograph all over their front pages, he was on a bus on the way back to Los Angeles, unaware that he had been identified.

He arrived safely and went into the bus station toilet to finish off the cocaine he had bought. No one seemed to be overly interested in him as he left the station and walked through Los Angeles. Ramirez was a Satanist, and had developed a belief that Satan himself watched over him, preventing his capture.

At 8.15 a.m. Ramirez entered Tito's Liquor Store at 819 Towne Avenue. He selected some Pepsi and a pack of sugared doughnuts; he had a sweet tooth that, coupled with a lack of personal hygiene, had left his mouth with only a few blackened teeth. At the counter other customers looked at him strangely as he produced three dollar bills and awaited his change. Suddenly he noticed the papers' front pages, and his faith in Satan's power must have been shaken. He dodged out of the shop and ran, accompanied by shouts of, "It is him! Call the cops!" He pounded off down the street at a surprising speed for one so ostensibly unhealthy. Within twelve minutes he had covered two miles. He had headed east. He was in the Hispanic district of Los Angeles.

Ever since the police had confirmed that The Night Stalker was Hispanic there had been a great deal of anger among the Hispanic community of Los Angeles. They felt that racial stereotypes were already against them enough without their being associated with psychopaths. Thus more than most groups, Hispanics wanted The Night Stalker out of action.

Ramirez, by now, was desperate to get a vehicle. He attempted to pull a woman from her car in a supermarket lot until he was chased away by some customers of the barber's shop opposite. He carried on running, though exhausted, into the more residential areas of east Los Angeles. There, he tried to steal a 1966 red mustang having failed to notice that the owner, Faustino Pinon was lying underneath repairing it. As Ramirez attempted to start the car Pinon grabbed him by the collar and tried to pull him from the driver's seat. Ramirez shouted that he had a gun, but Pinon carried on pulling at him even after the car had started, causing it to career into the gatepost. Ramirez slammed it into reverse and accelerated into the side of Pinon's garage, and the vehicle stalled. Pinon succeeded in wrenching Ramirez out of his car, but in the following struggle Ramirez escaped, leaping the fence and running off across the road. There he tried to wrestle Angelina De La Torres from her Ford Granada. "Te voy a matar! (I'm going to kill you!)" screamed Ramirez, "Give me the keys!", but again he was thwarted and he ran away, now pursued by a growing crowd of neighbours. Manuel De La Torres, Angelina's husband succeeded in smashing Ramirez on the head with a gate bar and he fell, but he managed to struggle up and set off running again before he could be restrained. Incredibly, when Ramirez had developed a lead, he stopped, turned around and stuck his tongue out at his pursuers, then sped off once more. His stamina could not hold indefinitely however, and it was De La Torres who again tackled him and held him down. It is possible that Ramirez would have been lynched there and then had not a patrolman called to the scene arrived. Coincidentally the patrolman was the same age as the killer, and he too was called Ramirez. He reached the scene just as The Night Stalker disappeared under the mob. He drove his patrol car to within a few feet of where Ramirez was restrained, got out and prepared to handcuff the captive.

"Save me. Please. Thank God you're here. It's me, I'm the one you want. Save me before they kill me," babbled Ramirez. The patrolman handcuffed him and pushed him into the back of the car. The crowd was becoming restless, and the car was kicked as it pulled away. Sixteen-year-old Felipe Castaneda, part of the mob that captured Ramirez remarked, "He should never, *never* have come to East LA. He might have been a tough guy, but he came to a tough neighbourhood. He was Hispanic. He should have known better."

"The Night Stalker" was in custody, at first in a police holding cell and then in Los Angeles county jail. While in police care he repeatedly admitted to being "The Night Stalker" and begged to be killed.

The case against Ramirez was strong. The murder weapon, a .22 semi-automatic pistol was found in the possession of a woman in Tijuana, who had been given it by a friend of Ramirez. Police also tried to track down some of the jewellery that Ramirez had stolen and fenced, by sending investigators to his birth-place El Paso, a spiralling town on the Texas-Mexico border. Questioning his family and neighbours revealed that Ramirez' early life had been spent in petty theft and smoking a lot of marijuana. He had never joined any of the rival teenage gangs that fight over territory throughout El Paso, preferring drugs and listening to Heavy Metal. It had been common knowledge that Ramirez was a Satanist; a boyhood friend, Tom Ramos said he believed that it was Bible-study classes that had turned the killer that way.

The investigators also found a great deal of jewellery, stashed at the house of Ramirez' sister Rosa Flores. The police were also hoping to find a pair of eyes that Ramirez had gouged from one of his victims that had not been found in any previous searches. Unfortunately they were not recovered.

The evidence against Ramirez now seemed unequivocal. In a controversial move, the Mayor of Los Angeles said that whatever went on in court, he was convinced of Ramirez' guilt. This was later to prove a mainstay in a defence argument that Ramirez could not receive a fair trial in Los Angeles.

The appointed chief prosecutor in the case was deputy District Attorney P. Philip Halpin, who had prosecuted the "Onion Field" cop-killing case twenty years earlier. Halpin hoped to end the trial and have Ramirez in the gas chamber in a relatively short period of time. The prosecutor drew up a set of initial charges and submitted them as quickly as possible. A public defender was appointed to represent Ramirez. However Ramirez' family had engaged an El Paso lawyer, Manuel Barraza, and Ramirez eventually rejected his appointed public defender in favour of the El Paso attorney. Barraza did not even have a license to practise law in California.

Ramirez accepted, then rejected three more lawyers, finally settling upon two defenders, Dan and Arturo Hernandez. The two were not related, although they often worked together. The judge advised Ramirez that his lawyers did not even meet the minimum requirements for trying a death-penalty case in California, but Ramirez insisted, and more than seven weeks after the initial charges were filed, pleas of Not Guilty were entered on all counts.

The Hernandez' and Ramirez seemed to be trying to force Halpin into making a mistake out of sheer frustration, and thus to create a mis-trial. After each hearing the Hernandez' made pleas for, and obtained, more time to prepare their case. Meanwhile one prosecution witness had died of natural causes, and Ramirez' appearance was gradually changing. He had had his hair permed, and his rotten teeth replaced. This naturally introduced more uncertainty into the minds of prosecution witnesses as to Ramirez identity. The racial make-up of the jury was contested by the defence, which caused delays. The defence also argued, with some justification, that Ramirez could not receive a fair trial in Los Angeles, and moved for a change of location. Although the motion was refused it caused yet more delays. It actually took three and a half years for Ramirez' trial to finally get underway.

Halpin's case was, in practical terms, unbeatable. The defence's only real possibility of success was in infinite delay. For the first three weeks of the trial events progressed relatively smoothly. Then Daniel Hernandez announced that the trial would have to be postponed as he was suffering from nervous exhaustion. He had a doctor's report that advised six weeks rest with psychological counselling. It seemed likely that a mis-trial would be declared. Halpin tried to argue that Arturo Hernandez could maintain the defence, even though he had failed to turn up at the hearings and trial for the first seven months. However this proved unnecessary as the judge made a surprise decision and denied Daniel Hernandez his time off, arguing that he had failed to prove a genuine need.

Halpin, by this stage was actually providing the Hernandez' with all the information that they required to mount an adequate defence, in order to move things along and prevent mis-trial. For the same reasons the judge eventually appointed a defence co-counsel, Ray Clark. Clark immediately put the defence on a new track: Ramirez was the victim of a mistaken identity. He even developed an acronym for this defence – SODDI or Some Other Dude Did It. When the defence case opened Clark produced testimony from Ramirez' father that he had been in El Paso at the time of one of the murders of which he was accused. He also criticized the prosecution for managing to prove that footprints at one of the crime scenes were made by a size eleven-and-a-half Avia trainer without ever proving that Ramirez actually owned such a shoe. When the jury finally left to deliberate however, it seemed clear that they would find Ramirez guilty.

Things were not quite that easy however. After thirteen days of deliberation juror Robert Lee was dismissed for inattention and replaced by an alternative who had also witnessed the case. Two days later, juror Phyllis Singletary was murdered in a domestic dispute. Her live-in lover had beaten her then shot her several times. She was also replaced.

At last on 20 September, 1989 after twenty-two days of deliberation the jury returned a verdict of guilty on all thirteen counts of murder, twelve of those in the first degree. The jury also found Ramirez guilty of thirty other felonies, including burglary, rape, sodomy and attempted murder. Asked by reporters how he felt after the verdict, Ramirez replied, "Evil".

There remained only the selection of sentence. At the hearing Clark argued that Ramirez might actually have been possessed by the devil, or that alternatively he had been driven to murder by over-active hormones. He begged the jury to imprison Ramirez for life rather than put him on death row. If the jury agreed, Clark pointed out, "he will never see Disneyland again," surely punishment enough. After five further days of deliberation, the jury voted for the death penalty. Again, reporters asked Ramirez how he felt about the outcome as he was being taken away, "Big deal. Death always went with the territory. I'll see you in Disneyland."

Any attempt to trace the source of Ramirez' violent behaviour runs up against an insurmountable problem. No external traumas or difficulties seem to have brutalized him. He had a poor upbringing, he was part of a racial minority, but these things alone cannot explain such an incredibly sociopathic personality. Ramirez seems to have created himself. He was an intelligent and deeply religious child and early teenager. Having decided at some stage that counter-culture and drug-taking provided a more appealing lifestyle, he developed pride in his separateness. In the El Paso of his early manhood, people would lock their doors, if they saw him coming down the street. He was known as "Ricky Rabon", Ricky the thief, a nickname he enjoyed as he felt it made him "someone". By the time he moved to Los Angeles, he was injecting cocaine and probably committing burglaries to support himself. He let his teeth rot away, eating only childish sugary foods. He refused to wash. He listened to loud Heavy Metal music.

It has been argued that it was his taste in music that drove him to murder and Satanism, but this would seem to be more part of the mood of censorship sweeping America than a genuine explanation. Anyone who takes the trouble to listen to the music in question, particularly the AC/DC album cited by American newspapers at the time of the murders will find that there is little in it to incite violence.

Ramirez' obvious attempts to repel others in his personal behaviour, and his heavy drug use seem more likely sources of violence than early poverty or music. His assumed "otherness" seems in retrospect sadly underdeveloped, having never progressed beyond a teenager's need to appal staid grown-up society.

This is not to say that Ramirez was unintelligent. His delaying of his trial and his choice of the Hernandez' to continue the delays shows that he had worked out the most effective method of staying alive for the longest period either before, or soon after he was captured. His remarks in court upon being sentenced were not particularly original, yet they are articulate:

"It's nothing you'd understand but I do have something to

say . . . I don't believe in the hypocritical, moralistic dogma of this so-called civilized society. I need not look beyond this room to see all the liars, haters, the killers, the crooks, the paranoid cowards – truly *trematodes* of the Earth, each one in his own legal profession. You maggots make me sick – hypocrites one and all . . . I am beyond your experience. I am beyond good and evil, legions of the night, night breed, repeat not the errors of the Night Prowler [a name from an AC/DC song] and show no mercy. I will be avenged. Lucifer dwells within us all. That's it."

Ramirez remains on death row. It is unlikely that he will be executed before the year 2000.

Jeffrey Dahmer

By the beginning of the 1990s, it began to seem that the American public had become shock-proof where serial killers were concerned. Killer "duos" like the Hillside Stranglers, or Lucas and Toole, killed to satisfy their sexual appetites. "Sunset Slayer" Douglas Clark and his mistress Carol Bundy confessed to a taste for playing with the severed heads of their female victims. In 1985, the suicide of a man named Leonard Lake, and the flight of his companion Charles Ng, led the police to a house in Calaveras County, California, and to a cache of videos showing the sexual abuse and torture of female victims – the number seems to have exceeded thirty. Ex-convict Gerald Gallego and his mistress Charlene Williams made a habit of abducting and murdering teenage girls, who were first subjected to an orgy of rape and lesbian advances, all in the search for the "perfect sex slave". In Chicago, a group of four young men, led by twenty-seven-year-old Robin Gecht, abducted at least fifteen women, and subjected them to an orgy of rape and torture – which included amputation and ritual eating of the breasts – in the course of "satanic" ceremonies. There was also evidence to link the New York Killer "Son of Sam" – David Berkowitz – who casually shot strangers in cars – with a satanic cult. It was hard to imagine how human depravity could go any further.

In spite of which, the revelations that burst on to television screens in late July 1991 caused nationwide shock. Just before midnight on 22 July, a young black man came running out of an apartment building in Milwaukee, Wisconsin, with a handcuff dangling from his wrist, and told two police patrolmen that a madman had tried to kill him, and threatened to cut out his heart and eat it. He led the police to the apartment of thirty-one-year-old Jeffrey Dahmer, where they demanded entrance. Dahmer – a white Anglo-Saxon – at first behaved reasonably, claiming to be under stress after losing his job and drinking too much, but when the police asked for the handcuff key, he became hysterical and abusive, and had to be taken into custody. The police soon realized that Dahmer's two-room apartment was a mixture of slaughter house and torture chamber. A freezer proved to contain severed heads, another some severed hands and a male genital organ, while five skulls – some painted grey – were found in various boxes.

Back at the police station, Dahmer confessed to killing seventeen youths, mostly blacks. He also confessed that the plastic bags of human "meat" in the freezer were intended to be eaten, and described how he had fried the biceps of one victim in vegetable oil. The threat to eat the heart of Tracy Edwards – the latest intended victim – had been no idle bluff.

The first problem was to find out the identities of the men to whom these skulls, bones and genitals belonged.

Back at police headquarters, Dahmer was obviously relieved to be co-operating; he seemed glad that his career of murder was over. It had all started, he admitted, when he was only eighteen years old, in 1978. That first victim has been a hitch-hiker. It was almost ten years before he committed his next murder. But recently, the rate of killing had accelerated – as it often does with serial killers – and there had been no less than three murders in the last two weeks. He had attempted to kill Tracy Edwards only three days after his last murder.

Dahmer was also able to help the police towards establishing the identities of the victims – which included twelve blacks, one Laotian, one Hispanic and three whites. Some of their names he remembered; the police had to work out the identities of others from identity cards found in Dahmer's apartment, and from photographs shown to parents of missing youths.

All Dahmer's confessions were sensational; but the story

of one teenage victim was so appalling that it created outrage around the world. Fourteen year old Laotian Konerak
Sinthasomphone, had met Dahmer in front of the same shopping mall where the killer was later to pick up Tracy Edwards;
the boy agreed to return to Dahmer's apartment to allow him
to take a couple of photographs.

Unknown to Konerak, Dahmer was the man who had enticed
and sexually assaulted his elder brother three years earlier.
Dahmer had asked the thirteen-year-old boy back to his
apartment in September 1988, and had slipped a powerful
sleeping draught into his drink, then fondled him sexually.
Somehow, the boy succeeded in staggering out into the street
and back home. The police were notified, and Dahmer was
charged with second degree sexual assault and sentenced to a
year in a correction programme, which allowed him to continue
to work in a chocolate factory.

Now the younger brother Konerak found himself in the same
apartment. He was also given drugged coffee, and then, when
he was unconscious, stripped and raped. After that, Dahmer
went out to buy some beer – he had been a heavy drinker since
schooldays. On his way back to the apartment, Dahmer saw,
to his horror, that his naked victim was talking to two black
teenage girls, obviously begging for help. Dahmer hurried up
and tried to grab the boy; the girls clung on to him. One of them
succeeded in ringing the police, and two squad cars arrived
within minutes. Three irritable officers wanted to know what
the trouble was about.

When Dahmer told them that the young man was his lover,
that they lived together in the nearby apartments, and that
they had merely had a quarrel, the policemen were inclined
to believe him – he looked sober and Konerak looked drunk.
They decided to move away from the gathering crowd, and
adjourned to Dahmer's apartment. There Dahmer showed them
polaroid pictures of the boy in his underwear, to convince him
that they were really lovers (the police had no way of knowing
that the photographs had been taken that evening), and told
them that Konerak was nineteen. Meanwhile, Konerak sat on
the settee, dazed but probably relieved that his ordeal was
over. His passivity was his undoing – his failure to deny
what Dahmer was saying convinced the police that Dahmer
must be telling the truth. They believed Dahmer, and went off

leaving Konerak in his apartment. The moment the police had left, Dahmer strangled Konerak, violated the corpse, then took photographs as he dismembered it. After stripping the skull of flesh, he painted it grey – probably to make it look like a plastic replica.

Back at District Three station house, the three policemen made their second mistake of the evening – they joked about the homosexual quarrel they had just broken up. But a tape recorder happened to be switched on, and when Dahmer was arrested two months later, and admitted to killing the Laotian boy, the tape was located and played on radio and television.

The story caused universal uproar. On 26 July, four days after Dahmer's arrest, the three policemen – John Balcerzak, Joseph Gabrish and Richard Portubcan – were suspended from duty with pay. (Later, administrative charges were filed against them, but finally dismissed.) Public anger was now transferred from Jeffrey Dahmer to the police department. Police Chief Philip Arreola found himself assailed on all sides, subjected to harsh criticism from his own force for not supporting his own men (in the following month, the Milwaukee Police Association passed a vote of no-confidence in him), and from Milwaukee's blacks and Asians for racism.

Dahmer's first murder had taken place in 1968, when he was eighteen. According to Dahmer's confession, he had found himself alone in the family house at 4480 West Bath Road; his father had already left, and his mother and younger brother David were away visiting relatives. He had been left with no money, and very little food in the broken refrigerator. That evening, he explained, he decided to go out and look for some company.

It was not hard to find. A nineteen-year-old white youth, who had spent the day at a rock concert, was hitch-hiking home to attend his father's birthday party. When an ancient Oldsmobile driven by someone who looked about his own age pulled up, the boy climbed in. They went back to Dahmer's house and drank some beer, and talked about their lives. Dahmer found he liked his new friend immensely. But when the boy looked at the clock and said he had to go, Dahmer begged him to stay. The boy refused. So Dahmer picked up a dumbbell, struck him on the head, then strangled him. He then dragged the body to the crawl space under the house, and dismembered it with a carving knife. It sounds an impossible task for an eighteen-year-old, but Dahmer was not without experience – he had always had a morbid interest in dismembering animals.

He had wrapped up the body parts in plastic bags. But after a few days, the smell began to escape. Dahmer's mother was due back soon, and was sure to notice the stench. He took the plastic bags out to the wood under cover of darkness and managed to dig a shallow grave – the soil was rock-hard. But even with the bags now underground, he still worried – children might notice the grave. So he dug them up again, stripped the flesh from the bones, and smashed up the bones with a sledgehammer. He scattered them around the garden, and the property next door. When his mother returned a few days later, there was nothing to reveal that her son was now a killer.

Unfortunately, Dahmer was unable to recall the name of his victim. The Milwaukee police telephoned the police of Bath Township and asked them if they had a missing person case that dated from mid-1978. They had. On 18 June, a youth named Stephen Mark Hicks had left his home in Coventry Township to go to a rock concert. Friends had driven him there, and they agreed to rendezvous with him that evening to take him home. Hicks failed to turn up at the meeting place, and no trace of him was ever found.

For nine years after killing Stephen Hicks, Dahmer kept his homicidal impulses under control. A period of three years in the army had ended with a discharge for drunkenness. After a short stay in Florida, he had moved in with his grandmother Catherine, in West Allis, south of Milwaukee. But he was still drinking heavily, and was in trouble with the police for causing a disturbance in a bar. His family was relieved when he at last found himself a job – in the Ambrosia Chocolate Company in Milwaukee.

Dahmer soon discovered Milwaukee's gay bars, where he became known as a monosyllabic loner. But it was soon observed that he had a more sinister habit. He would sometimes engage a fellow customer in conversation, and offer him a drink. These drinking companions often ended up in a drugged coma. Yet Dahmer's intention was clearly not to commit rape. He seemed to want to try out his drugs as a-kind of experiment, to see how much he had to administer, and how fast they worked. But other patrons noticed, and when one of Dahmer's drinking companions ended up unconscious in hospital, the owner of Club Bath Milwaukee told him that he was barred.

On 8 September, 1986, two twelve-year-old boys reported to the police that Dahmer had exposed himself to them and masturbated. Dahmer alleged that he had merely been urinating. He was sentenced to a year on probation, and told his probation officers, with apparently sincerity: "I'll never do it again." (Judges and probation officers were later to note that Dahmer had a highly convincing manner of donning the sackcloth and ashes.) This period ended on 9 September, 1987.

A year of good behaviour had done nothing to alleviate Dahmer's psychological problems; on the contrary, they had built up resentment and frustration. Six days after his probation ended, the frustration again exploded into murder. On 15 September, Dahmer was drinking at a gay hang-out called Club 219, and met a twenty-four-year-old man called Stephen Tuomi. They decided to go to bed, and adjourned to the Ambassador Hotel, where they took a room that cost $43.88 for the night. Dahmer claims that he cannot recall much of that night, admitting that they drank themselves into a stupor. When Dahmer woke up, he says Tuomi was dead, with blood coming from his mouth, and strangulation marks on his throat.

It was a terrifying situation – alone in a hotel room with a corpse, and the desk clerk likely to investigate whether the room had been vacated at any moment. Dahmer solved it by going out and buying a large suitcase, into which he stuffed the body. Then he got a taxi to take him back to his grandmother's house in West Allis, where he had his own basement flat – the driver helped him to drag the heavy case indoors. There, says Dahmer, he dismembered it, and stuffed the parts into plastic bags which were put out for the garbage collector. He performed his task of disposal so efficiently that the police were unable to find the slightest sign of it, and decided not to charge Dahmer with the murder.

Clearly, this second murder was a watershed in Dahmer's life. The earlier murder of Stephen Hicks might have been put behind him as a youthful aberration, commited in a mood of psychological stress. But the killing of Stephen Tuomi was a deliberate act – whether Dahmer was fully sober or not. Since Tuomi had gone to the room specifically to have sex, there could be no reason whatever to kill him – unless Dahmer's needs involved more than an act of mutual intercourse: that is, unless they actually involved killing and dissecting his sexual partner, as he had killed and dissected animals as a teenager.

As a result of the murder of Stephen Tuomi, Dahmer seems to have acknowledged that murder was, in fact, what he needed to satisfy his deviant sexual impulse. The fifteen murders that followed leave no possible doubt about it.

Precisely four months later, on 16 January, 1988, Dahmer picked up a white young male prostitute named James Doxtator at a bus stop outside Club 219, and asked him if he would like to earn money by posing for a video. They went back to West Allis on the bus, and had sex in the basement. Then Dahmer gave the boy a drink heavily laced with sleeping potion, and, when he was unconscious, strangled him. With his grandmother's garage at his disposal, getting rid of the body was easy. He told the police that he cleaned the flesh from the bones with acid, then smashed the bones with a sledgehammer, and scattered them around like those of his first victim. What he does not seem to have admitted is that the murder and dismemberment of James Doxtator was his primary purpose when he invited the boy back home.

The police interrogator looked up from his notebook to ask if there was anything distinctive about Doxtator by which he might be identified; Dahmer recalled that he had two scars near his nipples that looked like cigarette burns. Doxtator's mother later confirmed that her son had such scars.

Two months elapsed before Dahmer killed again. On 24 March, 1988, in a bar called the Phoenix not far from Club 219, he met a twenty-three-year-old homosexual named Richard Guerrero, who was virtually broke. Attracted by the graceful, slightly built Hispanic youth, Dahmer made the same proposals that he had made to the previous victim and, like the previous victim, Guerrero accompanied him back to his grandmother's house. There they had oral sex, and Guerrero was offered a drugged drink. When he was unconscious, Dahmer strangled him, then dismembered the body in the garage.

Guerrero's frantic family hired a private detective and circulated flyers with their son's description. They also hired a psychic. But they were still searching three years later, when Dahmer confessed to the murder.

Dahmer's grandmother was becoming concerned about the

awful smells that came from the garage. Dahmer said it was garbage, but it seemed to persist even when the sacks had been collected. Dahmer's father Lionel came to investigate, and found a black, sticky residue in the garage. Dahmer, confronted with this evidence, said he had been using acid to strip dead animals of their flesh and fur, as he had done in childhood.

In September 1988, Catherine Dahmer finally decided she could no longer put up with the smells and her grandson's drunkenness. On 25 September, Dahmer moved into an apartment at 808 N. 24th Street.

There can be no doubt that Dahmer intended to use his new-found freedom to give full reign to his morbid sexual urges. But an unforeseen hitch occurred. Within twenty four hours, the four-time murderer was in trouble with the police. 26 September, 1988, was the day he met a thirteen-year-old Laotian boy named Sinthasomphone, lured him back to his apartment, and drugged him. But the elder brother of later victim Konerak somehow managed to escape, and Dahmer was charged with sexual assault and enticing a child for immoral purposes. He spent a week in prison, then was released on bail. On 30 January, 1990, he was found guilty; the sentence would be handed out four months later.

But even the possibility of a long prison sentence could not cure Dahmer of his obsessive need to kill and dismember. When he appeared in court to be sentenced on 23 May, 1989, he had already claimed his fifth victim.

Anthony Sears was a good looking twenty-three-year-old who dreamed of becoming a male model; he had a girlfriend and had just been appointed manager of a restaurant. On 25 March, he went drinking in a gay bar called LaCage with a friend called Jeffrey Connor, and Dahmer engaged them in conversation. By the time the bar closed, Sears had agreed to accompany Dahmer back to his grandmother's home. (Dahmer seems to have been worried that the police were watching his own apartment.) Once there, they had sex, then Dahmer offered Sears a drink. The grim routine was repeated almost without variation; strangulation, dismemberment, and disposal of the body parts in the garbage. Dahmer seems to have decided to preserve the skull as a memento; he painted it, and later took it with him when he moved into the Oxford Apartments.

The Assistant DA, Gale Shelton, had recognized instinctively that a man who would drug a teenage boy for sex was highly dangerous, and needed to be kept out of society for a long time. Arguing for a prison sentence of five years, she described Dahmer as evasive, manipulative, uncooperative and unwilling to change. Dahmer's lawyer Gerald Boyle argued that the assault on the Laotian boy was a one-off offense, and would never happen again. Dahmer himself revealed considerable skill as an actor in representing himself as contrite and self-condemned. "I am an alcoholic and a homosexual with sexual problems." He described his appearance in court as a "nightmare come true", declared that he was now a changed man, and ended by begging the judge: "Please don't destroy my life." Judge William Gardner was touched by the appeal. This clean-cut boy obviously needed help, and there was no psychiatric help in prison. So he sentenced Dahmer to five years on probation, and a year in a House of Correction, where he could continue to work at the chocolate factory during the day.

From the Community Correctional Center in Milwaukee, Dahmer addressed a letter to Judge Gardner, stating "I have always believed a man should be willing to assume responsibility for the mistakes he makes in life. The world has enough misery in it without my adding to it. Sir, I assure you that it will never happen again. That is why, Judge Gardner, I am requesting a sentence modification."

Dahmer was released from the Correctional Center two months early – on 2 March, 1990. Eleven days later, he moved into the Oxford Apartments.

Two more victims followed in quick succession. Thirty-three-year-old Eddie Smith, an ex-jailbird, was picked up in the gay Club 219, drugged with one of Dahmer's Mickey Finns, then strangled and dismembered. A few weeks later, on 14 June, twenty-eight-year-old Eddie Smith was killed in the same way and his body disposed of in garbage bags.

So far, Dahmer's murders seem to have been due to a compulsive drive to kill and dismember. Now a new development occurred: psychological sadism. In April 1991, Eddie Smith's sister Carolyn received a telephone call from a soft spoken man who told her that Eddie was dead; when she asked how he knew he replied: "I killed him", and hung up.

Dahmer's career of slaughter almost came to an abrupt end on 8 July, 1990; it was on that day that he made the mistake of varying his method. He approached a fifteen-year-old Hispanic boy outside a gay bar, and offered him $200 to pose for nude photographs. The boy returned to room 213 and removed his clothes. But instead of offering him the usual drugged drink, Dahmer picked up a rubber mallet and hit him on the head. It failed to knock him unconscious, and the boy fought back as Dahmer tried to strangle him. Somehow, the boy succeeded in calming his attacker. And, incredibly, Dahmer allowed him to go, even calling a taxi.

The boy had promised not to notify the police. But when he was taken to hospital for treatment, he broke his promise. For a few moments, Dahmer's future hung in the balance. But when the boy begged them not to allow his foster parents to find out that he was homosexual, the police decided to do nothing about it.

When he saw his probation officer, Donna Chester, the next day, Dahmer looked depressed and unshaven. He said he had money problems and was thinking of suicide. She wanted to know how he could have money problems when he was earning $1,500 a month, and his apartment cost less than $300 a month. He muttered something about hospital bills. And during the whole of the next month, Dahmer continued to complain of depression and stomach pains, and to talk about jumping off a high building. Donna Chester suggested that he ought to find himself another apartment in a less run-down area. She was unaware that Dahmer was an addict who now urgently needed a fix of his favourite drug: murder.

It happened a few weeks later, on 3 September, 1990. In front of a bookstore on Twenty-seventh, Dahmer picked up a young black dancer named Ernest Miller, who was home from Chicago, where he intended to start training at a dance school in the autumn. They had sex in Apartment 213, then Dahmer offered him a drugged drink, and watched him sink into oblivion. Perhaps because he had not killed for three months, Dahmer's craving for violence and its nauseating aftermath was stronger than usual. Instead of strangling his victim, Dahmer cut his throat. He decided that he wanted to keep the skeleton, so after cutting the flesh from the bones, and dissolving most of it in acid, he bleached the skeleton with acid. He also kept the biceps, which he put in the freezer.

Soon after Ernest Miller's disappearance, his grandmother

began receiving telephone calls; the voice at the other end of the line made choking and groaning noises, and sometimes cried: "Help me, help me."

Neighbours were beginning to notice the smell of decaying flesh; some of them knocked on Dahmer's door to ask about it. Dahmer would explain politely that his fridge was broken and that he was waiting to get it fixed.

The last victim of 1990 died almost by accident. Twenty-three-year-old David Thomas had a girlfriend and a three-year-old daughter; nevertheless he accepted Dahmer's offer to return to his apartment in exchange for money. Dahmer gave him a drugged drink, but then decided that Thomas was not his type after all, and that he had no desire for sex. But since Thomas was now drugged, and might be angry when he woke up, he killed him anyway. But he filmed the dismemberment process, and took photographs of his severed head; Thomas's sister later identified him by the photograph.

He had committed nine murders; there were eight still to go.

The first murder of the new year was a nineteen-year-old black homosexual named Curtis Straughter, whose ambition was to become a male model; Dahmer picked him up in freezing, rainy weather on 18 February, 1991. While they were engaging in oral sex in the evil-smelling apartment, Straughter began to flag as the sleeping potion took effect. Dahmer took a leather strap and strangled him, then dismembered the body and recorded the process on camera. Once again, he kept the skull.

On 25 March, there occurred an event that psychiatrists believe may be responsible for the final spate of multiple murder. It was on that day that Dahmer's mother Joyce contacted him for the first time in five years. Joyce Dahmer – now Flint – was working as an AIDS counsellor in Fresco, California, and it may have been her contact with homosexuals that led her to telephone her son. She spoke openly about his homosexuality – for the first time – and told him she loved him. The call was a good idea – or would have been if she had made it a few years earlier. Now it was too late; Dahmer had gone too far in self-damnation.

The murder of nineteen-year-old Errol Lindsey on 7 April has a quality or *déja-vu*. The police report states bleakly that Dahmer met Lindsey on a street corner and offered him money to pose for photographs. Lindsey was drugged and strangled; then Dahmer had oral sex with the body. Errol Lindsey was dismembered, but Dahmer kept his skull.

Thirty-one-year-old Tony Hughes, was a deaf mute who loved to dance. When Dahmer accosted him outside Club 219 on 24 May, he had to make his proposition in writing – $50 for some photographs. Hughes was offered the sleeping potion, then strangled and dismembered. Dahmer had become so casual that he simply left the body lying in the bedroom for a day or so before beginning the dismemberment process – it was, after all, no more dangerous than having an apartment full of skulls and body parts.

With victim number thirteen, Dahmer again varied his method and came close to being caught. This was the fourteen-year-old Laotian boy – already mentioned – Konerak Sinthasomphone. Instead of strangling him after drugging him and committing rape, Dahmer went out to buy a pack of beer. Konerak woke up and almost escaped. But the Milwaukee police returned him, and his skull ended as yet another keepsake.

Sunday 30 June was the day of Chicago's Gay Pride Parade, and Dahmer decided to attend, taking a Greyhound bus for the ninety mile trip. After watching the parade, Dahmer went to the police station to report that a pickpocket had taken his wallet. But he seems to have had enough money left to approach a young black he met at the Greyhound Bus station, another aspiring model named Matt Turner. They travelled back to Milwaukee on the bus, then to Dahmer's apartment by cab. (Dahmer often earned more than $300 a week at the chocolate factory, which explains his frequent extravagance with cabs.) In his later confession, Dahmer said nothing about sex; but he admitted to drugging Turner, strangling him with a strap, then dismembering him and cutting off his head, keeping the skull.

Five days later, Dahmer was back in Chicago, looking for another victim. In a gay club on Wells Street he met twenty-three-year-old Jeremiah Weinberger, and invited him back to Milwaukee. Weinberger consulted a former room mate, Ted Jones, about whether he should accept. "Sure, he looks ok", said Jones. He was later to comment ruefully: "Who knows what a serial killer looks like?"

Dahmer and Weinberger spent Saturday in Room 213 having

sex; Dahmer appeared to like his new acquaintance. But when, the following day, Weinberger looked at the clock and said it was time to go, Dahmer offered him a drink. Weinberger's head joined Matt Turner's in a plastic bag in the freezer.

But Dahmer was nearing the end of his tether, and even drink could not aesthetize him for long. Neighbours kept complaining about the smell, and he solved this by buying a fifty-seven gallon drum of concentrated hydrochloric acid, and disposing of some of the body parts that were causing the trouble. All this meant he was frequently late for work, or even absent. On 15 July, 1991, the Ambrosia Chocolate Company finally grew tired of his erratic behaviour and fired him.

His reaction was typical. The same day he picked up a twenty-four-year-old black named Oliver Lacy, took him back to his apartment, and gave him a drugged drink. After strangling him, he sodomized the body.

But the murder spree was almost over. Four days later, the head of the final victim joined the others in the freezer. He was twenty-five-year-old Joseph Bradeholt, an out of work black who was hoping to move from Minnesota to Milwaukee with his wife and two children. But he accepted Dahmer's offer of money for photographs, and willingly joined in oral sex in Room 213. After that, he was drugged, strangled and dismembered. His body was placed in the barrel of acid, which was swiftly turning into a black, sticky mess.

That Dahmer's luck finally ran out may have been due to the carelessness that leads to the downfall of so many multiple murderers. The last intended-victim, Tracy Edwards was a slightly built man, and should have succumbed to the drug like all the others. For some reason, he failed to do so; it seems most likely that Dahmer failed to administer a large enough dose. Equally puzzling is the fact that, having seen that the drug had failed to work, he allowed Edwards to live, and spent two hours watching a video with him. Was the homicidal impulse finally burning itself out? Dahmer knew that if he failed to kill Tracy Edwards, he would be caught; yet, with a large knife in his hand, he allowed him to escape from the apartment.

It sounds as if he recognized that the time had come to try to throw off the burden of guilt and rejoin the human race.

On 27 January, Wisconsin's worst mass murderer came to trial in Milwaukee before Judge Lawrence Gram, entering a plea of guilty but insane. On 15 February, the jury rejected Dahmer's plea and found him guilty of the fifteen murders with which he had been charged. (In two cases, the prosecution had decided the evidence was insufficient.) He was sentenced to fifteen terms of life imprisonment (Wisconsin has no death penalty) which means that he can never be released.

CONCLUSIONS

Perhaps one of the most disturbing things about this survey of serial killers is that the majority of them – from Dumollard and Vacher to the Yorkshire Ripper and Jeffrey Dahmer, were caught by accident. This was the problem that made America's law enforcement agencies aware that a totally new approach was necessary.

Until the early 1980s, cooperation between states had been as loose as between, say, the various police forces in Europe. Clearly, something more like a single force was needed – linked by a single computer. That is why, in November 1982, various crime specialists put forward the idea of a National Centre for the Analysis of Violent Crime (or NCAVC), a proposal that was unanimously adopted seven months later. The result was the formation of the NCAVC at the FBI Academy at Quantico, Virginia.

The Centre was run by agents of the elite Behavioural Science Unit, sometimes known as the Psychological Profiling Unit, because its chief task was to attempt to assess the personalities of unknown killers from the crime itself. For example, in November 1979, when the New York police had appealed to the Quantico unit for help in solving the rape and murder of a schoolteacher named Francine Elveson, the unit had been able to suggest the killer's age, his educational qualifications and his psychological problems; this had led officers working on the case to recognize that the "profile" fitted a suspect named Carmine Calabro, an

The National Center for the Analysis of Violent Crime is in Quantico, Virginia, and includes an underground complex of banks, shops, service station, cleaners, restaurants and cinema. The cinema shows the same programme that was seen by the famous gangster John Dillinger (the Biography was showing *Manhattan Melodrama*, a gangster film with Clark Gable) before he walked out with "the Lady in Red" (Polly Keele) and was shot down by FBI agents.

unemployed actor. Calabro's tooth-prints established his guilt and he was sentenced to life imprisonment.

This was the unit that now became the central coordinator of the new programme, with its vast computer that gathers information on every murder that occurs anywhere in the United States, and looks for similarities that might establish whether the same killer has been responsible for more than one murder. As a result of these new methods, the FBI handbook *Sexual Homicide: Its Patterns and Motives* estimates conservatively that the success rate of the NCAVC has been about seventy-seven per cent.

Cases like the Dahmer murders make it clear that there is still a long way to go. If the disappearance of young blacks in Milwaukee had been recorded on the FBI computer, the presence of a serial killer would have been established long before Dahmer had disposed of seventeen victims. Yet the slowly increasing success rate of the NCAVC suggests that this problem, like the others, is amenable to the scientific approach. In 1986, special agent Roger Depue of the NCAVC expressed the new sense of optimism when he pointed out that the Quantico unit had already contributed significantly to slowing down the spiral of violent crime in America. "We are not only going to fight back – we are going to win."

The hunt for the "Yorkshire Ripper", Peter Sutcliffe, took so long (six years) because of the problem of storing and organizing 22,000 interviews and 150,000 suspects. As soon as murder hunts were computerized (after 1980) the success rate increased dramatically. John Duffy, the "Railway Rapist" and killer of three girls, was caught after he was selected by computer from a list of 4,900 sex offenders.

. *World Famous* .

ROBBERIES

Colin Wilson, Damon Wilson and Rowan Wilson

chapter one

"IF YOU THINK TODAY IS LAWLESS . . ."

When we complain about the rising crime rate, we speak as citizens who take the protection of the law for granted. Police patrol our streets and country lanes. Burglary and mugging may be on the increase; but at least the robbers take their freedom into their hands every time they set out to commit a crime.

If we are to understand the history of the past three thousand years we have to make an effort of imagination, and try to forget this notion of being protected by the law. In ancient Greece, the problem was not simply the brigands who haunted the roads and the pirates who infested the seas; it was the fact that the ordinary citizen became a brigand or pirate when he felt like it, and no one regarded this as abnormal. In the *Odyssey*, Ulysses describes with pride how, on the way home from Troy, his ship was driven near to the coast of Thrace; so they landed near an unprotected town, murdered all the men, and carried off the women and goods. Greece was not at war with Thrace; it was just that an unprotected town was fair game for anyone, and the war-weary Greeks felt like a little rape and plunder. This state of affairs persisted for most of the next three thousand years, and explains why so many Mediterranean towns and villages are built inland.

What is far more difficult to grasp is that "law abiding" countries like England were in exactly the same situation. Just before the time of the Black Death (as Luke Owen Pike

describes in his *History of Crime in England*, 1873), "houses were
set on fire day after day; men and women were captured,
ransom was exacted on pain of death . . . even those who paid
it might think themselves fortunate if they escaped some
horrible mutilation." And this does not relate to times of
war or social upheaval; according to J.F. Nicholls and John
Taylor's *Bristol Past and Present* (1881) England was "prosperous in the highest degree; populous, wealthy and luxurious . . ."
(p. 174). Yet the robber bands were like small armies. They
would often descend on a town when a fair was taking place
and everyone felt secure; they would take over the town,
plunder the houses and set them on fire (for citizens who
were trying to save their houses would not organize a pursuit) and then withdraw. In 1347–8, Bristol was taken over by a
brigand who robbed the ships in the harbour – including some
commissioned by the King – and issued his own proclamations
like a conqueror. His men roamed the streets, robbing and
killing as they felt inclined – the King had to send Thomas, Lord
Berkeley, to restore order. When a trader was known to have
jewels belonging to Queen Philippa in his house, he was
besieged by a gang led by one Adam the Leper and had to
hand over the jewels when his house was set on fire. The law
courts were almost powerless: when a notorious robber was
tried near Winchester, the gang waited outside the court and
attacked everyone who came out; the case was dropped.

The Age of Gin

Around the year 1650, a Dutch professor of chemistry called
Sylvius discovered that a powerful alcohol could be made by
distilling corn mash – which was cheap – and a sharp and
pleasant flavour could be given it with juniper berries. This
drink was called "geneva" (French for juniper), and this was
soon shortened to gin.

It was sold in small bottles in chemists' shops, and the Dutch
soon realized that geneva was as potent as good brandy, and
far cheaper. When William and Mary installed themselves on
James's throne in 1688, their countrymen began to export the

new drink to England. Since England was quarrelling with France, and was therefore reluctant to buy French brandy, geneva – or gin – quickly became the national drink. Because of the brandy embargo, a law was passed permitting anyone to distil his own drink, and the English soon improved on the Dutch original, distilling an even cheaper grade of corn mash, and producing a powerful spirit that would now be called

The most famous of British highwaymen, Dick Turpin, never actually made the famous ride to York on his mare Bonnie Black Bess. Neither was he the courteous and heroic outlaw depicted by legend.

Born in 1705, Turpin was a butcher who turned to sheep-stealing to stock his shop. Inevitably found out, he lived by robbery and petty theft until he joined the notorious Essex Gang in 1735. One of his two quoted utterances is to a widow who refused to divulge the whereabouts of her cash: "God damn you, you old bitch, if you won't tell us I'll set your arse on the grate." On another occasion the gang poured boiling water over a farmer – whose skull they had cracked – while they took it in turns to rape his maid.

The gang was finally betrayed in an alehouse when a reward of a hundred guineas was offered for each, but Turpin escaped by jumping out of a window. It was after this that he took up highway robbery in Epping Forest, soon becoming one of the most successful highwaymen in the country. Hiding out in a cave, he murdered a keeper who tracked him down.

Turpin retired on his ill-gotten gains and settled in Yorkshire, calling himself John Palmer. He was arrested for shooting a gamecock and sheep-stealing, but no one suspected his identity. Turpin wrote to his brother from prison in York, asking for help, but sent the letter without a stamp. His brother failed to recognize the handwriting and refused to pay the postman sixpence. But a local schoolmaster caught a glimpse of the letter, recognised the handwriting of his old pupil and claimed the £200 reward on Turpin's head. Turpin was tried and sentenced to be hanged.

In jail he became a celebrity, receiving many visitors. One of them swore he was not Turpin, whereupon Turpin told a jailer "Lay him a wager and I'll go you halves", his only other recorded utterance.

On the scaffold, he preferred to launch himself into eternity by jumping from the ladder.

moonshine. (It is also probably a safe bet that this was when someone discovered that beer could be distilled to produce whisky.) Gin shops opened all over England – one London street had six of them.

Queen Elizabeth's subjects had drunk sherry (Falstaff's "sack"), beer and wine, which were cheap – wine cost fourpence a quart. Then James I had succeeded in raising some of the money Parliament refused to grant him by taxing various commodities, including wine and sherry, so that the English working man of the seventeenth century could only afford beer. By 1688, the English working classes were alcohol-starved. The consumption of gin rose steadily, from half a million gallons around 1690 to three and a half million by 1727 and to nineteen million gallons by the middle of the century.

The result was a crime wave. Many gin shops carried the notice: "Drunk for a penny, dead drunk for twopence, clean straw for nothing." Crimes to obtain money for gin became as common as crimes to obtain money for drugs in our own society. Theft became so common that, in 1699, a particularly savage act was passed that made almost any theft punishable by hanging, provided the goods were worth more than five shillings. At the same time, anyone who helped to secure the apprehension of a thief could obtain various tax exemptions and rewards. The measures were desperate; but so was the situation. Quite suddenly, England was virtually in a state of war with criminals. The diarist Narcissus Luttrell mentions an endless series of highway robberies and similar crimes. On one Saturday in 1693, a highwayman named Whitney had been arrested after resisting for an hour, and another highwayman was arrested in St Martin's Church. A gang of seven broke into Lady Reresby's house in Gerard Street, tied her and her family up and then rifled the house. Three coaches were robbed coming from Epsom, and three rowdies had caused an affray in Holborn, broken windows and run a watchman through with a sword, leaving it in his body. The invasion of houses by robber gangs had become as common as it was before the Black Death. A few years later, the famous robber Dick Turpin – whose exploits were far less romantic than his legend – led a gang that specialized in breaking into country houses, torturing the householders to force them to disclose valuables and raping any maids. Turpin's fame rested on the flamboyant manner of his death, bowing and waving to the mob from his cart, and finally voluntarily leaping from the gallows ladder.

All this makes an interesting contrast with crime in the age of
Queen Elizabeth. It had been just as widespread, but far less
serious. London was then full of thieves and confidence men
(known as "cony catchers", a cony being a rabbit). The thieves
used to meet once a week in the house of their leader, who also
happened to be the brother-in-law of the hangman; there, like
an aldermen's meeting, they discussed "prospects" and ex-
changed information. In contemporary descriptions (Robert
Greene wrote several pamphlets about it), the London criminal
scene in the time of Elizabeth sounds rather like Damon
Runyan's New York, deplorable but fairly good-natured. A
century later, this had changed. Highwaymen infested the
country roads, burglars operated in the towns, and women
and children appeared in the courts as frequently as men.
Children were trained as pickpockets, and were also sent
out to earn gin money by prostitution – the novelist Henry
Fielding, who became a magistrate in 1740, wrote of the large
number of children "eaten up with the foul distemper". The
government's reaction was to execute almost every offender
who appeared in court. In 1722, a gang of Hampshire poachers
had murdered a keeper who had interrupted them; they had

Black Bess and Dick Turpin (1706–39)

blackened their faces so as to be less visible in the dark. Landowners in the Waltham area (where it took place) were so alarmed that the government was prevailed upon to pass an act – the "Waltham Black Act" – which enabled almost any poacher to be hanged. (If the act had been in existence when Shakespeare was arrested for poaching from Sir Thomas Lucy, his works would have remained unwritten.) The act included a list of more than three hundred other offences – including catching rabbits – for which a man could be hanged.

Yet these measures had no effect on the rising crime rate. They could hardly be expected to when a large proportion of the population was permanently drunk. Henry Fielding reckoned that a hundred thousand people in London alone lived mainly on gin. Another observer stood outside a gin palace for three hours one evening and counted 1,411 people going in and out. These "palaces" usually consisted of a shed, full of barrels of gin; the customers merely came to buy a pennyworth of gin, which explains the enormous number. Whole families, including, father, mother and children, then sat on the pavement and drank themselves unconscious; with gin at a penny a quart, it was not difficult. The artist William Hogarth engraved two famous pictures, "Beer Street" and "Gin Lane", to expose the evil. In Beer Street, a lot of jolly-looking men and women are drinking outside a tavern and obviously engaging in intelligent political discussion (there is a copy of the king's speech on the table). In Gin Lane, a drunken mother allows her baby to fall out of her arms into the area below, a madman impales a baby on a spit, and a man who has hanged himself can be seen through the window of a garret. Fielding remarked that the gin "disqualifies them from any honest means to acquire it, at the same time that it removes sense of fear and shame and emboldens them to commit every wicked and dangerous enterprise." The result was that pickpockets who had once relied on skill and light fingers now knocked down their victims with bludgeons in broad daylight. The novelist Horace Walpole was shot in the face by a highwayman in Hyde Park in 1752.

Punishments, both in England and on the continent, had always been barbarous; now they became sadistic. The sentence of being hanged, drawn and quartered was usually reserved for political criminals, although it might be applied to some particularly violent robber. The victim was dragged to the place of execution behind a cart; he was then half-hanged, and his bowels were torn out while he was still alive and burned in front of him.

After this the body was cut into four pieces. Female criminals were often burned alive, because it was regarded as more "decent" than allowing them to risk exposing their private parts as they swung from a rope. (In this respect our ancestors were remarkably prudish.) But it was common for women – as well as men – to be stripped to the waist before being whipped through the streets to the pillory or gallows. After the 1699 act, thieves were branded on one cheek to make their offence public knowledge – this was probably regarded as an act of clemency, since most thieves were hanged. Prisoners accused of offences that involved speech – perhaps preaching false religious doctrines – would have a hole bored through the tongue as they were held in the pillory. A confidence man named Japhet Crook was sentenced to have both ears cut off and his nose slit open, then seared with a red hot iron. The hangman, known as 'Laughing Jack' Hooper, cut off both ears from behind with a sharp knife and held them aloft for the crowd to see, then cut

Ask anyone to name a famous pirate, and the chances are that they will say: "Captain Kidd". The truth is that Kidd was never a pirate.

William Kidd was a forty-year-old sea captain with a respectable record when the British government asked him to head a "privateering" expedition in 1695. A privateer plundered the ships of nations with whom his government was at war, and England was at that time at war with France. Kidd was also supposed to hunt real pirates – the unofficial variety – in the Red Sea.

Kidd captured and plundered two Armenian ships with French passes – which he was legally entitled to do – and the owners complained in London. When he arrived in New York, Kidd found to his astonishment that he had been proclaimed a pirate. He protested that he was nothing of the sort (and hid some of his loot), but when he ventured ashore he was arrested and returned to London. In the two years before he came to trial, the passes that would have proved his right to plunder the Armenian ships disappeared, and Kidd was convicted of piracy. He was also convicted of killing a member of his crew whom he had struck with a bucket – during a mutiny, he claimed. Kidd was hanged on 23 May 1701. The best known of all pirates was actually an innocent man.

open Crook's nostrils with scissors; however, when he applied the red hot iron to the bleeding nose, Crook leapt out of his chair so violently that Hooper – who was a kindly man – decided not to carry out the rest of the punishment. On the Continent, sentences were even crueller; red hot pincers were used to tear out the tongues of blasphemers. A madman called Damiens, who tried – rather half heartedly – to stab Louis XV of France in 1757, was executed by being literally "quartered". He was carried to the execution because his legs had been smashed with sledgehammers. His chest was torn open with red hot pincers, and lead poured into the wounds. Then his hands and feet were tied to four dray horses, which were whipped off in opposite directions. They were not strong enough to tear off his arms and legs, so more horses were brought; even so, the executioner had to partly sever the arms and legs before they could be pulled off. Damiens remained conscious until he had only one arm left – during the early part of the proceedings he looked on with apparent curiosity – and his hair turned white during the course of the execution.

The Theft of the Crown Jewels

Another villain who certainly deserved execution cheated the hangman because the King of England – Charles II – entirely lacked the spirit of vengefulness.

The infamous Colonel Blood was born in Sarney, County Meath, in Ireland, in 1618, and christened Thomas. His grandfather lived in Kilnaboy Castle, and was a Member of Parliament. Blood's father was a prosperous blacksmith who owned an ironworks. When the Civil War broke out in 1642, Blood hurried to England to fight on the side of King Charles I. But as it became clear that Cromwell's forces were going to win, he changed sides and joined the Roundheads. The result was that when Charles was defeated in 1653, Blood was made a Justice of the Peace and granted a large estate.

His prosperity lasted only seven years; when Charles II returned to the throne in 1660, Blood had to flee back to Ireland. He was not entirely destitute – he had married a

Lancashire heiress, who had borne him a son. In Ireland he
joined a plot with other disgruntled Cromwellians to seize
Dublin Castle and take its governor, Lord Ormonde, prisoner; it failed and he had to flee again, this time to Holland. After
taking part in more political plots, he became a marked man
with a price on his head. A daring rescue of a fellow conspirator,
who was being taken to London under an escort of eight
soldiers, again made Blood one of the most wanted men in
the kingdom. In spite of this, he returned to England in 1670,
and, under the name of Ayloffe, practised as a doctor at
Romford.

He still dreamed of revenge on Lord Ormonde, who had
dispossessed him and crushed his Irish plot. On 28 May 1670,
Ormonde was on his way to a banquet in the Guildhall when he
was held up in his coach and dragged out by several men.
Blood then told him that he was going to be hanged at Tyburn,
and sent the others off to prepare the gallows. But the coachman raised the alarm, and servants ran to Ormonde's aid;
Blood fired a shot at him, then ran into the shadows of
Piccadilly. (It was rumoured that he escaped with the aid of
the Duke of Buckingham, who would have been glad to see
Ormonde hanged.)

Back in Romford, he decided on an even bolder scheme:
stealing the Crown Jewels, which were kept in the Tower of
London, behind a grating in a locked basement room.

The keeper, Blood learned, was a man named Talbot Edwards, who lived with his family on the floor above the jewels.
So one day early in 1671, disguised as a parson, Blood went to
see the Crown Jewels, and became friendly with Talbot Edwards. Next time he went he took his wife. But as they were
leaving the basement of the Martin Tower, Mrs Blood had a
sudden violent stomach ache, and was taken into the Edwards'
apartments to rest. The grateful Parson Blood returned a few
days later with four pairs of white gloves for Mrs Edwards.

Blood was soon a regular visitor. And since Talbot Edwards
had a pretty daughter, he was delighted when Blood proposed
a match with his own wealthy nephew, an idea that his
womenfolk also received with enthusiasm.

On 9 May 1671, Parson Blood arrived at 7 am with his
"nephew" and two more companions. While the good-looking
young man was making the acquaintance of the ladies, Blood
suggested that they might see the Crown Jewels. Edwards
thought it a good way of passing the time and led the way

downstairs. He unlocked the door of the room that held the jewels, led them in, and locked it behind him. At that moment, he was knocked unconscious with a mallet wielded by Blood.

The thieves wrenched away the grating that protected the jewels, and removed the crown, orb and sceptre. The crown was flattened with the mallet and stuffed into a bag, the orb stuffed down the breeches of one of the men. Edwards, who had been tied up, began to struggle at this point, and Blood ran him through with his sword. The sceptre was too big to go into the bag, and one of the accomplices – Blood's brother-in-law, Hunt – began to file it through with a mallet.

Then there was an interruption. Edwards' son had been serving in Flanders, and he now arrived unexpectedly. Blood's "nephew", looking out of the window, saw him approaching and made an excuse to go downstairs. Blood decided that it was time to leave; they dropped the sceptre and hastened away.

At this moment, Edwards regained consciousness, and began to shout "Treason! Murder!". The son, now upstairs with his mother and sisters, ran down to see what was the matter. When he found his father bleeding from a sword wound, he raised the alarm.

Blood shot a sentry who tried to stop him, then made a minor mistake that betrayed loss of nerve: instead of leaving across the nearest drawbridge, by the Bulwark Gate, he changed his mind and made for the Iron Gate, near which his horse was tied. Even so, he came close to escape – the sentries mistook other guards for the fugitives and attacked them. Fortunately, the commander of the guard recognized the mistake, and reached Blood as he was mounting his horse. Blood pointed his pistol and pulled the trigger; it misfired. Beckman wrestled with Blood and finally overcame him. By this time the three accomplices had also been arrested.

In custody, Blood refused to answer questions, repeating stubbornly: "I'll answer to none but the King himself." Blood knew that the King had a reputation for liking bold scoundrels, and reckoned on his Irish charm to save his neck.

He proved correct. Blood was taken to the Palace, where he was questioned by the King, Prince Rupert, the Duke of York, and other members of the royal family. Charles was amused by his roguery, and chuckled when Blood remarked that his escapade had not been worth it, since the Crown Jewels were certainly not worth the £100,000 they were usually valued at – £6,000 would be nearer to it. Blood then went on to invent a tale of a plot to murder the King in which he himself had taken part. They had hidden, he explained, in the reeds at Battersea when the King went to the river to bathe, but "such was the awful majesty of your unclothed form that the weapon fell out of my hand." The King may have taken this as a flattering reference to his natural endowments; at all events, he asked, "What if I should give you your life?", and Blood answered promptly, with the correct expression of deep humility, "I would endeavour to deserve it, sire!"

Blood was not only pardoned – to the disgust of Lord Ormonde – but granted Irish lands worth £500 a year. With his pockmarked face, short legs and little blue eyes, he soon became a familiar figure around central London, and made frequent appearances at court.

Talbot Edwards, who recovered, was also rewarded by the king, and achieved his own kind of celebrity as the man who had been robbed of the crown by Colonel Blood. He lived to a ripe old age, always delighted to tell the story to visitors.

Blood's downfall came eight years later, when, in 1679, he quarrelled with his former patron, the scheming Duke of Buckingham. Somehow, perhaps when drunk, Blood came to accuse Buckingham of "gross immorality". Buckingham sued him for £10,000 – which would have ruined Blood – and, to Blood's dismay, he was found guilty. But immediately after the verdict, Blood fell ill, and died on 24 August 1680, at the age of sixty-two.

Even death was quite not the end of the story. There was soon a rumour that Blood had arranged his own "death" to escape paying the fine, and that the coffin contained some other body. The coffin was dug up in the presence of the coroner; when the body had been identified at an inquest it was reburied – a disappointment to his enemies, who still hoped to see him hanged.

Farmer Porter and the Robbers

Nowadays, even in countries with a high crime rate, the countryside is at least safer than the town. In eighteenth century England, it was just as bad.

In the summer of 1751, a farmer named Porter, who lived near Pulford, in Cheshire, engaged some Irish labourers to help with the harvest. One August evening, there was a crash at the door as someone tried to force his way in; the farmer evidently kept it locked as a precaution. Five Irishmen smashed their way into the house, grabbed the farmer and his wife – who were sitting at supper – and tied them up. Porter was ordered to reveal the whereabouts of his cash box, and tried delaying tactics; at this the gang threatened to torture them both. A daughter who had been listening outside the door now rushed into the room, flung herself on her knees, and begged for her father's life; she was also tied up and threatened. She gave way, and told the gang where the valuables were kept.

The youngest daughter, a girl of thirteen, had hidden herself; now she escaped out of the rear door, tiptoed to the stable, led out a horse and rode across the fields to the village. She went to the house of her brother and told him what was happening. The brother and a friend armed themselves – probably with knives and hatchets – and hurried to the farm. A man was on watch; they managed to approach so quietly that he was taken unawares, and promptly killed him. Then they rushed into the parlour, and found the four men holding the farmer – who was naked – and trying to force him to sit on the fire to reveal where he kept his savings. One robber was promptly knocked senseless; the other three fled through the window. The rescuers organized a pursuit, and caught up with two of the robbers on Chester bridge; another man, the ringleader, was caught on a ship at Liverpool. All four men were tried and sentenced to death, but the sentence of the youngest was commuted to transportation for life. The ringleader, Stanley, managed to escape on the eve of his execution. On 25 May 1752, the other two – named M'Canelly and Morgan – were hanged, "their behaviour [being] as decent as could be expected from people of their station".

This kind of house storming was commonplace during the crime wave of the eighteenth century. The robbers organized themselves like military units. A house that was to be attacked was watched for days until the gang knew when they could burst in, and when they were likeliest to be safe from interruption. Stealth and skill were unnecessary in the actual operation; it was conducted like a siege of a town. The M'Canelly and Morgan case shows that the burglars of the mid-eighteenth century had already discovered a method of torture that became common in France at the time of the Revolution, when the robbers were known as *chauffeurs* – warmers. (Professional drivers were later called chauffeurs because the earliest cars were steam driven, so that the driver was literally a stoker, or "fireman".) We have seen that the streets of London were unsafe even by day; footpads operated openly in all the parks and open spaces, while highwaymen waited in every wood and thicket along every main road.

And what were the police doing while all this was going on? The answer is that there were no police. In the countries of Europe, the army kept some kind of order – that is why French policemen were later calls *gens d'armes* or gendarmes – men at arms. But England had no standing army, for it had not been invaded since William the Conqueror. And the British were deeply suspicious of the idea of a police force, believing it would erode their freedom. So in villages, there were local watchmen, and a parish constable – who was a local tradesman who did the job in his spare time. And, as Patrick Pringle points out in his introduction to Goddard's *Memoirs of a Bow Street Runner*, this system worked well enough in the country, but tended to break down in large towns. If a citizen was robbed, he himself had to pursue the robber, setting up a "hue and cry", and if he caught him, had to prosecute him at his own expense. The government tried to make up for the lack of law and order by the barbarity of punishments, so that as many as a dozen men at a time might be hanged at Tyburn (and on several occasions, as many as twenty). The *Gentleman's Magazine* for 1750 recorded: "Executed at Tyburn, July 6, Elizabeth Banks, for stripping a child; Catherine Conway, for forging a seaman's ticket; and Margaret Harvey for robbing her master. They were all drunk." As late as 1801, a boy of thirteen was hanged for breaking into a house and stealing a spoon; two sisters, aged eight and eleven, were hanged at Lynn in 1808. In 1831, a boy of nine was hanged for setting fire to a house, and two years later, another boy of nine was hanged for pushing a stick through a cracked shop window and stealing two pennyworth of printer's colour.

When better-off people left London in the mid-eighteenth century to go to the country, they locked up their houses and took their valuables with them, for they expected the houses to be broken into and robbed. And when someone wanted to recover stolen property, they went along to some dubious characters who knew the underworld, and offered a reward. In the previous century, a retired highwaywoman named Mary Frith, or Moll Cutpurse, set up a shop in Fleet Street to sell the goods stolen by her gang of pickpockets, and her best customers were the victims themselves; she was so successful that she drove every other fence out of the business. Moll died, rich and respected, in 1659, in her mid-seventies. A century later, Jonathan Wild set himself up in the same business, and soon achieved a success far beyond that of Moll Cutpurse. He became a kind of eighteenth century Al Capone, who divided London into districts, with a gang to each; any thief or highwayman who preferred to operate alone was hunted down and hanged on evidence supplied by Wild. He owned a London house and a country mansion, as well as a ship for taking stolen goods overseas; at one point, he even had the effrontery to ask the Mayor of London for freedom of the city in consideration of his great public services. When a law was passed making it illegal to take money for restoring stolen goods to their owners, he found ways around it, and became richer than ever. Eventually, the law caught up with him, and he was hanged in 1725. And within a year or so, London was in the grip of a crime wave that made it dangerous to walk in Covent Garden in broad daylight.

Gin was not the only cause. Others attributed it to the increasing number of sailors who flooded into London as Britain's trade with the rest of the world increased. But the novelist Henry Fielding came closest to the heart of the matter in a pamphlet enquiring into "the late increase of robbers" when he blamed "the vast torrent of luxury which of late years hath poured itself into this nation". England was becoming the richest country in the world, but its wealth existed side by side with appalling poverty. Naturally, the poor tried to divert a little of the wealth into their own pockets. The same thing had happened in ancient Rome and every other civilization that achieved wealth and success . . .

London went on a crime rampage, and it was not confined to the poor. The Mohocks, a society whose members were dedicated to the ambition of "doing all possible hurt to their fellow creatures", were mostly gentlemen. They employed their ample leisure in forcing prostitutes and old women to stand on their heads in tar barrels so that they could prick their legs with their swords; or in making them jump up and down to avoid the swinging blades; in disfiguring their victims by boring out their eyes or flattening their noses; in waylaying servants and, as in the case of Lady Winchelsea's maid, beating them and slashing their faces. To work themselves up to the necessary pitch of enthusiasm for their ferocious games, they first drank so much that they were "quite beyond the possibility of attending to any notions of reason or humanity". Some of the Mohocks seem to have been members of the Bold Bucks who, apparently, had formally to deny the existence of God and eat every Sunday a dish known as Holy Ghost Pie. The ravages of the Bold Bucks were more specifically sexual than those of the Mohocks and consequently, as it was practically impossible to obtain a conviction for rape and as the age of consent was twelve, they were more openly conducted. An expectation of inviolability was, indeed, shared by many, if not most young men of this class. One evening in the 1720s, Richard Savage, who claimed to be a son of the Countess of Macclesfield, quarrelled with some people playing cards in Robinson's coffee-house, lost his temper, and ran one of them through with his sword. He was tried for murder but he was subsequently pardoned. And when a young gentleman named Plunket called at a shop to collect a wig he had ordered he did not hesitate to pick up a razor from the counter and slit the wigmaker's throat from ear to ear, because he would not reduce the price by more than one guinea. Senseless murders such as this were as common as riots . . .

Things began to change for the better in 1729 when a half-pay captain named Thomas De Veil was appointed magistrate for Westminster and Middlesex. A decade earlier, De Veil had been well on the road to ruination with his taste for wine, women and song, which ran him up enormous debts. But he had the sense to retire to a country village and live cheaply before returning to London and setting up as a kind of scrivener, drafting petitions to the government. De Veil made no secret of the fact that he accepted his post as a magistrate because it offered him the opportunity to take bribes and indulge his immense sexual appetite with young ladies who had no other means to bribe him. He had twenty-five legitimate children and an unknown number of bastards, and next door to his office he kept a private room to which he could quickly retire with any attractive woman who appeared before him and was willing to buy her freedom on the couch. But in spite of being virtually a sex maniac, De Veil was also an efficient and hard-working magistrate. Ten years after the execution of Jonathan Wild, one of London's largest and most desperate robber gangs decided to kill him when they heard that he was collecting evidence against them, and well-armed groups of them waited for night after night around Leicester Fields (the present Leicester Square), where De Veil had his office. De Veil seems to have got wind of the plot, and all the waiting finally preyed on the nerves of one of the thugs, who secretly betrayed his companions to the magistrate. So one of London's most dangerous gangs was broken up.

De Veil's greatest triumphs came after he transferred his office to a house in Bow Street, in 1739. Already in his mid-fifties (and therefore, in eighteenth-century terms, an old man), De Veil began to build up a reputation as a detective. When an eating house in Chancery Lane was burgled, he found himself interrogating a suspect who professed total innocence of the crime. On a "hunch", De Veil asked the man casually for a loan of his knife, and he noted that the suspect's pocket knife had a missing point. He sent a constable round to the eating house with instructions to look in the lock; the missing point was found there, and the man convicted. As with most good detectives, De Veil's success rested upon this keen instinct about criminal behaviour.

After the death of De Veil in 1746, his position and his house in Bow Street were taken over by the novelist and playwright Henry Fielding, who had made the discovery that literature and poverty are almost synonymous. Fielding had made a living as a political playwright, until the Prime Minister, Sir Robert Walpole, grew tired of being satirized, and introduced a bill that required every play to be licensed by an official called the Lord Chamberlain – an office that aroused the fury of generations of playwrights until it was abolished in 1968. That put an end to Fielding's career as a dramatist, and novels like *Joseph Andrews* and *Jonathan Wild* failed to make up for the loss of income. So, with some reluctance, Fielding decided to accept the post of Justice of the Peace. His enemies set up a chorus of derision about the idealistic playwright who had become a "trading justice". But Fielding had no intention of lining his own pocket. In his few brief years of office (he was already ill in 1748, and died six years later) he became the most formidable enemy of crime that London had ever known.

His problem was simple: for every thief and highwayman who was sent to jail, there were a hundred more left on the street. With no police force except part-time parish constables, the London criminal had never known any organized opposition. Yet De Veil had shown that gangs could be destroyed by a determined magistrate. With half a dozen public-spirited friends, Fielding began to organize a group of "thief takers", all ex-parish constables who knew the villains by sight. To us, the system sounds hopelessly amateurish. Victims of robberies were urged to hurry to Fielding's house in Bow Street, whereupon the thief takers would set out in hot pursuit – which is why they soon became known as the Bow Street Runners. And since London's robbers were accustomed to immunity, and seldom bothered to leave their habitual haunts, they were captured in droves. Fielding described his satisfaction as he read the London newspapers, and saw reports of robberies diminishing day by day, until eventually they ceased altogether. He had been granted £600 by the government, and in putting a stop to London's crime wave, he used only half of it.

The next problem was the number of highwaymen and burglars who infested the roads around London. Again, it proved unexpectedly easy to solve. As soon as a few heavily armed constables patrolled the roads, the thieves became nervous, and moved elsewhere. One highwayman had become so accustomed to immunity that he returned regularly to rob the same coach just outside London. Finally, the coachman took a Bow Street Runner with him and when the robber rode up waving his pistol, the Runner fired and blew away half his jaw. The highwayman also fired, but missed; he was taken off to hospital, and thence to jail. This episode took place under the magistracy of Fielding's blind brother John, who continued to be the scourge of London's underworld for more than a quarter of a century after the novelist's death.

The Great Vidocq

At the age of 34, Eugène-François Vidocq was a short, powerfully built man with a scarred face and a jaw like a lion. Born in Arras on 24 July 1775, he had been in trouble most of his life; never serious trouble, but Vidocq had a quick temper and a powerful will, qualities that had led to a number of personal combats and jail sentences. Injustice enraged him, and his attempts to escape from jail had been determined and desperate. By 1808, when he found himself in Paris, the list of his offences was enough to ensure a lifetime in the galleys. He asked to see M. Henry, head of the criminal department of the Paris police, and made him an offer. If he could be guaranteed immunity, he would act as informer against a number of men that the police wanted far more than they wanted Vidocq.

Henry knew he had a bargain, but he felt it could be improved. He allowed Vidocq to go. And when, a few weeks later, Vidocq was denounced by criminal associates and appeared again in front of the chief of police, M. Henry drove a very hard bargain indeed. Vidocq was to become a police spy in one of Paris's toughest prisons, the Bicêtre. If Vidocq was even suspected of being a police informer, he would be found dead the next morning. But, as M. Henry knew, he had no alternative.

Vidocq's task was to obtain evidence against a burglar named Barthélemy Lacour, known to the police as Coco. He had stolen a quantity of silver from a police official. Now he was about to come up for trial, and the police had no evidence. Vidocq's task was to obtain that evidence.

It proved unexpectedly easy. Because of his reputation as an escaper, Vidocq was something of a hero to the other prisoners, and soon became a kind of unofficial lawgiver. One of the first "cases" brought before him in this capacity was, oddly enough, Coco himself, who was suspected of being a police informer. Vidocq saved Coco's life, and so became his trusted intimate. And soon Coco had confided in him that the police would never convict him, for the only witness was a street porter whom the police had failed to question. Coco did not tell Vidocq the porter's name, but he mentioned the street he lived in. Vidocq passed on this information to Henry, and the man was soon traced. Coco never knew how they obtained the evidence that convicted him . . .

For the next two years, Vidocq continued his career of betrayal. Then Henry kept his side of the bargain and allowed him to "escape" on his way to court – the other prisoners were delighted with Vidocq's latest exploit. After that, the great escaper apparently returned to his old habits, spending his days in low wine shops. But the criminals were baffled that the police seemed to know of their best laid plans in advance. No one suspected that the culprit might be the great escaper.

In due course, Vidocq's successes became so great that, in 1810, he was given his own police department; it was called the Sûreté. His priority was to establish a network of informers or "grasses" – a method most police forces now take for granted, but which was established by Vidocq. And from 1810 until he retired in 1833, he scored a remarkable series of successes.

One example will suffice to illustrate his methods. In 1821, a butcher named Fontaine stopped at a roadside inn, and fell into conversation with two respectable-looking travellers; the butcher was delighted when they said they were on their way to a fair at Corbeil, and asked if he could join them. He was carrying a large sum of money, and was worried about robbers. At a lonely spot a few miles further on, they beat him unconscious, stabbed him, and took his money, leaving him for dead. But the butcher survived, and was able to describe his assailants. At the scene of the crime, the police found a fragment of an envelope with part of an address, including "M. Raoul" and "Roche . . ." Vidocq knew a M. Raoul who kept a bar at the Barrière Rochechouart, and whose reputation was sinister.

The butcher had succeeded in delivering a powerful kick at the knee of one of the men, so Vidocq assumed he was looking for a man with a limp. His men kept the bar under surveillance, and soon observed a man with a limp who fitted the butcher's description of one of the robbers. When Vidocq saw him, he recognized a criminal named Court, whom he had arrested some time before for armed robbery. At dawn the next morning he went to Court's room. He told Court he had been accused of smuggling, and observed the expression of relief that crossed the robber's face. Court invited him to search the room, and Vidocq took possession of some weapons, then took Court to the nearest gendarme post.

Now Vidocq used the same technique on Raoul. He explained that Raoul had been denounced for holding anti-Government meetings and distributing seditious pamphlets. Raoul invited him to search the place. There was, as Vidocq expected, nothing. But Raoul had another apartment in Paris. And there, in a bureau, Vidocq found the other half of the envelope. He arrested Raoul and lodged him in prison.

Vidocq proceeded to question Court, carefully failing to mention the attack on the butcher; eventually, Court divulged that he had been concerned in the murder of a poultry dealer,

who had been robbed of four louis. Now, at last, Vidocq
revealed that the crime he was investigating was the attempted murder of the butcher. By now demoralized, Court
also confessed to this, but accused Raoul of the stabbing. Faced
with his confederate's admissions, Raoul also confessed. Both
men were condemned to the guillotine. Yet it is typical of the
close relationship that Vidocq was able to form with criminals
that he went to enormous lengths to make their last days
comfortable, and that when they knelt at the block, they
regarded Vidocq as a friend.

At the age of fifty-eight, Vidocq declined to retire into civilian
life, and became the first private detective in Europe. He wrote
his memoirs, and became a close friend of the novelist Balzac,
who immortalized Vidocq as the sinister but extraordinary
criminal Vautrin; in return, Balzac helped Vidocq to write
novels based on his early life.

• chapter two •

THE WILD WEST

The First Private Eye

The American equivalent of the great Vidocq was a Scottish-born detective named Allan Pinkerton. Like Vidocq, Pinkerton retired from the official police force to become a private detective, one of the first "private eyes" in the business. (In fact, the term private eye is probably derived from the Pinkerton symbol – an open eye bearing the legend "We never sleep".) But in the second half of the nineteenth century, the Pinkerton detective agency developed an efficiency that surpassed that of Scotland Yard or the Sûreté.

Allan Pinkerton was a radical, who fled from Scotland at the age of twenty-three – in 1842 – to avoid arrest. Working as a cooper in Dundee, Kane County, Illinois, he became an ardent advocate of the abolition of slavery, and helped to smuggle runaway slaves over the border into Canada. And in 1846, chance introduced him to his true vocation: detection. Walking in the woods on an island, he found the remains of a camp fire and trails in the long grass. Many men would have minded their own business; but Pinkerton had a social conscience. The local sheriff accompanied him back to the island, and decided that the camp belonged to a gang of counterfeiters. With Pinkerton's enthusiastic help, he uncovered a cache of fake money and arrested the gang. Only one of them escaped, and

Pinkerton, flushed with triumph, offered to help run him down. He tracked the man, pretended to be a fellow crook, and succeeded in getting him arrested. The result was an overnight reputation as a detective.

On Lake Michigan, not far from Dundee, there was a new city called Chicago – although this little collection of wooden cottages and rooming-houses, with a population of 4,000, was hardly more than a town. Soon after his triumph with the counterfeiters, Pinkerton was asked to become a deputy in Kane County and Cook County, which included Chicago. Like Vidocq, he proved to be a born detective, with a phenomenal memory for faces and a sure instinct for the ways of criminals. But the Chicago police were poorly paid, and when the Post Office engaged Pinkerton as a special agent, he saw that there was more money in private work. This is why, in 1850, he founded the Pinkerton detective agency.

This new, fast-expanding America needed efficient detectives. A fast-growing economy needs to transfer large amounts of money and valuables, and in the wide empty spaces, coaches and railway trains were a great temptation to bandits. The railway came to Chicago in 1852, and the new crime of rail theft

One dull afternoon in Reno in 1983, Eddie Blake decided to have a go at robbing a bank. "This is a hold-up," declared the note that he handed to the woman behind the counter, "put all the money into a bag and hand it over." Within seconds he was clutching the loot and running for it.

By the time he got home, the police were waiting outside his door to arrest him. He had scrawled the demand note on the back of one of his business cards. It contained his name, address and telephone number.

Clive Castro of Cooperville, Texas, did manage to get safely out of the bank that he had just robbed. He dived into the nearest passenger car, shouting "Drive off buster and make it snappy." The driver made it very snappy indeed. Castro had run into a patrol car which drove him straight to the nearest police station.

was soon costing the express companies and their customers enormous sums of money. In this vast country, Pinkerton often had to behave more like an Indian tracker than a policeman. In 1858, he was summoned to New Haven, where robbers had forced open the Adams Express car and prised open the safes with crow-bars, taking $70,000 in cash and jewellery. Near Stamford, Connecticut, Pinkerton found a bag containing $5,000, and knew he was on the right track. At Norwalk he heard of three men who had tried to hire a buggy, and tracked them down to a house where they had stayed overnight. When he learned that their host had been seen the next day on a train, carrying a heavy package that evidently made him nervous, he guessed that it contained the rest of the loot. He tracked the man to New York, but found that he had already left for Canada – but without the package. And under his questioning, the man's niece led him to the money and jewellery, hidden in the cellar. The gang was arrested, and Pinkerton completed the job by arresting the leader in Canada.

The Drysdale Bank Robbery

One early case from the Pinkerton archives is so incredible that it sounds like fiction. In 1855, a young bank teller named George Gordon was murdered late at night when working in his office; he was the nephew of the bank president. The bank vault was open, and $130,000 was missing. Gordon had been killed by a hammer blow dealt from the left. In the fireplace there were remains of burnt papers and clothing – the murderer had stayed on to burn his bloodstained coat. The only clues were two pieces of paper – a bloodstained page containing some pencilled figures – found under the body – and a partly burnt fragment of paper that had been twisted into a "spill" to light the fire. When Pinkerton unfolded this, he found that it was a note for $927.78, and that it was signed Alexander P. Drysdale, the county clerk, a man of unimpeachable reputation. The bloodstained page contained a subtraction sum – $1,252 minus $324.22 – the result being $927.78.

Pinkerton asked to see the bank balances of a number of

prominent local businessmen whom Gordon might have admitted to the bank after hours. Drysdale's account showed a
figure of $324.22. Now Pinkerton was able to reconstruct the
crime. Drysdale had come to the bank in the evening to request
a loan of $1,252. Gordon had agreed – but had subtracted from
this sum the amount already in Drysdale's account. Then he
had opened the vault. Overcome by sudden temptation, Drysdale had seized a hammer someone had left in the office and
killed his friend.

Pinkerton was certain that Drysdale was the killer, but how
to prove it? He began by finding an excuse to get Drysdale to
write something, and noted that he was left-handed, like the
killer. Next, he sent for three of his operatives from Chicago –
an older man, a woman, and a young man called Green. They
posed as visitors to the town, and began secretly investigating
Drysdale's affairs. Green, a good carpenter, found himself a job
in the local carpenter's shop, where all the old men gathered in
the evening to gossip. The older detective, who was calling

The most famous siege in criminal history began with a robbery
that went wrong.

On the freezing, windy night of 16 December 1910, a man who
lived next to a jeweller's shop in Houndsditch, East London,
heard the noise of hammering. Suspecting – correctly – that
robbers were trying to break through the wall into the jewellers,
he called the police. P.C. Piper knocked on the door of 11
Exchange Buildings and asked if the "missus" was there. A
foreigner told him she was out and he said he would call back.
Piper returned with several more policemen – all unarmed – and
knocked again. This time they were admitted, but as soon as they
were inside, shooting began. One policeman was killed outright,
two fatally injured, and four more wounded. Outside, a policeman
grabbed the gang leader, George Gardstein; another member of
the gang fired at the policeman, and hit Gardstein instead. They
hurried away, supporting Gardstein, who was bleeding to death.
Gardstein died that night at a nearby house – rented by a Russian
anarchist named Friz Svaars – at 59 Grove Street.

The doctor who had been called to attend Gardstein notified the
police, who found the body of Gardstein in the bed. Only one
member of the gang, a little hunchback named Sara Trassjonsky,
was still there, frantically burning papers. Her lover Peter Piatkow

himself Andrews, learned by chance one day that young Green bore a close resemblance to the dead George Gordon. And when Pinkerton learned of this, he formulated an incredible plan. Not far from Drysdale's home was a spot known as Rocky Creek, reputed to be haunted. "Andrews", pretending to be interested in a local plot of land, got Drysdale to take him through Rocky Creek at dusk, and as they rode among the trees, a ghostly figure walked across the path, its hair matted with blood. Drysdale shrieked; Andrews looked astonished and insisted that he could see nothing.

The woman operative had succeeded in getting herself invited into Drysdale's home as a guest of Mrs Drysdale, and she observed that her host was beginning to suffer nightmares and was prone to sleep-walking. Green, dressed as the ghost, kept up the pressure by occasionally flitting about outside the house when Drysdale was wandering around restlessly. Finally, Pinkerton appeared and arrested Drysdale, who protested his innocence. They took him to the

– who became known as Peter the Painter because he painted scenery for anarchist plays at a nearby club – had already escaped.

During the next month, a nationwide manhunt led to the arrest of eight gang members, including two women. On 2 January 1911, police received information that two more – Fritz Svaars and a man named Josef – were in the second floor room of Mrs Betsy Gershon at 100 Sidney Street. In fact, Mrs Gershon was a prisoner, and the men had taken her skirt and shoes to prevent her from going out. The police surrounded the house and evacuated the other floors. Early the next day they sent the landlady to go and ask Mrs Gershon to go and fetch a doctor, and the anarchists allowed her to go.

At dawn the police threw gravel at the window, and the anarchists opened fire. From the Tower of London the Scots Guards were sent, and the Home Secretary, Winston Churchill, arrived to watch the siege. The firing continued all morning. At one o'clock the house burst into flames, and the police refused to let firemen near it. One fireman was fatally injured as the house collapsed. The bodies of the two anarchists were found in the charred ruins, one shot in the head.

Peter the Painter was never caught, and is said to have died in America in 1914.

bank, and when the "ghost" appeared from behind the teller's counter, Drysdale fainted. When he recovered, he still continued to protest his innocence, and it began to look as if Pinkerton's bold strategy had failed. But when Drysdale was shown the two scraps of paper proving his involvement, he broke down and confessed. The stolen money was found hidden in a creek near his home.

The Reno Gang

But most of Pinkerton's early cases demanded persistence and courage rather than this kind of ingenuity. His most remarkable feat of the 1860s was undoubtedly his break-up of the Reno gang, America's first gang of organized outlaws. The five brothers – Frank, John, Simeon, Clinton, and William – were the sons of an Indiana farmer who lived at Seymour, Indiana. John left home at sixteen – in 1855 – and spent some time wandering around Mississippi, working on steamboats and learning to make a living by his wits. Back home, he propounded a scheme of amazing simplicity. The nearby small town of Rockford was prosperous and virtually unprotected. A series of arson attacks so terrified the inhabitants that they began moving elsewhere. Then the Renos bought most of Rockford at bargain prices.

During the Civil War, the Reno brothers served in the army; but most of them soon deserted. During the war, the bloodthirsty southerner William Clarke Quantrill led a band of guerrillas who were little more than robbers and murderers – it included Jesse James, "Bloody Bill" Anderson, and Cole Younger – and although most of the gang was wiped out in 1865, James and Cole Younger went on to become wandering outlaws. Meanwhile, back in Seymour, the Reno brothers formed their own outlaw gang, specializing in robbing county treasury offices. And in 1866, they invented a new crime – holding up trains. They boarded the wood-burning Ohio and Mississippi railroad coach as ordinary passengers at Seymour, then strolled down to the Adams Express car, forced the door, and held up the messenger at gunpoint. They pulled the communication cord, stopping the train, and rolled the safe off it. But they were still trying to burst it open in the woods when a posse drove them to abandon it. Nevertheless, John Reno had succeeded in seizing $10,000 in notes.

Pinkerton was asked to take on the case. The bandits had worn masks, but he had no doubt they were the Renos. A few weeks later, a new saloon was opened in Seymour – the amiable, round-faced man who ran it was really a Pinkerton operative called Dick Winscott – and the Renos soon became customers. Winscott even succeeded in persuading the brothers to allow him to take a group photograph – possibly the first time photography was used in crime detection. (Pinkerton had copies made and circulated.)

Seymour was an armed camp run by outlaws, and there was no chance of arresting the Renos on the spot. Allan Pinkerton enlisted the aid of Dick Winscott. The Renos were being sought for a bank robbery in Gallatin, Missouri, and had been identified by witnesses through their photographs. One afternoon soon after, the train stopped in Seymour, and Allan Pinkerton looked cautiously out of the window. On the platform he recognized the jovial figure of Dick Winscott, talking to John

In 1944, New York City police were baffled by a series of "phantom" bank robberies. The thieves were clearly expert safe crackers - using an oxy-acetylene torch to surgically destroy the lock mechanisms inside safe doors - but they also seemed to be able to pass through securely fastened bank doors without picking the locks.

Uncertain how to proceed, detectives were reduced to staking out random banks in the hope of seeing something suspicious. They struck it lucky, spotting two men standing by a bank door, seeming to discuss the bank's layout. A full-time tail was placed on the pair, Stanley Patrek and Joseph Stepka, and they were eventually caught red handed, walking away from a bank carrying a oxy-acetylene torch and $15,000.

The mystery of their method of entry and exit was cleared-up when police found a lock cylinder in Patrek's workshop. The pair had not been planning a heist when the police first saw them by a bank door; Stepka was removing a small screw from the lock. This allowed them, when they returned at night, to replace the original lock cylinder with their own, to which they obviously had a key. When they left they simply reversed the process and replaced the securing screw.

Reno. Six muscular men, accompanied by a sheriff from
Cincinnati – another city that held warrants for the Renos –
strolled casually off the train, surrounded John Reno, and
hustled him aboard. Reno bellowed for help, but although
the other Reno brothers commandeered another train and
pursued the kidnappers, John Reno was handed over to the
Gallatin authorities and sentenced to twenty-five years in jail.

In February 1868, Frank Reno – now the gang leader – led a
raid on the Harrison County treasury at Magnolia, Iowa, which
netted $14,000. Using his skills as a tracker, Pinkerton found
them hiding in the home of a pillar of the Methodist church in
Council Bluffs, and arrested them in a sudden raid. But the jail
in Council Bluffs was not strong enough to hold them, and
when the sheriff arrived the next morning he found the cells
empty and a chalked inscription: "April Fool" – the date being
1 April 1868.

Local citizens were becoming enraged at the impunity the
gang seemed to enjoy. The Reno brothers were not the kind of
jolly outlaws who became folk heroes; they were bullies and
killers. In desperation, some of the bolder Seymour residents
formed a Vigilance Committee. The Renos heard the rumours,
and made bloodthirsty threats.

After a train robbery at Marshfield, Indiana, which netted the
gang $96,000, Pinkerton decided they had to be caught by
cunning. He circulated rumours that $100,000 in gold was to be
shipped via Seymour. The train's engineer pretended to agree
to co-operate with the gang and tipped off Pinkerton exactly
where the robbery would take place. And as the outlaws
stopped the train and burst open the Express car, they were
met by a volley of shots from Pinkerton's men. Most of the gang
escaped, but the next day, three of them were captured in a
thicket and arrested. But one dark night a few weeks later, the
train on which they were being sent to their trial was stopped
by men waving red lanterns; the three bandits were dragged off
the train and lynched. A few weeks later, another three bandits
who had been tracked down by Pinkerton were intercepted on
their way to jail by a mob and lynched. The Reno gang left in
Seymour began to fight back; members of the Vigilance Committee had rocks thrown through their windows; there were
night raids, beatings, and mutilations. When Simeon and
William Reno were arrested by Pinkerton detectives in India-
napolis, Vigilance Committee members received messages: "If
the Renos are lynched, you die." The Vigilance Committee

decided that if the Renos were not lynched, things would remain as bad as ever. The authorities decided to transfer the two Renos to the more secure New Albany jail. On 6 September 1868, there was a determined attempt by vigilantes to break into the Lexington jail, but the Renos had already been moved. They were joined in New Albany by their brother Frank, who had been arrested in Canada, together with a gang member named Charles Anderson. But on 11 December vigilantes surrounded the jail and burst their way in with a battering ram. The sheriff was beaten unconscious, and his keys taken. Then the Reno brothers and Anderson were dragged from their cells and lynched. As the vigilantes dispersed, prisoners watched from their cells and saw Simeon gasping for breath on the end of his rope; it took half an hour before he ceased to struggle.

The Vigilance Committee issued a notice, naming other members of the gang still in Seymour – including brother Clinton – and declaring that if they wished to remain as honest citizens, they would be welcome; otherwise they would meet the fate of the others. The gang accepted the ultimatum sullenly, and the outlaws ceased to be a power in Indiana.

Jesse James

Pinkerton was altogether less successful in his attempts to catch Jesse James. Like the Reno brothers, Jesse and his brother Frank came back from the Civil War, in which they fought for the South, wondering whether the methods of Quantrill's guerrillas could not be applied with equal success in peacetime. On 13 February 1866, ten men rode into Liberty, Missouri, and robbed the bank; on their way out of town, one of them shot down an unarmed student on his way to college, then, whooping and firing pistols, the gang rode out of town. It was the first of many pointless murders committed by the gang led by this modern "Robin Hood". In December 1869, the James gang robbed the same bank in Gallatin, Missouri, that the Reno brothers had robbed two years earlier, and James shot the manager in cold blood.

The Pinkertons began trailing the James gang at about this time, but had no success. In February 1874, a Pinkerton operative, John W. Whicher, succeeded in infiltrating the gang, but was recognized and murdered. On 6 January 1875, the Pinkertons received a tip-off that Jesse was visiting his mother, Mrs Zerelda Samuel; they surrounded the house and tossed in a "smoke bomb". It killed James's eight-year-old half-brother, and blew off his mother's arm. The incident brought much sympathy for the James brothers and indignant criticism of the brutality of Pinkerton. Jesse James was so angry that he spent four months in Chicago trying to get Pinkerton alone so he could kill him; he was unsuccessful.

On 7 August 1876, an attempt to rob the bank in Northfield,

Edward "Ned" Kelly is remembered as an outlaw in the same tradition as Robin Hood, a national hero who stole as a protest against authority. He was the son of a man transported to Tasmania from Belfast in 1841, and he himself began his criminal career early. He stole cattle and horses, and while still in his mid-teens he served a three year prison sentence.

His criminal career really took flight when in April 1878, he wounded a police officer who had come to the family home in Victoria to arrest his brother, also on a charge of rustling. As a result, the warrant was extended to cover the both of them and they took to the bush to hide out and plan. While they were away, the remaining portion of their family were arrested, tried and imprisoned for theft and resisting.

The two Kellys joined up with two other criminals, Steve Hart and Joe Byrne, and as the Kelly Gang, terrorized the local area, avoiding capture through a network of sympathizers and informants that hated the police. The gang's robbery technique often involved rounding up most of the inhabitants of a town and holding them prisoner in the local hotel while they stole anything worthwhile that they could find. The gang had no reservations about killing any policemen that got near them.

Even after the police had arrested many sympathizers under the Apprehension of Felons Act, the gang continued to evade them. The officers did not dare arrest any women, for fear of the public outcry that this would cause, yet a large proportion of the gang's "Bush telegraph" consisted of female sympathizers and

Minnesota, went disastrously wrong; the citizens all rushed outdoors with guns, and most of the bandits were either killed or wounded; James's cousin Cole Younger and his brother Bob were captured soon after and sentenced to life imprisonment. James formed a second gang, but it never met with the same success as the earlier one. On 7 August 1881, the gang committed its last train robbery, netting only $1,500. Harassment by the Pinkertons was breaking their nerve. On 3 April 1882, Jesse James was planning another robbery with two new gang members, Bob and Charlie Ford, when Bob Ford pulled out his gun and shot James in the back. He had agreed to deliver Jesse James to the state governor for reward money and amnesty. The murder of Jesse James – at the age of 34 – made

thus remained intact. As the robberies continued the police were heavily criticized in all quarters.

Meanwhile the Kelly gang were planning an ambush in which they hoped to kill many officers. A former accomplice called Sherritt was being held under police protection. As a means to attract the police, Joe Byrne shot Sherritt dead, while the rest of the gang forced two railwaymen to sabotage the track outside town. The plan was to let the train carrying the officers de-rail, and then kill them while they were still confused and wounded. As usual the gang held the local population in a hotel, but a schoolteacher succeeded in evading them and warning the police. Soon they arrived in town by different means and surrounded the hotel.

Realizing that the situation was hopeless, Dan Kelly and Steve Hart took poison and died. Joe Byrne was shot dead by the police. Ned Kelly, determined to escape the police that he hated so much, made a break for the bush and, although wounded, succeeded in making a makeshift suit of armour out of plough mouldboards. Wearing this as protection, Kelly tried to break through the police line. He was brought down by bullet wounds to his legs, but not until he had withstood twenty-five hits on the armour.

Kelly was tried in Melbourne in 1880, and was hanged on November 11. The repeated failures of the police prompted an inquiry by the Royal Commission. Kelly still remains a hero for anti-authoritarians everywhere; at his trial he was described as a quiet, self-possessed man with a fanatical hatred of the police.

him more of a folk hero than ever, and his brother Frank was acquitted several times of crimes he had obviously committed (he died of old age in 1915). Allan Pinkerton died two years after Jesse James, at the age of sixty-five but the agency continued with unabated success under sons and grandsons.

The Dalton Gang

One of the great early classics of American crime is Thomas S. Duke's *Celebrated Criminal Cases of America*, published in 1910. Duke was a captain in the San Francisco Police Force, and his style is often rough and ready; nevertheless, it has a dramatic feeling of immediacy. Here is Duke's account of the Dalton gang.

After the extermination of the James–Younger gang, the Dalton brothers stepped in and occupied the place once filled by them in the ranks of bloodthirsty criminals. In the Dalton family were six boys, named Ben, Frank, Grattan, William, Robert and Emmet.

In April, 1889, the Territory of Oklahoma was thrown open. For weeks previous to that time, thousands of people were camped along the frontier so as to be located in the most advantageous position to rush in at the appointed time and stake claims on the most valuable land, which they afterwards purchased from the Government for less than two dollars per acre.

For many months after the rush, lawlessness reigned supreme in this Territory. Bob Dalton was performing the duties of a Deputy United States Marshal at this time, but he began to associate with the outlaws and finally became a leader among them. Emmet and Grattan joined the gang, but in 1890 the Territory became "too warm" for the Daltons, so they went to California, where their brother Bill had rented a ranch in Tulare County.

At 7:50 pm, January 6, 1891, train No. 17 left Alila, Cal., for Bakersfield, but had scarcely gone one mile on its journey when Engineer Thorn and Fireman Radliff were confronted by two masked men who stood on the tender of the engine. The engineer was ordered to stop the train and the frowning muzzle of a pistol placed against his temple caused an immediate compliance with the command.

The engineer and fireman were then ordered to accompany the robbers to the express car. The express messenger, suspecting what had happened, put out the lights in his car and lay on the floor. He was ordered to open the door, but his reply was a shot from his revolver which was followed by a fusillade, during which Fireman Radliff was mortally wounded. The desperadoes then gave up the struggle and fled. A pursuit was at once begun but all trace of them was lost until 12 March. On this date Sheriff O'Neil of Paso Robles arrested William Dalton on the strength of evidence he had gathered, and upon being interrogated Dalton made some damaging admissions, which led to the arrest of his brother Grattan a few days later.

Both were taken to Visalia and charged with this crime, but William was eventually acquitted. On 7 July Grattan was convicted, after having tried to throw the entire blame on his brothers, Robert and Emmet, who were still at large. His sentence was continued until 6 October, but on Sunday night, September 26, he in some mysterious manner obtained possession of the keys to the prison kitchen and cell door, and in company with one William Smith, a convicted burglar, and W.R. Beck, a notorious character, escaped.

Services were being conducted in a church nearby, and the team belonging to George McKinley, one of the worshippers, stood awaiting him, but the three desperadoes took possession of it and made good their escape.

On December 24, Sheriff Hensly of Fresno met Grattan Dalton in the mountains, and after an exchange of several shots the bandit again escaped. He then joined Emmet and Bob in the Oklahoma reservation.

Deputy United States Marshal Ransom Payne incurred the displeasure of this gang, because he had the "audacity" to attempt to capture them. Bob and Emmet Dalton and one Charlie Bryant learned that this officer would leave Wichita, Okla. Ter., on the evening of May 9, 1891, for his home in Guthrie, so they decided to rob this train and kill the officer. They went to a little station called Wharton and ordered the stationkeeper to signal the train to stop. When the train came to a standstill, one bandit took charge of the engineer and fireman, and the remaining two went through the train inquiring for Payne. That official being alone and not knowing the number of bandits in the party, and realizing that he would probably be killed if the Daltons were in the gang and discovered him, decided to evade them and left the train and hid in the brush near the track.

Failing to locate Payne, the two desperadoes proceeded to the express car, where they obtained about $1,500. The bandits then made their escape on horses, and when the train left Payne came out of hiding and ran to the stationhouse, where he found the stationkeeper bound and gagged. The next day a posse was organized and in August, 1891, Bryant was arrested. One of the posse named Edward Short took charge of him, while the remainder continued in pursuit of the Daltons. Short boarded the train with his prisoner, and when the train stopped at a little station he left Bryant, who was handcuffed, in the charge of Wells-Fargo's agent, to whom he loaned a revolver. The agent, believing the prisoner was asleep, laid the pistol down and continued with his work. Just then Bryant jumped up, seized the weapon and attempted to escape. Short saw him leave the car and instantly drew another revolver. A duel followed with the result that both men were killed.

The Dalton gang remained in seclusion until the night of June 2, 1892, when Bob, Grattan and Emmet Dalton, assisted by three or four others, held up the Atchison, Topeka and Santa Fe train at Red Rock Station, Oklahoma. As the passenger train stopped at this station only when signalled to do so, the stationkeeper was ordered to display the necessary signal. When the train stopped the engineer was overpowered by two robbers and the remainder of the gang proceeded to the express car, where $1,800 was obtained, after which they escaped in the darkness.

In the early part of the following July, the territorial police and railroad officials learned that the Dalton gang were rendezvoused near the Missouri, Kansas and Texas Railroad in Oklahoma, and as they had profited little financially from their recent raids it was suspected that one of the trains on this road would soon be attacked. It was therefore decided to put a heavily armed posse on each train. Thus prepared, the authorities rather welcomed an attack, feeling confident that it would mean the extermination of the gang.

On the evening of July 15, 1892, the three Daltons, reinforced by five others, rode up to Adair station in Indian Territory and after robbing the agent they ordered him to signal the train to stop. Conductor George Scales and Engineer Ewing were immediately taken into custody, and the party then went to the express car which was in charge of Messenger George Williams, who reluctantly opened the safe and several thousand dollars were stolen.

The "guards," who were lounging in the smoker instead of being with the messenger, did not appear very anxious to perform their duty, although some of them ventured out and opened fire in a half-hearted way. A stray bullet struck and mortally wounded a Dr W. Goff, who was at the time in a nearby drug store. Two of the guards named Kinney and La Flore were also shot, but their wounds were superficial. During the fusillade, a wagon was driven up to the train, the bags of money were thrown in and the bandits again escaped.

The next raid attempted by these bandits occurred at their old home in Coffeyvile, Kansas, on October 5, 1892. The gang on this fatal day consisted of Bob, Grattan and Emmet Dalton, Dick Broadwell and Bill Powers. They rode into town about 9:30 am, and were recognized by a merchant named Alexander McKenna, who quickly but quietly rushed about notifying everyone he met.

The five bandits proceeded to C.M. Condon's bank and Grattan Dalton, Powers and Broadwell entered the bank, where they found President Charles Carpenter and Cashier Charles Ball.

As soon as the three men entered this bank, Bob and Emmet Dalton hastened to the First National Bank across the street, as it was planned to rob both institutions simultaneously. In each bank the bandits were informed that the time lock would not be off for several minutes and the robbers decided to wait.

In the meantime the news of the movements of the gang had spread through the town like wildfire, and the gunsmiths were loaning weapons and ammunition to all who desired them. As a result both banks were soon surrounded by determined men, all heavily armed, and the bullets began to fly through the windows of the bank.

When the vault was opened at the First National, Cashier Thomas Ayers handed out the money, amounting to over $20,000. Bob and Emmet Dalton put this in a sack and escaped out of the back entrance. They ran in the direction of Condon's Bank, but when they observed the crowd of armed men in front of that institution, they began firing, with the result that a young clerk named Lucius Baldwin was instantly killed.

In the general battle that followed, two shoemakers, named

George Cubine and Charles Brown, were killed by Bob Dalton
when he saw them attempting to shoot him. Immediately after
killing these men, Bob saw Cashier Ayers of the bank with his
rifle raised, and Dalton shot him in the head, inflicting a serious
but not fatal wound.

At this time the three robbers in Condon's Bank rushed out
into the shower of bullets with about $3,000, and joining Bob
and Emmet Dalton, they ran to their horses, but did not have an
opportunity to mount.

John Kloehr, a stableman, and City Marshal Charles Connelly, both armed with rifles, then joined in the battle. Grat
Dalton killed Connelly and almost immediately afterwards
Kloehr killed Bob Dalton. Bandit Powers was the next to be
killed and Grattan Dalton was then killed by Kloehr.

All of the bandits having been killed except Broadwell and
Emmet Dalton, these two, realizing the great odds against
them, mounted their horses and attempted to escape. They
had only gone a short distance, however, when Emmet
wheeled about and in the face of a heavy fire, returned to
the body of his brother Bob, and as he was in the act of lifting
the body with the intention of carrying it away on his horse, a
load of buckshot was poured into his back and he fell unconscious.

Broadwell was fatally wounded as he attempted to escape
and his body was found a short distance from town. Several
horses were also killed and many citizens wounded.

Emmet Dalton finally recovered from what were diagnosed
as necessarily fatal wounds, and he was sentenced to serve the
remainder of his life at the State Prison at Lansing, but
Governor Hock pardoned him in January, 1907.

After the tragic death of his brothers, Bill Dalton reorganized
the gang and operations were resumed in Oklahoma Territory.
Their rendezvous was in the extreme eastern part of the
Cherokee strip, but considerable amount of their time was
spent in a little village called Ingalls. As they purchased their
provisions, ammunition and whisky in this village, they were
shielded by those who profited from their trade.

On September 1, 1893, Bill Dalton, Bill Doolin, Arkansas
Tom, George Newton and Tulca Jack were drinking at the bar
in the village hotel when the place was surrounded by a posse
consisting of ex-Sheriff Hixon, Deputy Marshals Thomas Houston, Lafe Hadley, Dick Speed and several other officials and
civilians. The outlaws ran out of the place and at the beginning

of the firing Deputy Speed was killed. Hadley killed Dalton's horse and the bandit fell and laid motionless on the ground. Hadley, believing him to be dead, approached, but as he drew near Dalton jumped up and shot the deputy in the head, killing him instantly. The bandit then mounted the murdered officer's horse, and although severely wounded, he escaped.

During the battle Deputy Houston and a clerk named Simmons were also killed, and S.W. Ransom, N.S. Murray and a twelve-year-old boy named Briggs were seriously wounded. All of the bandits escaped with the exception of Arkansas Tom, who was barricaded in the hotel and who subsequently surrendered on the condition that he would be protected from the mob. The next day it was ascertained that none of the bandits escaped without wounds.

The last raid committed by the Dalton gang occurred at the First National Bank at Longview, Texas, at 3 pm, May 23, 1894. At this time two roughly dressed men entered the bank and presented a note to President Clemmons, which read as follows:

"Home, May 23rd.
"This will introduce you to Charles Spreckelmeyers, who wants some money and is going to have it.   B. and F."

When Mr Clemmons read the note and looked up, he was covered by a rifle in the hands of one bandit while the other went behind the counter and secured $2000.00 in ten-dollar bills and nine twenty-dollar bills. City Marshal Muckley immediately learned of the raid and hurriedly gathered a posse who gave the robbers a hot battle. One of the bandits, Geo. Bennett, alias Jim Wallace, was killed as was also George Buckingham of the posse. Marshal Muckley and J.W. McQueen, a saloon-keeper, received serious wounds.

On June 7, 1894, a suspicious looking character, giving the name of Wall, came into the town of Ardmore, I.T., with two women who also acted quite mysteriously. They purchased about $200.00 worth of provisions and then called at the express office. The attention of the authorities was attracted by the peculiar actions of the trio, and while they made many conflicting statements, the information was elicited that they were living near a place called Elk. Sheriff Hart immediately organized a posse as he believed the provisions were purchased for some persons who feared to come to town, and as the Dalton gang was uppermost in his mind, he concluded that these three persons were connected with the gang. They were held prisoners and at 8 am the next morning the house where it was suspected that Dalton was hiding was surrounded.

Dalton came to one of the windows and seeing some of the posse he jumped from a window on the opposite side of the building and started to run.

Sheriff Hart called on him to halt, but as he ignored the command, one shot was fired from the sheriff's rifle and Dalton dropped dead without uttering a word.

The house was then searched and conclusive evidence was obtained, not only as to Dalton's identity, but also that he participated in the Longview bank robbery. The officials then returned to Ardmore and when the mysterious trio were informed of the death of Dalton, one of the women became hysterical and said she was Dalton's wife and that they were married at her home in Merced, California, in 1888.

The D'Autremont Brothers

In the mid-1920s, the most famous American sleuth was a man named Edward Oscar Heinrich, who became known as "the Edison of Crime Detection". Before he became Professor of Criminology at the Berkeley Campus of the University of California, Heinrich had been the city chemist in Tacoma, Washington.

The case that brought him celebrity began on 11 October 1923, when a train bound from Oregon to San Francisco was held up by bandits in the Siskiyou Mountains. The train was crawling through a tunnel when two men dropped off the roof of the engine tender and pointed guns at the engineer and fireman; they were made to stop the train and then marched up a slope at gunpoint and made to stand with raised hands. A third man placed a large package beside the mail car – which was half-way out of the tunnel – and ran. A moment later, there was a violent explosion, which blasted open the car and set it on fire. Then the engineer and fireman were ordered to pull the rest of the train out of the tunnel. This proved to be impossible. The bandits were becoming increasingly panicky, and when the brakeman ran out of the tunnel to see what was happening, one of them raised a shotgun and shot him dead. Then the engineer and fireman were deliberately executed. And the bandits, who realized that they were not going to get into the blazing mail car, disappeared. A mail clerk named Edwin Daugherty was burned to death.

Police from Ashland, Oregon, found a detonating device with batteries near the tunnel. Nearby there was a revolver, a pair of shoes, and a pair of greasy denim overalls.

Posses galloped off in all directions looking for the robbers. Meanwhile, the sheriff examining the detonator wondered whether its batteries might not have come from a nearby garage. He hurried there, and arrested the mechanic he found working in a pair of greasy overalls that looked very similar to those found near the detonator. But the mechanic maintained his innocence, and the police were unable to find the slightest shred of evidence to link him with the crime.

Edward O. Heinrich was obviously the man to approach, and the police sent him the overalls found at the scene of the crime. Within two days he told them over the telephone: "You are holding the wrong man. The grime on these overalls is not car grease. It is fir pitch. In the pocket I found particles of Douglas fir needles. The man who wore these overalls is a left-handed lumberjack. He is between twenty-one and twenty-five years of age, about five feet ten inches tall, and he weighs about 165 lb. His hair is medium light brown, his hands and feet are small, and he is a man of fastidious habits."

Later, Heinrich explained how he had made these deductions. The fir chips were in the right-hand pocket, which meant that the man stood with his right side towards the tree as he was chopping it down; a right-handed man stands with his left side to the tree. Besides, the left-handed pockets were more used than the right, and the overalls were buttoned on the left. The overall bottoms had been folded to fit into boots, and the position of the suspender buckles indicated the height and build of the wearer. A single hair adhering to a button told Heinrich that the man was white – Negro hair or Indian hair is quite different. Nail clippings that had been caught in a front pocket had been cut with a precision that indicated a man of fastidious habits. The size of the shoes had indicated a man with small feet, and it followed that his hands were also small.

Heinrich had found another clue. In the pencil pocket of the overalls he had found a scrap of folded paper that the police had missed. It was a receipt for a registered letter bearing a code number. The Post Office was able to tell the police that it had been issued in Eugene, Oregon, as a receipt for $50 sent by a man called Roy D'Autremont to Ray D'Autremont in Lakewood, New Mexico.

It was easy to locate Paul D'Autremont, the elderly father of the brothers, in Eugene. He told them that his three sons – the twins Roy and Ray, and their brother Hugh – had been missing since the day of the hold-up. And Roy was a left-handed lumberjack.

Heinrich's examination of the gun found near the detonator left no doubt that the D'Autremont brothers were the bandits. A hidden number led the police to the store in Seattle where it had been purchased by a man calling himself William Elliott. Heinrich, who was also a handwriting expert, was able to state that Elliott's handwriting was that of Roy D'Autremont.

Even the reward of $15,000 offered by the railway company failed to produce information of the brothers' whereabouts. But in March 1927, an army sergeant saw a "Wanted" poster, and thought that Hugh D'Autremont resembled a private he had known in the Philippines. Hugh D'Autremont was arrested in Manila. A month later, Roy and Ray were recognized at the steel mill in Steubenville, Ohio, where they were working. All three brothers were sentenced to life imprisonment.

• chapter three •

VICTORIAN VILLAINIES

The Great Gold-Dust Robbery

Until the end of the eighteenth century, most robbers were clumsy amateurs – footpads, highwaymen and burglars who lived from day to day, and usually ended on the gallows before they reached their thirties. But the Industrial Revolution created new wealth, and brought a new class of criminal: the bold planner who was willing to risk ten years in jail for an ambitious coup that might make him wealthy for life. And the simplest way to go about it was to find some underpaid clerk or warehouseman, and bribe him to take part – what we now call an "inside job".

The first of the great "inside jobs" happened in London Docks in 1839.

On 25 March 1839, two boxes of gold dust addressed to Hartley and Co. arrived at St Katherine's Dock from Brazil. They had just been forwarded from Falmouth by a shipper called Carne and Co. and the contents were worth £4,600. That same morning, Hartley and Co. received a letter from Carne and Co. telling them that the gold-dust was about to arrive, and that it would be collected by a representative of the agents of the Brazilian Mining Company.

Early that afternoon, the man they were expecting arrived to collect the boxes, and produced documents that described them in detail. A clerk named Lewin Caspar, who was in charge of the boxes, was heard to mutter that he hoped the papers were genuine. But he handed over the boxes, and the man drove off in a cab. Half an hour later, his employers were thrown into panic when another man arrived from the agents, and demanded the boxes, producing another set of obviously genuine documents. It seemed that Lewin Caspar had been right, and the first man was an impostor.

For Hartley and Co. it was a serious blow – they would have to reimburse the £4,600, enough to threaten them with bankruptcy. The London police force had only been in existence for ten years, and was not noted for its efficiency. Nevertheless, two detectives named Lea and Roe were given the task of tracking down the robber.

They began by tracing the horse-drawn cab in which he had escaped. The driver said he had been paid off in Wood Street, in the City, and that the man with the two boxes had then hired another cab and driven off towards Holborn. The second cabbie was finally traced, and told them that he had driven the man to a house in New Street. But the detectives arrived too late; the man had already left and moved to lodgings in Goodman's Fields. Now several days behind him, the detectives arrived to find that he had left this lodging too, this time without leaving an address. But, to their relief, he proved to be known to his landlord in Goodman's Fields. He was a married man named Henry Moss, and he worked as a foreman to a watchmaker in Goodman's Fields. Mrs Moss's female servant had been left behind, and told the detectives that on the morning of the robbery, Moss had left home wearing his best clothes, which was unusual. He came back to his New Street lodging with two large boxes. The next morning, the servant had noticed burnt fragments of these boxes in the grate.

The detectives picked up another important piece of information. Before the robbery, Henry Moss had been seeing a great deal of a Jewish watchmaker called Ellis Caspar, who had once been his employer. And Ellis Caspar was the father of Lewin Caspar, the clerk who had handed over the boxes of gold dust. This was too much of a coincidence, and both Caspars were promptly arrested.

While they were still searching for Henry Moss, the police decided that the next step was to find out what might have happened to the gold. A check among London's bullion dealers revealed that Bull and Co. of Cheapside had recently bought a large quantity of gold bars from a man called Henry Solomon. Solomon, a gold refiner, admitted that he had sold gold bars worth £1,200 to the bullion dealer, but claimed he had made them from melting down gold snuff-boxes. The police did not believe him, and when they told him so, Mr Solomon became sullen and uncooperative. These were the days when London was full of the kind of anti-semitism reflected in Dickens' Fagin – *Oliver Twist* came out the same year – and the *New Newgate Calendar* remarks that the gold-dust robbers "were of the Jewish persuasion, and the proverbial cunning and habits of cheating of these people were exemplified throughout the enquiry". There can be no doubt Mr Solomon's civil rights were violated in the course of his interrogation. Although the evidence against him was non-existent, he appeared before the magistrates, together with the Caspars, charged with receiving the gold dust.

Meanwhile, Henry Moss, who was hiding out in Peckham, had heard of the arrest of the Caspars. It also emerged later that he suspected the Caspars of intending to cheat him. So Moss decided to give himself up and turn police informer. His story was that he had acted in complete innocence. Ellis Caspar had approached him a year ago, and told him that his son Lewin now had a job as a clerk at a shipping agents. He wanted Moss to do him a small favour – take some papers, and go and collect some boxes from Hartley and Co. Moss was assured that he was doing nothing illegal, and agreed. But on this first occasion, something had gone amiss – Caspar said that a ship had failed to arrive. He was given ten shillings, and told they might need his help on some future occasion.

The occasion came a year later, when Henry Moss was finally given the necessary papers, and told to collect two boxes from Lewin Caspar at Hartley and Co. He followed his instructions, and took the boxes back to his lodgings in a cab. When he got there, he found Ellis Caspar waiting in a state of jitters. The police were on the trail, said Mr Caspar, and Moss would have to move the next morning. After this, the boxes were opened, and proved to contain a number of tins. Then the Mosses were told to burn the boxes.

Obviously, things had gone wrong. The whole swindle depended upon Lewin Caspar remaining unsuspected. The moment the detectives learned that the robber was a friend of Lewin's father, "the game was up".

Two more accomplices were arrested: a go-between called

Emanuel Moses, and his daughter Alice Abrahams, who had sold the gold-dust to Solomons. At the trial, it emerged that there was little honour among thieves: everybody was apparently out to swindle everybody else. Henry Moss had made a determined attempt to keep all the gold for himself, but was forced to hand it over to Moses and his daughter. They sold it to Solomons, who agreed to pay £3,700, but gave an IOU for £1,800 of this, which he then refused to pay. Alice Abrahams cheated her own father of £13 which she got for the gold dust shaken out of the bottom of the empty bags; her father cheated the Caspars by claiming he only received £2,000 for the gold. The Caspars intended to cheat Henry Moss by fobbing him off with an absurdly small part of the proceeds. And Moss – indignant when he learned that he was being cheated – decided to go to the police and give evidence against his

---

Around mid-1911, Paris was full of anarchists who declared that the corrupt social system could only be overthrown by violence. Among these was Jules Joseph Bonnot, the son of a poor family who had educated himself, and who at one time had been a racing driver. In Paris anarchist clubs Bonnot recruited a group of fifteen idealistic young men who agreed to follow him to the death. They obtained guns by raiding a gun shop, and stole a large, fast car from a garage. On 21 December 1911, Bonnot and four followers waylaid a bank messenger with typical brutality and violence, shooting him first in the chest, then in the throat, and firing shots over the heads of the crowd as they drove off. Their haul proved to be small, consisting mostly of useless securities. (Incredibly, the bank messenger recovered.)

When they knocked down a woman as they were driving a stolen car, they drove off at top speed; a policeman who tried to intercept them was shot to death.

In March 1912 they committed another typically brutal crime. They needed a car, so they waylaid the Marquis de Rouge, who was driving out of Paris in a new sports car at six in the morning. Rouge and the chauffeur were both shot dead and dumped in a ditch; the gangsters then drove to a bank in Chantilly, and while Bonnot waited with the engine running, the others went into the bank and fired indiscriminately, killing one man and seriously wounding two more. As they rushed out with their haul, Bonnot was trying to hold an angry crowd at bay by firing over their heads.

accomplices. (By this time, Moss had admitted that he knew he was involved in a crime from the beginning.) What seems certain is that if the Caspars had not tried to cheat Moss, he would never have gone to the police, and they would have gone free for lack of evidence.

Ellis Caspar and Emanuel Moses received fourteen years each, Lewin Caspar was transported for seven years, and Alice Abrahams received only four months, on the grounds that she had been influenced by her father. Henry Moss was sentenced to a day in prison.

This complicated affair – with its tale of mutual plunder – set all London laughing. No one noticed that something highly significant had happened: that a clerk in a position of trust had planned to become a wealthy man overnight with a brilliant and cunning scheme. If it had not been for the determination of

While they were driving away, a bullet grazed the arm of Francois Callemin; in a rage, he began shooting at random, luckily hitting no one. This robbery brought the gang its largest haul so far.

The Bonnot gang was now being hunted by the whole French police force, and the public clamoured for their arrest. More robberies followed, and the gang lived up to its reputation for brutal and unnecessary killings. One of them, Pierre Garnier – who had shot the bank messenger – wrote the police a defiant letter enclosing his fingerprints, and declaring: "I know you will get me eventually because you have force on your side, but I shall make you pay dearly for my life."

Other anarchists were shocked by all this violence, and the police began to receive tip-offs. Inspector Jouin arrested one gang member in March 1913, and another soon after. But Jouin himself was killed when he surprised Bonnot in a hideout in Ivry; Bonnot shot his way out, wounding another policeman.

Finally, Bonnot's hiding place at Choisy-le-Roi was surrounded after a tip-off from another hostile anarchist who felt that Bonnot was giving the cause a bad name. Dubois, the man who was sheltering Bonnot, was shot dead as he fired at the police while trying to escape on a motor bike. After six hours of shooting, the police stormed the house, and found Bonnot bleeding to death; he had time to shout "Bastards" as he lapsed into a coma.

Other gang members were arrested one by one, and many – including Callemin and Garnier – ended on the guillotine.

everyone involved to swindle everyone else, he might have succeeded. The gold-dust case is the first of the robberies that are usually preceded by the epithet "great".

The Great Bullion Robbery

It has to be admitted that the great gold-dust robbery lacks the stuff of high drama. This is certainly not true of the great gold bullion robbery that took place sixteen years later.

In fact, the story begins in 1848, when a remarkable theft occurred on the British railway; when a strong-box arrived by train in Bristol, the box was found forced open, and £1,500 in gold was missing. The case was never solved. But it attracted the attention – and admiration – of a suave gentleman forger named Edgar Agar. He knew that large quantities of gold bullion were sent by train, and that, with careful planning, he might make enough money to last him the rest of his life.

Agar was introduced to an unimpressive little clerk named William Pierce, who had sandy hair and a shifty look; Pierce worked for the South-Eastern Railway as a ticket printer, and he was a man of expensive tastes who never had the money to pay for them. So when Agar disclosed his interest in the gold shipments, Pierce showed himself eager to cooperate. He set out to learn all he could about the way the gold was sent, and at what point it might be vulnerable.

What Pierce learned was not encouraging. Large quantities of gold were often sent from London to Paris. But there were *two* keys to the heavy safe, and one was kept in London and the other in Folkestone. That obviously presented enormous difficulties to the most enterprising thief. Agar decided that forgery was easier, and dropped the idea.

In 1850, the shifty little clerk was discharged on suspicion of theft, which was probably justified. Now he was more anxious than ever to take part in the scheme. Accordingly he made the acquaintance of the station master at Margate, William George Tester, and persuaded him to help. This was in 1854, six years after Agar had dreamed up the plan. With Tester's help, it should be possible, he thought, to get a duplicate of both keys.

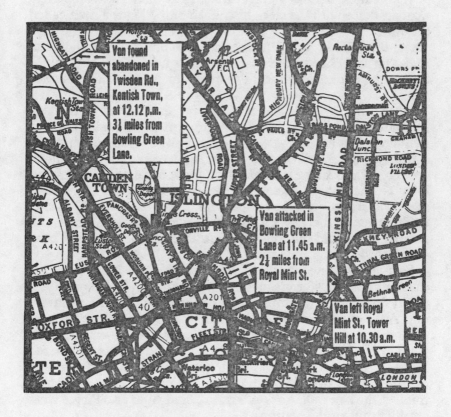

Map showing the details of a later Bullion robbery, May 1967

Agar, just back from America, where his criminal enterprises had flourished, thought this sounded promising. He and Pierce went off to Folkestone and took rooms there, then spent a great deal of time hanging around the station, trying to learn where the second key was kept. But the railway police noticed them, and took them for pickpockets. The down-at-heel Pierce fled back to London.

Agar stayed behind a short time longer, as he had scraped an acquaintance with the clerk in charge of the keys, a man called Sharman. The problem was how to find out which of the keys fitted the bullion safe. But the railway police were watchful, and warned Sharman that they thought Agar a villain. So Sharman suddenly ceased to respond to Agar's friendly overtures.

Agar now devised a clever scheme to find out about the key. He had £200 in gold sent from London to Folkestone, to be delivered to a Mr Archer – himself. This, of course, would be sent in the gold bullion safe. Then Agar went to Folkestone to collect it. The scheme should have failed, because Sharman had been warned about Agar. But luck was on Agar's side; Sharman was away on the day he called, and the young booking clerk went to the key cupboard – watched by Agar – and removed the gold bullion key. Obstacle number one had been successfully surmounted.

So was obstacle number two. Tester, the Margate station master, was transferred to London, and soon had the opportunity to take a wax impression of the other key. Now Pierce and Agar hurried back to Folkestone, and waited for the boat train to come in. For a few minutes, the office was empty while the various clerks came out and attended to the registered luggage. Pierce slipped into the office and grabbed the key; outside, Agar pressed it into a piece of soft wax. Within a minute, the key was back on its hook, and Agar and Pierce were strolling out of the station.

A fourth – and most essential – accomplice had now been enrolled – a guard named James Burgess, who was in charge of the guard's van that contained the bullion safes. Without him, the robbery would have been impossible. Burgess agreed that he would give a signal – wiping his hankerchief across his face – when there was gold bullion on the train.

Things were still far from straightforward. Both keys were cut from the wax impressions, but it took months – it was a complicated design – and when Agar tried them out, neither would fit. They had to modify them eight times before they would open the safe. Now that success was at last in sight, Pierce and Agar moved to new lodgings, and Pierce wore a false moustache and wig and changed his name.

There was still one more problem. Unless the stolen gold was replaced by something of equal weight, the loss might be discovered at Folkestone, where the bullion was weighed before it left England. That would be too soon. So Agar and Pierce bought two hundredweights of lead grapeshot from the Shot Tower, near Waterloo, packed it into carpet bags, and staggered back with these to their lodgings.

It was now the beginning of May 1855. Every evening the men followed the same routine. They drove to London Bridge Station in a cab, with their carpet bags, each weighing half a hundredweight, and then took up their position where they could watch the bullion train. But for two weeks, Burgess failed to make the signal they were waiting for, and they drove back home. They began to worry in case railway police should notice them again. But finally, on 15 May 1855, Burgess wiped his face with his handkerchief. Agar and Pierce immediately bought tickets, and went to the luggage van, where Burgess stowed their abnormally heavy bags. But only Pierce came out of the van. He went to a first class compartment. Agar crouched in a corner of the luggage van, covered with an apron.

As soon as the train started, Agar threw off the apron. From a leather bag strapped under his arm – and concealed by his cape-overcoat – he removed his tools: wedges, pincers, sealing wax and tapers. While Burgess acted as lookout, Agar opened the first of the two safes with the keys and removed two small and very heavy wooden boxes, sealed with metal bands. Working with feverish haste – the train would soon be stopping at Reigate – he used the wedges to prise up the bands on one of the boxes, then forced it open. It contained solid gold ingots. Four of these were removed, and bags of lead shot placed in the box. Then the nails were hammered down again and the bands replaced; finally, Agar lit a taper and melted the sealing wax to replace the seals. The box was locked back in the safe, and when the train stopped at Reigate, Burgess was ready to hand over a carpet bag to a man who came to the guard's van to claim it. William Tester strolled off the station carrying the four bars of gold.

As the train left Reigate, Pierce joined Agar in the guard's van, and they forced open the second box. This proved to contain American gold coins. Again, a quantity of these were removed and replaced with lead shot. After this, the second safe was opened. This was found to contain smaller gold bars. Regretfully – because he was running out of lead shot – Agar was forced to remove only a few of these. Their total haul was worth £12,000.

In Folkestone, two passengers holding carpet bags walked out of the station, climbed into another train, and continued their journey to Dover, where they arrived before midnight. There they went into a hotel and had a meal – their train back to London left at two in the morning. While Pierce guarded the bags, Agar took a stroll along the dock and dropped the safe keys and the tools into the water.

At the station, a porter offered to take their bags; when they declined, he became suspicious, and asked to see their tickets. But Agar had thought of everything, and produced two Ostend

---

William L. Carlisle – known as the "White Bandit" – stands out as one of the most amiable robbers in American history. Between 1916 and 1919, he robbed numerous passenger train across the east and central United States. Donning a handkerchief to hide his face and waving a revolver, he would relieve passengers of their valuables in much the same way as any other petty crook, but with one important difference: he would not steal from women. At times panicked ladies would even thrust their purses and jewellery at him, but he would always courteously refuse.

On one occasion, seeing that a man had only raised a single hand when commanded he moved closer to threaten him. However, he then saw that the victim had only one arm. Carlisle immediately apologised and left the man with his belongings.

His flamboyance was amazing. He not only wrote to the police to ask how the investigation was going, he even told them which trains he was going to rob beforehand. Even with this help, it took the authorities some time to catch him, and then he promptly escaped.

He was eventually recaptured and served seventeen years before being paroled in 1936. On release he turned over a new leaf, got a job and married. For the rest of his life he devoted all his spare time to campaigning against crime. Speaking at many public rallies he stressed the need to help young offenders, not to castigate them.

tickets – the return halves. The porter thanked him – then
remembered that there had been no Ostend boat that day, and
asked them when they came from Ostend. ("Yesterday") said
Agar breezily, holding out a tip. The porter saluted and went
away.

Two hours later they were back in London. Even now they
continued to take precautions. In case they had been followed,
they took three cabs in succession, arriving back at their
lodgings after dawn. There Tester was waiting with his carpet
bag. After seven years of planning, the great bullion robbery
was now successfully completed.

Meanwhile, in the Gare Maritime in Boulogne, the cross-
Channel steamer lay alongside the quay, and in the Customs
shed officials were checking the weight of the three iron-bound
boxes against the documents that accompanied them. In fact,
the boxes had been weighed at Folkestone, and one had been
found to be light; but since the other was too heavy, the
Folkestone Customs had decided that a simple mistake had
been made. The Boulogne authorities were less casual. When it
was realised that two out of three boxes were under-weight,
there was deep suspicion. Customs officials re-checked the
papers; there could be no possible doubt; the boxes were
dozens of pounds lighter than they should be. When the boxes
were finally opened, and the lead shot discovered, there was
consternation. The seals were intact. But on closer examination,
the officials discovered the marks of the wedges and pincers
that revealed that the boxes had been opened . . .

Back in London, the gang converted around £400 in American
gold sovereigns into English money, and it was divided equally.

The gold was now moved from the temporary lodgings to
Agar's house in Shepherds Bush. Here he lived with a young
woman called Fanny Kay, whom he had met working behind
the counter in the buffet at Tonbridge station, and persuaded to
move in with him. She had borne him a son. For the next week
or so, Agar and Pierce worked at a furnace in the upper room,
converting the gold ingots into smaller ones by running the
gold into iron moulds. They sliced up some of the smaller
ingots with a hammer and chisel. These smaller pieces they
were able to sell at £3 an ounce, bringing in £300. Then, very
slowly and cautiously, Agar began looking around for a
customer for a larger part of the loot. Tester and Burgess were
both given a share of the proceeds, after Agar had impressed
upon them the importance of continuing in their jobs and

displaying no sign of sudden affluence. A famous forger named James Townesend Saward – better known as Jim the Penman – bought £2,500-worth of the gold.

At this moment, Agar's luck turned – although he was not aware of it at the time. In spite of his new wealth, he continued in his old occupation of forging. He came across a young man named Smith, who seemed bright and willing, and employed him to do odd jobs. Smith seemed to be reliable – several lots of money were safely delivered by him – so Agar decided to employ the young man on a permanent basis. Although Smith was not told this, his job was to go to banks and cash forged cheques. In case Smith was caught, Agar made sure that he personally was untraceable; Smith did not know his real name, and he always met him at a hotel.

What Agar did not know was that Smith had spent twelve months in jail for receiving stolen goods, and had run a brothel, which had gone bankrupt. When Smith told a thief called William Humphries about his new job, Humphries advised him to be very careful, since Agar was a villain. In fact, Humphries himself had reason to dislike Agar. The latter had a roving eye, and had seduced Humphries's mistress, a girl named Emily Campbell. Fanny had found out, and after a quarrel, Agar had walked out on her and taken his new mistress to live with him elsewhere.

When Smith realised that he had been selected so that he could take all the risk, he went to the police. And the police arranged a trap. One day, Agar sent Smith to a bank in Lombard Street with a forged cheque for £700. Agar followed – in the event of Smith being caught, he wanted to make sure he was ready to disappear. The bank, apparently, handed over the £700 without suspicion; in fact, they had been tipped off by the police, and filled the bag with farthings. Smith then met his employer – whom he knew as Captain Pellatt – in Jockey's Fields (now Grays Inn) and handed over the bag. At this moment the police pounced and arrested them both. Agar was charged with forging the £700 cheque.

Agar was convinced that Humphries had "framed" him for stealing his mistress, and protested his innocence. But counterfeit notes and forged plates in his home made it clear that he was a professional crook. He was sentenced to transportation for life in Botany Bay. This was only five months after the great bullion robbery.

Now he began to feel remorse about abandoning Fanny Kay

and their son. He had £15,000 in the bank, and decided to settle it on Fanny. But he wanted to invest it and give Fanny a weekly income, rather than handing her the whole sum – being unaccustomed to handling money, she would probably spend it, whereas it could bring her an income of £2 a week for life. Agar now made his greatest mistake so far: he decided to entrust Pierce with the business of investing the money and making sure that Fanny received her income: the deed was signed in the Portland Convict Prison, where Agar was awaiting transportation. But the slippery Pierce had no intention of investing the money; since Fanny had not been told about it, he felt there was nothing to stop him from keeping it for himself.

In due course, Agar wrote to Fanny, asking her to buy a silver cup for his son, and another for Pierce's child; he also asked for a geography book with a section on Australia. Pierce, he said, would give her the money. Fanny – who was living with Pierce and his wife – asked him for money, but Pierce refused. Fanny stormed out, and went to the governor of Newgate prison, where Agar had originally been held. She had suspected what had been going on in the upper room with the furnace (although she knew nothing of the robbery), and wanted to make sure that Pierce went to jail too.

When a solicitor from the South-Eastern Railway arrived at Portland prison, and told Agar what was happening to his mistress and child, Agar was at first incredulous, then furious. Encouraged by the solicitor, he went on to tell the full story of the great bullion robbery. Pierce was arrested, and thousands of pounds were found buried under his front step and hidden in his pantry.

On 12 January 1857, Pierce, Tester and Burgess stood in front of the judge at the Bailey, and were duly sentenced – Burgess and Tester to fourteen years transportation to Botany Bay, and Pierce – amazingly enough – to a mere two years; Pierce had been charged as a member of the railway company, which he was not, and a lawyer was able to obtain a shorter sentence on this technicality. The judge said some extremely harsh words at his sentencing, but could do nothing about it. At least the judge succeeded in restoring Agar's money to Fanny Kay, who thereupon became rich.

Agar served five years of his sentence and was released, whereupon he married Fanny Kay. Unfortunately, he returned to crime, and was transported once more to Botany Bay. Shortly

before his death, a convict who had recently arrived told him
that he had become a legend in the London underworld; Agar
groaned: "That means nothing at all."

Fanny herself died penniless in a workhouse. What happened to Pierce is not known, except that he was badly beaten
up after he was released from jail – no doubt at Agar's request.

Tester, at least, succeeded in making good; after being
released from prison in Australia, he started a highly successful grocery business, and ended a wealthy man.

The Case of Orrock's Chisel

Unlike the previous two cases, the case that follows is of a
burglary that went appallingly wrong. But it has become one of
the great classics of Victorian detection.

On 1 December 1882, the cobbled, gaslit streets of east
London were wrapped in choking fog as a young constable
set out from Dalston police station on a beat that took him
down a narrow thoroughfare called Ashwin Street. As he
turned the corner, he came to a sudden halt as he saw a
man placing a lantern on top of the wall outside the Baptist
chapel, and beginning to scramble over. PC Cole took a swift
step forward, laid his hand on the man's shoulder, and asked:
"What do you think you're doing?" For a moment, the man –
who seemed little more than a youth – looked as if he was going
to resist; then he changed his mind and agreed to "go quietly".
But PC Cole and his captive had only gone as far as the pub on
the corner when the man broke loose and ran. Cole ran after
him and grabbed him by the left arm; as he did so, the man
reached into his pocket, pulled out a revolver, and fired three
shots. A woman who was walking towards them screamed and
fled; as she ran, she heard another shot. Moments later, she
encountered two policeman in Dalston Lane, and led them
back to the scene of the shooting. PC Cole was lying on the
pavement outside the Baptist chapel, his head in the gutter; a
trickle of blood ran from the bullet hole behind his left ear. He
died five minutes after being admitted to the local German
Hospital.

Inspector Glass, who took charge of the case, ordered a search of the area where the policeman had been found; on the wall of the Baptist chapel, the burglar had left his dark lantern; behind the railings, a chisel, a jemmy, and a wooden wedge had ben left on the ground. The only other clue was a black billycock hat, which the burglar had lost in the course of the struggle. The woman who had seen him running away described him as short and slightly built; another witness gave the same description.

There was one man in the Dalston police station who believed he knew the identity of the murderer. Only minutes before Cole had arrested the burglar, Police Sergeant Cobb had been walking along Ashwin Street with another sergeant, Branwell, when they had noticed a man standing under a streetlamp. Cobb recognized him as a young cabinetmaker named Tom Orrock, and when he saw the policeman, he looked furtive and uncomfortable. Orrock had no criminal record, but he kept bad company – thugs and professional criminals – and it seemed a reasonable assumption that he would one day try his hand at crime. As they passed Orrock that night, Cobb had been tempted to arrest him for loitering. But standing under a streetlamp was no crime, and Cobb had decided against it. Now he regretted it, and was inclined to blame himself for the death of PC Cole, who was a young married man with children.

Informed of Sergeant Cobb's suspicions, Inspector Glass was inclined to be dismissive – to begin with, he disliked Cobb, regarding him as too unimaginative and too conscientious. But he ordered Tom Orrock – who was nineteen – to be brought in for an identity parade. When the witnesses who had glimpsed Cole's captive failed to identify him, Orrock was released. Soon after that, he disappeared from his usual haunts.

Months after the murder, the investigation was at a standstill. The clues seemed to lead nowhere. The hat bore no marks of identification, and the chisels and the large wooden wedge might have belonged to anybody. But the bullets looked more promising. All four had been recovered – two from the policeman's skull, one from his truncheon, another from the truncheon case. They were unusual in that they had been fired from a revolver that was little more than a toy – the kind of thing ladies sometimes carried in their handbags. The science of ballistics was unknown in 1882, but the rarity of the gun suggested that it might one day provide a valuable piece of evidence.

When studied through a magnifying glass, one of the chisels also yielded an interesting clue. A series of scratches near the handle looked like an attempt at writing, probably with a sharp nail. And when the chisel was photographed for the case file, the letters could be seen more clearly, and they resolved themselves into a capital R, followed by what looked like an o, a c, and a k. Rock. Could it be short for Orrock? Cobb began calling in every tool shop in the Hackney and Dalston area, asking if they recognized the chisels, but met with no success.

Cobb refused to give up. A year after the murder, he was talking with an acquaintance of the missing cabinetmaker named Henry Mortimer, who occasionally acted as a police informer. And Mortimer's rambling discourse suddenly arrested the sergeant's attention when he mentioned that Tom Orrock had possessed a revolver – a nickel-plated, pin-fire miniature affair, Orrock had seen it advertised in the *Exchange and Mart*, and he and Mortimer had gone to Tottenham to purchase it from the owner for the sum of half a guinea. They had also been accompanied by two men named Miles and Evans, both professional – if unsuccessful – criminals. On the way home, the four men had stopped on Tottenham Marshes and used a tree for target practice. At Cobb's request, Mortimer accompanied him to Tottenham and showed him the tree. The following day, Cobb returned alone, and dug some bullets out of the tree with his penknife. One of them was relatively undamaged, and was obviously of the same calibre as the bullets that had been fired at PC Cole.

Now Cobb was sure he had his man, and that view was confirmed when Mortimer admitted that Orrock had virtually confessed to killing PC Cole. When Mortimer had expressed disbelief, Orrock had replied: "If they can prove it against me, I'm willing to take the consequences." This is precisely what Cobb now set out to do.

The first step was to lay the new evidence before his immediate superior. Inspector Glass was still inclined to be indifferent, but he agreed to ask for help from New Scotland Yard in trying to trace the shop that had sold the chisel. And, it was the Scotland Yard team that finally located a woman named Preston, a widow who carried on her husband's tool-sharpening business. She recognized the chisel because she always made a practice of scratching the name of the owner near the handle; she remembered the young man who brought in the chisel for grinding had given the name Orrock, which she had shortened to "Rock".

Now at last, they had the kind of evidence that might impress a jury. All that remained was to locate Tom Orrock. Scotland Yard was asked to circulate his description to every police station in the country. This would normally have brought prompt results, for in those days before the population explosion, most police stations were aware of any strangers who had moved into their district. So when another year failed to bring news of the wanted man, Glass was inclined to assume either that he was dead or that he had gone abroad. Cobb refused to believe it. And one day he had an inspiration. One place where a man could "lie low" with reasonable chance of escaping recognition was prison. Once again, Cobb began painstaking enquiries – enquiries that entitle him to be ranked with Canler and Macé as a distinguished practitioner of the needle-in-the-haystack method. And he soon learned that a man answering Orrock's description had been serving a term for burglary in Coldbath Fields for the past two years. Coldbath Fields, in Farringdon Road, was one of London's newer prisons, and had a reputation for severity. The name under which the prisoner was serving his sentence was not Tom Orrock, and when he was summoned to the governor's office, the man denied that he was called Orrock or had ever been in Dalston. Sergeant Cobb attended an identity parade, and had to admit reluctantly that he was unable to recognize Orrock among the seven uniformed convicts who now faced him. But as the men filed out again, they passed under a light, and Cobb suddenly recognized the profile of the man he had last seen standing under a gaslamp in Dalston more that two years earlier. He stepped forward and laid his hand on the shoulder of Thomas Henry Orrock.

Now it was a question of building up the web of circumstantial evidence. Orrock's sister, Mrs Bere, was questioned, and admitted that on the night of the murder her brother had returned home with a torn trouser leg, and without his hat, claiming that he had been involved in a street brawl. Orrock's two friends Miles and Evans were questioned separately. They admitted that they had spent the day of the murder drinking with Tom Orrock in various pubs, and that soon after 10 o'clock in the evening, the three had been in the Railway Tavern in Ashwin Street when Orrock boasted that he intended to embark on a criminal career by "cracking a crib" – stealing the silver plate of the Baptist church, which he attended regularly, and taking it to his brother-in-law to be melted down. Orrock had then left the pub. Not long after, Miles and Evans heard the sound of revolver shots, but claimed they had taken them for fog signals. All the same, they had left the pub and been among the crowd that gathered around the wounded policeman. Three weeks later, when a reward of £200 had been offered for information leading to the capture of the murderer, Orrock went to Evans and begged him not to inform on him; Evans swore that he would not "ruck" on a comrade even for a thousand pounds.

But all this was merely hearsay evidence. The vital link between Tom Orrock and the murder of PC Cole was the revolver. This had disappeared – one witness said that Orrock admitted throwing it into the River Lea. But the police were able to track down the man who had sold Orrock the revolver – his name was McLellan – and he unhesitatingly identified bullets and cartridge cases as being the calibre of those he had sold to a young man in the last week of November 1882, one week before the murder. McLellan's description of the purchaser fitted Thomas Henry Orrock.

A few decades later, all this corroborative evidence would have been unnecessary. Examination of the bullets under a comparison microscope would have proved that the bullet found in the tree at Tottenham was identical with the bullet that killed PC Cole.

But in the year 1884, no one had yet thought of studying the pattern of rifle marks on the side of a bullet; it would be another five years before Edmond Locard's mentor, Professor Alexandre Lacassagne, would provide the evidence to convict a murderer by studying bullet grooves under a microscope. Nevertheless, when Tom Orrock came to trial in September 1884, it was the bullet evidence that carried most weight with the jury. The bullet found in the tree at Tottenham was "precisely similar to the one found in the brain of the dead constable", said the prosecution. "If the prisoner purchased the revolver, where was it? A man did not throw away a revolver that cost him 10 shillings without good cause." The jury was convinced. On Saturday 20 September 1884, Thomas Orrock was convicted of the murder of PC Cole and sentenced to be hanged. The jury added a special recommendation to Sergeant Cobb for his persistence in tracking down the killer. But the chronicler relates that, in after years, Inspector Glass liked to claim credit for capturing Orrock, and "has often remarked that the man who in reality put the police in possession of their information to this day is ignorant that he disclosed to them this knowledge" – from which it would appear that Glass continued to resent the success of his subordinate and to deny him any of the credit.

chapter four

THE AGE OF DETECTION

Fingerprints

The greatest single advance in crime-fighting was the discovery of fingerprints. As long ago as the 1820s, it had been noticed that no two fingerprints are ever alike. But what good was that when there was no method of classifying them? This had to wait until the 1890s, when Sir Francis Galton and Edward Henry finally worked out a way of classifying them according to "loops" "arches" and "whorls". But it was not until 1902 that Henry set up a fingerprint system at Scotland Yard. It proved its value on Derby Day, 1902, when the police were able to prove that twenty-nine arrested men were pickpockets with previous convictions. Later the same year, a burglar named Henry Jackson was caught when he left his fingerprints on some fresh paint in a house in Denmark Hill.

The first major crime solved by fingerprints in England was committed by two brothers named Alfred and Edward Stratton; early in the morning of 27 March 1905, they broke into a shop in Deptford, East London, hoping to find a large sum of money. They knocked out the shopkeeper and his wife with a jemmy, hitting them so violently that both died. But Alfred Stratton left behind a fingerprint on the cash box – in which there had only been a few pounds – and both brothers were hanged.

The Great Bertillon

In France, fingerprinting took longer to establish itself; this was largely because the French had already invented their own method of criminal identification, called "Bertillonage", after its inventor, Alphonse Bertillon.

Bertillon's story would be ideal for Hollywood. He compared photographs of criminals to see if there was some way of classifying noses and faces. Then he thought it might be a good idea to take measurements of criminals when they were arrested – height, reach, circumference of head, height sitting down, length of left hand, left foot, left leg – Bertillon chose the left-hand side because it was unlikely to be affected by work. He was subject to constipation, stomach upsets, headaches and nosebleeds; but he had a certain stubbornness that made him ignore the knowing smiles of colleagues. A doctor named Adolphe Quetelet had asserted that the chances of two people being exactly the same height are four to one. If that was so, and the same thing applied to the other statistics, then you needed only two or three measurements of each criminal to raise the odds to a hundred to one. When the prefect of police ignored Bertillon's letter about this method, Bertillon bought himself a set of filing cards, and started to work on his own, staying in the office until late at night. Macé revealed a lack of insight when he read Bertillon's report, and said it was too theoretical. The prefect, Andrieux, told Bertillon to stop making a nuisance of himself. And three years went by before Bertillon could persuade a new prefect Jean Camecasse to give him an interview. Camecasse was as sceptical as his predecessor, but he was impressed by the clerk's persistence. He told Bertillon that they would introduce his method experimentally for three months. This was obviously absurd; it would take more than three months to build up a file, and a method like Bertillon's depended on accumulation. He knew his only chance lay in working on and praying for luck. His card index swelled at the rate of a few hundred a month. But with more than twenty thousand criminals in Paris alone, the chances of identifying one of them was low. Towards the end of the third month, Bertillon had towards two thousand cards. Theoretically, his chance of identification was one in ten – fairly high. But it must be remembered that a large number of his criminals were sent to jail, often for years, so most of his file was lying fallow, so to speak.

On 20 February 1883, luck was with him. His system led him to identify a petty criminal who had been measured three months earlier. It was a very small triumph, but it was enough to make Camecasse decide to allow the experiment to continue. This was not far-sightedness. The post of prefect was a political appointment; Camecasse was hoping for fame. Unfortunately, a new prefect had been appointed by the time Bertillon became a celebrity; but history allows Camecasse the credit. As the file swelled, identification became more frequent. Before long, it averaged one a day.

Bertillon's system was soon being used by most of the major police forces of the world. And when fingerprinting arrived, Bertillon immediately incorporated this into his system, making sure that the file on every criminal included his fingerprints. Unfortunately, Bertillon refused to face up to the truth: that fingerprinting had completely superseded his own methods.

On 22 July 1934, John Dillinger, a farm boy turned bank robber, went to the Biograph cinema in Chicago with his girlfriend Polly Hamilton and her friend Anna Sage to see Clark Gable in *Manhattan Melodrama*. Anna Sage, who was under threat of deportation, had decided · to try and curry favour with the authorities by betraying the gangster, and was wearing a bright red dress. As they left the cinema, FBI agents surrounded him, and as Dillinger sprinted away, three agents fired, killing him.

But did he really die? The autopsy notes reveal that the corpse's eyes were brown; Dillinger's were blue. The dead man suffered from a heart condition; Dillinger did not. Neither did the corpse possess various marks and scars that Dillinger was known to have on his body.

Crime writer Jay Robert Nash has argued that the dead man was a small-time hoodlum called Jimmy Lawrence, and that J. Edgar Hoover was too embarrassed to acknowledge the mistake. Lawrence, he believes, was "set up" by the "lady in red" so Dillinger could escape. A fellow gang member, Blackie Audett, claims that Dillinger married and escaped to Oregon. The rest of Dillinger's gang was wiped out not long after their leader's "death".

He refused to take the obvious step and classify fingerprints so they could be identified immediately. If a French policeman wished to identify a burglar who had left his fingerprint at the scene of a crime, he had to go through every single file until he found it. It was the sheer cumbersomeness of this method that led to Bertillon's downfall.

The Theft of the Mona Lisa

On 21 August 1911, someone stole Leonardo's *Mona Lisa* from the Louvre. It should, of course, have been a total impossibility, with so many guards; but it happened on a Monday, when the Louvre was closed to the public. The painting, which is on a panel, was housed in a case with a glass cover. This case was found, empty, on the service stairs.

Bertillon was immediately summoned, and careful examination revealed fingerprints. A fingerprint is made by sweat – that is to say, the skin's secretions which include fatty substances; this comes from sweat pores along the papillary ridges, and also from contact of the fingertips with parts of the body where there are sebaceous glands, such as the face. Latent or invisible prints on smooth surfaces can be made visible by dusting the surface with fine powder, such as talc, aluminium, or lead powder. (On white surfaces, such as china, a black powder is used.) And when Bertillon dusted the glass with powder, he realized with delight that the thief had left behind a good set of fingerprints. And now if the thief happened to have a criminal record, it should be a matter of the utmost simplicity to identify him . . .

And if the theft had taken place in London or Berlin or Madrid, it would have been. But Bertillon's fingerprints were still unclassified. And since 1902, when he had solved the Scheffer case, he had accumulated more than 100,000 additional cards. So, in fact, it was an impossible task. Bertillon and his assistants searched for weeks and months – Bertillon was such an obsessive that he probably went through every card individually. But after a few hundred prints, the eyes grow tired, and the attention flags. Bertillon must have ended day after day in a state of exhausted defeat. Nothing could have brought home to him more clearly that his system was a waste of time, and that he should have adopted Henry's fingerprint classification, as improved by Inspector Collins.

Two years later, the thief was arrested in Florence. The police had been tipped off by an art dealer named Alfredo Geri, who had been offered the painting in a letter signed "Leonard". Leonard proved to be an Italian house painter named Vicenzo Perrugia, and he was carrying the *Mona Lisa* with him. His story of the theft caused astonishment, and some amusement at the expense of the Louvre authorities. The crime had not been planned. Perrugia had been a friend of a painter working in the Louvre, and the guards were familiar with him; they let him past without question. Finding himself quite alone in the Salon Carré with the famous painting, the temptation had been too much. He had simply lifted the case off the wall, walked down the service staircase, and extracted the painting, leaving his fingerprints on the glass. Then he had hidden the painting – which is small – beneath his smock and walked out unchallenged. For the next two years the *Mona Lisa* lay hidden under his bed.

Dr Abraham Bredius, a Dutch art-historian, was very boastful about his expertise in the seventeenth-century artist, Vermeer. In 1938, he discovered a new painting by his hero called *The Disciples on the Road to Emmaus*, which was immediately bought by the famous Boymans Museum in Rotterdam for the huge sum of £58,000.

Unfortunately, The Disciples was actually the work of Hans van Meegeren, an art student, who had specifically painted the picture to expose Bredius and the art cognoscenti in The Netherlands. Bredius was later taken in by ten other paintings by van Meegeren and the fraud was only discovered when the latter owned up to selling an imitation Vermeer to Goering in 1945 and subsequently confessed all.

Bredius' influence was so powerful that nobody believed van Meegeren until he painted another Vermeer, *Jesus and the Scribes*, under their very noses.

But for Bertillon, the final bitterness must have been that he had Perrugia's card in his file, for Perrugia was a petty thief who had been arrested several times.

Significantly, in this same year 1913, Bertillon was found to be suffering from pernicious anaemia; he died in February 1914, and France immediately accepted the same fingerprint classification as the rest of the world.

The Great Pearl Robbery

In fact, fingerprint evidence played no part in the most famous robbery of 1913, which was a kind of throw-back to the "great" robberies of the Victorian age.

The story begins on 16 July 1913, in the office of a diamond merchant called Max Mayer, in Hatton Garden. Mr Mayer was anxious to go away on holiday, but first he wanted to replace in his safe his most precious possession: a pearl necklace worth £130,000, which he had built up over many years. The necklace had been in Paris, in the hands of a dealer named Henri Salomons, who had been showing it to a wealthy customer. Unfortunately, the deal had fallen through, and the necklace had been returned back to Mr Mayer by registered post. This was not the first time that the famous necklace – whose existence was known to the whole of the jewellery trade – had been back and forth across the Channel, and so far, it had been perfectly safe.

But when Mr Mayer opened the sealed package on that July morning just before the First World War, he was shocked to find that it contained only several lumps of sugar. Scotland Yard was notified immediately, and a telegram despatched to M. Salomons in Paris. He immediately rushed to London, and confirmed that he and his wife had packed the pearls themselves, and sent them from the local post office in the Rue de Provence. Salomons was above suspicion. So it was obvious that the necklace had been stolen in transit. The sugar lumps were French, which suggested that the substitution had taken place in France, probably on the mail train. Clearly, the theft had been carefully planned, for the package had been re-sealed with identical string, and with sealing-wax that bore Mr Mayer's seal, MM.

The Paris police were also informed, and immediately began tracing the passage of the necklace from the post office to the Cross-Channel ferry. They ended by admitting their bafflement. There was simply no point at which the registered package could have been opened.

Fortunately for Mr Mayer, the necklace was insured. Nevertheless, it was his most precious possession, and he longed – against all the odds – for its return. Mr Mayer therefore offered a £10,000 reward for its recovery.

To the delight of Scotland Yard, this worked. They received a letter from an Antwerp jewel dealer named Samuel Brandstater, who said he and his cousin Meyer Quadratstein – another diamond merchant – had been offered the necklace. In due course, Brandstater and Quatratstein arrived at Scotland Yard. Brandstater then explained that he had been contacted by a relative from London, a diamond broker named Leiser Gutwirth, who had offered him the pearl necklace – admitting it was stolen – for one and a half million francs. Brandstater had offered 300,000 francs, which Gutwirth had indignantly rejected. So Brandstater told him he would try and raise more money, and Gutwirth had returned to London.

So now Scotland Yard knew the name of at least one of the thieves. And now that Brandstater had betrayed his relative, they could rely on his help to recover the necklace and earn the reward. But the whole transaction obviously required care. If the thieves suspected they were betrayed, they would scatter, and Mr Mayer would never see the return of his necklace.

Now began the long and nerve-wracking business that Chief Inspector Ward of Scotland Yard – who was in charge of the case – called "playing the fish". First the informer Brandstater met Gutwirth at Charing Cross station, and raised his offer to half a millon francs. Gutwirth replied angrily: "Go back to Paris. The necklace cannot be bought at less than a million francs." Brandstater said he would try and raise more money, and agreed to meet Gutwirth again.

And so it went on – meetings at Gutwirth's home, at Lyons tea-shops, and various hotels. Usually, two policemen were sitting a few tables away, carefully observing everything. One by one, the other members of the gang revealed themselves. They were all "diamond merchants" who were also known to the police as high-powered crooks: Simon Silverman, Joseph

Grizzard and James Lockett. The police (and insurance company) enlisted the aid of a Paris diamond merchant named Max Spanier, who agreed to meet the thieves and make them an offer. At one meeting in a Strand tea-shop, Grizzard asked Lockett: "Have you got a match?", and Lockett tossed him a match box. Grizzard opened this and revealed three beautiful pearls lying in cotton wool. This was merely to prove that they really had the pearl necklace.

To convince the crooks that he was serious, Spanier bought two of the pearls for 50,000 francs each, and promised to buy the rest in a few days' time. Spanier, Brandstater and his cousin Quadratstein knew they were taking their lives in their hands every time they met the crooks in some hotel room, and the police provided them with loaded revolvers.

Unfortunately, the members of the Scotland Yard team were not all equally skilful at the art of shadowing. One day, the crooks spotted four obvious plain-clothes policemen watching the hotel. They lost no time in fleeing to the Continent, and for a while it looked as if the clumsiness of the police had destroyed months of patient work. But after a few weeks, the crooks were lulled once more into a sense of security, and when Spanier told

In Preston Crown Court in November 1983 a man accused of the theft of a large amount of jewellery was in mid-trial. His defence was mistaken identity. He wasn't there, didn't know anything about it and it wasn't him. As the Prosecuting Counsel, Peter Oppenshaw, began his cross-examination of the defendant, a large commotion was heard at the back of the courtroom. The defendant's wife had just walked in with several of her friends.

Suddenly one of the victims of the burglary began to shriek hysterically. The wife of the accused had turned up at court wearing most of the victim's family heirlooms. Mr Oppenshaw turned slowly to the jury and, savouring the moment for all it was worth, he declared:

"Ladies and gentlemen, I am sure you will agree that this turn of events has given the accused's line of defence something of a hollow ring."

them that he had a wealthy Indian prince who was interested in the necklace, they allowed themselves to be lured back to London. This time, Scotland Yard pounced immediately. It was at the British Museum tube station, and Gutwirth, Silverman, Lockett and Grizzard were all present when the police quietly took their arms and told them they were under arrest.

But now once again there was dismay at Scotland Yard. The thieves were not carrying the pearls. And although the police had enough evidence to convict them – the two pearls sold to Spanier – the case would certainly be counted a failure if the rest of the necklace was not recovered.

Then, totally unexpectedly, the necklace turned up – lying in the gutter in St Paul's Road, Highbury. A piano-maker named Horne picked up a match box wrapped in paper, and found that it contained some white beads. He took them to the local police station, where the police agreed they were probably valueless. When he got home, Horne found that one of the beads had fallen into his pocket, and in the local pub, offered it to anyone who wanted to buy it for the price of a pint – one penny. No one did. And later, Horne lost it. In fact the missing pearl was the largest in the necklace, and was worth thousands of pounds. It was never recovered.

The Highbury police finally realized that the box of ''beads'' might be the missing pearls that everyone was talking about, and asked someone from Scotland Yard to come and look at them. And so Mr Mayer finally received back most of his necklace, minus its largest pearl.

Now the story slowly emerged. The gang, led by Silverman, often ate in a Hatton Garden restaurant known as the ''Diamond Club'', where diamond brokers met and talked shop. It was there that they planned the coup – almost certainly overhearing Mr Mayer telling someone that his necklace was on its way back from Paris. But how could they get their hands on it? The answer was simple and obvious. When the necklace was on its way back, in a registered parcel bearing French stamps, the postman merely had to be bribed to take it to Silverman's office, where it would be opened and re-sealed. A craftsman had even made a replica of Mayer's MM seal for a shilling. Sugar would be substituted for the pearls – French sugar, to give the impression that the substitution had taken place in France – and the postman would then deliver it to Mr Mayer's office, and collect his receipt.

The gang refused to admit that there had been a postman

involved, but Gutwirth had told the informer Brandstater that
£400 had been set aside as "expenses", to pay two postmen
£200 each. No postman was ever charged as an accomplice.

The gang was let off surprisingly lightly. Lockett and Grizzard received seven years each, Silverman (who planned it) a
mere five years, and Gutwirth only eighteen months, because
he had no police record.

The final puzzle remains: how did the pearls end up in a
London gutter? The answer, almost certainly, is that the gang
had given them into the care of some accomplice, who heard
that the thieves had been arrested, and suspected that he was
next on the list. When the piano-maker Horne picked up the
packet, he saw a man and a woman just climbing on to a nearby
bus, and called to them to ask if they had dropped it; they did
not reply. No one has ever learned whether the pearls were
dropped in the gutter by accident or design, and Mr Mayer
certainly did not care one way or the other.

The First Cat-Burglar

Fingerprinting had the effect of making burglars more careful.
The old-fashioned Bill Sikes, with his checked cap and jemmy,
was soon an endangered species, and a new and more sophisticated type of burglar appeared on the scene. The first to draw
the attention of Scotland Yard is described by ex-Superinten-
dent Robert Fabian, in his book *Fabian of the Yard*.

> Robert Augustus Delaney will be remembered at
> Scotland Yard as the man who started a new fashion
> in crime that was to become known as "cat-bur-
> glary". Delaney trod the crags and precipices of Park
> Lane's roofs with nonchalant skill. Wearing faultless
> evening clothes, he could apparently climb the sheer
> side of a house. I think he imagined himself a kind of
> acrobatic Raffles.
>
> He certainly made the great criminals of the past –
> like Charles Peace, who carried a collapsible ladder
> disguised as a bundle of firewood – look clumsy. In

his pocket was a slender steel tool like a putty-knife for slipping window catches – it could also open jewel-boxes. Around his trimly tailored waist coiled four yards of black silk rope. Two men died trying to imitate Delaney: "Irish Mac" impaled himself on spiked railings, and "The Doctor" – who should have known better – fell forty feet from a portico in St James's. He had £8,000 of jewels in his pocket and crawled grimly for two miles before dying.

In 1924, when the rich and noble residents of Park Lane were trooping splendidly in to dinner, Delaney would crouch beneath their windows, unwinding his gossamer rope. The tinkle of polished cutlery . . . or was it the clink of a dulled steel hook catching in the balcony drain gutter . . . and Gussie Delaney robbed their bedrooms like a wraith and departed before coffee wafted fragrantly into the victim's drawing-room and cigar smoke hazed the wine.

The thefts were reported to us in Vine Street, where I was a probationer detective fresh from training school. We questioned indignant flunkeys, far haughtier than their masters, but they knew nothing, and next week another robbery from a Park Lane bedroom – and so on at weekly intervals.

It was not really my case, nor was my probationer pal, Tommy Symes (now Chief Inspector), assigned to it. One night we sat stirring police-canteen coffee, waiting to go out on a routine club raid, but the Park Lane mystery burglaries intrigued us more.

"One each week for the past five weeks," I said. "A total of £30,000. He should be ready to retire soon. And none of us will have caught a whiff of him!"

Tommy leaned forward. "Keep it to yourself," he murmured. "I've been putting in some spare-time work on those burglaries – I've been making a sort of map . . ."

I had to laugh. "So have I, Tommy!" We compared efforts, and found that both of us had the same idea – a map of the Park Lane district, indicating those houses where residents were known to be outstandingly wealthy and where the dining-room could be kept under observation.

"And it looks as if he's working in some sort of sequence, too," I said quickly. "See – top end of Park Lane, then the bottom end, then St James's. Fourth burglary top of Park Lane again, fifth burglary at the bottom end . . ."

"And the next one around here!" Tommy's broad thumb covered Arlington Street at the Ritz Hotel corner. "It might be tonight," he added.

We left the canteen and went into the CID main room. The duty inspector called: "Oh, you two – that club job – it's off for tonight. We shan't be needing you."

We looked at each other. It was a crisp, starlit October evening, just gone dark. "Care for a bit of fresh air, Tommy?" I asked casually. He grinned. "Green Park it is!"

Concealed in the shadow and shrubbery of Green Park, we knew we could keep watch on the backs of all those tempting mansions by the Ritz corner. Three hours later we were chilled, cramped, disap-

---

For a brief period in the 1920s, the gang led by brothers Matt and George Kimes and Ray Terrill was one of the most successful in America. The members were all farm boys, many of whom had decided that bootlegging was more profitable than ploughing.

Terrill persuaded the Kimes brothers that bank robbery would be even more profitable than bootlegging, and so it proved. A raid at the Farmer's National Bank in Beggs, Oklahoma, netted $20,000. They were captured when their car hit a tree but Terrill and Matt Kimes escaped and robbed the same bank again, this time taking $18,000.

In Pampa, Texas, in 1927, the gang learned that the huge old iron bank safe was almost uncrackable, so they rolled it outside – while customers were held up by other gang members – loaded it on to a truck and drove away with it. It proved to contain $35,000.

Matt Kimes was caught soon after this and sentenced to life. Terrill teamed up with Herman Barker, eldest of Ma Barker's sons, but in September 1927, after a shoot-out during which they escaped, Barker was found dead in a ditch. (Ma Barker always claimed he had been "executed" by the police.) Terrill was captured soon after and spent most of his life behind bars.

pointed. Nothing had happened.

The next night was cloudy. Once again Tommy took the Green Park bandstand, while I waited in the garden behind Wimborne House. Faintly we heard the austere chimes of dinner gongs from the big mansions. One by one, bedroom lights winked out from costly chandeliers. I fumbled for a peppermint and stared into the shadows until my eyes felt aglow like a stoat's . . . A dark figure was creeping along the nearest garden boundary. Quick, agile as a cat, it vaulted the high railing and disappeared.

We next saw the shadowy intruder flit across one of the white balconies. How did he get up there? Tommy, flattened against the wall beneath the balcony, turned as I crept near him.

"Did you see that?" His voice was hoarse with suppressed excitement. "Like a blooming cat!"

"I'll wait for him here," I whispered. "You give the alarm inside."

The lights began to flash on in each of the spacious upstairs rooms as Tommy Symes raced through the bedrooms and corridors, with alarmed householders behind him. I heard excited voices – then the repeated thud of sturdy shoulders at an equally sturdy thick mahogany door. The thief had jammed it with a wooden wedge, ready for such an emergency. He reappeared on the balcony, made no attempt to descend into the garden, but ran light-footed along the balcony, leapt a nine-foot gap to the next, and alighted soundlessly. He threw something up on to the gutter of the neighbouring roof and in six seconds was across the slanted tiles, away . . . For hours we scoured the district, but our quarry had vanished among the chimneys. All I had seen was the glint of a diamond stud in what was obviously a dress-shirt front.

The Inspector was scathing. "You really must forgive me for intruding upon your beautiful partnership," he said. "But I would like to know about all this before it happened, so we could have one or two more men on the scene – " Upon me he cast a withering glance. "You say you saw him – but you can't describe him – except he climbed like a cat – he didn't have fur by any chance?"

Afterwards I said solemnly: "Tommy, we've got to catch that blighter – that cat-burglar – and rub butter on his paws!" That was not all I said.

We went to the scene of the previous night's burglary. Jewels valued £2,000 were missing, which didn't make us feel better. By daylight that leap from one balcony to its neighbour seemed no less remarkable. We measured it, Tommy throwing the end of a tape-measure across the space to me. And as I leaned to catch it I noticed something . . .

It was a footprint on the balcony ledge – so small and so exquisitely pointed in the toe that it might have been made by a woman's dancing shoe. We got a ladder and in the soft mould of the drainage gutter on the roof found another imprint of the wedge-shaped shoe, the smooth tiles showing clearly the porous tread of crêpe soles. "Rubber-soled evening pumps!" said Tommy. "He'd need to get those made specially!"

I spent the day visiting those exclusive shoe emporiums of Jermyn Street, York Street (as it was then), Dover Street and Shepherd's Market, where craftsmen took pride in hand-made shoes to suit clients' whims. In Albemarle Street I was lucky.

"Most remarkable," said the proprietor earnestly, "that any gentleman should require crêpe rubber soles, however thin, on patent-leather evening shoes. I remember strongly advising the gentleman against it – but he was insistent." The order-book showed name and address as: "R. Radd, 52, Half Moon Street. Five guineas – paid."

A good address. I went to Half Moon Street, but the numbers stopped at 42, and there had never been a 52. A stranger to the district would have been unlikely to know that. It seemed worth investigating the bars and lounges around Half Moon Street. Those were the days of evening clothes for gentlemen in London's West End, so my laundry bill became staggering . . . and the days passed.

More than a week afterwards I walked into the Range Bar. My dress shoes clacked like sabots on the polished parquet corridor. A man passed me. He wore good evening clothes, a diamond sparkled in his laundered shirt-bosom, and as he walked it occurred to me that his feet were making no noise at all! I glanced quickly – and saw tiny pointed toes . . . Outside he hesitated at the taxi-rank, then decided to walk. I jumped into the cab at the tail of the rank.

"I'm a police officer. Follow that man. Don't put your flag down. I'll lie on the floor."

We rolled after the man with the pointed shoes – round the corner from Half Moon Street, up another side street, then: "He's gone into No. 43, Gov'nor," said the taxi-driver.

"Right," I said. "Don't stop. Keep going to New Scotland Yard."

I took the lift to the Criminal Record Office, but there they knew nothing about the address. I searched some picked photo files. There was no record on the man. Still . . . back at Vine Street I made a report.

For two days we trailed our man without success. Then he strolled down to Hatton Garden, met a man in a café, and went with him in a taxi to Southgate, where they entered a comfortable-looking private house. After about twenty minutes the man with the pointed shoes came out alone. I left a colleague to make inquiries at the house and followed him back to No. 43.

In a brown van a concealed spark morse receiver buzzed and stuttered: "Inquiries at house in Southgate – occupier known – admits receiving jewellery – has just paid £800 – jewellery answers description of part proceeds from Park Lane thefts."

That did it. We called at No. 43, and a middle-aged woman answered the polished bell and regarded us haughtily. She was dressed pompously in rustling black, and a black taffeta ribbon at her throat held a cameo brooch.

"Have you a man living here . . . ?" I described my suspect. The woman considered me as though she suspected some fault with the drains.

"That may well be Mr Delaney, who has the upstairs flat. Is he expecting you?"

I brushed past her. "We'll just find out!" I called

cheerfully from the stairway.

She gasped, "I think you're very rude!"

So did Mr Augustus Delaney, as his engraved name-plate described him, who looked up coolly as we entered without knocking. "What the blazes do you want?" His accent was slightly Canadian.

"Quite all right," I said, soothingly. "We're just looking for some money and jewellery. You don't mind, do you?" He stood up, suddenly pale, and then his mouth twitched into a wistful smile. "I suppose – it's too much to hope that you gentlemen are burglars?" The £800 was hidden under the mattress. Stolen jewels were concealed in the dressing-table, behind the drawer backs.

On his first conviction he received three years' penal servitude at the Old Bailey for those six Park Lane burglaries. That was in 1924. Would you like to know what this daring, well-educated and quick-witted young man did with the rest of his life and with that superb acrobat's body that fate had given him? By the time he died in Parkhurst Prison on 14 December 1948, he had spent twenty years in various gaols. In his brief intervals of freedom his pointed, immaculate shoes had scarcely time to become worn down at the heels!

The Count of Gramercy Park

Gerald Chapman, the "man prisons couldn't hold", the crook who wore tailor-made suits and spoke with a near-impeccable English accent, was regarded by the American public as a modern Robin Hood, and accordingly lionized. One writer speculates that his parents were comfortably off and that he had a good education. It was all untrue. Chapman was born in Brooklyn in 1890, of Irish parents, and had the usual criminal apprenticeship of petty theft and reformatories. When he was fourteen a judge prophesied he would end in the electric chair. In fact, he was hanged.

It was when he was eighteen, and was transferred from Sing Sing to Auburn, N.Y., that Chapman met a man he came to admire passionately, George "Dutch" Anderson, a graduate of Heidelberg and Uppsala Universities, who spoke several languages. (His real name was Ivan Dahl von Teller, and he was a Dane.) Anderson was a swindler and a "gentleman crook", and he advised Chapman to give up armed robbery and use his brains. Chapman began to educate himself with books and acquired an English accent.

Released from prison, he went back to robbery, and this time was so successful – for a time – that he was able to buy himself expensive clothes, rent a fashionable apartment, and dine in good restaurants. He decided that being a gentleman suited him. But in 1911 he received ten years for armed robbery, and was sent back to Sing Sing. There he became friendly with a man named Charles Loerber, who was in for armed robbery, and who was totally lacking in any kind of finesse.

In 1919, Chapman, Anderson and Loerber were all paroled. Chapman joined Anderson on a tour of the Midwest, and was soon convinced of the soundness of Anderson's methods when they managed to acquire a fortune of $100,000 through confidence trickery. Chapman rented an apartment in New York's exclusive Gramercy Park. Here he called himself G. Vincent Colwell, and acquired a pretty English "wife" called Betty, who was as much a born lady as he was a born gentleman.

It was Charles Loerber who persuaded Chapman to return to armed robbery. He had been observing the mail trucks on Wall Street, and noted that they had minimum security, and that their wire-mesh sides gave a good view of the amount of mail they were carrying.

On the cold, foggy night of 14 October 1921, Chapman, Anderson and Loerber, driving a stolen black touring car, followed one of these post office vans along Wall Street, which becomes deserted after the offices close. Suddenly Loerber accelerated and pulled alongside the mail van as it halted at a red light. Within seconds, Chapman was on the running board, holding a gun to the driver's ribs. This was the dangerous part, when someone might have seen him and given the alarm; fortunately, no one did, and he pulled open the door and sank into the passenger seat. The driver, Frank Havernack, obeyed his instructions to pull over into a quiet side street – Leonard Street. The stolen car pulled up behind them, and Anderson demanded the keys to the van. Then, while Chapman sat with his gun in the driver's ribs, Anderson and Loerber located five sacks of registered mail and tossed it into the car. They drove off leaving Havernack tied up, with a mail bag over his head.

In a hideout across the river – a farm belonging to an uncle of Loerber's – they opened the sacks, and counted out the money and bonds. It amounted to $2,643,720 – the biggest haul so far in American criminal history. More than three hundred thousand of this was in cash, and more than twice that amount in traveller's cheques.

While the police were searching frantically for leads, and Federal agents kept a watch on all the ports, G. Vincent Colwell was back at 12 Gramercy Park, throwing parties to which his wealthy neighbours were invited. He even organized the theft of an expensive pearl necklace from one of his guests. Then the driver identified Chapman and Anderson from "mugshots", and their pictures appeared in "wanted" posters in every post office. But still no one thought of looking in Gramercy Park. Chapman, impeccably dressed, with a neat moustache, often stood in front of the wanted poster, and reflected how little this rough-looking character looked like Vincent Colwell.

Prohibition had arrived. Chapman and Anderson invested some of their money in the bootleg business, and prospered. And in another robbery at an American Express office in Niagara Falls, the gang added a further $70,000 to their capital.

Loerber was their undoing. He was picked up while trying to "fence" some of the securities, and gave away his associates in exchange for a lighter sentence. On 3 July 1922, Chapman and Anderson were arrested. But while Chapman sat alone with a detective in the Federal Building on Broadway, he pretended to have some kind of attack, slumping in his chair and gasping for water. As the detective rushed out of the room, Chapman rushed out of the window, ran along a narrow cornice – his hands shackled – and climbed in at another window. But he was soon located and re-arrested. The escape attempt made the headlines, and Chapman was delighted to see himself described as a modern Robin Hood.

In the Atlanta penitentiary, faced with a twenty-five-year sentence, Chapman swore he would escape. The governor assured him he wouldn't. But with immense patience, Chapman stole small pieces of cord from the workshops and braided them into a rope, which he buried in a flower bed. From stolen cutlery he made a file and a crude hook. Then he began to complain of stomach pains. After several days he was admitted to hospital for observation. There he was placed in a room with a "trusty" named John Grey. He soon persuaded Grey to join him in an escape attempt. They filed through the bars, severed an electric cable – plunging the prison into darkness – then used a rope of bed sheets to get to the ground. Five minutes later, both men were over the wall.

Two days later, Chapman was tracked by bloodhounds as he lay in a field; as he tried to run away, he was shot twice, then handcuffed.

In a civilian hospital in Athens, Betty came to visit him. She succeeded in smuggling in a gun, and Chapman used it to force an intern to give him his white coat. Then, after binding and gagging the intern, he walked out of the hospital and climbed into the waiting car driven by a fellow-crook, Charlie Wolfe. Betty joined him a few minutes later and they drove away – and vanished.

In fact, they made their way to a hideout in Muncie, Indiana, where Chapman recovered from his wounds in the home of Dr Harry Spickerman – a man he had met in Atlanta. Then he persuaded a farmer named Ben Hance to take him in as a boarder. There, in January 1924, he was joined by Dutch Anderson, who made an equally remarkable escape from Atlanta. Anderson had managed to get himself assigned to the tubercular unit, and was housed in a tent in the prison grounds – the notion being that plenty of fresh air would cure tuberculosis. He and a number of other prisoners had tunnelled their way sixty feet under the prison yard and wall.

Chapman now stole himself an expensive car from a showroom in Stanton, and changed the numberplates. Then he and Anderson drove east, committing burglaries and robberies as they went along. Their aim was to set up in the counterfeiting business, but in New Britain, Connecticut, they decided that the department store of Davidson and Leventhal looked as if it would be easy to burgle, and that early on Sunday morning would be a good time, when the safe would be full of Saturday's takings. They were accompanied by a new confederate, Walter Shean, the spoiled son of a businessman in Springfield, Mass., who enjoyed hanging around with two famous robbers.

In the early hours of 12 October 1924, Chapman blew one of the store's safes with nitro-glycerine; to his disgust, it contained ledgers and an envelope with a few dollars. And while he was working on the other safes, the police arrived, alerted by a local livery-stableman, who had become suspicious of the well-dressed men entering a large store at dawn on a Sunday. As two armed policemen blocked the doorway of the room in which he was hiding, Chapman fired, then made his escape, followed by flying bullets. The shot policeman, James Skelly, died on the operating table two hours after Chapman and Anderson had escaped.

When the police arrived in force a few minutes after the shooting, they found Walter Shean dozing in the car, and the incriminating envelope containing a few dollars on the back seat. In the warehouse of Shean's advertising agency in Springfield, police found a large quantity of stolen goods, including fur coats, oriental rugs and jewellery. There were also firearms. It took a large removal van to transfer all the loot to police headquarters.

It was while going through this loot for the hundredth time that Detective Ed Hickey noticed a loose label on a carpet bag, and steamed it off to reveal another underneath; this carried the name of Dr Harry Spickerman of Muncie, Indiana. Spickerman was the doctor who had cured Chapman's bullet wounds. Hickey and his team moved into the Braun Hotel, opposite the surgery of Dr Spickerman, and waited patiently for two months. And in the lobby of the Braun Hotel, on 17 January 1925, one of Hickey's men noticed a well-dressed man with an English accent buying a newspaper. He immediately recognized Chapman. The following morning, shortly after leaving Dr Spickerman's house, Chapman was arrested. He put up a fierce struggle and succeeded in firing one shot before he was overpowered.

When the gun was turned over to the forensic lab, it proved to be the same weapon that had killed officer Skelly. Chapman was extradited to Connecticut to stand trial for the murder. His defence was that he was in Holyoke, Mass., at the time of the shooting, but Walter Shean testified against him. So did his former landlord Ben Hance, on whose premises more incriminating evidence was found. On 4 April 1925, Chapman was sentenced to death. In spite of appeals, he was hanged a year later, on 6 April 1926.

By then, Dutch Anderson was already dead. On 15 August 1925, Anderson and a gunman named Charlie Wolfe sought out Ben Hance and his wife Mary, the farmer who had sheltered Chapman and Anderson; they shot them both in their car. Mary died immediately; her husband died later in hospital – but not before he had named his killers. Charlie Wolfe was quickly arrested, and was sentenced to life for the murders. Anderson moved on through northern Michigan, leaving behind a trail of counterfeit bills. On 31 October 1925, he passed a counterfeit twenty-dollar bill in a cafe in Muskegon, Michigan. The manager called a policeman, who caught up with Anderson a few streets away, and Anderson agreed to accompany him for questioning. Suddenly, Anderson darted away into the crowd; the policeman, Charles Hammond, followed him. In a deserted street, Anderson hid under a loading platform behind an empty factory, and as Hammond approached, shot him down. As Anderson ran out from under the platform and took to his heels, Hammond fired after him and brought him down. Both the policeman and the counterfeiter died.

The Inside Job of All Time: The Rondout Heist

Late on the night of 12 June 1924, mail train No. 57 of the Chicago and Pacific Railroad was just passing through the small town of Rondout, Illinois; thirty-two miles northwest of Chicago. The eleven-coach train was ten minutes behind schedule and the driver had pushed the speed up to sixty-five miles-an-hour to try to make up time. So intent were he and the fireman on keeping the boiler at full steam, they completely failed to notice two intruders entering the engine compartment. The fireman looked up from his shovelling to see the muzzle of a rifle levelled at his head and at the same moment the driver felt a pistol in his back.

"Do as I say and you won't get hurt," they were told. "Put on the brakes then flash your headlight three times." As they coasted to a stop the gunman looked back down the train and shouted: "Now back the train three car-lengths." The driver co-operated, positioning the third mail coach over a level-crossing. Four armed men then jumped from two cars parked on the road and ran to the train, firing into the air like archetypal Mexican bandits.

Showing no interest in the other coaches, the robbers made straight for the one straddling the crossing. They dealt with the mail clerks inside by throwing a tear-gas grenade through the upper window. Then, as the agonized clerks stumbled out the door, two robbers in gas masks stepped forward to ransack the coach.

It was at this moment that the men on watch saw a dark figure approaching along the path that skirted the train tracks.

"Who the hell is that?" one demanded.

"I don't know," replied another.

Then someone shouted: "Let him have it." The bandits opened fire and the figure staggered and fell to the ground. The robbers ran to the slumped figure and carried it to one of the cars. From their swearing it was evident that they had accidentally shot one of their own people.

Undeterred, the thieves looted the mail coach then sped into the night. They took with them $50,000 in jewellery, $450,000 in newly issued currency and $1,500,000 in readily negotiable bonds; a neat two million dollars in all.

The police started with little to go upon. The train crew were so frightened they reported seeing twenty bandits in all – far too many to fit into the two getaway vehicles. As such their testimony would stand for little at any trial. This, and the lack of any physical evidence, left the police with only two leads.

The first was the wounded man – if he was still alive – he would be difficult to conceal. The police informers were told to keep their eyes open for any underworld medical activity.

The second was the apparent efficiency of the actual robbery. The thieves had known which of the eleven coaches held the richest plunder and in which mail bags to search most thoroughly. This suggested an inside job.

Fortunately, the Chicago police had an expert in such matters on their staff. He was Inspector William Fahy, on secondment from the investigative branch of the US Post Office. He had been sent to put a stop to the growing influence of organized crime in the dealings of the Chicago Post Office – a role similar to the one in which the gangbusting Eliot Ness was to later bring down Al Capone.

At thirty-six, Fahy had an excellent record. Known as the "Lone Wolf" by colleagues for his habit of working alone, he had caught numerous "inside job" robbers, including "Big Tim" Murphy.

Murphy – both a labour racketeer and popular State Senator – had been involved in several major robberies from the Post Office, but had covered his tracks with great care. However, despite much pressure to drop the case, Fahy eventually secured a conviction and lengthy sentence for the mobster. At the time of the Rondout robbery, Fahy was one of the most highly thought of officers in the city. There was no question of anyone else handling the Post Office side of the investigation.

The case soon took a turn for the better. An informant reported that someone who had "soaked up a lot of lead", was secretly being treated at an address in the North Washtenaw sector of the city. The police arrived and found a badly shot up man attended by a friend. In the pocket of the second man they found $1,500 in brand new bills, just like the ones taken at the train heist. A stake-out at the house over the next twenty-four hours netted two more visitors, one being a well-known bootlegger named James Murray.

Inspector Fahy interrogated the suspects personally and it was not long before one broke. Willis Newton identified the wounded man and his nurse as his brothers Willie and Joe. They, Murray and two men called Holliday and Glasscock – from the infamous St Louis gang "Egan's Rats" – had been in on the robbery. Unfortunately, he did not know the identity of the Post Office informer. Only the "Boss", James Murray, had any contact with this person, Newton said.

The engine driver and fireman easily identified Willis and Joe Newton as being two of the robbers. Then, soon afterwards, the police picked up Holliday and Glasscock as well as a fourth Newton brother called Jessie, who Willis had left out of the confession.

Jessie confessed as well and led the police to his stash of the cash. Investigation of the other gang members' haunts also turned up much of the stolen money. However, the investigation into the criminal informant got nowhere. Then the case took a very surprising turn.

One day, a woman calling herself Nan Ryan walked into the office of Police Captain William Schoemaker. She told him that she was the wife of Jerry Ryan, a man William Fahy had recently arrested for robbery. Convinced of her husband's innocence she had set out to find evidence that Fahy was corrupt. Pretending that she had hated her husband she had started to date the officer – he was apparently totally unconcerned that she might be trying to destroy him.

Eventually her self-sacrifice had paid off. Fahy, when drunk, had complained that she always wore the same dress. She replied that she had no money to buy another and Fahy had said; "You just be patient for a couple more days. I'm going to get $14,000 tomorrow."

Incredulous though they were, the Chicago police had to take the accusation seriously. They had Fahy secretly followed and it was soon realized that he was spending far more than he earned. To settle the matter a fake telegram concerning the undercover surveillance of the bailed James Murray was planted on a detective's desk. As soon as he saw it, Fahy sneaked out and rang Murray to warn him. Fahy had not been informed that the bootlegger's telephone was bugged.

The detective was arrested and charged with aiding and abetting the Rondout train robbers. At the subsequent trial, he and Murray – both insisting on their innocence – were sentenced to twenty-five years each. The other robbers were sentenced to between twenty-five years and a year-and-a-day, depending on their co-operation in recovering the stolen loot. Jerry Ryan, husband of the unofficial undercover agent Nan Ryan, was quietly released without trial.

Of the valuables taken from mail train No. 57, all were eventually accounted for but $14,000 – the sum William Fahy had told Nan he was due to receive.

chapter five

THE AGE OF GANGSTERS

Prohibition, which began in 1919, brought the era of gangsterism to the United States. But at least it also brought prosperity to men like Dutch Schultz, Dion O'Banion and Al Capone, and made bank robbery unnecessary. The repeal of Prohibition in 1933 meant that America was full of out-of-work gangsters. Worse still, the great slump of 1929 brought widespread poverty and misery to the wealthiest nation in the world. The inevitable result was a steep increase in crime. And since banks were the places that held the money, bank robbery became the profession of some of the most ruthless of Al Capone's successors – John Dillinger, Pretty Boy Floyd, Clyde Barrow and Bonnie Parker, Alvin "Creepy" Karpis and the Ma Barker gang. Their story belongs in a volume on gangsters rather than robbers, who regard themselves as a specialized fraternity. But it is worth mentioning that much of their success depended on an absurd law that did not permit police officers to pursue bandits over a state line (ie bank robbery was not a "Federal offence".)

The largest bank theft so far was made at the Lincoln National Bank in Lincoln, Nebraska, in September 1930, which broke bank-robbery records with a haul of more than two million dollars in cash and securities – it actually forced the bank to close down. The man who planned this coup was a remarkable character called Harvey Bailey, who had been a respectable farmer until he returned from the First World War, and became a bootlegger. Trouble caught up with him when he lent his car to four bank robbers and they got caught; he was indicted, and skipped his bail. It was this mischance that turned him into a full-time bank robber – although periodically he tried to retire and live quietly with his family. The Lincoln National Bank robbery was the high point of Bailey's career. After that he became – to his regret – involved with the Barker gang and a bumbling gangster called Machine Gun Kelly, whose ambitious wife Kathryn was determined that her husband should be America's foremost law-breaker.

Bailey made two daring prison escapes. But his downfall came when he was on the run with a wounded leg, and took refuge in the Shannon Ranch, in Paradise, Texas, just after Machine Gun Kelly had kidnapped a wealthy oilman, Charles Urschel. Urschel was released on the payment of a ransom of $200,000 – Machine Gun Kelly overruled suggestions that they should kill him anyway. When de-briefed by police, Urschel was able to help them with a series of brilliant deductions and observations he had made while blindfolded in captivity – in particular, the precise time that a commercial plane flew over the ranch every day. This enabled the police to pinpoint Paradise, Texas. Bailey was captured there, with a $500 bill that one of the fleeing gangsters had given him. It proved to be from the ransom money, and Bailey was sentenced to life in Alcatraz for a crime he had no part in.

When Kelly was finally captured in a hideout in Memphis, Tennessee, newspapers reported that he yelled "Don't shoot, G-men", so coining the popular abbreviation for government agents.

The Rubel Ice Company Robbery

One of the boldest robberies of the 1930s took place on the morning of 24 August 1934 in Brooklyn, New York. Just after noon, an armoured car from the United States Trucking Company arrived to collect cash from the Rubel Ice Company on Bay and Nineteenth Street. Before leaving the vehicle the guards scanned the area; everything looked normal, and one guard entered the building while the other waited outside. At this moment, a kerbside pedlar threw a sack off his cart revealing two machine guns. Other men who had looked like innocent loiterers ran up with drawn guns. In a few minutes, bags of money were transferred from the armoured car to two cars belonging to the robbers. By the time the guard emerged from the Ice Company, the cars were speeding away. The New York police were on the scene within minutes, looking for the two cars, but the gang was already unloading the money at a pier less than a mile away into two waiting boats. The gang took their haul to a New Jersey hideout, and found that they had netted just under half a million dollars. The robbers then split up, taking an oath not to speak of their part in the hold-up.

Two years later, the police began to learn the names of men they believed had taken part in the robbery: John Manning, a top criminal, Joseph Kress, who had stolen the cars, two ex-bootleggers called John Hughes and Thomas Quinn, John and Francis Oley, kidnapper Percy Geary and forger Stewart Wallace. Most of these men were later imprisoned for other crimes, but remained loyal to their oath of denying all knowledge of the crime. John Manning, who was almost certainly the planner, was shot and killed in a gang feud on 6 July 1936.

The Invisible Bank Robbers

For sheer skill and planning, the case of the "invisible bank robbers" remains one of the most memorable in America's criminal history.

These thieves were not gangsters, but cracksmen of unusual ability, high-skilled professionals who burned their way into bank safes with an oxy-acetylene torch. But the real mystery was their apparent ability to walk through solid doors. In the majority of cases, the police were unable to discover how the men had broken into the bank. Moreover, the thieves were able to walk the streets with heavy oxygen tanks, apparently without attracting attention. These abilities led one reporter who worked on the case, Edward Radin, to christen the robbers "the phantoms".

Albert Spaggiari had been a hired gun for a right-wing terrorist organisation and had served in the paratroopers in French Indochina. By 1976, however, he was running a photographic supply shop in Nice, ostensibly a settled man. Yet he was planning one of the biggest and most daring bank robberies ever.

The Société Générale Bank in Nice had an ancient vault, built in the 1900s, and Spaggiari knew that this made it a relatively easy target. He surveyed the bank for hours, looking for a way to get to the vault without having to go through the modern building above ground. One day he saw his chance: a team of city cleaners were leaving the sewer from a manhole in a direct line with the vault. If he could tunnel through the underground masonry into the bank while the vault was locked, he could loot the safe deposit boxes and bullion almost at his leisure.

He recruited accomplices of equally dubious backgrounds, including Gaby Anglade, who in 1962 had tried to assassinate Charles De Gaulle, and Jean Kay, a conman who once cheated a rich industrialist out of 6,000,000 francs.

The tunnel was started in an underground parking facility opposite the bank, and took two months to complete. The diggers worked by the light of a fluorescent strip light attached to half a mile of cable, and Spaggiari catered the excavations, regularly bringing large amounts of food and wine down into the tunnel for his partners.

The tunnel complete, the robbery was carried off on 20 July 1976, France's independence holiday. The gang moved sixty million francs in cash, bonds and jewellery from the vault, leaving the vault's doors welded shut to delay discovery of the crime. Supposedly the gang found some pornographic photographs belonging to a blackmailer in one of the deposit boxes, and pinned them up all around the vault. They also left a message that read: "Without weapons, without hate and without violence."

By October the police had found some of the stolen bonds being sold by a garage owner in Nice. Following this lead, they arrested Spaggiari at Nice Côte d'Azur airport, where he had just returned from a holiday in New York, Hong Kong and Bangkok.

He remained in custody for only four months. Expecting a fifteen to twenty year jail sentence, he broke free of the court security and dived through a loosely secured window onto the street below. As his defence lawyer shouted: "No! not that!" he was picked up by a waiting motorcyclist and driven to freedom.

The first robbery took place on the night of 19 October 1944, at the Long Island City Savings and Loan Association. But the thieves had either been interrupted, or forced to abandon the job because of defects in their equipment. A hole had been burned neatly through the door of the safe, but the contents remained untouched. And the door of the building was locked, exactly as it had been when the manager had left the previous evening. There were no fingerprints – the police did not expect any, since all burglars wore gloves as a matter of course.

In the days of the D'Autremont brothers, safe-breakers had used explosives – usually nitro-glycerine – or "can-openers", huge jemmies that can rip off a safe door. In 1944, oxy-acetylene was the most sophisticated method.

Twelve days later, the "phantoms" broke into a safe in Brooklyn and removed sugar coupons and rationing stamps; again, there was no sign of forced entry. An almost identical robbery took place in Queens thirteen days later. Twelve days after that, the thieves got away with $11,000 in cash and $5,000 in war stamps; this time they had entered by a rear window. A robbery at another Brooklyn Savings and Loan Association in January was less successful – the thieves got away with blank war bonds. But again, the detectives could find no obvious means of entry.

The police interviewed every bank burglar in New York and eliminated most of them from their enquiries; the rest were kept under surveillance. This seemed to deter the "phantoms"; there were no more robberies for two months, and the next one occurred in Newark, New Jersey; the thieves drove off with the safe containing $7,000, and it was found the next day, with the neat burn-hole that had become the trademark of the raiders. But in March 1945, after the retirement of Captain Richard A. Fennelly, the man who headed the "Safe and Loft" Squad – specializing in safe-crackers – the "phantoms" moved back to New York and committed a series of robberies. Fennelly's assistant, Lieutenant Maguire – now promoted to chief of the squad – decided to keep a watch on all savings and loan associations. It required a vast number of officers, but it seemed to be the only way to approach the baffling case.

One day, two policemen sitting in a car in downtown Manhattan noticed two men standing outside a bank. Neither of the men was a known safe-breaker, but the policemen nevertheless felt they looked familiar. Then one of them remembered: they had seen them a week before near a savings and loan association. One was big and muscular, the other small and slim. Now the policemen watched them enter the building, pick up an advertising booklet, then stand by the door, apparently deep in conversation, while they glanced around the room. After this they strolled across to a restaurant opposite. Within a few minutes, two additional police cars had been summoned. When the men emerged from the restaurant and entered a grey Dodge sedan, a plain-clothed detective strolled past and noted its number.

A check with the Bureau of Identification revealed that it was registered in the name of Stanley Patrek, of Clay Street, Brooklyn. A check with the Motor Vehicle Bureau uncovered Patrek's driving licence, complete with a physical description. The Bureau of Criminal Identification was then able to tell Maguire that Patrek, who had been born in 1915, had a record as a hold-up man. He had been paroled in the previous year. His description indicated that he was the shorter of the two men.

Patrek and his companion were shadowed to a garage in Astoria, and later to their separate addresses. The following day, a plain-clothed detective in an unmarked car saw the heavily-built suspect come out of his apartment building, looking as if he was on a shopping errand. The detective slipped into the building and waited on the stairs. When the man returned, he observed which apartment he entered. A name on the door identified him as Joseph Stepka. He, it seemed, had a criminal record as a burglar as well as a stick-up man.

Now the two men were carefully shadowed; it was the constant aim of the police to make sure they had no suspicion they were under surveillance. If they were suspicious, both had sufficient money from robberies to lie low indefinitely. Both men seemed to be happily married, and spent much time at home playing with their children. But they also spent a good part of most days patrolling the streets and surveying loan association offices. One night, the detectives observed them having dinner with two attractive blondes, and deduced that they were deceiving their wives – the women proved to be a dance-hall hostess and a cigarette girl.

On 28 May 1945, a night of torrential downpour, the men left home late at night and returned to their Astoria garage. Three police cars proceeded to trail them as they drove off in the Dodge sedan. But near the Triboro Bridge, the suspects began

A New York bank computer programmer realised in 1970 that if he stole a few cents each month from all the customers in his bank he would become very rich without anyone noticing. In order to do this, he wrote a programme that rounded everyone's balance down to the nearest ten cents each month and transferred the balance into the account of whichever name was last in the alphabetical list of account holders. He then opened an account for himself in the name of A. Zyglit (an anagram of Lazy Git) and settled down happily to become a millionaire.

Things went wrong for the fraudster when a Polish immigrant named Zyzov moved into the neighbourhood and opened an account at the same bank. After a couple of months he politely wrote to the bank to ask why they appeared to be paying such enormous interest on his very small savings. The whole sham was discovered and the programmer was sent down for a number of years. If only he had called himself Zyzyzyk.

to weave in and out of side streets, and the police lost them. The following morning, Maguire learned that the "phantoms" had struck again at the Whitestone Savings and Loan Association, and got away with a safe containing $9,000. Again, there was no sign of forced entry, and the door was locked normally when the manager came to open the bank.

The following day, detectives trailed the two men from bank to bank as they made small deposits totalling $9,000. And when Maguire checked with the banks, he discovered that similar deposits had always been made in the past on days following the "phantom" robberies.

On the night of 1 June 1945, Patrek and Stepka again left home late in the evening and drove to the Astoria garage, lifting a bulky suitcase into the trunk. Once again they were shadowed as they followed a circuitous route to their destination, which proved to be Yonkers. The police lost them again, but eventually found the grey sedan parked not far from the Yonkers Savings and Loan Association on Broadway. For the next three hours they waited in darkness. Then the two men returned, both carrying heavy objects. The police ordered them to halt, and both men turned to run. Shots fired in the air made them change their minds. Stepka proved to be carrying the oxy-acetylene equipment, while Patrek held a briefcase containing more than $15,000.

The two men surrendered philosophically, and admitted that they had no idea they had been under surveillance for months. The Astoria garage proved to contain elaborate and expensive safe-breaking equipment – the most elaborate the police had ever seen.

But although they had been caught red-handed, there was no conclusive proof that Patrek and Stepka were the "phantoms" who had committed the previous robberies; understandably, they preferred to leave this problem to the police. The Astoria garage was studied carefully, and the detective in charge noticed some metal filings on the floor. These were turned over to the Technical Research Laboratory. The safe from the Whitestone Savings and Loan Association, which had subsequently been found abandoned, was also handed over. Under the microscope, the floor sweepings were found to consist of asbestos as well as metal filings, a strong indication that they came from a safe – most safes at that time were fire-proofed with asbestos inside the door, and often in the rear wall. Then samples of the filings and asbestos were compared with samples from the safe by means of the spectroscope. In emission spectroscopy, the sample is placed between two carbon electrodes, and a spark struck between them; the light from the burning sample is then split into a spectrum, whose emission lines are as distinctive as a fingerprint. The spectroscope revealed beyond all doubt that the filings and asbestos came from the Whitestone safe.

The chief mystery remained: how had the phantoms succeeded in walking in and out of locked doors? They refused to say; but a small box in their garage workshop finally revealed the secret. The box contained a well-known make of lock, together with an extra cylinder – the part the key slips into – and a tiny screwdriver. If the lock could be approached from the inside – the side that became accessible when the door was open – the screwdriver could be used to loosen a screw in the cylinder. Once this screw had been loosened, the cylinder could be worked out of the lock by pushing in a key, and twisting it back and forth. Eventually, it could be slipped out of the lock, and another cylinder – to which the thieves had the key – substituted. When the robbery was over, the original cylinder was replaced, the screw tightened, and there was no sign of the substitution.

Another lock in the box, partly sawed away, revealed how the thieves had stumbled upon this interesting secret. One of them had obviously made a scientific study of every make of lock until he found one with this flaw. When the watching detectives had observed Patrek and Stepka engaged in earnest conversation as they stood in the doorway of the bank, they had assumed that the men were simply observing the layout of the place; in fact, Patrek was unobtrusively inserting the screwdriver, using the big man's body as cover, and loosening the screw. Here was a case in which the thieves applied to crime the same scientific techniques that forensic experts were applying to their solution. It was a relief for the New York police when both men received long prison sentences for grand larceny.

The Brinks Bank Robbery

Not be be confused with Brinks-Mat, which we shall discuss in a moment, the Brinks bank robbery achieved another record, with a haul of nearly $3 million.

On 17 January, 1950, in the early evening Thomas Lloyd and his fellow employees were checking the day's consignment of cash and cheques. They worked for Brinks Incorporated, the American money-moving firm, in the Boston branch. They worked in the locked wire cage that surrounded the vault, among over three million dollars worth of different forms of money. As they counted and checked, Lloyd was distracted by faint sounds of movement on the other side of the wire. Looking up, he saw seven masked men wearing similar uniforms to his own. Each held a pistol; they were covering all the Brinks staff.

One of the men shouted: "Open up this door. This is a stick-up! Don't give us no trouble."

They had entered the room so quietly that they had given Lloyd and his co-workers no time to reach for the loaded shotguns that rested in a rack by the safe. Thus the Brinks men had no choice but to cooperate.

Lloyd opened the mesh door and, at the gang's command,

lay on the ground with the others. Their hands were bound with cord and their mouths sealed closed with adhesive tape. Over the next twenty minutes the robbers worked hard, stuffing sacks with the money that lay around and also blowing open the vault door with a 20 mm anti-tank weapon. At the end of this time, around seven pm, they left quietly and almost nonchalantly.

It took half an hour for Lloyd to wriggle free of his bonds and activate the alarm. The signal went direct to the police, and they were on the premises by eight. The gang had taken a staggering amount: $1,218,211.29 in cash and $1,557,183.83 in money orders and cheques. Among the haul were bundles of cheques intended for war veterans and half a million belonging to the Federal Bank Reserve. This meant that the robbery was accounted a Federal crime, and soon the bank was filled with FBI agents.

The ease with which the criminals had slipped into the central vault of the holding bank seemed to indicate help from an employee. The locks were intact; somehow the intruders had got hold of duplicate keys for most of the building. Checks on the branches employees revealed nothing, and the police and FBI turned to other methods. They pulled in hundreds of people and questioned them all.

The answer to the puzzling question of how the gang had got in without inside help was actually rather simple. About two years before the robbery, two men, Joseph "Specs" O'Keefe and Stanlet "Gus" Gusciora had been asked by a friend, Anthony Pino, to scout out the Brinks building, with a view to seeing if it was possible to rob it. When O'Keefe and Gusciora checked the bank late one night, they were astounded to find that the outer lock could be turned with only an ice pick, and that the inner doors opened when a strip of celluloid was slid through between the frame and the handle. Using these two simple burglary techniques, the prowlers were able to get right into the vault. There, the alarm was evidently switched on, and the safe door bolted. Hanging on a nail close by was a clipboard with the total amount of money in the vault scribbled on it. The two men let themselves out silently and reported back to Pino.

The main problem, then, was that at the time of day that they could easily use burglary techniques to gain entry, the alarm was always activated. In order to rob the bank, they would have to catch the employees before they left, and this would require a respectable and quiet means of entering the vault. The solution was simple – one night, O'Keefe and Gusciora stole all the locks from the Brinks Incorporated doors and had a fast and discreet locksmith create keys for them. They then sneaked back and replaced the locks well before the morning shift arrived.

Equipped with keys, Pino and associates gathered a group of accomplices and began planning the rest of the crime. They acquired uniforms that resembled the Brinks standard outfit, so that people on the street would not think twice about seeing them loading fat Brinks sacks into their getaway vehicle. Pino ordered that they get some rope, but that it must be stolen so that the police could not trace it. In the event those told to acquire the rope were too lazy to steal it and instead mail ordered it from Sears and Roebuck.

All signs pointed to 17 January being a very busy day for Brinks and consequently a very lucrative day upon which to rob it. Seven men including O'Keefe and Gusciora were detailed to enter the building and commit the robbery while two men, among them Pino, attended the getaway car in the street. One man was to keep watch from a roof top; the final, eleventh man was to dispose of all the evidence that they brought away from the crime, including the truck.

As we have seen, all went very smoothly, and late that evening the gang met to divide up the profits. They gathered at the house of one of the robbers' parents, a couple that spoke no English and were apparently unaware that their son's business activities took place on the wrong side of the law. In a back room the gang divided the usable money from the unusable, which was to be burnt. $98,000 was new, sealed and sequentially numbered, and thus useless without a massive money-laundering operation. Nearly all the cheques and money orders were "trouble money" too, being far too risky to attempt to cash. In all about $1,100,000 was salvageable, making each share worth $100,000. Each of the eleven wandered off into the night rich.

They did not have long to enjoy it however. Within two days all of the eleven had been questioned by the police in their massive sifting operation. Two gang members were given safekeeping of all the shares, during this difficult time. After they had all been released due to the lack of any evidence against them, $35,000 was found to have disappeared. The keepers maintained that the money had gone while they were being questioned, and thus that they knew nothing about it. Grudgingly the gang accepted this and took back their depleted shares. Soon however the police were back, centring their attention upon O'Keefe. After first removing $5,000 for spending money, O'Keefe handed his money to another gang member, Adolph Maffie, to keep while he and Gusciora temporarily left town.

They set out westward, into Pennsylvania, and it was not long before they began to practise their trade again. They broke into a hardware store and stole five handguns. They then used these to hold up a clothes shop and steal six suits. The fact that there was already FBI and police interest in the pair, coupled with the fact that they were careless, soon led to their apprehension. O'Keefe was given three years, while Gusciora received five to twenty years in prison.

Meanwhile the Boston police had found pieces of the getaway truck in local scrap yards. The gang had intended to bury the sections, but the frozen ground that January had frustrated their efforts. On the strength of evidence gained from examination of the truck parts and also on close observation of some of the gang, the FBI produced a list of eight suspects, including O'Keefe, Gusciora and Pino. As the Statute of Limitations on robbery as a Federal crime means that no criminal can be tried more then three years after the event, the FBI were forced to subpoena the eight men to appear before a Grand Jury in late 1952. They had little chance of success because they lacked solid evidence, and sure enough the prosecution failed early in 1953.

The gang seemed to have escaped punishment; the only chance that the police had was to acquire more evidence and try them under Massachusetts state law. In Massachusetts, the Statute of Limitations occurs only after six years. There seemed little chance however that new evidence would surface after such a long interval, and by the time of O'Keefe's release from jail in 1954, the case was all but closed.

O'Keefe returned expecting to receive his $93,000 dollars from Maffie. Maffie had, unsurprisingly, spent the lot. O'Keefe showed great restraint and did not do anything to Maffie, saying that he could not kill him because he might "get lucky again and pay me back". Instead, O'Keefe tried to extort money from Pino. He kidnapped Pino's brother-in-law and demanded $25,000 from his old boss "for starters". Pino gave him $2,500, and O'Keefe, oddly obliging, gave Pino's brother-in-law back.

His all-but-failed extortion was a mistake in more than one way; soon afterwards his Oldsmobile was sprayed with sub-machine gun bullets and O'Keefe only escaped injury by flinging himself to the floor. A second attempt on his life left him with gunshot wounds in his chest and wrist. It must have almost been a relief when he was jailed for twenty-seven months on an old offence.

The FBI had heard of O'Keefe's problems, and agents visited him in prison, off-handedly telling stories about the new cars and houses that his old compatriots had been purchasing with their new-found wealth. Within three visits O'Keefe was ready to name his fellow Brinks robbers and testify against them. He was put under twenty-four-hour armed guard, and the re-mainder of the gang were arrested. O'Keefe's old accomplice Gusciora did not survive to stand trial. While being held in Boston he experienced fits of unconsciousness and vomiting. Within weeks he had died of a brain tumour.

With the testimony of one of the robbers, the rest of the gang were doomed; each received a life sentence. O'Keefe's counsel plead for leniency on the grouds of the help that he had given to the authorities:

"Where would we be – the Commonwealth of Massachusetts or the FBI – if it weren't for Specky?"

O'Keefe was released in 1960. The vast majority of the haul was never recovered.

Hermann Goering, the head of Hitler's Luftwaffe, deserves to be included a book on robbers, since he was one of the most successful art thieves of all time. A member of the German "junker" class and a highly educated man, he was passionately fond of art; so whenever German troops marched into some city with a famous art gallery or museum, Goering had its art treasures sent back to Berlin, many for his own private collec-tion. In late twentieth century currency the value of the plunder would run to billions; even in the 1940s it reached millions.

In 1945 Goering took refuge in Bavaria and tried to take control from Hitler, who denounced him as a traitor. Captured by the allies, Goering was sentenced to death as a war criminal at Nuremberg; he committed suicide by poison before he could be executed.

Emile the Nut

Across the Atlantic, gangsters in Paris and Marseilles were studying the exploits of their American counterparts with admiration. One of these was perhaps France's most notorious and dangerous gangster since the far-off days of the Bonnot gang: Emile Buisson.

Buisson's heredity seems to have been extremely bad. His father was a drunkard, a builder of bakers' ovens, addicted to absinthe. Only four of his nine children survived, and one of them was a weak-minded deaf-mute girl. The two criminals of the family, Jean-Baptiste and Émile, were its only two healthy members; a third brother died of tuberculosis at the age of twenty. The mother, worn out by overwork, starvation, and continual brutal beatings from her husband, was taken to an asylum. The father took to exhibiting his deaf-mute daughter in cafés for money; he was sent to jail for carnal knowledge of minors – including his daughter – and died in an asylum.

Émile was born at Paray-le-Monial, in the Sâone-et-Loire department of southern France, on 19 August 1902. His elder brother fought in the war, deserted, and was sent to a penal battalion in Algeria. Released in 1921, he promptly became a pimp in Paris.

Émile served his first term in jail at the age of sixteen, and then twenty months' imprisonment for theft. He was due for military service, and so sent out to a penal battalion in North Africa. The brutality of these battalions was unspeakable. However, Émile managed to distinguish himself in the fighting, and got the Croix de Guerre. Back in France, he took up a life of petty crime and served many short terms in jail.

In 1932, he helped to rescue his brother from jail. The plan was bold. Jean-Baptiste got himself transferred to Strasbourg model prison at Ensisheim by confessing to a crime in Strasbourg and getting three years added to his eight-year sentence. He there broke his leg by smashing it with a table leg. He was transferred into the hospital, and the same night jumped from a first-floor window, breaking it again. However, with the help of Émile he made a clean getaway.

Émile Buisson committed his first big robbery on 27 December 1937, and got himself the nickname "Mimile le Dingue" – Crazy Mimile. He was driving a "traction avant" Citröen – front-wheel drive (known generally simply as "tractions"), and he and a gangster named Charles Desgrandschamps (known as "Bigfooted Charlie") robbed two bank messengers outside the Banque de France in Troyes. Émile fired at one messenger, wounding him in the thigh, and then, to the surprise of Bigfooted Charlie, began to fire at random down the street and into the bank.

He was arrested a month later. French justice was slow, and in 1940, at the time of the invasion, he was still awaiting trial in Troyes Prison. He escaped. In early 1941, he robbed the Credit Lyonnais bank in Rue Notre Dame des Victoires, Paris, killing two bank messengers in cold blood.

Shortly after this he was caught by the Gestapo carrying arms and sent to a military prison; he was then sentenced for the Troyes hold-up in 1937. He escaped by simulating lunacy until he was transferred to the asylum. In 1947, with four associates, he robbed a café in the Rue Lesueur (site of Petiot's crimes) and later executed one of his associates who kept back a brooch. This gave him such a terrible reputation in the underworld that he was not betrayed by professional informers in the usual way, and stayed at liberty a great deal longer than he might otherwise have done.

Over the next few years he took part in many hold-ups, always using sten-guns and Citröen "tractions". After the war, Paris had become a great deal more dangerous than Chicago in the Prohibition era, and gang killings were commonplace. Finally, the police were armed with sub-machine guns, but after accidentally shooting up an old gentleman who was drunk and a bus full of passengers, they were forced by public opinion to be a little more cautious. Finally, a special bandit squad was formed, adequately financed, and run by Charles Chenevier of the Sûreté, who had arrested Buisson in 1937. There was one unsuccessful attempt to arrest Buisson, when a whole convoy of heavily armed police cars rushed out of Paris towards a hotel at Arpajon; but their spectacular exit from Paris excited attention, and someone phoned Buisson, who escaped. However, he was finally arrested in 1955; and tried for the murder of the gangster whom he had "executed". He was guillotined in 1956.

His brother, Jean-Baptiste, nicknamed "Fatalitas" because of his fatalism, shot a restaurant proprietor, Jean Cardeur, when the latter cast aspersions on his dead brother's memory. Maître Carboni, who defended him, turned to the jury as they filed out and said pathetically: "Do not let me have two heads from the same family on my conscience for the rest of my life." (He had defended Émile.) The appeal was successful; Jean-Baptiste was found guilty with a recommendation to mercy, and sentenced to a life sentence of hard labour in Melun Prison.

Jacques Mesrine: "Public Enemy Number One".

At the time of Buisson's execution, a young Frenchman named Jacques Mesrine was already contemplating a career of crime that was to make him for a while the most famous criminal in Europe. Like so many of his larcenous predecessors, Mesrine liked to think of crime as a way of achieving the fame he deserved, and he revelled in his reputation as a modern Robin Hood.

Mesrine was born in Clichy, Paris, in 1937. In 1940, his mother moved her family to Château-Merle, near Poitiers, where she had been brought up, while her husband was in the army. Mesrine was an attractive child, and his biographer Carey Schofield reports that he was usually able to get what he wanted from adults by smiling at them. But he was also solitary. Once, when asked to go and play with other children, he replied; "No, I always have a nicer time on my own."

After the war, the Mesrines returned to Clichy. Mesrine later claimed that he never had enough affection from his father, who worked hard in a textile designing business. He was a poor student at school, but made a strong impression on his schoolmates with his charm, his prowess at fighting, and his love of argument. His constant absenteeism led to his expulsion from two schools. He began joining other teenagers stealing cars for joyrides. At the age of eighteen, he married a beautiful black girl from Martinique, and they moved into a small flat. But he soon found marriage boring and when his wife had a baby, decided that his mother could bring it up.

At nineteen, Mesrine was conscripted into the army, and asked to be sent to Algeria, where the French were trying to put down a Muslim revolt. There was much brutality on both sides.

Mesrine thoroughly enjoyed being in action, and received the Military Cross for valour. While in the army, he was divorced from his wife.

His return to civilian life was an anticlimax. He soon committed his first burglary. With two other men, he broke into the flat of a wealthy financier. When a drill broke off in the lock of the safe, he went out to a hardware shop, broke in and got more drills. They escaped with twenty-five million francs.

When de Gaulle came to power in 1958, he began seeking a political solution to the Algerian problem. Mesrine, like many Frenchmen, regarded this as a betrayal. The right-wing General Salan set up a secret organization, the Organisation Armée Secrète. Mesrine became involved, and it reinforced Mesrine's attitude to law and order – the typical criminal attitude that it is a question of individual choice and that men who can think for themselves should make up their own minds whether to obey the law.

In the spring of 1962, Mesrine was arrested when on his way to rob a bank, and sentenced to three years in prison. He was released on parole a year later. For a while he decided to ''go straight''. He married a second time, had a young daughter, and now with his father's help, began to study to become an architect. There is evidence that he was a good architect. But when, in late 1964, he was made redundant, he went back to crime. His cool nerve served him remarkably well. Once, in the course of holding up a jewellery shop, the police arrived. Mesrine ran into the back yard, unlatched the gate to make it look as if he had run through, then hid in a dustbin until the coast was clear. On another occasion, he escaped from a flat he was burgling through a lavatory window, and escaped across the roof-tops, walking out of a building further down the street, and asking the police what all the commotion was about.

In 1967 another attempt to ''go straight'' as an innkeeper – financed by his father – again proved to be a failure as he found respectability too unexciting. He went off with a woman, Jeanne Schneider, and together they carried out a daring robbery at a hotel in Switzerland. In 1968, as one of the most wanted robbers in France, he decided to move to Canada.

He and Schneider went to work for a Montreal millionaire, Georges Deslauriers, as chauffeur and housekeeper, but the gardener took a dislike to Jeanne, and Deslauriers dismissed them. Mesrine's response was to kidnap Deslauriers, and hold him for a $200,000 ransom. Deslauriers managed to escape before the ransom was paid, and Mesrine and Schneider moved to a small town, Percé, where they made the acquaintance of a wealthy widow called Evelyne le Bouthillier. After an evening spent with the pair, Mme le Bouthillier was found strangled. Mesrine always claimed that he knew nothing about the murder.

They slipped over the border into the United States, but were arrested by a border patrol and taken back to Canada. There they were charged with the murder of Mme le Bouthillier. Mesrine was furious at being accused of the murder of an old woman. He claimed that he *had* committed several murders, and tortured people who had insulted him, but that he would have been incapable of this particular crime. Held in the Percé prison pending trial, Mesrine succeeded in escaping by attacking a guard and stealing his keys. He also released Jeanne. They were recaptured only two miles away. Mesrine was given ten years for the kidnapping of Georges Deslauriers; Schneider was given five. But they were acquitted of the murder of Evelyne le Bouthillier.

A year later, Mesrine led a number of other prisoners in a spectacular escape from the "escape-proof" prison of St Vincent de Paul at Laval. He became a celebrity in Canada and it gave him the idea of a still more daring exploit. After robbing a bank in Montreal, he and another escaped convict drove back to the St Vincent de Paul prison with the intention of freeing the remaining prisoners in the top security wing. But when a police car approached them on the way to the prison, Mesrine opened fire. With bullets whistling past them, they escaped back to Montreal. A week later, Mesrine and two accomplices were in the forests near Montreal where they were stopped by two forest rangers. One of the rangers recognized Mesrine, and made the mistake of showing it. Both were shot down, and their bodies dumped in a nearby ditch and covered with branches.

There were more bank robberies – on one occasion, Mesrine robbed the same bank twice because a cashier had scowled at him as he walked out after the first robbery. Then Mesrine met a beautiful nineteen-year-old, Jocelyne Deraiche, who became his mistress. With two accomplices, they crossed the border again into the United States, continuing south to Venezuela where they were able to live comfortably on the profits of their bank robberies, aided by ex-OAS men living there. When a police official told them that Interpol was on their trail, Mesrine and Deraiche flew to Madrid.

All the publicity he had received in Canada had given

Mesrine a taste for fame. He decided to become the best known criminal in the world. In the remaining seven years of his life, he achieved that ambition.

Back in France, in 1973 Mesrine committed a dozen armed robberies, netting millions of francs. He gathered around him a gang he could trust. As the hunt for him intensified, he made preparations for the future by examining the courthouse at Compiègne. The precaution proved useful. When police finally caught up with him on 8 March, Mesrine staged a spectacular escape from the Palais de Justice in Compiègne, getting hold of a gun that an accomplice had left in a lavatory, then holding up the court, and escaping with the judge as a human shield. He was shot in the arm in the course of his escape, but had the bullet removed when he was safe in a hideout.

Once again at his old occupation of robbing banks and factories, he carefully nurtured the image of the gentleman crook, the modern Robin Hood. When a female bank clerk accidentally pushed the alarm button, Mesrine commented courteously, "Don't worry, I like to work to music", and went on collecting the money. When he heard his father was dying of cancer in hospital, he made a daring visit to see him dressed as a doctor in a white coat with a stethoscope round his neck. Not long after this, a bank robbery went wrong, and the accomplice waiting in the getaway car was arrested. As a result, the police tracked down Mesrine to his flat in the rue Vergniaud and placed him under arrest.

La Santé prison proved to be escape-proof, and Mesrine passed the time by writing a book, *L'Instinct de Mort* (*The Killer Instinct*), which was smuggled out and appeared in February 1977. In it Mesrine admitted that a previous claim to have killed thirty-nine people was a lie, but it contained detailed descriptions of other murders – for none of which a body had been found. After three and a half years, the prosecution finally opened in May 1977. Mesrine astounded the court by telling his audience that it was easy enough to buy the keys that could open any pair of handcuffs, then extracted a matchbox from the knot of his tie and within seconds had removed his handcuffs. The gesture brought him the kind of publicity that he had now come to crave. He was nevertheless sentenced to twenty years.

A year later Mesrine staged another of his spectacular escapes. An accomplice named Francois Besse squirted soapy water into the eyes of a guard, and Mesrine, who was in the interview room with his lawyer, grabbed some guns from a ventilation shaft. Two warders were made to undress, and the convicts dressed in their uniforms. They let another prisoner, Carman Rives, out of his cell, and then all three rushed across the prison yard. Mesrine and Besse escaped over the wall with a ladder, but Rives was shot.

The police commissioner, Serge Devos, was placed in charge of the squad whose business was to recapture Mesrine. Mesrine moved to Deauville, a seaside resort in Normandy. He was unable to resist the temptation of walking into the local police station, announcing that he was a police inspector from the Gaming Squad, and asking to see the duty inspector. They were told he was not there. As they walked out, one of the policemen said, "That's Mesrine", and the other told him that was impossible. Mesrine then robbed a casino in Deauville, and in the desperate chase that followed, was almost caught. After this, he invaded the home of a bank employee who had given evidence against him at his trial, and forced him to go to the bank and hand over nearly half a million francs.

A Paris department store was the scene of another one of Mesrine's typically quixotic gestures in the summer of 1978. He saw the floor-walker seizing a shoplifter – a boy of fifteen. Mesrine announced himself as a police inspector with special responsibility for juvenile affairs, flashing a fake identity card, then grabbed the boy by the scruff of the neck and led him out of the store. There he let him go. In August, he gave an interview to a journalist from *Paris Match*, which caused a sensation. Then Mesrine came to London where he spent several weeks undisturbed by police. There he planned another astonishing crime – to kidnap the judge who had sentenced him to twenty years in prison. On 10 November 1978 Mesrine and an accomplice returned to France, went to the judge's flat and held up his wife, daughter and son-in-law. But the accomplice was inexperienced, and the daughter succeeded in getting word to the judge's son when he came to the door. Mesrine saw the arrival of the police, ran down the stairs, and as he came face to face with several policemen, pointed behind him. "Quick, Mesrine's up there." And they went rushing past. A young policeman who recognized Mesrine outside was handcuffed to a drainpipe.

In hiding, Mesrine wrote an open letter to the French police denouncing conditions in French prisons and claiming that this had "evoked a fanatical passion for human rights". During his last year there was an obvious deterioration in Mesrine's character. "Mesrine believed in his lies more than anyone else did," said his biographer. "Any suggestion, even from his closest friends, that perhaps he was exaggerating a little, could send him into an uncontrollable fury. He had always been subject to fits of rage, and these were becoming more and more frequent . . . He would smash everything that was in his way, and it is extraordinary that he never killed anyone while in a rage." Mesrine explained to journalists – whom he still allowed to interview him – that he now "identified ideologically with the extreme left".

When the police finally located his hideout, in a flat in the rue Belliard, they decided to take no chances. Mesrine had sworn never to be taken alive. On 2 November 1979 Mesrine came out of the building with his girlfriend, Sylvie Jean-Jacquot, and walked towards his BMW, parked nearby. At a road junction, a blue lorry signalled that he wanted to cut across him and turn right. Mesrine waved him on. The lorry stopped in front of the car, and another lorry drew up behind. Four policemen climbed out, and within seconds, twenty-one bullets had shattered the windscreen. Mesrine was killed immediately. Sylvie Jean-Jacquot was shot in the arm, and her dog was also hit. The police flung their arms around one another and danced for joy.

The Great Train Robbery

If Mesrine was the most famous bank robber since World War Two, the most famous single "heist" was undoubtedly the Great Train Robbery. In fact, the *New York Herald Tribune* of 21 January 1964, described it in a headline as "History's Greatest Bank Robbery", followed by the unfathomable comment: "There'll Always Be An England."

On the night of 7–8 August 1963 the mail train travelled southwards as usual, making scheduled stops to load letters and packages into its twelve coaches. Packed into the second coach from the engine on this particular night were 128 large bags filled with paper money, mainly five and one pound notes. The cash had been spent over the August bank holiday that had just passed, and was returning to the head offices of several banks in London. The driver of the train, Jack Mills, and his fireman David Whitby, had taken over the running of the train at Crewe at about midnight. By 2 am they were past Leighton Buzzard in Bedfordshire and were only about half an hour from Euston. Unexpectedly however a signal showed amber rather than green, a sign that the driver should slow down in anticipation of a red signal soon. Sure enough the next signal at Sears Crossing showed red, and Mills brought the train to a halt.

In order to find out what had caused the stoppage, Whitby jumped off the train and made his way to a trackside telephone that was connected to the nearest signal box. The line was dead, the wires having been deliberately severed. Whitby shouted to the driver that the phone had been sabotaged, and ran back towards the engine. As he reached the second coach however a figure stepped from the rear. Thinking that this must be one of the postal workers on the train, Whitby asked, "What's up, mate?" Without replying the figure beckoned him over to the embankment. Suddenly the figure shoved Whitby down the slope where he was overpowered by two waiting accomplices.

"If you shout, I'll kill you," threatened one, holding a cosh

A criminal psychopath called Dr R. H. Hales escaped from the Indiana lunatic asylum in which he was being held by stowing himself away in an empty ice-box. When he emerged into the outside world, he immediately applied for the position of Senior Medical Adviser at the Indiana State Prison and, astonishingly, was given the job. "Dr Hales gave a brilliant interview," said a prison spokesperson. "We therefore followed our policy that we did not require references and gave him the job at a salary of $35,000 per annum." The bungle wasn't discovered until Hales was recognised by his new employer from a wanted picture in the local press.

over Whitby's head. Panicked, he replied, "All right mate, I'm on your side."

Whitby was taken back to the engine where he found Mills on his knees and bleeding copiously from a head wound. The cab was full of men in boiler suits and balaclavas. The robber who was evidently the train expert was having difficulty operating the engine – it was a new design. Finally Mills, still bleeding, was forced to drive the engine and its first two carriages down the track for about half a mile, to Bridego Bridge where the track goes over a road.

The gang smashed the windows of the second coach with an axe, and overpowered the postal workers inside. All but eight of the bags were unloaded and thrown to a lorry waiting below. Mills and Whitby were handcuffed together and left in the smashed coach; the lorry sped away with over two million pounds.

The police were called from the nearby village of Linslade by two of the postal workers after they judged that the gang were no longer watching the coach. Scotland Yard arrived and began the process of interviewing everyone in the district about new-comers or strange activities.

Within five days, the police had found the gang's abandoned base, Leatherslade Farm, about twenty miles from the robbery location. Neighbours had seen many cars coming and going until up to three days after the crime. They also reported that the windows had been habitually covered while the occupants were at home, and that they had claimed to be decorating the farmhouse. A Mrs Brooke was found, who had actually handed the keys over to the gang so that they could examine it with view to a sale.

The farm was bursting with evidence; almost every surface carried fingerprints. The gang had left a collection of personal objects lying around, including a can of paint, a monopoly set and two Land Rovers with identical number plates.

While the police were cataloguing the bewildering array of clues from the farm, two of the robbers were being captured in Bournemouth. The owner of a lock-up garage on Tweedale Road had become suspicious when the two men had wanted to pay for three months rental in advance with a huge sheaf of notes. While they were moving their van into the garage the owner called the police saying that she thought that she was in the company of two of the Great Train Robbers. Two plain clothes officers arrived and began questioning the owners of the van. Suddenly one of them dashed off down the road.

While the officers were tackling this one, the other also tried to make his escape. Both were recaptured with relative ease and taken into custody. The two men's names were Gerald Boale and Roger Cordrey, and their van proved to be stuffed with money, £141,000 in used notes.

At this point the rest of the gang evidently panicked. Two walkers in Redlands Wood, near Dorking in Surrey, found two holdalls by the side of the path. They were filled with bank notes. Police sniffer dogs also turned up a suitcase around the same location; altogether the bags contained £101,000.

Arrests based upon the evidence from the farm followed quickly, six more men identified by their associates and their carelessly distributed fingerprints. Also the lawyer that organized the sale of the farm to the gang, John Wheater, was charged with conspiracy and the harbouring of Leonard Field, one of the arrested men.

Lastly the police raided the flat of Bruce Reynolds, a man believed to be the organising force behind the crime. The police did not find Reynolds at home, but they did find Roy "The Weasel" James, a man also wanted in connection with the robbery. The police were forced to chase James across the length of St John's Wood before they could capture him. In all, thirteen men had been apprehended.

The trial opened on 20 January 1964, in Aylesbury assize court. The Crown had over two hundred witnesses and a network of circumstantial evidence that seemed incontrovertible. Among the witnesses called to the stand was Jack Mills, the driver of the train. The savage beating that he had received had permanently disabled him; his speech was halting and he had difficulty walking. British Railways had paid him £25 compensation. His evidence was however inconclusive, as he could not identify any of the accused.

Nearly all the defendants had left some fingerprints in Leatherslade Farm and this evidence alone was near damning. Only John Daly successfully overturned the evidence of his prints: his lawyer argued that although they were present on the Monopoly set, the Crown could not prove that they had got there while the set was in the house. He was discharged.

On 26 March 1964, eight of the defendants were found guilty of conspiracy and armed robbery. Three further were found guilty of conspiracy only. The final defendant was Ronald Arthur Biggs, who had succeeded in having his trial held separately from the other men.

The sentencing followed and it was shocking in its severity. Roger Cordrey, who had helped the police extensively, was sentenced to twenty years. All those convicted of armed robbery received thirty years, except Boale, who was given twenty-four years. Brian Field and Leonard Field, convicted only of conspiracy, also received twenty-four years. John Wheater, the gang's lawyer, was treated leniently because of his conduct in the Second World War, and was sentenced to only three years. Appeals were lodged, and in four cases these eventually resulted in reduced sentences.

The press was disgusted with the length of the terms handed down. The *Guardian* described them as "out of all proportion with everything except the value of the property involved". The *Daily Herald* calculated that the prisoners would have been punished less for a combination of manslaughter, blackmail, and breaking a baby's arm.

Three of the gang were wanted at the time of the trial and later tracked down. Bruce Reynolds, James Edward White and Ronald "Buster" Edwards received between fifteen and twenty-five years each upon their eventual capture. Ronald Biggs was sentenced to thirty years in prison, but he succeeded in escaping with Charles Wilson, another of the armed robbers. Wilson was recaptured, but Biggs left the country. He narrowly avoided arrest in Australia, and eventually settled in Rio, where he leads a relatively rich and high-profile life, running his own nightclub and even appearing as himself in Malcolm Maclaren's film *The Great Rock 'n' Roll Swindle*.

The Brinks-Mat Bullion Robbery

In November 1983, robbers in England created another world record.

At 6:40 am on Saturday 26 November 1983, the men of the day security shift had just entered the Brinks-Mat high security warehouse in Houndslow, West London, and were preparing the day's orders. The nondescript factory unit was a stop-off point for valuable shipments travelling to and from nearby

Heathrow airport and contained one of the country's largest vaults. As such, its security systems were state of the art and an undetected entry would have seemed next to impossible.

Nevertheless, as four of the six security guards stood chatting in the locker room a bizarre figure stepped through the entrance. He was wearing a black suit and tie with a trilby on his head. He was also wearing a yellow balaclava and brandishing a 9 mm Browning automatic pistol.

"Get on the floor or you're fucking dead", he roared. Three of the guards complied immediately, but the fourth, Peter Bentley, just stared. The intruder crossed the room and struck him over the head with the weapon, hurling him to the floor with a badly gashed scalp. More armed, balaclavaed men ran into the room and proceeded to bind the guards' arms and legs with tape and to cover their heads with black cloth bags tied at the neck with drawstrings.

The two other guards, Tony Black and Michael Scouse, were in the radio room at the time and were similarly surprised and bound. At this point the man who appeared to be leading the intruders ordered that a radio be tuned to the police waveband to pre-warn them of any alert. The security guards noted that he had a clipped, well-spoken voice with no discernible accent – unlike the others who sounded cockney.

Whoever the raiders were, they knew the Brinks-Mat security systems intimately. The only way to open the vault and safes was with two different keys and two different sets of combinations. These were held by the senior security guards, Robin Riseley and Mick Scouse; the robbers demanded these "keymen" specifically *by name*. Also, on the way to the vault the raiders used *their own key* to open an intervening door.

Outside the vault, Scouse and Riseley were subjected to a fresh incentive to cooperate. Their trousers were cut open and petrol was poured on their bellies and genitals. Scouse was then told: "You better do as I say, or I'll put a match to the petrol and a bullet through your head."

The keymen were given no opportunity to "accidentally" set-off the alarms as they proceeded to access the vault and its safes. The robbers gave specific orders as to which systems had to be deactivated and in what order. This, and other facts, later convinced the police that the criminals had been working with inside information.

Entering the vault they were forced to clamber around a large number of shoebox-sized, grey cardboard boxes to gain access to the three safes. Here the raiders' plan broke down. Riseley had become so frightened he was unable to remember his half of the codes for the safes and no amount of blows or threats could make him remember the numbers.

In frustration the robbers demanded what was in the little boxes. Scouse, realizing that they might kill Riseley if there was nothing to distract them from the safes, replied that the boxes contained gold ingots. Some of the boxes were torn open and the fact was confirmed. In their haste the thieves had almost missed three tonnes of purest gold bullion with an approximate market value of twenty-six million pounds.

Soon afterwards, the other guards – lying in blindfolded darkness – heard the familiar squeak of the loading trolley, the sound of the entry bay doors opening and a vehicle entering. Then they heard one of the robbers shout, "We're going to need another van." Evidently they had come prepared, because another vehicle roared in moments later.

The two keymen were brought back as this went on and one of the robbers sympathetically asked Scouse, "Are you all right, Mick?" Riseley, on the other hand, who the raiders had though was being "a hero", was dismissed with a derisive, "It's a good job it's Christmas."

The vault was emptied and the robbers jumped into the vans. Just as the guards started to relax a little, one of the raiders re-appeared in the doorway. "Merry Christmas!" he shouted, then ran to the departing vehicles.

The six man gang got clean away with £26 million in gold plus £160,000 of platinum, £113,000 worth of rough diamonds and £250,000 in untraceable traveller's cheques. It was the most profitable robbery in British history.

The police had little firm evidence to go upon. The security guards all agreed that the gang was made up of white males between thirty and forty years old, but so were most of the London armed robber fraternity. However, during the hour-long raid some of the thieves had lifted the lower half of their balaclavas to speak more clearly. The guards thought that they might be able to identify the "Bully" and the "Boss", if they saw them again. These were the man who had clubbed Bentley to the ground and the well-spoken leader.

The insurance company that had to shoulder the burden of the robbery issued a £2 million reward for the identities of the thieves, but nobody came forward. The police were left with only one solid line of enquiry, the fact that somebody on the inside of the Brinks-Mat organization seemed to have fed the robbers security secrets.

Although many people had access to this information, there was the fact that the robbers had passed under several security cameras to gain access to the building to consider. This suggested that the two men in the radio room – which also housed the monitors – had not been doing their duty. Interrogation showed that Mick Scouse had been engrossed in organizing the day's shipments, leaving Tony Black to watch the screens alone.

An investigation of Black's background revealed an interesting fact. Although he had a clean criminal record, he was the brother-in-law of Brian Robinson: one of the top ten suspected armed robbers in the country. Robinson's nickname in the criminal underworld was "The Colonel", due to his excellent organizing abilities and military-style, accentless voice.

After intensive interrogation Black broke down and admitted he had been the informant. He had been meeting regularly with his brother-in-law to hand over information, photos of the warehouse security systems and even a copy of the entrance key. Black, thereafter, cooperated fully with the investigation, but in one matter he could not help the police: he had no idea where the bullion was hidden.

The police quickly arrested Robinson and several other suspects. The security guards, at identity parades, singled Robinson out as the "Boss" and a second man, Michael McAvoy, as the "Bully". On 29 October 1984, these two and a third suspect, Tony White, were sent for trial at the Old Bailey under heavy security.

At the trial, Tony Black – who had already been given seven years for his part in the robbery – testified for the prosecution wearing a bullet-proof vest. It was rumoured that the man the press had dubbed "The Gold Mole" had a million pound contract on his head; perhaps the very money he had been promised as his share of the criminal proceeds.

He told the court that neither he or the robbers had any idea that the vault would contain so much loot when they agreed the date of the raid; it had been a matter of pure luck.

Eventually, on 3 December, the trial came to a close. Robinson and McAvoy were both found guilty, but White was acquitted. Outside the court he told reporters: "The evidence against us was the same. We should all have been acquitted." As the judge passed down twenty-five year sentences on

Robinson and McAvoy they both smiled: they had expected life imprisonment.

As the months passed the press interest in what had happened to the king's ransom taken in the raid decreased. It was rumoured that both the gold and the unprosecuted thieves were now safely abroad in countries with no extradition treaty with Britain. The police, of course, continued to investigate with vigour. Such a vast sum of gold was bound to leave some trace of its passing.

Most armed robberies can only hope to net a few thousands of pounds. The safes in the Brinks-Mat vault had held several hundred thousand pounds in used notes on the day of the robbery, and this in itself would have been an excellent haul. Millions of pounds worth of bullion, on the other hand, was quite another matter. The London underworld would not have had the resources to launder such a huge load, so the police began an extensive, national investigation to find those who were handling the gold.

Fourteen months after the robbery, on a freezing evening in January 1985, an incident took place at the Kent country home of wealthy property dealer and businessman Kenneth Noye, which reawakened public interest.

The police had been keeping Noye under surveillance for just over two weeks. They had reason to believe that he was an important link in the Brinks-Mat "gold chain", a group of seemingly legitimate businessmen who were re-casting and selling the gold for the absent robbers. The police team included men from the elite C11 squad – espionage-level experts in covert surveillance – whose job it was to hide as close to Noye's grounds as possible.

On that evening the two C11 officers were Detective Constables John Fordham and Neil Murphy. At 6:15 pm the order was give for them to close in on the house, entering the grounds, to reconnoitre. It has not since been made clear if this was just a standard check of the area or the preliminary to the serving of a search warrant on the Noye property. Either way, the two men were surprised by Noye's young Rottweiler guard dogs and DC Murphy retreated back to the fence. This was standard procedure in such a case and he did not bother to look to see if his partner was following. For some reason though, Fordham continued into the property, despite the barking dogs.

Kenneth Noye heard the dogs and went to investigate. Since darkness had already fallen he first went to his car to get a torch. He also picked-up a kitchen knife, which he later told the police he had been using to scrape clean a battery terminal. He said that as he walked to where his dogs were barking a terrifying figure loomed out of the shadows.

It is true that Fordham would have looked a fearsome sight that evening. He was wearing several thick layers of clothes under a combat style jacket and must have looked huge. He was also wearing a dark coloured balaclava through which only his eyes and mouth could be seen.

Noye stabbed him ten times in the heart region of the chest. He was still conscious when other officers arrived, but was pronounced dead on arrival at Queen Mary's Hospital in Sidcup.

At the subsequent murder trial the prosecution tried to prove that Noye, and another man called Brian Reader, had gone out with the deliberate intention of killing D.C. Fordham. As evidence they produced eleven re-moulded 1 kilo bars of gold found at Noye's house and pointed out to the jury that Reader, who had been visiting the house at the time, was a fugitive from justice – he had been on the run in Spain for some years, trying to avoid a burglary charge at home. To stop Fordham discovering these facts they had, said the Crown, cold blood-edly killed the officer.

Noye replied in the witness stand that he had been unaware of Reader's criminal status. He freely admitted that he was involved in the illegal smuggling of gold bullion, but he was not, he insisted, a murderer. Fordham, he said, had reared up at him in the darkness and struck him across the face. In a panic, and thinking he was about to be killed, he had stabbed wildly at the figure, but it just kept coming towards him. Later he realized that Fordham had been collapsing from the wounds.

Medical evidence showed that Noye had indeed suffered some battering to the face, but could not ascertain if this had happened before or during the knifing. A defence forensics expert also testified that after the killing, Fordham's balaclava had been clumsily tampered with, by persons unknown, to make it look less frightening. This was, presumably, to under-mine Noye's claim to striking out of fear.

In the absence of any immediate witnesses to the killing and the lack of any conclusive physical evidence, the jury found both defendants not guilty. However, Noye had admitted to gold smuggling and thus had little chance of avoiding jail.

He, Reader and a third man, called Garth Chappell, were

later found guilty of conspiracy to handle stolen bullion and evasion of VAT payments. Noye was sentenced to a total of fourteen years imprisonment and was fined £500,000. Reader and Chappell were jailed for nine and ten years respectively.

Since that time the police have failed to retrieve any of the Brinks-Mat bullion or catch any of the other robbers. For a short time a deal was struck with the imprisoned McAvoy and Robinson that if they returned the gold they would greatly increase their chance of early probation; but, in the end, this came to nothing.

The prisoners trusted their associates to keep their shares until they were released, but when they asked for their portions early, they were refused. The authorities offered them a similar deal for the names of the other criminals, but up to now they have maintained the underworld code of loyalty and kept silent.

It is believed that most, if not all the bullion has now been converted into legitimate property and cash and with interest it must now be worth many times the original value of the haul. Much is rumoured to have been invested in London's Dockland refurbishment project.

The identities of the four remaining thieves and many of their associates are now said to be known by the police. They are believed to be living in Spain's Costa del Sol. At the time of writing, August 1993, Britain has no extradition treaty with Spain.

The Knightsbridge Safe Deposit Robbery

Nothing seemed less likely than that someone would break the record established – albeit accidentally – in the Brinks-Mat robbery. But within three years, the gang who robbed the Knightsbridge Safe Deposit had almost doubled it. This may also be regarded as *the* "inside job" of all time, since the man who planned it was the manager and part-owner.

Security Deposits of Brompton Road, Kensington, catered for the kind of customer who found banks a bore. The business provided lockable safe deposit boxes in a secure building and also a discreet lack of curiosity as to their customers' affairs. The owners, Zahid Adamjee and Parvez Latif, had spent £825,000 acquiring the business in 1986, believing that the economic boom of the time would lead to huge demand for high security storage. Things had not gone well however, and in their first year they lost £400,000 and rented out only a quarter of their capacity. Latif stood to lose most, as his background was far less wealthy than that of his partner. He had a £100,000 overdraft, and little prospect of paying it off.

Around this time, Latif became friendly with a client of the firm, a man named Valerio Viccei. Viccei was a conspicuously wealthy young man, with a taste for Ferraris and rich living. He was also wanted in his native Italy, for bank robbery, and was also suspected of involvement with ultra-right wing terrorism. He remained financially afloat in London in much the same way as he had in Italy, robbing banks when he was short of cash. Unsurprisingly, he himself used Latif's business rather than entrust his money to a bank.

The two men socialized, often going to restaurants together. At some stage the fact that Viccei's main skill was the answer to Latif's main problem occurred to them both, and they set about planning the robbery of *Security Deposits*.

Latif increased the value of the business's insurance to £1 million, while Viccei gathered four accomplices and contacted a fence, Israel Pinkas, to help him dispose of any expensive items that the crime might turn up. At around 3 pm, on Sunday 12 July 1987, Viccei rang *Security Deposits* posing as a prospective customer, and asked to be shown around.

That Sunday the business was being run by Latif with only two security guards. One of these took Viccei's call and told his employer that a customer was coming to look at the arrangements. Around 3:15 pm, Viccei arrived with one of his team, and was shown into the secure area by Latif, who all the time was playing the attentive manager eager to acquire a new account. Viccei pulled out a pistol, and in a performance that the police later described as "worthy of an Oscar" Latif "panicked" and allowed the thieves to do what they liked.

Viccei smashed the locks of each box with a sledgehammer, while his accomplice followed with a crowbar and a sack, wrenching open the wrecked doors and grabbing the contents. In the rush, Viccei cut his hand badly, but carried on his work in a very professional manner. At around 5 pm the gang left the building, about £40 million richer.

For the moment however Viccei and the others were not sure of how much they had taken. £2,500 was given out to each of the accomplices as spending money, and the gang split.

It is not known exactly how much was stolen that day. Estimates are low as £20 million and as high as £60 million. Rumours suggested that the gang also got away with some of the laundered money from the Brinks-Mat Bullion robbery two years earlier. The police were, naturally, desperate to apprehend the gang.

The ease with which the crime was achieved seemed to indicate inside help, but for the moment the police did not suspect Latif. He continued his performance, returning to work every morning and trying to deal with the flood of outraged customers.

Some things about the business puzzled the investigating officers. For example there was no video-taped surveillance of the robbery. Latif pointed out, not unreasonably, that many of his customers objected strenuously to being filmed, and that the lack of this security feature was a positive selling point of his service. The absence of any alarm that connected directly to the police was more difficult to explain; Latif's answer to this query was that his staff dialled 999 if there was any problem. For the time being the police were stumped.

Forensic examination of the smashed lockers soon provided a hugely significant clue. There was a fingerprint in blood on one of the doors. The print was so clear and prominent that at first the police imagined that it might be a kind of arrogant challenge from the robbers. Although their attempts to identify the print at first were unsuccessful, searching the records of foreign criminals thought to be in the UK soon produced the name "Valerio Viccei".

Police next set up surveillance on a group of people thought to be Viccei's friends. Among them was Israel Pinkas, who had been very busy since the robbery. Officers observed that some of the group, including Pinkas, frequented White's Hotel on the Bayswater Road. Pinkas seemed often to be looking out for a black Ferrari that regularly parked in the Hotel's drive. The police checked the car's details in their computer, but it showed that the owner was not Viccei.

Observation finally paid off however, and one day the officers recognized Viccei leaving the hotel and climbing into the black Ferrari. Viccei *had* bought the car only a few weeks before, for £87,000 cash. The registration documents had not yet been processed. As the Ferrari pulled into a virtually stationary queue of traffic, an officer tried to reach in through the open window and take the ignition key. Viccei dragged the policeman about twenty yards down the road before another officer succeeded in getting on the car's bonnet and smashing the windscreen with his truncheon. Viccei was under arrest.

Having trapped the man that they believed to be the kingpin of the gang, the police set about following the trails of evidence to his accomplices. While searching Viccei's flat, they came upon an interesting piece of paper: a phone bill from Viccei's room in an Israeli hotel. Among the calls to Pinkas and to other people that the police already suspected was a call logged to Parvez Latif, the owner of the robbed business and supposed victim of the crime. This was damning evidence, and he too was soon arrested, along with Israel Pinkas, Latif's girlfriend and all but two of the rest of the gang.

The trial took place at the Old Bailey, and there was little doubt as to the outcome. Viccei received twenty-two years, Latif eighteen. One of the gang testified against his fellows, and was given only five years. Sixteen months later another gang member, Eric Rubin, was caught and sentenced to twelve years.

The capture of Viccei, and the consequent arrests of the others, could have been avoided entirely were it not for the black Ferrari. Viccei had planned to travel to Colombia and to lie low there. He would not go, however, without his new car. The Colombian embassy were making bureaucratic difficulties, and it seemed that the license to import the car would not be granted for many days. Viccei determined to wait, and in doing so doomed himself and his accomplices to long prison sentences.

The Whitchelo Case

The 1980s witnessed the advent of a new type of crime: consumer terrorism, in which large companies were blackmailed by criminals who threaten to tamper with their products and so cause a slump in their sales. One of the most memorable practitioners of this new dimension in extortion was an ex-police sergeant called Rodney Whitchelo, who was inspired to try consumer terrorism after hearing a lecture about it at the Detective Training School in Ripley, Derbyshire, in the summer of 1986.

Soon after hearing the lecture, Whitchelo – still in the force – opened three building society accounts in the names of John and Sandra Norman. The cash-cards and statements were sent to a mailing address in Hammersmith, so no one ever saw the face of the account holder.

During the course of the next two years Whitchelo was transferred from the Regional Crime Squad to the CID in Hackney; but he took care to keep up with his old mates.

In August 1988, the Managing Director of Pedigree Petfoods in Leicestershire received a tin of his own firm's pet food, together with a letter which demanded £100,000 to prevent its products from being contaminated. The tin of pet food had been injected with poison. If they did not pay, said the letter-writer, dozens of similarly contaminated tins would appear on supermarket shelves. It instructed the company to insert an advertisement in the personal columns of the *Daily Telegraph*.

Pedigree contacted the police, who told them to obey the instructions. So a happy birthday message to "Sandra" was inserted in the *Telegraph*. They added a telephone number suggested by the police.

In a second letter, the blackmailer explained how the "ransom" was to be handed over. It was to be paid into three building society accounts that were in the names of John and Sandra Norman. Here Whitchelo revealed something like criminal genius. Most consumer terrorists, like most kidnappers, were caught during the hand-over of cash. But he could go and draw out money from thousands of cash machines all over the country.

Here the police scored their first minor triumph. Detective Inspector Ian Leacey, who was in charge of the case, authorized some of the money to be paid into only one of the Normans' three accounts – the Halifax. This at least limited the number of machines he could use to nine hundred.

The blackmailer soon began to withdraw cash, at the rate of £300 per day (the maximum). Withdrawals were as far apart as Wales and Scotland. And there was no obvious way to catch the blackmailer except by placing a constant watch on all nine hundred cash machines.

In spite of his success, the blackmailer was furious that the police had restricted him to the Halifax account. He telephoned four supermarkets, warning them that their pet food had been tampered with. Three of the calls turned out to be hoaxes; but the fourth – to a supermarket in Basildon – was not; several tins with minute holes proved to contain injections of salicylic acid. Then he wrote to Pedigree Petfoods again, warning them that in future he would contaminate their tins with razor blades. But Leacey kept his nerve, and declined to authorize payment of ransom money into the other accounts.

In March 1989, Heinz Babyfoods became the target of the blackmailer; they were told that if they failed to pay £100,000 a year for five years, their products would be contaminated with caustic soda.

Now the operation to trap the gang (as the police assumed it to be) was transferred to Scotland Yard, and placed in the hands of Chief Superintendent Pat Fleming. And Fleming decided that he had only one option: to organize a huge operation to watch all nine hundred machines. It would be impossible to mount the watch all the time – the cost would have been prohibitive. But since withdrawals were being made virtually every day, it should be enough to watch all machines on the same day.

The immense operation was a failure. For what Fleming had failed to take into account was that he might be dealing with a blackmailer with "inside" knowledge. Whitchelo had, in fact, resigned from the force in 1988 on health grounds – asthma – but he kept in touch with his old colleagues, who spoke freely in front of him. So whenever detectives – three thousand of them – were engaged in watching cash machines, Whitchelo stayed home. As soon as the operation ceased, he started withdrawals again.

Fleming installed video-cameras at some of the cashpoints. One day, a withdrawal was made at one of these. The tape was rushed to London, and eagerly wound to the right time. The watchers groaned as they saw that the blackmailer was wearing a crash helmet with a tinted visor; he had outsmarted them again.

The blackmailer again tried to force his victims to put money into other accounts. He had so far netted over £14,000, but he wanted bigger sums. Heinz became aware that he was putting on the pressure when a baby in Cowley, Oxford, began to bleed from the mouth as his mother fed him pear yoghurt; the forensic lab found it to be full of tiny fragments of razor blade. A lady in Rayleigh, Essex, was luckier: she had poured

Heinz beef dinner onto a plate for her puppy when she saw a
piece of paper that said: "Poisoned with NaOH" in the bottom
of the jar. (NaOH is the chemical formula for caustic soda.)

Fleming now tried telling the Halifax to make their machine
swallow the card of John and Sandra Norman next time it was
presented; they were hoping to get a fingerprint from it. In fact,
the card had been handled with gloves; but Whitchelo's
response was to threaten to put cyanide in the food. In doing
so, he forced Fleming to "go public"; at a press conference on 27
April 1989, he called a press conference and told the reporters
about the blackmail. The result, of course, was a slump in the
sale of Heinz babyfoods. Oddly enough, it also led to two
thousand copycat offences.

Now his account had been closed, Whitchelo's cash supply
had been cut off. But when Heinz offered a reward of £100,000
for information about the blackmailer, he saw his chance. He
contacted Heinz – using a stencil – and claimed to be someone
close to the blackmailers, who would cooperate with the police
if the reward money was paid into two building society
accounts held in the name of Ian and Nina Fox. Police attempts
to trace who opened these accounts were as unsuccessfull as in
the case of John and Sandra Norman, which convinced them
that this was no informant, but the original blackmailer.
Fleming authorised Heinz to pay the reward into the building
societies the blackmailer had named.

Fleming was now beginning to suspect that the blackmailer
was *too* lucky – that is, that there was some kind of leak. His
response was to set up a new and secret operation, code-named
Agincourt, and to allow the rest of the force to believe that the
cooperation was being run down. Fleming's hunch was confirmed when the blackmailer grew lazy, and began limiting
himself to cash machines in and around London. It looked as if
he was a Londoner. In which case, he could be caught with a
much more limited operation. Fleming's secret group consisted
of only enough men to watch fifteen cashpoint machines. The
operation was set for 20 and 21 October. Fifteen Woolwich
Society cashpoints were staked out, since the blackmailer
seemed to favour the Woolwich.

At this point, "Agincourt" was struck by what – at the time –
seemed appalling bad luck. A workman with a drill sliced
through a cable servicing the Woolwich computer, putting
many machines out of action. But since the men were now
in position, Fleming decided they might as well press ahead.

Whitchelo had decided on one of his favourite tactics: to go out just before midnight and withdraw £300. Then he could wait until a few minutes after midnight, and withdraw another £300 – the limit being £300 on any specific date.

He chose the machine in Uxbridge, Middlesex. As it happened, this was not covered by a surveillance team. But it was also one of the machines put out of action by the severed cable. Whitchelo drove on to Enfield.

At half past midnight, the surveillance team – of two – at Enfield saw a Peugeot pull up and a man in a crash helmet climb out. They watched him withdraw £300, then stepped up to him as he climbed back into his car. Detective Constable Mark Kiarton asked what the crash helmet was for; the man said that it was raining. Meanwhile, the other constable had found the cashcard in the name of Ian and Nina Fox. "We are placing you under arrest." As he spoke, Rodney Whitchelo slumped in a faint.

Whitchelo pleaded not guilty, but the typewriter on which he had typed the "ransom" demands was found in his bachelor flat in Hornchurch, Essex. So was a tape he had made with a journalist friend with whom he intended to collaborate on a book. Its subject: how to commit the perfect crime.

On 17 December 1990, at the Old Bailey, Whitchelo was found guilty of blackmail and contaminating food products, and sentenced to seventeen years in prison.

. *World Famous* .

GANGSTERS

Ian Schott

• chapter one •

THE SICILIAN DONS

Sicily is a parched, mountainous and pitiless country. Despite its small size, it possesses a peculiar sense of remoteness; it is full of wild, empty places, for hundreds of years the haunt of the infamous Sicilian bandits (these, often mafiosi on the run, were still customarily holding up vehicles in the 1960s). Apart from one or two cities favoured by the tourists, the morose and introverted island is covered by dull, crumbling towns, into which the rural population has traditionally huddled for mutual protection from the elements and from brigands.

It is an innately feudal society, and though the Sicilian princes and their houses have passed away, the Mafia has long since filled that power vacuum, and the Mafia dons have bought up the estates of the impotent aristocrats.

No one knows where the name "Mafia" originates. Sicilians say that when Sicily was occupied by the French in 1282, a young Sicilian woman was raped by a French soldier on her wedding day. Her distraught mother ran through the streets shouting *"Ma fia! Ma fia!"* (my daughter, my daughter). The Sicilians immediately rose up and massacred their French oppressors. It is also said that the name "Mafia" derives from a similar word in Arabic, which means "place of refuge".

But the Mafia, the very existence of which has been frequently denied, not only by its members but by prominent politicians, has been an integral part of southern Italian culture for centuries. For two thousand years the peasants of Sicily and southern Italy struggled against bitter poverty, rapacious land-lords, and endured constant changes of master as a conse-quence of territorial battles between princes; Sicily has been invaded no less than six times.

It was an anarchistic world, in need of order. But the law was the oppressor of the peasants, not their defence. As a conse-quence, a system of underground government evolved, run by men outside the law. These were often violent and committed criminals, but to the peasants their word was their bond, and they could be expected to arbitrate in local disputes, protect the people from outside marauders, preserve the integrity of the local culture and intercede with the nominal rulers of the land. Such a man, who had to be strong enough to avenge any insult to himself and his friends, took the title of *un uomo d'onore*, a man of honour, or *un uomo di rispetto*, a man of respect. They became the Mafia, the most closed and ruthless of secret societies.

Though the Mafia has long been driven by the pursuit of wealth, it has continued to rely for its support on this tradition of "honour". In addition, certain traits in the Sicilian character make it wholly suited to the temperament required of mafiosi. As an isolated race, the Sicilians have clung to the ties of blood and soil with a savage ferocity, in a fashion both atavistic and tribal; indeed some of their customs are echoed in the remote tribes of Africa and Asia.

When the Italians emigrated to America, the men of honour went with them, and were initially a useful defence against an often hostile American society. They protected the Italian commu-nities, ran the lotteries, dealt with the authorities and offered loans. The Italians were ambivalent about the Mafia, or, as it was also known, *amici nostri*, meaning "our friends" (*cosa nostra*, another branch of the Mafia, literally means "the things we have in common"). They venerated these paternal criminals, while praying that their children would never enter into this strange, violent world, the detritus of which they would come across in the shape of unrecognizable corpses strewn over the local waste-lands. Many families noticed, when burying some aged and withered relative, how heavy the coffin was. They would know that alongside their grandmother in the coffin lay some victim of a Mafia dispute, whom the undertaker had been asked to squeeze in.

The Sicilian tradition of the *vendetta* – a fight to the death between clans until honour is satisfied – is a mainstay of the Mafia mentality. Vendettas have made for some of the bloodiest episodes in the island's history. The worst vendetta of them all took place in the neighbourhood of the poor, dusty towns of Bagheria and Monreale between 1872 and 1878.

The two Mafia clans involved were the Fratuzzi and the Stoppaglieri, who were both active in the same area but had hitherto kept hostilities to a minimum. Then, in 1872, Giuseppe Lipari, a member of the Fratuzzi clan, committed what in Mafia parlance is called *infamità* by denouncing a member of the Stoppaglieri to the police. The Stoppaglieri duly sent word to the Fratuzzi that they should, in time honoured fashion, execute Lipari. This they failed to do, and a vendetta was born. Within months all the close relations of the original disputants had been killed, and the more remote kin were being compelled to participate in the tit-for-tat murders. When everybody who was officially a Fratuzzi or a Stoppaglieri was dead, the entire population began fearfully rummaging through its ancestry to find out if they too had some distant blood links which would compel them to participate in the round of killings. Within a few years, a man walking down the street would find himself approached by a withered old crone swathed in black mourning who would inform him that he

They say that there is nothing personal about a proper Mafia execution. These are the words of Nick Gentile, an American mafioso from Sicily, discussing the ethics of eliminating an uncontrollable young hood from his native country: "There was nothing we could do about him so he had to be rubbed out. We embalmed the body and sent it back to his people in Sicily. His folks were poor – they didn't have anything – so we put a diamond ring on his finger, the way they'd see it the moment they opened the casket. I guess we did the right thing. We figured otherwise that he'd end up in the electric chair or the gas chamber. That way they wouldn't even get his body back." The Sicilians regard the retrieval of the body after a murder to be of the greatest importance. For vengeance must be sworn "in the presence of the corpse". If the body cannot be found, the anger of the relatives has no ritual outlet. Hence the most perfidious of crimes are kidnappings in which the victim disappears altogether.

Even in this century, some towns have been decimated by prolonged vendettas. The Mafia stronghold of Corleone, a tiny sullen town set in an unforgiving rocky landscape, experienced no less than 153 murders in the years between 1944 and 1948. Most of the bodies were never recovered. The town of Favara suffered 150 Mafia-vendetta killings in a single year; between 1914 and 1924 only one male inhabitant died of natural causes in old age (residents were not sure whether to be proud or not of this absurd statistic). Mass emigration to escape involvement in vendettas resulted in Sicily losing one-tenth of its adult population between 1953 and 1961; some towns became virtually uninhabited.

might not be aware, but he was now the surviving head of the Fratuzzi or Stoppaglieri clan, and was therefore in state of ritual vendetta.

In vain, many distant relatives of the decimated clans tried to emigrate, or conceal themselves; the area was becoming depopulated and reverting to wilderness. But the inheritors of the vendetta were always tracked down and forced to continue the feud, though the original ground for it had long since been forgotten. By 1878, the supply of able-bodied men was almost exhausted, and boys were being pressed into service. On one occasion a child was informed that in the absence of living seniors, he was now a clan leader, and, presented with a loaded blunderbuss, he was escorted to a point where he might attempt an ambush.

In the end, one of the few surviving Fratuzzi, a man called Salvatore D'Amico, who had lost all his family and was sick of the slaughter, offered his own life to end it. He went to the police and, in a repetition of the events that sparked the feud, informed on the Stoppaglieri, thus giving his own clan a ritual means to end the vendetta. The Fratuzzi understood D'Amico's noble intent; this time they made no mistake and duly killed him, displaying his body so that the Stoppaglieri might see that after six years and the blood of several hundred people the infamità had finally been paid for. Thus the vendetta was halted.

Another tradition of the Sicilian Mafia is that of *omertà*. Omertà is a complex notion. At one level it simply means "manliness", but at another it is to do with silence and self-

This gives an interesting insight into the beginnings of crime - and of gangs. It is known that most of man's earliest cities, some of which sprang up 5000 years B.C., contained overcrowded slums. This may sound strange; after all, the world of those days had a tiny population. So why didn't the people spread themselves out more? The answer is simple. Men built cities for mutual protection; they preferred to be huddled together. Moreover, these cities were often in river valleys where there was a limited amount of space to expand. The result was inevitable - crime on a large scale. To people from quiet country villages, the wickedness of the cities must have seemed terrifying - as is instanced in the Bible, with its stories of Sodom and Gomorrah, and those godless cities of Mesopotamia that were destroyed by the Flood (which actually took place about 4000 B.C.). The city, therefore, literally created crime - at least, large-scale crime. And, unfortunately, the pestilence soon overflowed into the surrounding countryside; travellers were robbed and murdered; small villages were overrun by robber bands who killed the men, raped the women, and burned the houses.

It can thus be said with some confidence, that the first gangsters appeared soon after the first cities. But at this point, an important distinction must be made. There are two distinct kinds of gangster which, for convenience, can be labelled the bandit and the true gangster. Bandit obviously means the same as gangster (since a gang is a band); but their motivations are different. To put it simply, the gangster tends to be crueller and more vicious than the bandit. The bandit lives in rural areas; he has space. He may have taken to crime for a variety of reasons; but one of these is not overcrowding. He prefers to be a member of a band because being a loner in wide open spaces is a demoralizing business. (Criminal loners often commit far more atrocious crimes than 'bandits', because boredom and solitude make them lose their sense of identity.)

restraint. When the police would come across a seriously wounded mafioso and ask him to identify his attacker, the reply would traditionally be couched in the followed terms: "If I die, may God forgive me, as I forgive the one who did this. If I manage to pull through, I know how to settle my own accounts." Such a response displays omertà. If wronged, a true man of honour will not wreak his vengeance in a rash, bloody act, or betray his anger; he will certainly not tell the authorities. Instead he will wait, for years if necessary, to avenge himself in the coldest way possible, often striking when he seems to be on excellent terms with the man he intends to destroy.

Although it stands outside Christian morality, the uncorrupted form of the feudal Mafia that survives in Sicily has a strict morality of its own. Mafiosi don't see themselves as petty criminals, but as lawgivers; they do not steal from the community, but take what is rightfully theirs in return for offering their continued protection. Killing is a pragmatic and at times inevitable action; a punishment.

The position of strength that the Mafia has achieved in this century, as it progressed from a federation of outlaws into a consolidated money-making machine, is largely the work of two formidable dons: Don Vito Cascio Ferro and Don Calogero Vizzini. These men struck the deals that brought the Mafia out of the shadows into the abandoned palaces of Sicily's lost aristocrats, and into the town halls.

In the early part of the century, Don Vito Cascio Ferro was for twenty-five years the undisputed master of Sicily. In his youth he had emigrated to America, where he had become a leader of the "Black Hand", an amalgamation of fugitive mafiosi and members of the Naples-based *Camorra*. While in America, he picked up a taste for smart expensive clothes and on his return to Sicily sported dashing, anachronistic garb: frock coat, wide-brimmed fedora, pleated shirt and flowing cravat. While other Mafia dons still dressed like surly peasants, Don Vito cut a sartorial swath through Sicilian society. He became an honoured guest at the salons of Palermo, opened exhibitions, romped with Dukes and Duchesses, frequented theatres, bought himself a phonograph and even took a hot-air balloon flight to demonstrate his interest in scientific advancement. Society women trembled with a strange passion when they spoke his name, and Don Vito had to reprimand his barber severely for selling off his hair cuttings as sacred amulets.

In the eighteenth century it was the Mafia, casting itself as a supporter of the popular leader Garibaldi, that whipped up the Sicilians into the violent frenzy that finally broke the shackles of the Bourbon state. When, before the turn of the century, democratic elections were held in Sicily, the Mafia took control of the political machinery and gradually drew apart from the people, blatantly compelling them at gunpoint to elect the Mafia's own chosen creatures. With political power assured, Don Vito was free to develop the system of *pizzi*. *Pizzo* refers to the beak of a small bird, and Don Vito adopted this term as a euphemism for racketeering, describing Mafia tolls and levies as "wetting the beak" – taking his cut.

Don Vito organized beak-wetting at the expense of the farmers, whose produce the Mafia bought dirt cheap and then sold at vast profits in the markets (where only those who had paid a levy were allowed to own a stall, and all prices were fixed by the Mafia). The Mafia also wet its beak in the meat, beer, and fish industries; in the sulphur mines, salt mines, building industry and cemeteries. It also took up a large portion of the tobacco smuggling racket and cornered the market in stolen Roman artifacts. The owners of country houses and estates were invited to employ mafiosi as guards against the otherwise inevitable arson attack. The Mafia sold and managed the monopolies in every area of trade; even beggars were obliged to pay for their right to occupy a prominent pitch.

The Mafia effectively replaced the police force as the arbiters of law and order and thereby established one of its most consistent sources of income: the recovery of stolen property. If a horse, mule, jewel or, latterly, motor-car was stolen, the victim would be approached by a mafioso who would offer to recover the lost object for a commission of up to thirty-three per cent of its value. If the commission was agreed upon, the object would be virtually guaranteed to reappear without delay. The original thief would be compelled to sell the object back to the mafioso at a small price (but would be grateful to escape with his life) and the mafioso would profit at the expense of both parties. It was a popular service; the police charged nothing but could only recover stolen property in one case out of ten. The Mafia might be expensive, but was successful ninety per cent of the time.

This happy state of affairs continued until Mussolini and the Fascists came to power. Although the Mafia had contributed to the Fascists' funds (an insurance policy; besides, Fascism was preferable to any form of Communism), Mussolini was wholly distrustful of the Mafia, realizing that its members habitually turned on their allies. More importantly, the power of the Mafia presented a direct challenge to the arrogance of his authority. Il Duce made a most unhappy trip to Sicily in 1924. He saw that the Fascist administrators were powerless in the face of the Mafia, that the police could obtain no witnesses to any crime, and that the Mafia-elected deputies to Parliament devoted their time exclusively to composing speeches denying the existence of their criminal masters.

Some of the rackets Don Vito established were quite fantastic. The Mafia imposed a tax on lovers, so that a young man going to court a girl who sat – as was the custom – behind a barred window, had to pay what was known as "the price of a candle" to guarantee his safety. The Mafia also exploited the financial opportunities offered by religion. It controlled the standing committees of the various cults of the Sicilian saints (the committees had access to the funds raised in the saint's name), and had a virtual monopoly on the manufacture of devotional candles. Later the organization began manufacturing religious artifacts, producing holy statues, medallions and even relics by the thousand; one Italian newspaper reported that there were in existence seventeen embalmed arms attributed to St Andrew, thirteen to St Stephen and twelve to St Philip. There were also no less than sixty fingers said to belong to St John the Baptist and forty "Heads of St Julian". All these had been manufactured and sold by the Sicilian Mafia, who discovered a vast market for these bogus relics in the United States. In areas where there was no saint and no holy relic to be prostituted, a convenient "miracle" would be arranged – the appearance of the Madonna to a child for example – to bring the pilgrims flocking in, who would buy their passage on Mafia-run coaches and stay in Mafia-owned guesthouses. The cult of Padre Pio, the "stigmatized" monk of San Giovanni Rotondo, who supposedly bore wounds similar to Christ's, was one such scam. The Mafia created this peculiar attraction, and fleeced the faithful, who journeyed hundreds of miles to see this monk, of a fortune. It even sold acres of bandages asserting that they were soaked in the monk's miraculous blood (in 1960 it was analysed and revealed to be the blood of chickens).

On a tour of the island, Mussolini suddenly announced that he wished to visit the grubby town of Piana dei Greci, then run by a Mafia potentate named Don Ciccio Cuccia – an ugly man noted for his acute vanity. Since it was an unscheduled visit, the police had no time to make elaborate security arrangements, and they realized that the only guarantee of Mussolini's safety was to suggest that he ride in Don Ciccio's car. When Mussolini sat next to Don Ciccio, with the police motorcycle escort lined up on either side, Ciccio turned to Il Duce and asked him why he was bothering to surround himself with police; "Nothing to worry about so long as you're with me . . ." he gloated. It was then that Mussolini understood that he had no power in Sicily.

On his return to Italy, the furious Mussolini immediately declared war on the Mafia and assigned Prefect Cesare Mori to the task of extermination. Mori was a stupid, pompous and cruel man. Given *carte blanche*, he measured success solely in terms of numbers arrested and confessions extracted; his onslaught naturally provided an unprecedented opportunity for the settling of old clan feuds. Hundreds of anonymous denunciations poured in; thousands were arrested on the basis of rumour and vindictive gossip and shipped off to penal colonies. Mori would frequently descend on a village and arrest the whole male population. After a while, the people worked out that the only way of pacifying this vain monster was to erect a banner on his approach to the village, bearing the words "HAIL CAESAR".

In 1927, Mussolini proudly announced to the Fascist Parliament that his heroic colleague, Prefect Mori, had won the battle against the Mafia. In reality, it had been a bloody but ineffectual campaign. Most of the important "Men of Honour" had either made their escape or gone underground, or disguised their loyalties by joining the Fascist Party; they would be back. But at least many of the Mafia dons had been deprived of their quasi-feudal authority, and for the next few years – until the Allied invasion of Sicily – the peasants were better off than they had ever been.

One Man of Honour that Mori had managed to arrest was Don Vito Cascio Ferro. Charged with smuggling (on bogus evidence), the old don spent most of his trial disdainfully ignoring the proceedings of the court, becoming animated only when his defence counsel pleaded for leniency. "That," barked Don Vito, "is in conflict with my principles and offensive to my authority."

Prefect Mori reintroduced the use of the *cassetta*, a traditional tool of the Inquisition, to extort confessions. A small, low-standing box, it was used as a platform across which a torture victim could be painfully spread-eagled. Brine was then poured over his body and he was scourged; if he failed to confess, he was then forced to drink gallons of sea-water. Next his fingernails would be removed, then slivers of skin. If he still persisted in claiming innocence, his genitals would be crushed.

Asked if he had anything to say before he was sentenced, Don Vito stood up and, after carefully considering his position, said: "Gentlemen, since you have been unable to obtain proof of any of my numerous crimes, you have been reduced to condemning me for the only one I have never committed."

He had indeed over the years been charged with sixty-nine major crimes, twenty of which were killings, but no case was ever sustained. He only ever admitted to one murder, that of Jack Petrosino, an American detective whose researches into the Mafia had brought him to Italy in 1909. Don Vito, dining one evening with an influential politician, suddenly announced that he had to return home to attend to an important matter. He would borrow the politician's carriage and return immediately. He was driven into Palermo where he shot Petrosino, and then returned to his dinner. The politician happily swore that Don Vito had never left his house.

Locked up in the Ucciardone prison, Don Vito was the most beneficent of men, preoccupying himself with the welfare of his fellow inmates, who made his bed and cleaned his cell (thereafter something of a shrine, and only given to prisoners of equal honour). He even hired and fired the prison warders. He did not complete his sentence, but died of a heart attack. His death made Don Calogero Vizzini the acknowledged head of the Mafia and it was "Don Calò" who would engineer its resurgence.

The son of a peasant farmer, Calogero Vizzini was born in the small, shabby Sicilian town of Villalba in 1877. His family had some prestige locally, not only because they had the rare distinction of owning a few grim acres of barren land, but because Calogero's uncle was a bishop, and his brother the parish priest of Villalba – important considerations in a place where the church shares power with the police and the Mafia.

Young Calò was not a good student, and remained an

illiterate all his life, perversely flaunting his ignorance and parochial bigotry. His first brush with the law came at the age of seventeen, when he was charged, unsuccessfully, with criminal assault. It seems that he took a fancy to the pretty daughter of a neighbouring family, the Solazzo clan. Though he had no intention of marrying her, he nonetheless forbade her to have dealings with any other man. When his honour in this affair was threatened by the girl's association with a rising young magistrate, Calogero and his gang burst in on the courting couple and beat the unfortunate suitor senseless. He nearly died, and the girl remained a spinster all her life.

At eighteen, Calogero went into business escorting grain shipments from peasant farmers across the remote, bandit-infested countryside to the flour mills. He did well, having struck a bargain with one of the most notorious of Sicilian bandits, Paolo Varsalona, who ran an extremely elusive band of brigands. Far from living their lives as roaming outlaws and making themselves an identifiable prey for the authorities, Varsalona's men maintained the outward appearance of respectability; they lived in the towns and pursued the traditional lives of peasants. At his call they would assemble, commit whatever crime was on the agenda, and then melt back into the workaday world. Calogero was so impressed with the bandit that he spent a number of formative years in Varsalona's gang, before they were finally caught in a police trap. Calogero was acquitted of murder on the grounds of "insufficiency of proof", and having made a sufficient impression on the necessary figures, was formally invited to become a member of the "Honoured Society" – the Mafia.

At the age of twenty-five, Calogero took the title of *zu*, meaning "uncle", and by the outbreak of the First World War was head of the Mafia in the Province of Caltanissetta. During the war he made a fortune from selling broken-winded and clapped out nags to the Italian cavalry; he also charged the farmers of his region to guarantee that their fit horses were not requisitioned.

Shortly afterwards, faced with claims that the army had become the country's largest receiver of stolen goods, the Italian authorities sought to put Calogero on trial. His inevitable acquittal brought him further prestige as the scope of his enormous influence was seen; he was allowed to take the title of "don" and so became, after Don Vito Cascio, the second most important member of the Sicilian Mafia.

When Mori's purges took place, Don Calò (as he was universally known) was sentenced to five years, but he had fostered good relations with a young Fascist administrator, and was quietly released a few days after he entered prison.

The years between Mori and the Allied landings in Sicily were a time of retrenchment for the Mafia. But from the early days of the Second World War, it was clear to the Mafia that there was much to be gained from co-operating with the Americans and the British. Firstly, the eviction of Mussolini and the end of domination by Rome (many mafiosi dreamed of Sicily becoming, if not an independent state, then a colony of the US or Britain); and secondly, the suppression of Communism, which threatened the feudal stranglehold of the Mafia. Furthermore, an invasion and the ensuing power vacuum would provide the necessary opportunity for the Mafia to reassert itself. Indeed, it was to be expected that the Allies would need the services of the Mafia, and would willingly make concessions in return for assistance in taking first Sicily, then Italy itself.

The full history of the Allied involvement with the Mafia has never been disclosed, but that it happened is no secret. Sadly, in some ways it is the US that is responsible for the dreadful Mafia rule that has so traumatized post-war Italy.

It seems fairly certain that the initial connection was made through the don of all dons, "Lucky" Luciano, who was imprisoned in America at the outbreak of the Second World War. He was released at the cessation of hostilities and deported to Italy, and it is believed that the price of his release was that the Mafia assist the American authorities in a number of areas. One such area was the surveillance of suspected Nazi agents and insurgents in America's docks, another was the invasion of Sicily. From Luciano the message was passed to Don Calò, and it all came to pass as planned.

When, on 10 July 1943, the Allies landed on the south coast of Sicily and began to push northwards, their forces were divided into two bodies. The British and Canadian troops ploughed up the east coast – in theory the easier invasion route – and encountered a poorly equipped and inexperienced enemy who nevertheless fought back well, compelling the battle-hardened British troops to a tough, five-week campaign. The Americans, on the other hand, were allocated the mountainous terrain of central and western Sicily, which appeared on paper to be a much more arduous task. Surprisingly, they obtained their objectives at startling speed, reaching the north coast with barely a casualty.

The key point in the Italo-German defence of the route was a series of fortified positions near the towns of Villalba and Mussomeli, commanding the route along which the Americans had to come. Here, under the command of Colonel Salemi, a man noted for his courage, the Italians and Germans gathered together a substantial force of artillery, tanks, anti-tank guns and foot soldiers. Though Salemi had no illusions as to the probable outcome of any battle, he knew that, given the strength of his position, he would make the Americans fight a long and bloody battle; he might be able to halt their advance for weeks.

But Villalba, as one will recall, was the home town of Don Calò, the beloved Mafia potentate of all Sicily. A few days after the Allies landed, American planes could be seen dropping strange packages into the town, which, it was later disclosed by a man who saw Don Calò unwrap one, contained yellow silk handkerchiefs embroidered with the letter "L". This stood for Luciano. It was a pre-arranged signal. On 20 July three American tanks made a dash into Villalba, flying yellow handkerchiefs, and bore away the invaluable Don Calò, who then went to join the US Army as guide and passport to bloodless conquest. It is reported that the meeting between the Americans and the don took place in utter silence; he knew precisely what the agreement was.

The following morning, Colonel Salemi awoke to discover that two-thirds of his troops had deserted. They had been approached in the night by mafiosi who had courteously informed them of the hopelessness of their position and given them civilian clothes in which to escape. Salemi himself was them ambushed and held in the Town Hall of Mussomeli by the Mafia. The Americans strolled through without firing a shot. Don Calò returned to Villalba to be greeted by cries of "Long live the Allies; long live the Mafia!". He was elected Mayor of the town and was thereafter accompanied by a guard of "anti-fascists" armed by special permission of the Allied Military Government.

He subsequently cornered the trade in olive oil, and divided his time between this lucrative area of the black market and controlling the post-war direction of Sicilian politics. The fall of the Fascists brought thirty-two alternative political parties into existence; the Mafia threw its weight behind the Separatist

Party (later it would consider the Christian Democrats most suitable for its purpose). Don Calò considered it absolutely necessary that all left-wing parties be suppressed. When the socialist Popular Front asked permission to hold a rally in Villalba, they were most surprised to find the don warm to the idea. On 16 September 1944, as Girolamo Li Causi, the left-wing leader, began to address the crowd gathered in the town square of Villalba, the Mafia opened fire and wounded Li Causi and thirteen others.

Worse was to come. In 1945, the Separatists decided that an armed rising was necessary to guarantee their power, so Don Calò brokered a deal between them and the most famous of all Sicilian bandits, Salvatore Giuliano, who for many years had opposed the Mafia, but was to end up as its pliant tool. Giuliano offered, for a large sum, to attack the carabineri outposts and precipitate the anarchy necessary for an uprising. But the Separatists had big plans: they raised a volunteer force, and dispatched it to join up with the bandits. Under Giuliano's command, this force was to await the chosen moment and then commence all-out insurgency. The order never came. Eventually the bandits left the volunteer army, which dwindled to fifty-eight men. The volunteers were then attacked by Italian military forces (sanctioned by the Allies) of 5000 men accompanied by tanks and artillery. It was an extraordinary battle. The Separatists were dug-in on a hill, and their assailants, though out-numbering them fifty to one, exhibited the most remarkable caution. The fight went on for over a day, and apocalyptic reports of it filled the press. When it was over, each side had lost only six men and most of the surviving Separatists had escaped.

Don Calò abandoned his support for the lost Separatist cause, but Giuliano continued to rage around the countryside, well equipped with weapons and explosives of American origin, shooting, robbing and blowing up all non-patriotic elements. The authorities made no serious effort to eliminate him: he was too useful a loose cannon. His violence had the effect of quelling peasant unrest.

Giuliano's moment of infamy came on 1 May 1947, the day of the elections to the Regional Parliament. Sicily was to be allowed independent status within the Italian state, and, since the Separatist movement was now defunct, the Church, the landlords, the Mafia and the Allies put their weight behind the Christian Democrats; the other parties supported the principle of land-reform, and were therefore considered dangerously left-wing.

For decades the people of the neighbouring towns of Piana dei Greci and San Giuseppe Jato had held a rally on May Day, at the mountain pass of Porta della Finestra. Quite apart from any political significance, it was a holiday, and the feast of Santa Crocefissa. But despite the Mafia's warnings, there was an increasingly upbeat Communist movement among the peasants, and they wound their way to the high mountain pass in a cheerful mood, singing and waving banners. It was a brilliant, quiet morning. By 9.30 a.m. there were over 2000 of the poor and oppressed gathered at Porta della Finestra. They would listen to some speeches and then enjoy themselves, eating and drinking the day away. At 10 a.m., the leader of the Popular Front took the stand to make the first speech. Fifteen minutes later, as he opened his mouth, a seventy-year-old woman in the crowd fell over, shot dead. Behind her lay a thirteen-year-old girl, half her face blown away. Old men tumbled over, their intestines spilling out. Concealed in the rocks above the crowd, Giuliano's men were carrying out a massacre. Ten minutes later, it was all over. There were eleven killed outright and fifty-five others wounded, some of whom died later.

Shortly afterwards, three young men and a local prostitute who were on their way up to the meeting saw a strange sight: twelve armed men in American uniforms, and one in a white raincoat, came scrambling down the mountainside. The onlookers concealed themselves. They had just seen Giuliano and his band returning from their bloody work. His actions were wholly successful: the Popular Front had a disastrous election.

For the next two years, Giuliano was a popular man among the landlords, the Mafia, and (however distasteful it was) the occupying American forces; there would be no Communism in Sicily. But Giuliano finally outlived his usefulness, and became an embarrassment to his former allies. The police could not catch him, or find witnesses to testify against him. But they finally managed to buy the treasonable services of his lieutenant, Pisciotta. For fifty million lire he agreed to kill the bandit king. At 3.19 on the morning of 5 July 1950, Pisciotta shot Giuliano twice in the chest as he lay sleeping in a safe house in the town of Castelvetrano. The police then hastily hauled the dead bandit out of bed, dressed him, took him outside and sprayed him with machine-gun fire to try and conceal Pisciotta's treachery, so that he might live to enjoy his reward. Unfortunately, the corpse refused to bleed dramatically enough, and they were obliged to slit the throat of a chicken and pour its contents all over Giuliano.

Don Calò was relieved to see the bandit die. Latterly, his power had been so great that when he was disowned by his Christian Democrat supporters, Giuliano had openly threatened to abduct and kill its backers, including Don Calò. The latter, having helped create this monster, was reduced to hiding from him and travelled concealed in the backs of vegetable lorries. A year after the bandit died, Don Calò also went to the grave, though somewhat more peacefully.

Inclined to over-indulge and take little exercise, he had grown sluggish and corpulent. While travelling to Villalba one day, he asked that his car be stopped so that he could assume a comfortable supine position on the verge. Lying there, his vast belly pointing skywards, he sighed deeply, murmured "How beautiful life is!" and promptly expired. His funeral was a state occasion attended by all of significance, and his plaque in the church at Villalba declares, without irony, his many virtues; he was chaste, temperate, forbearing, tireless in his defence of the weak and, above all, a gentleman.

chapter two

FROM "LUCKY" TO GOTTI: A MISCELLANY OF AMERICAN MAFIOSI

The American Mafia, the most powerful criminal organization in the world, owes its present strength to the pioneering efforts of Charles "Lucky" Luciano, who in the first half of this century transformed a collection of feuding extortionists and racketeers into a multi-billion dollar corporation.

He was born Salvatore Lucania in East Harlem, New York, into a large and poor family; his father was a construction worker and his mother supplemented their meagre income by taking in laundry. At the age of fifteen, he was thrown out of the house by his father who despaired at his son's drift into crime; not even the severest of beatings seemed to inhibit him. His mother continued to adore him, and smuggled jars of her home-made pasta sauce (the one thing he missed) to her errant son.

He rented his own apartment and formed his own *borgata*: a gang of young, street-wise criminals. Many of the New York Mafia's foremost members began their careers in Luciano's borgata: Frank Costello, Gaetano "Three Fingers Brown" Lucchese, Albert Anastasia and Vito Genovese.

For fear of shaming his family name, the embryonic mobster changed his surname from Lucania to Luciano. He also decided he hated being called Salvatore, as it was too often shorted to "Sal", and re-christened himself Charles; he later acquired his nickname "Lucky" by surviving an assassination attempt by knife. Lucky stood head and shoulders above his confederates; he possessed extraordinary business acumen and a capacity for organization. By the age of eighteen he was a czar of petty crime and was formulating plans for a nation-wide confederacy of hoodlums. He even made the unprecedented move of forming an alliance with two Jewish mobsters, Meyer Lansky and Benjamin "Bugsy" Siegel, from the Lower East Side.

Within a few years, Lucky went to work for the don of the "amici", the boss of the Mafia, Giuseppe "Joe the Boss" Masseria, who insisted on patronizing Lucky by calling him *bambino*. Masseria, who was rampantly anti-semitic, hated Siegel and Lansky and insisted that Lucky "get rid of those fucking hebes". Lucky detested Masseria and had the pleasure of arranging for him to be murdered on the orders of Salvatore Maranzano, who succeeded him to the throne of power. Masseria was shot in a restaurant where he thought he was joining Lucky for a plate of pasta. Lucky got up mid-way through the meal and went to the toilet; while he was in there the restaurant was raked with gunfire.

Maranzano, an elegant figure, was something of a Sicilian traditionalist, and Lucky, while having nothing personal against him, could see that there was little prospect of the man instigating any of the modern business plans that Lucky had his heart set on. Maranzano read Roman history for inspiration, whilst Lucky dreamed of a modern empire of crime, sheltered by accountants and lawyers. Lucky had to take the throne by force: in September 1931 Maranzano and his supporters died, on an occasion that was thereafter remembered as "The Night of the Sicilian Vespers". Four men, disguised as members of the Internal Revenue, visited Maranzano and knifed him to death; some forty of his associates were also murdered. At the age of thirty-four, Lucky Luciano was the head of the New York Mafia, which he eventually welded into the most powerful criminal organization ever known.

He was finally brought down by the efforts of a determined District Attorney, Thomas E. Dewy, who nailed him on charges of running a prostitution ring; but Lucky's luxurious sojourn in New York's Clinton State prison set the tone for incarcerated

From its earliest days in America, much of the Mafia's wealth was founded upon illegal gambling rackets, the most basic of which was the "numbers" game that predominated in the black ghettos. Tickets, costing between twenty-five cents and a dollar, were sold at barber shops and candy stores. It was a simple variety of lottery: the participant would select up to three digits from one to ten, with odds thus ranging from ten to one to a thousand to one. The winning number was determined by the last three digits of an established daily number that could not in theory be fixed, such as the circulation of a newspaper or the day's sale of US Treasury stocks. The profit was the difference between tickets sold and winnings paid out. With no tax and low overheads the income could be vast.

mafiosi. He had a private cell with an electric stove, curtains over the cell door and a pet canary. Dressed in a tailor-made prison uniform of silk shirt and highly polished shoes, he was guarded round the clock by paid bodyguards, and held formal audiences in the prison exercise yard, bestowing favours like a monarch.

Perhaps his greatest achievement – for it enabled the uninterrupted pursuit of illicit wealth – was the peace he forged between the Mafia clans. But as the network of organized crime expanded, his position – that of *capo di tutti i capi* (the boss of all bosses) – became an increasingly attractive post.

When he was sent to prison, the Second World War had started, and the Mafia was approached by the US Government for assistance at home and abroad. They wanted the cooperation of the Sicilian Mafia in the event of Allied landings and they also wanted the Mafia to provide the eyes and ears for a counter-intelligence operation along the New York waterfront, to balk anticipated acts of sabotage by German and Italian agents. The Mafia agreed; its secret pay-off was to be the release of Lucky Luciano, to which the Government acquiesced on condition that he was returned to Italy.

On 9 February 1946, Luciano was transported from his upstate New York prison cell to Brooklyn where he was to be put on an ocean-liner with a one-way ticket to Italy. The entire high command of the New York Mafia turned out to see Lucky off: Albert Anastasia, Vito Genovese, Joseph Profaci, Joseph Bonanno, Frank Costello and Joe Adonis. Also present were two fast-rising mobsters, Carlo Gambino and Thomas Lucchese.

Lucky stayed put in Rome for a while, but then began to creep back towards the US and turned up in Cuba, run by the corrupt Batista, where the Mafia had invested heavily in casinos and hotels. But he was too close for the comfort of the US authorities, and they encouraged the Cubans to return him to Italy. In January 1962, Lucky Luciano went to the Naples airport to await the arrival of an American film producer interested in making a film based on the gangster's life. To general consternation, he dropped dead of a heart attack in the airport lounge.

Lucky had been concerned that in his absence the Mafia would begin to tear itself apart. No sooner was his ship out of the harbour than his worst fears came true. The arrogant Vito Genovese was not only making a pitch for the position of "capo di tutti i capi", but was also demanding that the Mafia move into the rapidly expanding narcotics market, and wanted to see the fruitful partnership that Lucky had formed with the Jewish mobsters broken. His demands found little favour with Frank Costello, the Mafia don of Manhattan, who had been one of those closest to Lucky and who commanded great influence and respect, both inside and outside the Mafia. Costello was known as the "prime minister of the underworld" for his skill in defusing potentially explosive disputes. He was an affable and cautious man who detested violence, and had assiduously courted police and politicians so that New York's authorities turned a blind eye to Mafia activities, so long as they stayed clear of drugs and kept the violence internal and to a minimum. Moreover, he liked the Jews and appreciated their business acumen. The Mafia had learned much from them, particularly the importance of maintaining a quasi-legality in its activities, infiltrating legitimate businesses wherever possible.

Costello made an enemy in Genovese, who in turn found an ally in Anastasia. Their resentment – and ambition – festered, and in 1957 they decided to make a play for power. On 2 May Costello was attacked in the lobby of his hotel by a notoriously stupid hood, an ex-boxer called Vincent "the Chin" Gigante. He shot Costello at point-blank range in the head. He hit him squarely in the temple, but, miraculously, the bullet pierced only the skin, made a complete circuit of the head under the surface, and finally re-emerged at its entry point. The Chin was unaware of this: he left Costello for dead. Costello told the

In the United States, the gangster era began long before Prohibition. New York was America's first major city, and as early as 1790 it had slums that were as foul and miserable as any in the world. In the hundred or so rooms of the Old Brewery, human beings were packed like rats, and murders averaged one a night. When the district was demolished in 1852, the builders filled numerous sacks with human bones and remains. There were many tough and colourfully-named gangs: the Dead Rabbits, the Roach Guards, the Shirt Tails, the Plug Uglies (which referred to their huge plug or top hats). Then, during the 1840s, Tammany Hall politicians discovered that gangsters could be useful allies, threatening rivals and drumming up votes. And it was from this period that the real history of American gangsterdom began.

At the time, most of the gangsters were Irish - and, oddly enough, Chinese. The Chinese were accustomed to their 'Triad Societies' at home. When they came to settle in America - mostly on the West Coast - they naturally formed themselves again into 'tongs' for mutual protection.

The Chinese were also among the first to practise gang assassination. In 1897, a rich Chinese gangster, Little Pete - owner of several gambling houses - was sitting in a barber's chair in San Francisco. He had made the mistake of sending his bodyguard out to find the result of a horse race. Two men who had been trailing him for months, awaiting their opportunity, came in and literally filled him full of lead. The killers were never caught. A similar scene was to be repeated half a century later when, in October 1957, Albert Anastasia, one of Murder Incorporated's assassins, was shot in a Manhattan hotel barber's shop.

police that he had no idea who would want to kill a dull businessman such as himself, and immediately made plans to retire. He had got the message, and died peacefully twenty years later.

Anastasia was a wholly deranged individual and the failure of the attempt on Costello sent him off the deep end. He became paranoid that he would be killed in retribution, and took steps to eliminate anyone he thought posed a physical threat to him. It was a blood-bath. As his violence and demands for power increased, it was decided that something must be done. Finally one of his capi, Carlo Gambino, arranged for the elimination of Albert Anastasia, nominally on the grounds that he had been charging a $40,000 fee for entry into his Mafia family – an unforgivable lapse in traditional protocol. Gambino turned to the most infamous killers around, the Gallo brothers: "Crazy Joe", "Kid Twist" and "Kid Blast". In October 1957 they walked into a barber's in a Manhattan hotel, where Anastasia was having his morning shave, and, while a towel was over his head, blew his brains out.

Gambino died peacefully in 1976, and his son-in-law Paul Castellano, also from the Gambino family, became "capo di tutti i capi". Castellano was a man very much in the mould of Carlo Gambino. He was diplomatic by instinct and liked a quiet life, unlike Gambino's long-time lieutenant, Aniello Dellacroce, the mentor of John Gotti, future head of the Gambino clan and Mafia don in the making.

Aniello Dellacroce (which literally means, in Sicilian Italian, "little lamb of the cross") was Gambino's number two for many years. His unadulterated sadism provided an admirable foil for the smooth charms of the don. Born in Italy, Dellacroce drifted into crime while still a boy and by his late teens was a Mafia hood specializing in strong-arm work and killing, for which he had a considerable gift, and which he obviously enjoyed. He

---

Salvatore "Sally" De Vita was a most unusual hood. An incredibly ugly man, he was the only known Mafia transvestite, and spent much of his time off duty trying to disguise himself as a woman. He wore blonde wigs, rouge, mascara, lipstick and a padded bra, and owned wardrobes full of stunning designer dresses, mostly stolen. But it was unwise to tease him excessively: he invariably carried a loaded pistol in his Gucci handbag.

would fix his bulging eyes on his victim and, in carefully modulated tones, would tell the man exactly how he was going to die; first he would shoot him in the knees, then in the stomach, and, after pausing to savour the pain he had inflicted, he would occasionally consent to administering a *coup de grâce* in the head. When an enforcer for the vicious hood Alberto Anastasia, Dellacroce had been delegated to "manage" his casinos. He would punish bent dealers and croupiers by smashing their hands with a sledgehammer.

Once, upon finding the corpse of one of his victims, police were convinced it had been decapitated. Pathologists later found the remains of the head beaten into the chest cavity.

Carlo Gambino, the figure said to have inspired Brando's portrayal of Don Corleone in *The Godfather*, arrived in America as a twenty-two-year-old stowaway in 1924. He was a loyal Mafia member from the start, a waterfront hood, a leading capo and finally a brilliant strategist who took control of the entire Mafia. His business intelligence was second to none. During Prohibition he managed to corner the market in distilled alcohol, buying at fifteen dollars per tin and selling at fifty. During the Second World War he set up a huge black market racket using forged ration stamps, netting himself millions of dollars. He took the Mafia further into the twilight world of quasi-legality, where the profit from illegal activities could be laundered and invested legally to create yet more money. Under him, the Mafia consolidated its grip on the unions, some of whom were happy to let their pension funds be invested at his discretion. A modest, soft-spoken man, Gambino was the subject of police investigations for forty years, but his last stint in prison was in 1937. They never pinned anything on him after that: it was impossible to find anyone insane enough to testify against this endearing, kind old gentleman. When police came to question him at his unassuming Brooklyn house they could always count on being received courteously and offered some of Mrs Gambino's excelle home-made cookies. But while he detested flashiness and unnecessary violence in business, as a Mafia disciplinarian Gambino was utterly ruthless, and countless numbers died on his whispered orders. One man who attempted to seduce wives of imprisoned mafiosi was subjected, on Gambino's orders, to the most horrible death, being slowly fed while alive into a large meat grinder, feet first.

Another corpse could only be identified by teeth found inside its stomach. Curiously, when travelling incognito, Dellacroce liked to dress up as a catholic priest.

Dellacroce – and, under him, Gotti – made millions for the Mafia from dealing in heroin. Publicly, the Mafia has always forbidden its members to deal in drugs, upon penalty of death. It has given the impression that gambling, protection rackets and large-scale swindles were the foundation of its wealth, and that its activities have become increasingly legal. One reason to discourage its members from dealing in narcotics is the long sentence the crime carries. Faced with forty years in prison, a criminal can be tempted to turn informer in exchange for immunity.

But in reality, the Mafia has from its first days in America been involved with narcotics. There is too much money to be made, too easily: a kilo of the opium base for heroin costs $12,000 at its source in the Middle East or Southeast Asia. After being processed and cut with other substances until it is only three and a half per cent heroin, the same kilo will fetch two million dollars on the streets.

Mafia bosses generally stayed carefully in the background, and avoided being seen to be involved in the trade. Instead, the Mafia would normally operate in association with some other branch of organized crime. Since the mid-1950s, the Mafia has controlled the American heroin trade at a discreet distance. It reorganized the supply line, linking up with the powerful Corsican heroin dealers, and established processing laboratories in Sicily staffed with French drug chemists. The "French Connection" was created and the Mafia flooded the streets of urban America with high-quality "smack". The number of heroin addicts in the United States rose from fifty thousand in the 1950s to something near half a million.

The son of poor immigrants from Southern Italy, John Gotti was born in New York in 1940. Brought up in East Harlem and Brooklyn, he quickly became known for his volcanic temper. He seemed to be in a constant rage, and was uncontrollable at school, though he was by no means unintelligent and had an IQ of around 140. A born leader, he soon attracted a group of equally wild companions and formed a "borgata".

After his father, John Gotti, moved his family to the violent waterfront district of Brooklyn and then the even meaner streets of East New York, Gotti joined a tough gang, the "Fulton Rockaway Boys". They ran minor extortion rackets, stole and hijacked, organized a little illegal gambling (taking care in all of these not to intrude on Mafia territory), and, above all, fought territorial battles with other gangs for the right to parade up and down their grim home turf.

Gotti was soon leader of the "borgata". Quite apart from his canniness and naked aggression he stood out for his appalling taste in clothing: he wore anything, so long as it was loud, colourful and stolen. Purple suits were a favourite. He attracted the attention of Carmine "Charley Wagons" Fatico, an associate of the late Alberto Anastasia. Although only seventeen, Gotti quickly proved his worth as a strong man, performing one or two spectacular beatings, and became one of the 120 men Fatico had working for him. Fatico had a well-established organization, which grossed him around thirty million dollars annually. The money came from hijacking, illegal gambling and loan-sharking, but Fatico had a special line in gay bars. Homosexuality was still illegal in America, and Fatico's discreet string of private gay clubs, where exotic stage acts could be seen by men prepared to pay exotic prices for admission and drinks, was highly lucrative. Ironically, it would be at one of his bars, the Stonewall Inn, that gay men in 1969 began the gay rights movement.

Throughout his early years Gotti was in and out of prison, principally on charges of theft and hijacking. His time in jail gave him the opportunity to meet a whole host of mafiosi, who, in turn, remembered the explosive and capable young man. When Carmine Fatico began to ail, Gotti was put in charge of the outfit, and along with a number of other middle-ranking hoods he successfully organized a lucrative narcotics channel into New York. He went to great lengths to ensure that Castellano was not aware of the narcotics trade; he even publicly banished one of his crew on the grounds that he was a drugs dealer. By 1979 Gotti, although little more than a Mafia soldier, was already rumoured to be Dellacroce's chosen successor as underboss of the Gambino clan, a remarkable rate of progress since he had only been "made" (formally initiated into the Mafia) two years beforehand.

Gotti's principal weakness was gambling. He could blow $30,000 a day on betting and at one point in the 1982 American football season Gotti had lost a quarter of a million dollars. He and his brother ran an illegal casino in Little Italy. Gotti could not resist betting against his own house and on one night lost $55,000.

Dellacroce died of cancer in 1985. At the same time, Gotti's

In 1980 Gotti's already unstable temperament was heightened by personal tragedy: his twelve-year-old son Frank was accidentally run over by one of his neighbours, a man called John Favara. Favara was utterly distraught, but his expressions of remorse and sympathy met with angry silence. Later, his car was stolen, and "murderer" scrawled across it. He found a black-edged picture of the dead boy in his mail-box. Rumours began circulating that he was about to be killed. He decided to move, but on the very day that he sold his house, three men in a van rolled up to his work-place. He pulled a gun, but his shots went wild. Bludgeoned insensible, he was thrown into the back of the van and never seen again.

narcotics network had been uncovered by the police and he and several other Mafia members were facing trial. Castellano, furious at the heroin-trafficking, had come to regard Gotti as a substantial embarrassment. It was only a matter of time before he had him killed. With his protector Dellacroce gone, Gotti felt exposed and decided to strike first. He rapidly established the necessary support for his actions throughout the Mafia membership, alternately seducing and threatening, and convinced many that the ageing Castellano was too afflicted by conscience and needed replacing.

On 16 December 1985, Castellano arrived outside Sparks Restaurant in New York. Getting out of his chauffeur-driven car, he encountered three men in identical overcoats and fur hats. They fired six shots into his body. He died instantly. The men then shot his chauffeur dead and melted away. Gotti did not attend his funeral.

By Christmas 1985, John Gotti was head of the most powerful criminal organization in the world. In April 1992, he was convicted of murder and racketeering, and sentenced to life without parole. His case is currently under appeal.

Castellano's funeral was a modest affair, unlike most Mafia funerals. The standard for these events was set in 1928 by the spectacular last rites of Brooklyn mobster Frank Uale, who was shot to death. There were two hundred cars in his funeral procession, thirty-eight of which carried the flowers, and several thousand mourners. He was buried in a casket of silver and nickel, costing $15,000; the whole occasion cost $200,000.

• chapter three •

MURDER INCORPORATED

Just before the First World War, the overcrowded population of the predominantly Jewish quarter of the Lower East Side in New York's Manhattan and the Italian neighbourhoods of Little Italy and East Harlem began to overflow and move eastwards, across the East River and into the vast interior plains of Brooklyn. Here for generations the quiet villages of Williamsburg, Brownsville and East New York had existed in a rural torpor which was soon dispelled. With the immigrants came organized crime, and by 1930 the Italian Mafia and the Jewish mobs were flourishing alongside one another. Though they had often fought, they were, for the most part, content to come to mutually beneficial arrangements in the pursuit of profit.

The Italian Mafia concentrated on its conventional interests, primarily loan-sharking and illegal gambling, while the Jewish mobsters derived their wealth from extortion, principally targeting the small garment manufacturers. Many of these had fled over the river in order to escape from the Garment Center in Manhattan, which had for years been under the control of mobsters like Louis "Lepke" Buchalter, who was used by the manufacturers to break strikes, and then found that he could make money by charging the manufacturers for his protection.

The manufacturers who fled across the river did not elude Buchalter for long. He came after them, but in Brooklyn he found that seven local punks were already attempting to run a protection racket involving clothing manufacturers. Buchalter was deeply offended at this intrusion into his private territory, and accordingly made plans to have them eliminated. But the killing of the seven posed problems. While he was blessed with strong-arm men who could be relied on to break heads effectively, Buchalter was short of talented, discreet killers who could perform their task efficiently, without upsetting the authorities and leaving a trail of bloody footprints that would lead the police to his door.

To solve this problem, Buchalter opened negotiations with the Mafia, represented by its rising star in Brooklyn, Albert Anastasia, a capo from the waterfront rackets. Buchalter proposed that the Italians and the Jews should pool their talents and create a combined force of Italian and Jewish professional killers, who would work – for a price – for both individuals and organized crime syndicates. Anastasia accepted, and Murder Incorporated was born.

The organization fused murder with corporate methods. Buchalter was president and Anastasia chief executive officer, and they had a staff of selected, smart killers, who were put on annual $12,000 retainers. There were strict corporate rules: murder was only to be committed for "business reasons", and "civilians" were not to be harmed in the course of the hit.

The policy on each job submitted was jointly agreed by president and chief executive, who rationally and coldly considered the ramifications of requests for killing within the sphere of organized crime. If they accepted the job, the execution was assigned to a team of assassins.

The organization's star killer was Abraham "Kid Twist" Reles. Fat, five foot two inches tall, with thick lips, a flat, broken nose and gangling arms, Reles derived his nickname from his habit of munching boxfuls of chocolate candy twists.

By the mid-1930s, Louis Buchalter was extorting nearly fifty million dollars a year from the New York garment manufacturers in return for guaranteeing that there would be no disruption of labour. He had nearly 250 vicious hoods in his employment, including the infamous Jacob Shapiro, his chief lieutenant, who walked around with lead window-sash weights in his pockets with which he used to smash in the skulls of manufacturers and union leaders unwilling to cooperate.

He specialized in the use of the ice-pick, which he jammed into his victim's heart. Reles showed no mercy, and when people saw him walking down the street they were inclined to cross to the opposite pavement. Everybody knew that Reles had once openly killed two black men without any provocation: one of them had worked at a car wash and failed to spot a small smudge on the front fender of Reles' car, the other had worked at a parking lot and had failed to move fast enough when Reles ordered him to fetch his Cadillac.

It will never be known how many people Murder Incorporated killed during the peak years of business, between 1935 and 1939. Some estimates are as high as 300, but only about a dozen or so murders – including that of Arthur "Dutch Schultz" Fleigenheimer – have actually been laid at its door. Its "employees" swaggered around the streets of Brooklyn, untroubled by the police, who generally avoided them. There were nearly 200 "employees", because, apart from the elite killers, there were "fingermen" who charted the movements of prospective victims, "wheelmen" who stole the cars used in the hits and "evaporators" who tidied up after the crime and ensured that the body of the victim disappeared.

Murder Incorporated might still be terrorizing America, were it not for the arrest of the erratic Abe Reles. The lethal Kid Twist was forever committing non-sanctioned murders, casual killings over and above his Murder Incorporated quota. The police picked him up for one of these; the evidence was indisputable, and Reles faced the electric chair. In return for immunity from prosecution, Kid Twist agreed to turn stool-pigeon and tell everything he knew about Murder Incorporated. His sensational revelations allowed the police to crush

Each assignment was called a "contract", a euphemism which rapidly passed into common usage, along with "hit", the Murder Incorporated official parlance for the actual killing. The killers retained by Murder Incorporated were the cream of New York's hit-men. Among them were Vito "Chicken Head" Gurino, who earned his nickname because he perfected his aim by blasting the heads off live chickens, and Frank "The Dasher" Abbanando, so called because once, when his gun misfired during a hit and the victim pursued him around a building, Abbanando was faster, and succeeded in lapping him; he came up behind his pursuer and shot him in the back of the head.

Trapped between the sea and steep hills, Hong Kong is one of the most overcrowded cities in the world, and its murder rate has always been high. After World War II, the population quickly rocketed from half a million to more than two and a half million. Consequently, there was a terrifying wave of gang murders - murders so atrocious that the police speak of them as the work of 'horror cults'.

In 1958, there were more than 900 murders - five times the American murder rate, and 150 times the English. These 'horror cults' are, in fact, Chinese 'tongs', or 'Triad Societies'. (The earliest tongs were called 'Three Harmonies Societies'.) Like their American counterpart, the Mafia, they operate prostitution, drugs rackets, protection, and extortion. But their methods of ensuring obedience depend upon terrorism.

For example, in 1958, a rich merchant named Ko Sun Wei, together with four of his family, were horribly murdered in his house in Kowloon. The victims were staked out, with their arms and legs spreadeagled. Three women - the merchant's two daughters and his daughter in law - were raped repeatedly, then tortured to death with knives. One woman was still alive when the police arrived, but was unable to speak - her tongue had been cut out.

These were only five among 350 murders that took place in Hong Kong in September 1958. Sergeant Arthur Ogilvie, of the Hong Kong Police, who gives these figures, also mentions that during the riots of 1956, Triad Societies took the opportunity to pillage more than $25,000,000 worth of goods. With a figure of this size involved, it can be seen that crime in modern Hong Kong is an even bigger business than it was in the Chicago of the 1920s. The interesting point here is the verification of observations about overcrowding. It produces true gangsters - men who are adepts in cruelty and violence, because they are unable to experience human emotions.

the organization, and Louis Buchalter went to the electric chair.

But Reles never lived to enjoy the new life the authorities had promised him. After spilling the beans on Murder Incorporated, he began to blab about the Mafia, and mentioned specific people, including Albert Anastasia, to the Brooklyn District Attorney, William O'Dwyer. Too late he learned that O'Dwyer had allegedly gone straight out and sold the glad news of Reles' revelations to Anastasia. The Mafia boss paid the corrupt attorney $100,000 for the silencing of Kid Twist.

On 11 November 1941, Kid Twist mysteriously fell from the seventh-floor window of a Coney Island hotel, where he was being concealed by the District Attorney's office under a twenty-four hour guard. Although the murder case remains officially unsolved to this day, it was alleged that O'Dwyer or Anastasia arranged for two or three corrupt police officers to defenestrate the stool-pigeon before he said any more.

The death ended any further investigation into Murder Incorporated, but Reles remained a legendary figure in New York. Throughout Brooklyn, gangsters would raise their glasses and say: "Here's to Abe Reles, a great canary. He could sing, but he couldn't fly."

Albert Anastasia, the Mafia's "King of Brooklyn", was also known as "The Mad Hatter" or "The Executioner". A homicidal maniac with a violent temper, he liked killing for the sake of killing and ordered deaths on the slightest pretext. After reading in the newspaper that a local citizen had recognized the famous bank robber Willie Smith and turned him in to the police, Anastasia ordered that this conscientious citizen be immediately killed. "I hate a rat," he said, "no matter who he is." He liked to have murder victims hideously tortured before their death and when unable to participate himself he insisted that every detail of the torture be later recounted to him; he particularly relished it when they begged for mercy. He lived like an emperor near New York Harbour in New Jersey, in a vast house surrounded by a seven-foot barbed-wire fence, a pack of Dobermans and a permanent bodyguard. His money came from the waterfront rackets: extortion, theft, gambling, loan-sharking and kick-backs. The 40,000 longshoremen who worked in the port were all under his thumb. Also, his brother "Tough Tony" was president of the biggest union and he was thought to have the entire roll-call of local police and politicians on his payroll.

• chapter four •

"BUGSY" SIEGEL: CASANOVA MOBSTER

Benjamin "Bugsy" Siegel (he hated being called Bugsy, a name he acquired in his early mob days) was the most suave and charming of criminals. Intelligent, cosmopolitan, Jewish and handsome, he effortlessly infiltrated American society. The titled loved him, and he enjoyed the trust of the most hard-bitten and cynical of businessmen. To movie stars he was tangible proof of the reality of the romantic hoods they played. Many, such as Cary Grant, were close friends though sometimes they became frightened as to where their friendship with this man might take them. Siegel once told Del Webb that he had personally killed twelve men. When Webb's face betrayed his fear, Siegel looked at him and laughed.

"There's no chance that you'll get killed," he told him. "We only kill each other."

Benjamin Siegel was born on 28 February 1906 in the Jewish Williamsburg district of Brooklyn, then a labyrinth of crowded tenements, street pedlars, delicatessens and synagogues. He left home without finishing school, and joined a band of other juvenile delinquents who prowled the East Side in Manhattan at night. His first crime was a stick-up in a loan company office, and he was soon "rolling" drunks, committing burglaries and vigorously participating in the perpetual, violent gang wars.

On one foray he met another young hood, George Ranft, who later changed his name to Raft and became the Hollywood star. Siegel and Raft became the closest of buddies. Many years later, when Raft was a national celebrity, his aging mother saw him being escorted into a cinema by an honorary guard of four policemen. So accustomed was she to thinking of her son as a criminal that her first reaction was to shout "Run, Georgie, run!"

From Siegel's earliest days he became known for his love of horse-play and his sheer effrontery towards the police. Later, when a major player in crime, he would still amuse himself by leaning out of the windows of hotels and dropping water-bombs on the heads of the snooping police.

By rights, Siegel should have remained a petty crook and tearaway, just one of the other thousands of struggling street bums from the Jewish and Italian ghettos. But during the days of Prohibition – there was never a single edict more favourable to organized crime – he made the transition from punk to swaggering gangster.

During this era the Lower East Side was dominated by two ruthless mobs: the Italians – the Mafia – led by Lucky Luciano, Vito Genovese and Albert Anastasia, and the Jewish mob, headed by Louis Buchalter and Jacob Shapiro, known as the "Gold Dust Twins". It was as part of this group that Siegel encountered Meyer Lansky, his long-time associate. Together they split away and formed the "Bug-Meyer Mob".

Little hard evidence of the extent of his early criminal activities survives, though his mob had a fearful reputation. He was regularly picked up by the police for such offences as possessing concealed weapons, and at the age of nineteen was accused of rape by a local girl. When the case came to court, the witnesses had mysteriously vanished. The only conviction he ever suffered was for illegal gambling, when he was picked up by the police during a raid on a Miami hotel. Even then he gave a false name and was fined only $100.

Furthermore, as Siegel ascended the hierarchy of crime, his file at New York Police Department, which should have bulged with the records of his arrests and various suspected offences, grew perversely thinner. Over the years, this smartest of gangsters managed to wipe his past record clean, arranging, by legal and illegal means, to have past offences deleted, pictures withheld and charge sheets appropriated. The only official memento of his early career now remaining to the New York Police is a solitary mugshot.

Still in his twenties, Siegel already had a suite at the Waldorf-Astoria, two floors below his mentor, Lucky Luciano. He wore coats with velvet collars, handmade shirts and sharp, pointed and highly glossed shoes. He had a special line in hats and favoured a snap-brim, a style he had picked up from the Broadway columnist, Mark Hellinger, one of the first of many friends in show-business. Broadway was a great melting-pot for the legal and illegal sectors of society. Criminals, celebrities, politicians, magnates, actors and actresses – anyone who was news – mingled and networked at the same parties and the same restaurants and clubs. They dressed alike, and thought alike. They were drawn by the same things: the craving for success, recognition and the good life that money could buy. More than one major movie or Broadway show was financed by the proceeds from speakeasies, extortion and murder.

The Siegel-Meyer mob hauled liquor and supplied armed convoys for other groups trucking it between New York and Philadelphia. The gang also had a wholesale liquor business of their own and operated a string of illicit stills and a smuggling network. They were in business for money, and though they happily committed robberies, hijackings and murders these were less for profit than to assert their identity and discourage any major competitors in the truly lucrative field of bootlegging. Siegel's earnings were near the one million dollar mark. He once told a friend that, had he not taken a beating in the Wall Street crash, he would have happily gone "legit".

Like any high profile gangster he had his enemies and his life was always at risk, and in these early years Siegel was constantly on the move, shifting between his apartment on Eighty-fifth Street, the Waldorf, his headquarters near Lewis Street on the Lower East Side, and the various hideouts and offices of his criminal associates. He kept his family – his wife Esta and his two daughters – tucked out of sight in an expensive house in Scarsdale. In the early 1930s, Bugsy survived a number of attempts on his life: his car was shot up by machine-gun fire, and a bomb was placed in a room in which he was hosting a meeting of senior mobsters (he escaped with minor injuries, and apparently was able to slip unseen out of the hospital to avenge himself on the would-be assassin, before returning to his sick bed – a perfect alibi).

Siegel, like many Jewish mobsters, preferred to settle disagreements by negotiation, but would not hesitate to order the execution of problematic individuals. In 1934 Joey and Louis "Pretty" Amberg, minor drug pedlars and extortionists from Brownsville, who had already demanded a cut of a fee charged by Siegel's gang for a piece of strong arm strike-breaking in their territory, exasperated his patience when they killed one of his henchmen. Joey was called into Bugsy's office, forced to confess and then summarily shot; Louis was finely diced with an axe.

When Prohibition came to an end, the Mafia and their associates – and Siegel was still an ally – needed to replace their lost income. They began to look more closely at the previously minor areas of narcotics, prostitution, casinos, union enforcement and even wholesale murder for the right money (Murder Incorporated was one result). They also looked to expand westwards, into California.

In 1936 Bugsy Siegel moved to California. California seemed a territory ripe for crime and Bugsy didn't want to stay in New York and end up dead on the streets, nor did he enjoy the company of fellow gangsters. He always thought a little more of himself, and craved respectability. For Siegel, Hollywood was a natural home: here people could re-invent their pasts freely, and a little urbanity, good looks and a lot of money bought acceptance. Furthermore, he had a weakness for actresses, and had recently formed an association with Ketti Gallian, a French starlet. He was to spend $50,000 vainly trying to launch her career in movies.

Siegel settled down in Beverly Hills, living in a house rented from the famous singer, Lawrence Tibbet. He styled himself a "sportsman" and bon viveur, and joined the exclusive Hillcrest Country Club. His daughters attended the best private school and he socialized with George Raft, Jean Harlow and Clark Gable. Jean Harlow had a particular affection for Bugsy and was thought to have been the godmother of his daughter Millicent. Siegel also made the acquaintance of the million-airess and socialite Countess Dorothy Dendice Taylor DiFrasso. Tired of her marriage, and jaded with her fortune, this buxom and frosty eyed woman frequently visited her mansion in Beverly Hills, where she organized elaborate entertainment – such as bare fist boxing – for her celebrity guests. She had an unhappy affair with Gary Cooper, and was casting around for something a little out of the ordinary, when she was introduced to Siegel. Within days, the semi-literate gangster from New York, driven by an enormous need for social acceptance, was in her bed. He was literally sleeping his way to the top.

Siegel still had "business" interests in New York, mainly protection rackets, from which he derived a steady income. But

Ned Kelly, was definitely a bandit. Kelly, the son of an Irish farmer and former convict, became Australia's public enemy Number One when he killed three constables at Stringybark Creek in 1877.

From then on, he lived the traditional life of the bandit on the run, moving around the countryside with his gang - which included his brother Dan - and robbing banks. He made himself head and body armour, weighing 97 lb, and was wearing it when the police finally ambushed his gang in Glenrowan He was only 24 when he was executed in 1880. Asked why he had decided to confront the police at Glenrowan, Kelly made a reply that was to be echoed by many American gangsters of the Bonny and Clyde era: 'A man gets tired of being hunted like a dog... I wanted to see the thing end.'

The most significant feature about Kelly is that he was a man who thought he had a grievance against the law - and in this he resembles many of the famous 'bandits', from Billy the Kid to John Dillinger. Whether the grievance is real or not is beside the point; but it starts the bandit off on the road that leads to the gallows, or the final bloody shoot-out with the police.

with his taste for the glamorous life, the cost of the mansion he was building, the education of his family and the endless string of girlfriends to be discreetly maintained, he always needed more. He was also a compulsive gambler who could spend $2,000–$5,000 a day on football and horses. But for the moment, he was on a winning streak.

He had interests in pieces of property in California, which brought in a little, but his first major coup was to invest heavily – with money borrowed from unfortunate friends like George Raft – in a series of off-shore, floating casinos: gambling ships, which stood outside the state's jurisdiction. He made a small fortune, but Raft, who was always in money troubles and had been virtually forced to invest in the ship, never saw a cent of profit. Indeed he was lucky to get his original stake back: his $20,000 was returned to him in tiny instalments over a period of months. Bugsy might have been extravagant, but he was never unduly generous.

Siegel, the most assiduous social climber of his day, kept lists of people he wished to meet – and bed – and even managed to inveigle his way into the house of Jack Warner, the movie mogul, quite against Warner's wishes. Siegel managed to conceal his criminal association from his new Californian neighbours, but a reporter on the *Los Angeles Examiner* received a tip-off from a mysterious informant and a front-page exposé followed; Bugsy found that his local reputation was taking a dip. He decided to spend some time away and, leaving his family behind, he took off with the Countess DiFrasso to Italy and thence all over Europe. Initially, the reason for the trip was to try and sell the patent of a new explosive, "Atomite", which he had interested the Countess in, to Mussolini. The Countess, feeling that she should be seen to be travelling with someone of her own class, bestowed a bogus baronetcy on Bugsy, who enjoyed going under the title Bart Siegel, English aristocrat. The explosive was another expensive disaster for the Countess, and they had to cut short their stay in Rome because Siegel, seeing that Goering and Goebbels were also paying a visit, decided that one or both of them needed killing. Whatever his crimes, Siegel always possessed a healthy attitude towards Nazis, and to his dying day regretted that he had not killed Goebbels when he had had the opportunity.

Returning to California, Siegel found himself pitched into the roughest waters he had hitherto experienced.

Harry Greenberg was a minor mob member of Polish

parentage, who was also an illegal immigrant. Deported by the American authorities, he jumped ship and found his way back to California, where he started threatening to talk to the police about the mob unless a lot of money was forthcoming. Siegel was called upon by his New York associates – men like Albert Anastasia and Buchalter – to help them to shut the mouth of the fat, overwrought Greenberg before he blabbed. Greenberg was located by a hood named Whitey Krakower, and assassins were imported from the East. But, for some unknown reason, Siegel himself – perhaps because he needed to reassert his authority in the underworld – decided to participate directly in the killing. In November 1939, Greenberg was gunned down outside his apartment. The naïve Krakower then began to talk freely about Siegel's involvement in the killing, and in July 1940 he too was found shot dead. Bugsy did not like bad publicity.

Then Abe "Kid Twist" Reles was arrested. When he turned stool-pigeon, he implicated Bugsy in the Greenberg murder, and the police felt fairly certain that they could also get him on the death of Whitey. Siegel was arrested and held in a County jail awaiting trial. This made little difference to his lifestyle. He

---

The Countess DiFrasso was in love with Siegel and in 1938 bankrolled one of his more extravagant schemes: the search for a legendary ninety-million-dollar treasure supposedly buried on an island off Costa Rica. Equipped with a treasure map supplied by an old soak called Bill Bowbeer, the couple assembled an extraordinary entourage of fellow speculators, chartered a boat and set off for Cocos Island, where, Siegel told the company, concealed in a cave was this fabulous treasure. After several weeks of sailing, the motley crew of socialites and crooks reached the deserted, inhospitable island. Its shore was rocky, and the land was covered by thick jungle and creepers. They spent ten horrible days looking for the gold; few on board had actually expected to find anything, but it quickly became apparent that Siegel had been in deadly earnest. His temper rose rapidly as the fruitless search continued. They dug everywhere in temperatures approaching ninety degrees, eaten alive by mosquitoes and plagued by tropical sickness. The Countess retreated to the boat and sat in the shade, drinking champagne and wilting. Finally, having dynamited large portions of the island, the furious Siegel was forced to abandon the search. The expedition cost the Duchess at least $50,000.

was idolized by other inmates, who would queue up to polish his shoes. He had a specially made uniform, which another inmate regularly pressed, and he was able to order his meals from outside; roast pheasant was a particular favourite. It was election year, and Siegel was a vociferous supporter of the Democrat President, Roosevelt; he was allowed to wear a Roosevelt badge on his prison uniform. Social life presented no problems. On the pretext of visiting his dentist or conferring with his lawyer, Siegel was able to make countless trips outside prison, much to the consternation of the police, who believed they'd put him in the can and instead would come across him holding court in clubs, restaurants and movie-theatres.

In December 1940, the District Attorney dropped the charges against Siegel. The authorities now thought they had little evidence against him, but it was also murmured that Siegel had made one or two useful contributions to the re-election funds of certain people, and that, furthermore, the New York authorities didn't want to risk putting Reles in the witness stand against Siegel; they wanted to keep him alive to testify against the big New York mafiosi.

Bugsy walked free, with all the glamour the whiff of crime bestowed, but without the taint of a conviction. He was considered even more desirable, and he was further sought after by the ladies. The Hollywood stars invited this poisonous but charming curiosity to their houses, and even the local police developed an affection for him, often giving him lifts back from the race track, their sirens wailing as they escorted the cosseted

---

Bugsy Siegel was supremely vain. A fanatic on the subject of physical fitness and virility, he smoked and drank little, worked-out in the boxing ring and spent every afternoon in the gym, where he held many of his business meetings. At night-time he rubbed beauty cream into his face and put on an elastic chin strap to keep his features from sagging. Unless he was out on the town he went to bed at 10 p.m., having spent an hour or so struggling with a self-improvement book (he was continually trying to extend his vocabulary and lose the New York accent that betrayed his origins). He had a horror of going bald, and nobody was allowed to mention his receding hairline. Anyone with a full head of hair would be aware of his jealous gaze and he once paid an associate who had a full complement of hair $2500 to allow him to cut a mass of it off.

gangster home. Later, when the police thought they had more evidence against him, he was re-arrested, but the untimely death of Kid Twist ensured his release.

At some point in 1941 Siegel met Virginia Hill. Hill, the daughter of poor, small-town folk from Alabama, had slept her way across America and Mexico, marrying at least twice, and breaking a host of hearts. She had no regard for thrift, and spent the considerable sums of money admirers lavished on her on lingerie and parties. One man, Joe Epstein, a good-natured and short-sighted accountant from Chicago with lucrative connections to a gambling syndicate, used to send her weekly packets containing wads of thousand dollar bills; he continued to do so for years. Hill was very beautiful; her auburn hair and grey eyes – and her extravagant and generous personality – could reduce the most rational of men to cringing sexual supplicants. She and Siegel were a natural pairing. When he came calling for her – as he did every day – she would bath in Chanel No. 5. Her kid brother, Chick, whom she had rescued from the drudgery of rural Alabama and took everywhere with her, stayed on hand to provide constant room service for the lovers. They also used a host of hotels and apartments under a variety of pseudonyms. When the government finally went looking for Hill over a small matter of several hundred-thousand dollars in unpaid taxes, they issued a wanted poster on which they described her as a "paramour and associate of gangsters and racketeers" and gave a list of twenty aliases she had used over the years.

Hill had a wardrobe a queen would have envied: a hundred pairs of shoes, a series of $5,000 designer dresses, a dozen mink stoles, a pair of persian-lamb coats. Her winter-wear was imported from England, she had $15,000 diamond rings and each year bought herself a brand-new Cadillac. Most of the money came from Epstein. But Bugsy paid too, and put a $30,000 deposit on a house at Miami Beach for her. When questioned by the Revenue, she said that she only had an income of $16,000 a year, from betting on the horses. She did bet large sums, and won huge amounts too; but it was nothing compared to the flow of money from Epstein. Chick Hill once reckoned that his sister got through around five million dollars in these years. She didn't just spend it on herself: at times she literally threw it at people, tossing sheaves of it out of the window. No one has ever satisfactorily explained why Epstein sent her so much; some say she had a share of his gambling syndicate, others that she was one of the most successful blackmailers ever. But the truth is probably that Epstein not only was smitten, but also felt responsible for her: she became his mistress when she was only seventeen. Before her death, Hill told a friend that she hated Epstein, that he never gave her any peace, and never gave up trying to buy her back.

During the Second World War, Siegel declined to fight for his country. They probably wouldn't have let him into the Army anyway. With the nation's eyes turned outwards, he was able to expand his criminal activities, encouraging bookies to subscribe to his Trans-America race-result wire service. Most bookies already subscribed to a rival service, the Continental. But the threat of physical violence generally opened their eyes to the advantages of Siegel's wire.

He bought interests in racetracks and illegal gaming clubs in California, and, across the state line, began to acquire legitimate gambling interests in Las Vegas, where he had investments in a number of small clubs. His annual income was conservatively estimated to be around $500,000, but it was never enough. His gambling and his women saw to that, and he was forever borrowing money.

Bugsy was still married to Esta, but spent most of his time with Hill, to whom he was by no means faithful. Virginia Hill was no more faithful to Bugsy: she needed, and devoured, men but she did love Bugsy Siegel. When the attention of the police became too much for him, he decided to move out of the Hollywood mansion and escape to Nevada. Virginia was keen to get away from Hollywood too, and Bugsy even intimated that despite his need to keep up pretences of married respectability he was considering divorcing his wife. The movie star

Naturally, Siegel wanted to be a movie star. He figured he spent all his time acting, and it seemed inevitable to him that he would one day be paid for doing so. He began turning up in the studio where George Raft was making a film with Marlene Dietrich, first watching, then going to Raft's dressing room and acting out the sequences he had witnessed. He purchased a 16mm camera, and had one of his tame hoods film his impromptu performances. He let it be known that he was interested in appearing in films and spent months trying to improve his diction and perfect his appearance. But the offers never came. He could only impersonate; he could never act.

Loretta Young offered to buy his house for $85,000, but pulled out after Bugsy refused to pay $350 to have the termites in the cellar exterminated. Bugsy, irascible as ever, took her to court, lost the case, appealed and lost again. His peculiar meanness was much in evidence when he finally moved out of the house: he forced George Raft to pay him $500 for an assortment of decaying garden furniture not worth twenty dollars, which the movie star had no need for; but one didn't refuse Bugsy. "I guess he needs the money" sighed Raft, counting out the bills.

One summer day in 1945, Bugsy Siegel took his old friend Little Moe Sedway on a trip to Las Vegas, then a poky little desert town in a sea of burning sand with a collection of run-down gambling clubs. Most of the Californians who crossed the border to gamble would head for the smarter resort of Reno. Las Vegas was for ranchers, cowpokes, poor Indians and the occasional lost tourist.

Bugsy drove Moe to a remote and bleak spot seven miles outside town, where a dilapidated motel rotted in the sun. He told him his plan: he was going to buy these thirty acres of wasteland for a few cents and build a hotel and casino costing two million dollars. It would be called "Ben Siegel's Flamingo". When Moe protested at the absurdity of the idea – what possible incentive could there be for anyone to come here? – Bugsy simply stared dreamily at the desert haze and told him that one day people would drive hundreds of miles just to see the place he planned.

Fronted by his friends, Siegel bought up the land over the next few months, and floated the Nevada Projects Corporation, raising one million dollars through a share issue, all of which were bought by close associates; Meyer Lansky took shares, as did Louis Pokross, another member of the old Bug-Meyer gang. In effect, the Flamingo was financed by the Mafia. In December 1945, building began.

Bugsy was beside himself with excitement. He engaged the popular Del Webb to build the hotel, and pulled every political string he could to obtain the necessary supplies of copper, marble and steel; wartime stringencies still applied, but while veterans down the road returned from the fighting to find that they couldn't get bricks with which to build houses, the Flamingo was made a priority building project. Truly, Bugsy Siegel was a master of graft.

In the midst of this, Bugsy forgot that he hadn't seen his family for months, and Esta finally sued for a divorce from the man who was now an utter stranger, wrapped up in his twin passions of the Flamingo and Virginia Hill. She got an unusually generous settlement: Bugsy was in an ebullient mood and signed an alimony agreement worth $1,500,000 to his ex-wife.

He was being profligate on the building, too. He flew plasterers and carpenters in from other cities, and paid them fifty dollars a day. When materials weren't forthcoming, he would obtain them at extortionate prices on the black market. Lorry drivers were turning up and delivering materials which they would return at night to steal and then sell back to him the following day. He ordered that the walls be of double thickness. When it transpired that the supporting beam of the penthouse suite he intended for his own use was only going to be 5'10" off the ground and he would have to duck humbly under it every time he entered the room, he ordered this central piece of structure to be ripped out and re-designed. His vanity cost $22,500. Bugsy decided that the layout of the kitchens was wrong: it cost $30,000 to alter. Then he complained that the boiler room was too small: another $115,000. He insisted that the ninety-two bedrooms all had their private sewage systems: the plumbing bill came to $1 million. The building was his obsession, his final play for recognition; he was going to run the most glitzy hotel and casino in the country and therefore everything must be as he desired it. He was out of control.

Throughout 1946, as the hotel took shape, his temper grew fouler and his aggressive outbursts of frustration and fury more regular. He reverted to being an irascible hood, made uglier by his imperial ambitions; the workmen who battled in the sweltering Nevada heat to finish the hotel in time for a Christmas opening were afraid of his megalomania and of the boots and guns of henchmen like Hymie Segal and Little Moe Sedway. The atmosphere was fraught.

In the summer, on impulse, Bugsy and Virginia Hill flew to Mexico and were married. Siegel gave her a ruby and diamond ring. He never mentioned the wedding to anyone else; it was five years before Hill told reporters that she had once been Bugsy's wife. Bugsy was never an emotionally articulate man, and rarely expressed any sort of tenderness. But though they might not talk about it, they both knew that theirs was the love of kindred spirits. Bugsy even wrote Hill a poem once.

The Flamingo was due to open on 26 December. Realizing that the day was fast approaching, Siegel began frantically to try and publicize the hotel. He hired press agents in Los Angeles, who inundated the newspapers with photographs of the nubile beauties that would be on display at the hotel. In Las Vegas he took full page advertisements in all the region's newspapers and hired Henry Greenspun, the editor of a monthly magazine, *Las Vegas Life*, to manage his publicity (he wanted, most particularly, to ensure that he was never again known as "Bugsy"). He assiduously courted the press, sending them cases of whisky, promises of free sex at the casino and sometimes envelopes full of cash; there was many a newspaperman who disengaged himself from a firm handshake with Bugsy to find himself holding a $100 bill. He drew up a list of movie stars he wanted present for the opening and ordered Billy Wilkerson, his long-time associate in Los Angeles, to make sure they turned up and chartered a fleet of aircraft to bring them to the door of the Flamingo.

But Siegel's luck was about to run out. Randolph Hearst, the newspaper magnate, let it be known that he was none too keen on either Siegel or the Flamingo. The press kept their distance, or wrote sniping articles about Siegel's shady past. The movie stars he wanted – Joan Crawford, Spencer Tracy, Greer Garson – were advised by influential figures to stay away. In despair, Siegel contemplated cancelling the opening; but Virginia Hill had just spent $3,500 on a new dress and was not going to have her big night ruined.

On 26 December the weather was appalling. A driving wind and a foul storm kept the chartered aircraft and most of the willing celebrities grounded in Los Angeles. The spectacular ornamental waterfall outside the hotel – visible for miles – wouldn't work, because a cat had had a litter of kittens in the tap, and Siegel believed it would be bad luck to flush the kittens out. When the doors opened, it was apparent that there were more staff than customers, and only two or three names of any sort – including the faithful George Raft – had made the journey by car or train. The great occasion was a disaster.

So long as the gambling side of things could hold its own, there was hope. Casinos do have runs of bad luck, but if managed with a modicum of care, they should be money-making machines: after all, the odds are invariably in favour of the house. But Siegel was on a losing streak: the casino's losses in the first week were unprecedented. Some say that the local opposition joined up to try and bust the Flamingo in its first forty-eight hours, pouring money in to break Siegel with big early winnings. But everybody – except George Raft, who went down $65,000 on the Chemin de Fer – made a small fortune. Siegel was frantic; he switched the dice, changed the cards and moved the confused dealers from table to table. Nothing changed his luck and he was even being clipped by his own staff, who were openly playing rigged games.

Siegel stalked the still unfinished hotel and casino, pumping with adrenalin, his eyes bloodshot, his temper exhausted. He began to look for fights, and tried to sock Chick Hill. He and Virginia had a vicious scrap in which she flew at him with a stiletto heel, cutting his face badly. Hill went back to Los Angeles, took a new mansion, bought new clothes and indulged herself with new lovers. She hated the desert, and was going crazy herself. One night a policeman was called to her house, to find her stalking round in her night dress, clutching a gun and announcing that she intended to kill everybody present.

Siegel's rivals in Las Vegas and Los Angeles began to spread rumours about the volcanic temper of the thug who ran the Flamingo; they said that visitors were putting their lives at risk. Finally, facing ruin, Siegel announced that he would close the Flamingo and re-open it, completely finished, in March.

He began to suspect that his backers might seriously be contemplating ridding themselves of him and might even be involved in the process of ruining him so that they could take the Flamingo over. He surrounded himself with armed hoods and lashed out wildly at anyone whom he suspected of disloyalty. He needed money so badly that he stung everyone he knew for whatever they had: George Raft was persuaded to lend him $100,000, which he never saw again.

The re-opening night in March was a downbeat, panicky affair. There were no firework displays or razzmatazz, and Siegel, his friends and their wives spent the evening running from bedroom to bedroom, frantically trying to help the workmen and chambermaids to finish preparing them. At

---

After two weeks, the Flamingo had lost $300,000. The building costs of the complex stood at four million dollars, and there were still ninety-two bedrooms to furnish at $3500 each. The mob wanted to hear some good news about their investment. Siegel was looking down the barrel of a gun.

eight p.m. there were still guests in the lobby, waiting to check into rooms that had no furniture. But, on the face of it, business looked much better. Siegel had ridden the adverse publicity, and people were making the trek across the desert to visit this fabulous, glowing palace.

But Siegel's bad luck persisted. The guests were playing in the casino, but they were still winning. The net loss for the first six months was approaching one million dollars. There was a series of other disasters too. On one hot afternoon, the occupants of the swimming pool were alarmed to see all the water disappear down a vast crack which suddenly opened up. Many mumbled about the hand of God and checked out immediately. It was just an engineering flaw, and was soon repaired, but by then the word was out: the Flamingo was cursed.

Virginia Hill was becoming more unstable. One night, after convincing herself that Siegel was sleeping with a blonde hat-check girl, she launched herself at the woman, and put her in hospital with a dislocated vertebra and severe facial lacerations. Siegel was furious: his arbitrary explosions were adverse publicity enough. The couple argued; Hill took an overdose. She was taken to hospital in time to save her life, but it was only the first of many suicide attempts, and one day she would succeed.

Hill was exhausted. Siegel had become a raging insomniac. He now knew that his position was hopeless, that he had insufficient experience to run the Flamingo, that his vanity and bad taste had contributed to the disaster, and that he could find no more money from anywhere. But when Hill told him to sell up and move with her, he refused.

His death was inevitable. The backers wanted him out. He had long parted company with two of the mob's contacts with the project, Gus Greenbaum and Little Moe Sedway (the man he had first taken to see the windblown, desolate site). These

When the movie starlet Marie McDonald (a close friend of Siegel and Hill) came to Las Vegas they were surprised that she did not visit the Flamingo. She told them that the room clerk at her hotel, one Ray Kronsen, had flippantly said that the place was full of gangsters and murderers. Siegel was beside himself. He took Hymie Segal and Chick Hill and went round to the hotel where the clerk worked and clubbed him insensible with gun-butts.

two seem to have been remarkably well-informed about the time-table the Mafia drew up for Bugsy's last days.

Over the few days leading up to 20 June 1947 Siegel seemed to be almost constantly on the telephone. Nobody will say who he was speaking to. Sometimes the conversations were violent disagreements, sometimes he seemed to be imploring, sometimes he was rational and friendly. On 19 June Siegel called a sidekick called Fat Irish Green into his office and showed him a briefcase containing $600,000.

"I'm going to Los Angeles for a couple of days," he said. "I want you to look after this case. If anything happens to me, just sit tight and then some guys will come and take the money off your hands."

Then he called Virginia Hill's house on Linden Drive in Los Angeles. He got hold of Chick and told him that he would be over that night, accompanied by his associate, Alan Smiley. He said that he was going to have a meeting at his lawyer's the next day.

He arrived, slept, had his meeting and then went to a barber's and had a leisurely lunch. He also had a talk with an old mob friend, Mickey Cohen, and asked him if he could get hold of some guys with "equipment". Cohen dropped a couple of names, and Siegel said he'd see them the following day. To Cohen, it looked as if Siegel was even now planning to fight back. After dinner at Jack's Restaurant in Ocean Park, Siegel and Smiley returned to Linden Drive. Siegel opened the door with the solid gold key that Virginia had given him, and he and Smiley sat in the lounge, which was decorated in a curious mixture of English chintz and American camp, talking over the grim state of business.

At 10.20 p.m. on 20 June 1947, as the two men talked, Chick was upstairs, fumbling with the clothing of his girlfriend Jerri Mason. Suddenly, he heard what sounded like gunfire downstairs. When he reached the lounge, Al Smiley screamed at him to turn the lights out. He did so, and both men stood in the dark, trembling, with Jerri Mason screaming in the background. They heard a car pull away. After a while, they switched the lights back on. Chick saw that Smiley was hiding in the fireplace, and on the floor, his head nearly severed by nine shots from a .30-30 carbine, was the corpse of Benjamin "Bugsy" Siegel. His right eye was found plastered to the ceiling fifteen feet away, and his eyelids with their luxuriant lashes were glued to an adjoining door jamb.

The front-facing window of the lounge was shattered by bullets. The killer had come very close to the house, and had carefully rested his gun on the tasteful lattice-work frame that shielded the house from the road. Siegel had been a sitting target because, curiously, the curtains had been open, as if by arrangement.

Within twenty minutes of his death, Greenbaum and Moe Sedway strolled through the doors of the Flamingo and took control of the complex. Later, a group of businessmen called on Fat Irish Green, and relieved him of the cash that Bugsy had deposited with him. The Flamingo was refinanced, and given a respectable front man. In a short time, it began to make vast profits, and all along the bleak road where it had once stood as a lonely memorial to the grandiose dreams of a dead mobster sprang up a host of other, glittering gambling palaces. The modern city of Las Vegas was born.

Siegel had a handsome coffin, made of scrolled silver and bronze and lined with silk, costing $5,000. Few of his associates attended the funeral; the police and press outnumbered the mourners. Virginia Hill didn't come, nor did George Raft, nor the Countess DiFrasso. Just his family – his ex-wife, his daughters, his sister.

Virginia Hill was in Paris when Siegel was killed. She checked out of her hotel and drove to Monaco, where she sat alone in the Casino. Later that night she took an overdose of barbiturates. She survived, then returned to Paris where she took a suite in the Ritz and again tried to kill herself. She flew back to America, but the pattern of attempted suicide persisted. On each occasion she was saved only by fortunate intervention, mostly by Chick. Pursued by the Internal Revenue and eaten by depression and loneliness, she finally fled the United States and made her way, via Mexico, to Europe.

Hill went to live in the ski resort of Klosters, outside Zurich. She was increasingly unstable, and regularly assaulted her

Little Moe Sedway died of multiple ailments and was buried in the same cemetery not fifty feet from Siegel, his bitter enemy. Gus Greenbaum was not so fortunate: he fell out with his Mafia masters and in 1958 was decapitated with a butcher's knife while asleep in Las Vegas; his wife was then knifed and strangled for good measure as she lay beside him.

brother's girlfriends (throughout her life she possessed a formidable right jab). Before leaving America she had married Hans Hauser, an Austrian-born ski-instructor reputed to have the looks and body of Apollo. She even had a child, Peter, by him. But she was never happy with Hans, and soon despised him. The Revenue had already seized everything she owned in the US – her house, her cars, her mink coats. Now she tried to strike a deal with them. She would come back, try and settle her tax and serve a nominal sentence. But the deal fell apart. She lurched on: to Salzburg, then Prague and then Cuba, from where she was immediately sent back to Prague (she was unaware that Castro was now in power). Epstein stopped sending her money; she was broke, and raged against the world.

Finally, in March 1966, Hill drove to the small, beautiful mountain village of Koppl outside Salzburg and, by a waterfall, swallowed twenty-eight barbiturates and quietly died. She was forty-nine years old.

chapter five

AL CAPONE: PUBLIC ENEMY NUMBER ONE

Contrary to popular belief, Al "Scarface" Capone, the most infamous of the Chicago gangsters, was unconnected to the Mafia. He was not a Sicilian, and he spent his active life quarrelling with the "Mob". Capone came from a Neapolitan family and was born in Brooklyn in 1899, the fourth son of Gabriele and Teresa Capone, who had emigrated from Naples some six years previously. Like all gangsters, he was involved in crime from an early age, running with the so-called "Five Points Gang", which was led by another Italian, John Torrio, a future partner in violence. At the age of fifteen, young Alphonse discovered that The Black Hand, a Camorra/Mafia murder squad, was extorting money from his father. He tracked down the two men responsible, shooting them dead. Torrio was impressed.

In 1919 the Volsted Act was passed, and America began its long and ultimately disastrous experiment with Prohibition. Torrio had been in Chicago for a few years already, establishing himself as a serious gangster. In Chicago, illegal drinkers were kept supplied by one of a dozen big gangs, each of which had its own clearly defined territory. Torrio controlled the South Side of the city, in conjunction with the Irish Duggan-Lake gang who supplied the Inner West Side. The rest of the West Side was run by the Genna brothers, Sicilians from Marsala, who were noted for the pleasure they derived from killing. The North Side of Chicago was the province of Dion O'Banion, a small time thief who ran a flower shop opposite the Holy Name

Cathedral. He worked in conjunction with two Poles, George "Bugs" Moran and Hymie Weiss.

At first there was little trouble between the gangs; there was enough business to go around, and the gangs' energies were devoted towards organizing themselves into efficient units. But within a year, they began to look for opportunities to muscle in on each others' profits, and the murders began. Torrio suddenly acquired rivals on the South Side, the O'Donnell gang, who started hijacking his beer trucks and smashing up his drinking dens. He had several of their drivers killed, but he realized that in the circumstances attack was the best form of defence. If he did not exert control over the whole of Chicago, it was unlikely that he would survive at all. He needed skilled, violent men who were prepared to kill without remorse and casting his mind back he remembered the young Capone, now twenty-one and a lieutenant in the Five Points Gang. Torrio lured him to Chicago with an extraordinary offer: Capone would get twenty-five per cent of all existing turnover and fifty per cent of any further business.

Within two years Capone had gained control of the middle class Chicago suburb of Cicero, which became his personal headquarters. The local police and town authorities were in his pocket, and through the classic mix of bribery and intimidation his illegal casinos, brothels and bars were left alone to flourish. He also killed in public with impunity. Nobody would testify against him and he and Torrio were raking in $100,000 a week apiece.

Both Torrio and Capone agreed that absolute control of Chicago was there for the taking but Capone, no diplomat, wanted to shoot his way to the top in an all-out gang war; Torrio was more circumspect and tried to persuade his irascible partner to bide his time. Then, in October 1924, a dispute broke out between the Gennas and the O'Banion gang. The Sicilians had stolen a cargo of the Irishman's whisky. O'Banion swore revenge, but on 4 November was himself mown down in his flower shop by three men posing as customers. The murder was almost certainly the work of Capone and Torrio, but both they and the Gennas had convenient alibis, and although the street outside the shop had been crowded, once again no one had heard or seen anything. The coroner was forced to return a verdict of "unlawful killing at the hands of a person or persons unknown".

O'Banion had a lavish funeral. His body lay in state at the

undertakers for three days. Silver angels stood at the head and feet of his corpse, bearing in their hands ten candles that burned in solid gold candlesticks. Mounted police had to maintain order as the vast procession wound its way to the cemetery; there were twenty-six trucks of floral tributes, valued at $50,000. Capone sent a bunch of red roses, with a dedication: "from Al". Both he and Torrio attended the funeral.

O'Banion's organization was taken over by Hymie Weiss, his trusted lieutenant. Weiss adored O'Banion, and wept buckets by his grave. He swore revenge and a few days later Capone's car was swept by machine-gun fire. He escaped unhurt, but Torrio was not so lucky: two weeks later he was gunned down by another of the late O'Banion's men, Bugs Moran, in front of his wife. He recovered, but soon found himself in jail on charges of operating an illegal brewery. In prison, his nerve began to crack. He had steel screens fitted to the windows of his cell and paid for three extra sheriffs to stand guard; he wanted out of Chicago. In 1925, on his release from prison, he announced he was leaving town. Chicago, he said, was "too violent". At the age of forty-eight, Torrio took retirement and Capone, then only twenty-six, inherited his criminal empire. Shortly after his ascent to power, three of the six Genna brothers – Angel, Mike and Antonio – died in gun-battles. The others decided that life in Sicily was preferable to death in America, and retired hastily to Marsala. Only Weiss and Bugs Moran now stood between Capone and absolute control of Chicago.

Weiss fought back in spectacular style. In broad daylight, no less than eight car-loads of his henchmen descended on Capone's headquarters at the Hawthorne Inn and within the space of a few seconds they pumped over a thousand bullets into the

One of Capone's first victims in Chicago was Joe Howard, a small time crook, who unwisely stole two consignments of Torrio's alcohol. The following night, as he sat enjoying the "happy hour" in his neighbourhood drinking hole, Capone walked in and shot him six times at point-blank range in front of a gallery of witnesses. The police arrested Capone, but had to release him when, after a series of personal visits from smartly-dressed men in large cars, all the witnesses became uncertain as to what, if anything, they had seen.

building. Capone escaped, but decided to bring the dispute to a swift conclusion and on 11 October 1926 Hymie Weiss was gunned down on the steps of Holy Name Cathedral. Ten days later, Capone called a meeting of the Chicago gang leaders. "We're a bunch of saps to be killing each other" he told them. They nodded their assent, and agreed to a peaceful carve-up of the whole of Cook County.

For a while there was peace, and everybody made money. Capone became fabulously wealthy. Within Cook County he controlled no less than 10,000 illegal drinking dens, or speakeasies, each of which purchased an average of six barrels of beer and two cases of liquor a week from him. The beer reputedly brought him about three and a half million dollars a week; the liquor another one point eight million. When the proceeds from his gambling and prostitution rackets were added to this, his income was estimated at six and a half million dollars a week. Though his overheads were vast, his profits still made him a multi-millionaire.

Capone thought that Chicago was no place to bring up his children. By 1928, he felt secure enough about his position to look around for a second home, somewhere away from the city. Not every state was keen on having him as a resident. He was thrown out of California, and tried Florida instead. Its citizens objected vociferously, but Capone succeeded in buying a palatial residence on Palm Island, Miami, where he quietly passed Christmas and New Year of 1929.

While he was away, Bugs Moran, the man who had shot

Capone was now a pillar of the establishment, most of which was on his payroll (it is thought that he spent some thirty million dollars annually on back-handers and bribes and blatantly bought favourable politicians, financing the re-election campaign of Mayor "Big Bill" Thompson to the tune of $260,000). A conservative man, strong on family values, he dressed immaculately, in hand-made silk shirts, and sported diamond tie-pins. He gave generously to charities, and church restoration funds. He contributed $100,000 to a fund for striking miners, and during the Depression opened a string of soup kitchens and gave more than two million dollars to help ease the plight of the poor. When an old woman was blinded in the cross-fire of an assassination attempt on him, he paid $10,000 to have her sight restored.

In the early years of the century, most of America's most formidable gangsters, were Chinese. By comparison, the Irish were relatively amateurish and badly organized. But another racial group was slowly achieving ascendancy - the Italians. Fleeing from the poverty of their homeland - and from its chronic political troubles - they also had their tradition of secret societies. The word 'Mafia' originally described a Sicilian outlaw who had taken to the hills, covered with low scrub (mafia), to hide from justice (either at the hands of the police, or of the family of someone he had killed).

The Mafia came to New Orleans - under the name of 'the Black Hand' - in the 1880's. Almost without exception, mafiosi preyed upon their fellow citizens, who, in turn, were too terrified to appeal to the police of their adopted country. Similarly, the Irish gangsters tended to prey upon their fellow Irish, and the Chinese on the Chinese.

As the century progressed, the Chinese slowly lost their reputation as gangsters - perhaps because many of them succeeded, through hard work and intelligence, in escaping from the slums - and the Irish, and their bitter rivals the Italians, took over. Then came the double-edged sword of Prohibition. Chicago's crime industry was run by men like the O'Donnell brothers, and the flamboyant Dion O'Banion, who was quoted as saying angrily: 'To hell with them Sicilians!'

On November 10, 1924, three men walked into O'Banion's flower store, and unceremoniously gunned him down. The man who arranged the murder commented ironically: 'O'Banion's head got away from under his hat.' His name was Al Capone. The United States had entered its third and most lethal era of gangsterdom. It is still in the midst of it.

Torrio in revenge for the murder of O'Banion, decided to settle his long-standing score with Capone. He began to muscle in on Capone's activities, regularly stealing his consignments of liquor, and threatening the other, more legitimate businesses that Capone had poured his illicit wealth into. When the source of the trouble became apparent, Capone acted swiftly. He called his right-hand man, Jake Guzik, and gave orders for the elimination of Moran. The time and place of the killing were fixed: it was to be 10.30 a.m. on 14 February 1929, St Valentine's day.

On that cold and grey Chicago morning, six of Moran's men – and one other man, an optician called Doctor Richard Schwimmer, whose presence has never been explained – were standing nonchalantly in a garage on North Clark Street, waiting for a truck-load of stolen whisky to arrive. Shortly after 10.30 a.m., a local resident, Mrs Max Landeman, heard the sound of shots coming from the adjoining garage. Looking out of the window, she saw a man leave the garage and get into a large black touring car. Another woman, Miss Josephine Morin, who lived in the flat below, saw two men come out of the garage with their hands raised above their heads. They were followed by two uniformed police officers, who had their guns drawn. She presumed she was witnessing an arrest. The four men got into a large black Cadillac and drove off.

Curiosity got the better of Mrs Landeman, and she hurried over to the garage. The doors were shut. Pushing them open, she saw seven men piled in a bloody heap on the floor. In addition to the optician, the bodies were later identified as being those of Frank and Peter Gusenberg, Moran's principal hit-men; James Clark, Moran's brother-in-law; Al Weinshank, his accountant; Adam Heyer, his business-manager; and Johnny May, a burglar. It looked as if Capone's men had entered, disguised as policemen, lined them up facing the wall and then massacred them. Frank Gusenberg was still alive when the police arrived. They tried to persuade him to talk, but he refused to say who the killers had been. He died three hours after entering hospital, without breaking the gangster's sacred code of silence.

Bugs Moran was lucky. He should have been with his men, but had been unexpectedly delayed. By the time he arrived, it was all over; he saw the police cars and ambulances and made himself scarce. He had no doubts about who had ordered the killing: only Al Capone would contemplate such a massacre. At the time of the shooting, Capone was in the office of a Miami official, arguing about his right to reside in Florida. The police picked up some other members of his gang, but they too had alibis. Jack "Machine-Gun" MacGurn, Capone's prize executioner, claimed to have been with his girlfriend at the time of the killing, and even married her so that she could not be forced to testify against him. In the end no one was ever charged in connection with the St Valentine's Day Massacre, but Moran was finished as a force.

Gang members began to whisper that there was something a little unstable about Capone. His temper had become shorter, his use of violence less selective. The killings grew indiscriminate, and men from all walks of life were gunned down, knifed and garrotted for the most petty of offences.

In the spring of 1929, Capone found himself under unusual pressure. Herbert Hoover had been elected President, and had promised the nation an onslaught against organized crime, naming Al Capone Public Enemy Number One. In addition, Capone discovered that there was a highly enticing contract out on his life. Its possible source was Moran, but it might just as easily have emanated from the families of Scalise and Anselmi, or one of the hundreds of others whose relatives had been destroyed by Capone; even his own men thought that he was becoming a liability.

Capone decided to drop out of circulation for a while, and contrived to have himself arrested for a minor firearms offence. He expected thirty quiet and safe days in jail, but was horrified to find that he had been put away for a whole year. It made

---

Capone came back from Florida in high spirits, only to discover that two of his trusted lieutenants, John Scalise and Albert Anselmi, had ambitions to take over the "outfit". Capone organized a communal gang meal, inviting the two to join him and other favourites in a private room at a restaurant in Hammond, Indiana. To those present, Al Capone seemed in an uncommonly good mood. He laughed and joked and kept the drink flowing. Then, towards the end of the meal, he got up and sauntered around to where Scalise and Anselmi were seated. Leaning over the backs of their chairs, he smiled sweetly at them. "I hear you boys want my job," he said. "Well come and get it!" Picking up a baseball bat that was positioned on an adjoining table, he smashed in their skulls.

little difference to his life, as he soon managed to establish good links with his Chicago operations, and continued to control events from the security of his prison cell.

Meanwhile, Hoover embarked on a series of meetings with various arms of his administration: the Prohibition Bureau, the FBI and the Treasury Department. The officials discussed how they might be able to put Capone away permanently. Since Capone had most of the police in his pocket it was impossible to find witnesses to his crimes and orthodox methods were unlikely to succeed. For a while the Justice Department launched an all-out war on his organization, smashing up his breweries and trucks, but it had little long-term effect: Capone had the resources to absorb the attacks and come back.

By far the most successful department in the fight against organized crime was the Treasury. Frank Wilson, the senior investigator of their Special Intelligence Unit, had already succeeded in putting away a number of Capone's associates, including Frank Nitti (his deputy), Jack Guzik (his accountant), and his brother Ralph; all got sentences of between eighteen months and five years.

Since Capone had no bank account in his own name, and all his assets nominally belonged to others, Wilson had little to go on. He would have to prove that Capone's lavish lifestyle indicated undeclared income and unpaid taxes.

Gangsters can't declare the source of their earnings and have a natural aversion to paying taxes. Capone claimed that he lived off $450 a month; because his earnings were therefore less than $5,000 a year, he had never filed a tax-return.

Wilson began piecing together the record of Capone's personal spending. He found that between 1926 and 1929 Capone had purchased more then $25,000 of furniture for his various homes; he had also spent $7,000 on suits and another $40,000 on telephone calls. In all, Wilson found that in that period Capone had spent some $165,000, which clearly indicated undeclared income. It would only be enough to put Capone away for three years; they needed more. Finally Wilson persuaded some of Capone's casino employees to talk, and the Treasury was able to charge Capone with failing to pay taxes on one million dollars of undeclared earnings, meriting a possible thirty years in prison.

At first Capone's attorney struck a deal with the prosecution: if his client pleaded guilty he would get no more than two years in prison. But when the Judge heard about the arrangement he was disgusted and refused to accept it.

Capone went on trial. The jurors were subject to persistent threats and attempts at bribery, which necessitated a last minute change of the entire jury. On 24 October 1931, Capone was found guilty on all counts and was sentenced to eleven years in prison and fined $50,000, the most severe sentence ever imposed for a tax offence. He was imprisoned in Cook County jail while his lawyers lodged an appeal. It failed, and in May 1932 he was shipped to Atlanta Federal Penitentiary and from there he was moved to the infamous prison on Alcatraz in San Francisco Bay.

Shortly after he began his sentence, Capone was diagnosed as suffering from syphilis. All attempts at a cure failed and by the time he was released in 1939 the disease had reached its debilitating tertiary stage: at the age of thirty-eight, Al Capone was going mad. He went to live at his home on Palm Island, Florida. Surrounded by his family, and under constant medical supervision, he survived for another seven years, a grim, haunted figure, his mind slowly consumed by syphilis. In 1947 he died following a brain haemorrhage and his body was returned to Chicago, the scene of his triumphs, where he was buried, at great cost, in a marble mausoleum in the cemetery at Mount Olive.

· chapter six ·

BONNIE AND CLYDE: DEPRESSION MOBSTERS

During the drab, poverty-stricken years of the Great Depression, the Great Plains became the hunting ground for a number of celebrated gangsters who specialized in motorized crime. Although criminals like any others, their poor backgrounds and their reputation for robbing banks rather than other struggling individuals gave them the image of latter-day Robin Hoods. As much as anything, the stories of their doomed and violent lives made good news in an otherwise dull decade.

Foremost amongst them were the young lovers Bonnie Parker and Clyde Barrow, now folk heroes and the subject of many works of fiction. In reality they were a little less scrupulous about killing than the legends suggest. Clyde Barrow, who was born on 24 March 1909 into an impoverished Texan farming family, had a particularly vicious streak, and it was claimed that from an early age he took great pleasure in torturing farm animals.

His future partner, Bonnie Parker, two years his junior, came from a devout Baptist environment. Her father died when she was four and the family moved to the gruesomely named Cement City, Texas. A pretty, petite blonde, Bonnie was much sought after and when only sixteen married a Dallas bum

Arriving in London about 1710, at the age of 22, Wild quickly made the discovery that the man who makes most out of crime is not the thief, but the man who finances him.

At this time, there was an extraordinary loophole in the law; a receiver of stolen goods could not be prosecuted. Wild set up as a receiver, and soon became so prosperous that he was able to buy an inn. By the time an Act of Parliament changed the law on receivers, he had already devised a way to operate legally. He would approach men who had been robbed, and offer to buy the stolen goods back from the thief, for a small commission. This was so successful that he set up a shop where people who had been burgled could come to inquire about their property.

For five shillings, Wild would enter their names on his books; a few days later, in exchange for a reward, he would restore the goods. The peace officers - employed by the City of London had no objection. Wild was one of their best informers. So long as he helped to send highwaymen and thieves to the gallows at Tyburn, they didn't care what he did.

Wild would probably have died comfortably in his bed if he hadn't over-reached himself. He organized some of the robberies himself. Business was so good that he had to store some of the stolen property in warehouses. Jealous confederates finally betrayed him. The law had to act. In May 1725 he was taken to Tyburn - now Marble Arch - in a cart, peked and jeered at by the mob; there he was hanged on the triangular gallows. It was probably his reputation for betrayal, rather than dishonesty, that prompted the crowd's hostility.

named Roy Thornton. He was soon in jail, doing life for murder, and at the age of nineteen she met the handsome, polite and pleasant Clyde, whom her mother thought a lovely boy. Her illusions were shattered when Clyde was arrested on seven counts of burglary and car theft. But her daughter was smitten and helped Clyde to escape from jail, smuggling in a gun. A few days later he was picked up again, this time for robbing a railway ticket-office at gunpoint, and sentenced to fourteen years in a grim Texas prison.

There was nothing Bonnie could do this time, so Clyde got to thinking and came up with the ingenious idea of persuading another inmate to cut off two of his toes with an axe. Thus crippled, he was deemed to have suffered enough, and re-leased. He hobbled straight back to Bonnie. He tried going straight, but the work was dull, the pay bad and you still died at the end of it all. Crime held less prospect of such prolonged disappointment. He and Bonnie headed for West Dallas; they picked up a friend of Clyde's, one Ray Hamilton, acquired two other gang members and hit the road.

They rarely struck gold – the biggest haul was a mere $3,500 – and after a few minor heists Clyde committed his first murder, when he shot a jeweller in Hillsboro, Texas. They got away with the grand total of forty dollars. Bonnie was in custody at the time, on suspicion of auto-theft. By the time she was released, three months later, the gang had signed their death warrants by gunning down a Sheriff and his Deputy outside a Texas dance hall.

Some of their murders were the result either of a surprisingly casual attitude to killing or of sheer nerves; little else could explain the occasion on which Bonnie shot a Texas butcher three times in the stomach, or the unnecessary death of the son of a car owner whose vehicle they were stealing. The police stalked them relentlessly. In 1933, they went to hide out in Missouri, where they were joined by Clyde's hitherto respect-able brother, Buck, and his neurotic wife, Blanche. Such a large group made it all the easier for the police to find them. They were duly surrounded but, by now heavily armed, they shot their way out, killing two policemen.

On the run, the two became increasingly morbid; aware that they would inevitably die, they were concerned that they would never see their parents again. A certain desperation crept into their behaviour, and the killings became even more arbitrary. They survived a nasty car crash, and escaped again

"Pretty Boy"Floyd was so christened by an affectionate whorehouse madam in Kansas City. Named Charles Arthur, he was a tall and muscular farm labourer from Oklahoma who one day tossed aside his shovel and decided on a career as a gangster. A contemporary of Bonnie and Clyde, he ploughed exactly the same furrow, robbing banks and shooting anyone who opposed him. Caught and sentenced to fifteen years for the one killing they could pin on him, Pretty Boy hopped off the train taking him to prison and went back to work. He was finally gunned down by the FBI in Ohio in 1934.

from a police assault, before they were once more cornered in Missouri. Again they managed to escape, but this time the police scored: Buck was shot in the head, and Blanche was blinded. Bonnie was still crippled from the car crash. When Clyde stopped driving to buy water and food, the police were on them. Buck was riddled with bullets and died in hospital six days later. Blanche stayed with her dead husband, and was sentenced to ten years in prison.

Bonnie and Clyde eluded the authorities for the next three months. Betrayed by a former gang member, the police staked them out and ambushed their car as they returned from shopping. On 23 May 1934 the Ford V8 sedan they were driving had nearly a hundred rounds pumped into it. They died instantly, very young and very pretty. When they were buried in Dallas, they pulled crowds from all over the country.

chapter seven

THE KRAYS

Charles Kray was a small, dapper man with sharp black shoes, gleaming black hair and an easy smile. A dealer in second-hand clothes and scrap precious metals, from Hoxton, East London, he came from a family of wanderers, and in the 1930s was happy to travel hundreds of miles to buy stock, knocking on doors and "pestering" people. Charles Kray was considered one of the finest "pesterers" in the business and his neighbours said that the Krays had gypsy blood and were descended from horse-dealers who had settled in this poorest part of London; a drab, depressed area, famous for its pubs and thieves. Here Charles's earnings – twenty or thirty pounds at least most weeks – were riches indeed.

At the age of twenty-four, he married Violet Lee, a seventeen-year-old blonde with blue eyes, whom he met in a dance hall in Hackney. One of three attractive sisters from Bethnal Green in the East End, Violet was a headstrong and romantic girl who had effectively eloped with Charles. When she found out a little more about him, she was content to make do. A good wife, quiet and resourceful, she tolerated his gambling and drinking and their relationship was as equable as these things came. Her own father was a celebrated street-fighter and alcoholic who ruled his family with Victorian severity, and she was grateful to escape.

They lived with Charles's parents over a shop in Stene Street, Hoxton, and Violet was soon pregnant. The doctors told her that she should expect twins. In the event, she gave birth to a single child, who was named Charles David. Three years later she was pregnant again.

On the night of 17 October 1934, Violet gave birth at home to male twins who arrived within an hour of each other; she called the first Reginald, and the second Ronald.

Violet adored her twins. Their older brother was a placid, easygoing child, but the twins were a demanding pair, and brought out their mother's protective pride. Assailed by the grinding poverty of the time, dreadful housing, disease, malnutrition and inevitable male drunkenness, East End working-class families were more often than not held together by the canniness and sheer persistence of their women, and Violet was to make an exacting matriarch.

Violet dressed her beloved twins in identical clothes. They were pretty babies, swathed in their white angora woolly hats and coats, and everybody clucked over them. They were unusually healthy children for those times, but at the age of three they contracted diphtheria. They were hospitalized – the first time they had been separated from their mother – and Ronald did not make a particularly good recovery. Afterwards, his mother began to worry about him and pay rather more attention to him than to his brother. Young children can be adversely affected by an early dose of diphtheria, so it was perhaps no coincidence that Ronnie was quieter and slower than Reginald; he also began to display a tendency to sulk, and as a toddler made quite violent demands on his mother's affections. The brothers vied for her attention, and watched each other closely, determined that neither should receive more love than the other.

As the pair grew up, they became a strange beast with two heads and four fists, always allied against the world, but often fighting savagely between themselves (though ten minutes later it would all be forgotten). From an early age they fought all-comers. They were surprisingly vicious, and happily took on older boys. Ronnie was the more overtly aggressive. He may have looked for opportunities to denigrate Reggie in his mother's eyes, but he knew he could count on him in a scrap.

Much to Violet's delight, the family moved back to Bethnal Green, her old neighbourhood. They took a house in Vallance Road, where they were surrounded by members of Violet's close family. The area possessed its own morality, its private code of honour, and a long tradition of villainy. For those

involved in the incessant pub fights, street brawls and stabbings, it was a violent world. But so long as the "decent" folk
were left alone, the police were inclined to turn a blind eye.

During the Second World War the Krays' father went into
hiding to evade the call-up; many others in the area did the
same, so much so that the street gained the name of "Deserter's
Corner". The twins became adept at lying to the police when
they came looking for their father. There were few men
around. Ronnie and Reggie spent long hours in the company
of Violet's now reformed and teetotal father, who regaled them
with the folklore of local fighters and thieves. Violet's sister,
Auntie Rose, who lived round the corner, became a favourite of
the twins. She was a tough, street-fighting woman herself, and
from the beginning she lacked Violet's sentimental illusions
about the twins. She loved them, but she knew and prized their
darker nature and spoiled them rotten. "You're a born devil,"
she said to Ronnie. "You know what those eyebrows of yours
mean, meeting in the middle like that? That you're born to
hang . . ."

Violet aspired to respectability and decency; the twins were
imbued with these virtues. This entailed proper behaviour in
public, and the local schoolteacher and vicar were hard pressed
to find fault with Reggie and Ronnie. They were polite, helpful,
punctilious and respectful to their elders. But increasingly they
had other, distinctly violent, aspirations. They formed juvenile
gangs and fought extended campaigns across the Bethnal
Green wastelands. Their elusive father introduced them to
old-time cockney villains, like Dodger Mullins, the "old guv-
nor" who taught them the code of the East End criminal.
Toughness, pride in one's fighting name, contempt for women
and their family values, a willingness to go to the limits in a
fight and an utter disregard for the law; the eleventh command-
ment in Bethnal Green was "thou shalt not grass on thy
neighbour".

Aged ten, the Kray twins began to box. Their first fight was in
a fairground ring, against each other, and they fought with
furious intensity. The bout was declared a draw, with Ronnie
taking a black eye and Reggie sporting a bleeding nose. Not
only did the fight indicate their prowess at a traditional East
End skill, but it also gave the pair an unforgettable taste of
notoriety. They were quickly snapped up by a local trainer, and
a year later were again fighting each other in the Hackney
Schoolboys Final. Reggie won on points, but the violence of the

From 1894 onwards, there have been major investigations into police corruption about every two decades. In New York, the most recent of these was the Knapp Commission of 1971. In spite of the sensational nature of the revelations, the hearings excited little coast-to-coast attention. The final report which came out in December 1972 colourfully divided 'bent cops' into 'meat-eaters' and 'grass-eaters'. Meat-eaters are policemen who aggressively misuse their power for personal gain; the 'grass-eaters' simply accept the pay-offs that come their way. The vast majority of corrupt policemen, said the report, are grass-eaters.

In an area like New York's Harlem, with its illegal gambling, a bent cop could make $1500 a month. If he was transferred to another command, this payment would continue for another two months - giving him time to adjust to his 'lower income'. It could explain how, when the police seized heroin, it was likely to find its way back into the drugs market - and how of $137,000 seized from drug traffickers, $80,000 went into the pockets of the arresting officers. In one police precinct, over 68 pounds of 'French connection' heroin had vanished from the police laboratory - $7 million-worth at current prices then.

The figures poured out regularly, and no one was very shocked or very surprised. Americans had heard it all before. They *expected* their police to behave like that. They might be roused to protest occasionally if the misbehaviour became too public - as when Mayor Daley's Chicago policemen were seen- on television beating up anybody who looked like a demonstrator during the Democratic Convention of 1968. But generally speaking the feeling is that the police have got a tough job, and that a little brutality and corruption is inevitable - if not, occasionally, necessary.

contest frightened the spectators, and Violet made them promise that they would never fight each other again.

Until the age of sixteen, when they turned professional, the
twins never lost a bout. Ronnie was tough, but Reggie was
canny, and was clearly the one to place the money on, if one
was sufficiently familiar with the pair to be able to tell them
apart. The twins received a lot of publicity, which fed their
appetite for power. At sixteen, they were dominant in the local
gang fights. Their commitment to violent force was outstanding: their opponents' serious injuries were caused not only by
fists and boots, but by coshes, bicycle chains and broken bottles,
which the twins were quick to employ. Ronnie had perfected
the technique of cutting an enemy in the face, for which
purpose he preferred to use a large sheath knife rather than
the traditional razor. The twins bought their first gun, a
revolver, and hid it under the floorboards in Vallance Road.

One of their victims, a sixteen-year-old named Harvey,
nearly died. There were witnesses, and the twins were re-
manded in custody. But, by the time the case came to trial,
the witnesses, reputedly subjected to veiled threats, were
unwilling to testify, and the twins walked free.

Already, Ronnie was getting out of hand. His father had felt
his fist, and had become wary of him. He had once had hopes
for the twins' future as professional boxers, but he now avoided
the increasingly undisciplined pair. Then Ronnie slugged a
policeman. Reggie hated the thought of his brother sitting alone
in the cells and, acting on the perverse sense of loyalty that was
to characterize their relationship, went out and hit the same
constable, successfully joining his brother down the local nick.
They got off on probation, but Ronnie's reputation as a loose
cannon effectively put paid to his professional boxing aspirations. Indeed, despite the good impression these well-man-
nered boys continued to make on naïve figures of authority, the
only people who really exerted any control over them were
their Auntie Rose and their beloved, precious and all-forgiving
mother, Violet.

In 1952, the twins were called up for National Service in the
Royal Fusiliers. Their behaviour on their first day set the tone of
their relationship with the Army. They were still being shown
around the barracks by a corporal when they announced they
didn't care for the environment and were off home. When the
corporal tried to stop them, he was hit.

Over the next two years they proceeded to make a mockery

of the machinery of army discipline. They were constantly in the guardroom, in military prisons or on the run. They were unafraid of punishment; spartan conditions were merely a trial of their manhood, and their insolent fortitude and skill of fist ensured that all attempts to re-shape them were soon abandoned.

There was something increasingly self-conscious and contrived about the way they presented themselves to the world, dressed in smart blue suits, their tight politeness and control giving way to sudden bouts of orchestrated violence. Their experience of the army sharpened this double act. When, as frequently happened, they were charged with assaulting an officer, it was customary for both to plead ignorance. The authorities found it impossible to ascertain which of these identical, stony-faced young men had actually thrown the punch. Later, towards the end of their relationship with the army, they were incarcerated in the guardroom at Howe Barracks, Canterbury, where they wreaked havoc. Ronnie amused himself by pretending to be "barmy", throwing wild tantrums; Reggie handcuffed the guards; they both burned their bedding and together roundly humiliated a succession of hardened soldiers set on subduing them.

Those with wisdom saw that the best way to treat the twins was with weary forbearance, and looked forward to the day when they could be shot of them. The only man who exerted any significant control was a long-serving, aristocratic adjutant, a languid ex-public schoolboy who had been a prisoner of the Japanese. He appeared untroubled – even bored – by their antics and thus earned their respect. They could be sentimental about a proper gentleman.

Ronnie and Reggie had by now decided that what they wanted was a piece of the "good life". Though not yet certain as to what this was, they nevertheless knew that it wasn't going to come by legitimate means but through the exercise of power in the criminal world. Ronnie was an aficionado of gangster literature and movies; he idolized the organized criminals of Chicago, like Capone, who behaved like emperors.

Military prisons enabled Ronnie and Reggie to meet a whole generation of the criminal fraternity from all over the country. They were to remain excellent networkers. Among the more local of the new friends was Dickie Morgan, a villain from a family of villains. While on the run with him they stayed at his family house in Clinton Road in the East End, a regular thieves' kitchen, where the Krays were able to mingle with a host of habitual petty criminals. While hiding from the army they also hung around the less salubrious areas of Soho, and made a useful impression on its underworld. Though they were barely nineteen, the twins appreciated that it was in the underworld of the West End, with its gambling clubs, strip joints and drinking holes, that easy money was to be made. If they were to be more than minor criminals from Bethnal Green they need a reputation out West. Out East they would give occasional, breathtaking displays of bar-room fighting. People remembered them, and began to talk about the strange atmosphere that hung around them: an impressive odour of evil.

One Christmas Eve, when the twins were on one of their spells of unauthorized leave from the Army, a policeman named Fisher (who had arrested and returned them to the army once before) came across them sipping a cup of tea in a cafe in Mile End. He invited them to accompany him to the station. They agreed and, once outside, promptly slugged him and ran off. On their capture they were tried for assaulting a policeman, and were sent to Wormwood Scrubs for a month. It made a refreshing change from military prison. Inside, they found themselves accorded a degree of respect generally reserved for important villains. They appreciated the photographs of themselves that appeared in local papers during their trial, sticking the cuttings in their personal scrap-books as evidence of their growing notoriety.

The army finally court-marshalled and ignominiously dismissed the twins. Back in the East End, they began looking for a locus for their career as professional criminals, and fixed upon the Regal, a dilapidated billiard hall in Mile End. A haunt of local gangs who would come, boozed up, to fight and extort, the place was already in trouble. When Reggie and Ronnie started hanging out there, the violence inexplicably increased to such a level that when the twins offered the owners five pounds a week for the tenancy it was gratefully accepted.

The twins made an unexpected success of the place. The violence stopped abruptly, and the hall was efficiently managed and maintained. It remained open day and night, and the twins began to enjoy a heathly income from the billiard tables. They themselves were the main attraction. Their friends began to drop in regularly and hang around just to see what might happen: life was never dull. There might be a fight on the premises, as when the Maltese gang called in, looking for protection money, and were cut to ribbons with cutlasses; or the twins might form up a raiding party and drop in on a neighbouring pub for a brawl. Watching them punch, kick, slice and stab, their friends were consistently struck by the intent and serious nature of Kray violence. Despite the twins' small stature, they were never to come off worse in a fight. They developed specialities. Reggie perfected a trick he called his "cigarette punch", for which he would sucker the prospective target by offering him a cigarette with his right hand. When the man opened his jaw to put the cigarette in his mouth, Reggie would catch him with a left hook. An open jaw shatters very easily and the "cigarette punch" floored many. Ronnie preferred to cut people, though he considered the razor an inadequate weapon, and preferred a knife or sharpened cutlass. He also fantasized about using guns, of which he had an expanding collection. It was undoubtedly Ronnie who was the more frightening of the pair.

At first there was little organized purpose to the twins' violent forays. But the loose groupings of admirers and minor criminals soon began to form into a distinct gang. Ronnie had found new role models in Lawrence of Arabia and other

The Regal gave them a stage on which to parade their theatrical personas. Ronnie was to the fore in this, playing the Chicago mobster, sitting impassively in a chair clad in dark, double breasted suit, small knotted tie and heavy jewellery, occasionally summoning a henchman for a quiet word. He ensured the lights were low, and demanded that the atmosphere be smoky and conspiratorial, as in the movies. He would hand out packets of cigarettes and urge people to gasp away until the room was choked with a fug. He had a liking for the weird and freakish, and would drag in a circus giant or a pair of dwarves to amuse his entourage.

He also liked young boys. Initially, there was an air of philanthropy about his interest in lads culled from the streets. Sometimes he would justify his relationships by pointing out that the kids were also part of a network of informants. But, though he always despised effeminacy, Ronnie was homosexual. It was shortly common knowledge. Later he would bed lads from the area and then give them five pounds to take their girlfriends out for the night, provided they told him which experience they had preferred.

military heroes. He began to organize, and instil obedience into, the evolving gang. He learned the value of intelligence and propaganda, and began to plan raids in detail, evolving complex tactics. One day somebody christened him "the Colonel". The nickname stuck.

The Krays were often seen as one personality split between two identical bodies, and in this collective psychology it was the violent aspect of Ronnie that was in the ascendant. The aspect of reason, and a modicum of self-restraint, represented by Reggie, was gradually being suppressed.

For the moment, the gang – which would one day become known throughout London as "the Firm" – served as a form of publicity for the Krays. Their aura of control made the Regal into a safe house and meeting place for criminals, who could make contacts, exchange information and conceal their stolen goods. The twins took a cut from the crimes they helped arrange; Reggie generally negotiated. They began to pull complicated con-tricks, and extort regular protection money from pubs, illicit gambling dens and bookmakers.

As their activities took shape, they presented a challenge to some of the established local gangs. Three dockers, all brothers, who unofficially ran Mile End and Poplar, issued a challenge. They were big men – much bigger than the Krays – and all good amateur boxers. To the disappointment of their followers, the Krays refused to talk about the affair. As the appointed date – a Sunday morning – approached, many began to think that the twins were opting for discretion rather than valour. Ronnie and Reggie seemed wholly unconcerned. They spent the Saturday night as usual, getting thoroughly drunk (their capacity for alcohol was stupendous), and lounged around the Regal quietly on the Sunday morning, sipping tea and chatting amiably. Then, with a nod to each other, they strolled down the road to the pub where, in an empty bar, the dockers were waiting. By the time the manager of the pub thought the twins must have had a good hiding and went back into the bar, it looked like an abattoir. Two of the dockers were laid out and Ronnie was carving some finishing touches on the third.

The twins looked forward to the day when they would assume control of London's gangland. Nor were they content to take it in the discreet way in which these matters were customarily handled. None of the old criminals would start a gang-war if it could be avoided. Not so Reggie and Ronnie. They longed for confrontation; they were convinced of their invulnerability, and in the face of this boundless confidence, most of their opponents simply melted away.

They allied themselves with an old villain, Jack Spot, who with another, Billy Hill, ruled the town, and constantly tried to precipitate an all-out struggle for power in the Chicago style. Armed to the teeth with guns, they prowled the streets in their car, looking for trouble. Finally, Ronnie got a chance to shoot a gun. Spot and Hill had both retired and there were new Italian gangs moving in on the West End. The twins believed they were on a hit-list of potential opponents. Ronnie took his favourite Mauser, drove to the Italians' pub and discharged three shots. Fortunately, despite his passion for guns, he was a notoriously bad shot, and missed everybody.

The "Firm" grew. By 1955 there was a buzz of money around the twins. Funded by an ever-growing protection racket, they looked like they might be on their way to wealth and now drove big American cars. Their henchmen did well too. Each could expect some forty pounds a week as their share of the proceeds from extortion, and both Reggie and Ronnie were lavish with the cash: they enhanced their charitable reputation by looking after the families of those doing a stint in prison and were always approachable for a hardship loan.

Then, on 5 November 1956, Ronald Kray was sentenced to prison for three years. He had been convicted of inflicting grievous bodily harm on a young man named Terry Martin, a member of a gang from neighbouring Watney Street. Martin's

The money didn't make Ronnie happy. Increasingly, he wanted to kill somebody. He fantasized about it, drawing up lists of those who merited death, and cutting the ends of his unused bullets to make them into dum-dums capable of blowing a man to pieces. When a local car-dealer got into a spot of bother with a client and asked for help, Ronnie went after him with a Luger and shot the man in the leg, just as he was apologizing to the dealer for his rash behaviour. Reggie had once again to do the tidying up. He bought time by letting himself be arrested in Ronnie's place. By the time he got round to telling the police that they had arrested Reginald, not Ronald, Kray, his brother was safely hidden away, and the victim and all witnesses were suffering from amnesia. Reggie was not best pleased with Ronnie, who retaliated by telling him that he was an amateur who'd never have the balls to kill a man.

gang had beaten up an ex-boxer named Joe Ramsey. Ramsey was important to the Krays: he had just secured them their first toe-hold in the West End as his partners in The Stragglers, a shabby drinking club. Martin was the only member of the gang the twins could get their hands on. They held him while Ramsey sliced him up with a bayonet, and then put the boot in. Martin nearly died. Reggie went home. Ronnie, still attired in blood-stained clothing and armed to the teeth, was stopped by the police, as he drove frantically around the area, looking for more trouble. Ronnie went to Wandsworth gaol, where he seemed quite happy. He was respected by both prisoners and staff, and lacked for nothing. With help from outside, he soon had the traditional prison trade in tobacco under his thumb, ate well and did no work.

With the erratic Ronnie safely under lock and key, Reggie began to prosper. He missed Ronnie, but at last it was not necessary to sacrifice business interests for the sake of theatrical violence. Reggie opened a club, The Double R (after Ronnie and himself) on the Bow Road. He had always felt that the East End lacked a decently run club with a bit of glamour. The club was respectable, and had good singers and a lively atmosphere. Its association with two men popularly believed to be violent criminals also gave it a sheen of fashionable, sexy violence. One or two playboys and pop-stars began to roll in, looking for something to stimulate their jaded palates. The legitimate world and criminal world, high life and low life, the overtly proper and the covertly perverse mingled freely at the Double R.

Charlie Kray, the twins' brother, began to work alongside Reggie. They opened another club in the East End, and then started a gambling den next to Bow Police Station. Later they formed a friendship with their former enemy, the retired gangster Billy Hill. Hill had interests in illicit gambling throughout the West End that he still needed to have minded, and gave Charlie and Reggie a stake in the lucrative business. With Parliament on the verge of legalizing gambling, the Krays realized that they could soon quit the East End and be wealthy and powerful on a grand scale, without having to resort to Ronnie's style of violence. Ronnie could be thoroughly misogynistic; free from his influence, Reggie began to enjoy the company of women. He had nights out in the West End and moved in society. He looked happy.

Ronnie was not having an enjoyable time. His good behaviour had secured his transfer to a prison on the Isle of Wight. It was easygoing, but Ronnie was lost without the familiar criminal company and respect he had been accorded in Wandsworth. He grew depressed, and then paranoid. He thought that people believed he was an informer; then he saw the outlines of a conspiracy and imagined that he was under constant surveillance by people who wanted to torture him. He retreated into himself and spent days sitting in the corner of his cell. He finally broke and, after a bout of terrifying violence, was put in a straitjacket. Then his beloved Auntie Rose died of leukaemia. Ronnie slid into madness, and shortly after Christmas 1957 was certified insane.

He was diagnosed as paranoid schizophrenic. Transferred to a Surrey mental institution, he began to make a recovery, assisted by large doses of the drug Stematol. But so long as he was certified insane, there was no prospect of his release.

Under prison regulations, anyone who was certified insane, escaped and stayed at large for longer than six weeks had to be certified again on recapture. If Ronnie could escape, and appear sane on recapture, he would be allowed to complete his original sentence.

In the summer of 1958, Reggie helped his brother to escape, and hid him in the Suffolk countryside. The twins had spent a spell there during the Blitz, and the country seemed to calm Ronnie down. He lived in a caravan deep in woodland, accompanied by a trusted bodyguard who did the cooking and cleaning. Reggie kept him well supplied with boys and alcohol and Ronnie amused himself by getting his bodyguard to play "the hunting game" in which they stalked each other with air-guns. But he was soon bored. He was jealous of Reggie's public prominence and missed London. He implored Reggie to let him make the occasional late-night foray to the Double R. Against the better advice of his brother Charlie, Reggie agreed. Soon Ronnie was dressing up as Reggie and strolling through the streets of Whitechapel.

But each time he returned to the country, Ronnie fell back into his former depression. He brooded, and began to mutter ominously about murder. He was moved from the caravan into a neighbouring farm. After the police called to make a routine check, he lapsed once more into paranoia, accusing Reggie of being an impostor: he was not his brother, but a Russian spy.

Even Reggie was frightened. The family discreetly consulted psychiatrists and doctors, but the drugs prescribed had a limited effect. Ronnie was contained by the consumption of two bottles of gin a day.

After Ronnie attempted suicide, the family realized that he had to be returned to a secure mental hospital; they must surrender him to the authorities. Reggie let the police know that if they came around to Vallance Road they could pick his brother up. Ronnie was unsuspecting, and when the police called, he went without a murmur.

With treatment, he was allowed to finish his prison sentence and was released in the spring of 1959. He immediately suffered a fit of paranoia and, convinced that the Russians were coming to get him, was sedated in a hospital. Again he recovered, but his personality was irrevocably altered. Before his breakdown he had been an unnerving presence. Now he was hysterically excitable, wholly crazed and dangerous, devoid of any vestige of conventional conscience and trapped within his own grotesque fantasies.

As a consequence of one of Ronnie's rash pledges of loyalty, Reggie found himself embroiled in a dispute over money between a shop-owner and a small-time crook. He went to prison for eighteen months. Charlie Kray melted into the background and Ronnie was free to indulge his taste for open warfare, slowly destroying the business they had built up.

Income plummeted. Then, quite coincidentally, something profitable happened. Ronnie fell out with Perac Rachman, later notorious as a landlord specializing in extortion. In order to get Ronnie off his back, Rachman showed him how the Krays

Ronnie liked to have the local barber come over to his house and shave him in the morning, something he had read that Chicago gangsters did. The tailor also had to call personally, and he had his shirts and suits delivered to the door. He took up riding and spent the weekends playing the country squire in a Suffolk village. He had a pet Doberman, which he adored. But he remained contemptuous of the moderate policies of Reggie and Charlie and wanted an immediate return to the old days of violence and petty extortion. He upset people, careering drunkenly around the East End, demanding protection money from clubs in which the Krays already had a stake and publicly insulting the Italian gangs with whom Reggie had carefully forged peace. He accused Reggie of having gone soft, which he blamed on his brother's taste for women.

could get their hands on Esmerelda's Barn, a Mayfair gambling club, the haunt of stars and minor royalty.

The twins now had a business advisor, Leslie Payne. A canny man, who had just been declared bankrupt and badly needed the work, "Payne the Brain" was a principal factor in the rise of the Krays. Latterly he had managed to exert some control over Ronnie. Reggie was out of prison pending appeal and, together with Payne, the twins called on the owner of Esmerelda's Barn. Acting on information Rachman had given them, Payne made the man an offer. After a glance at Reggie and Ronnie, the man decided not to refuse it. The club did well. Soon the twins were making £40,000 a year each, without having to lift a finger. But Reggie lost his appeal, and went back to prison.

Ronnie carried on playing the role of king gangster. He had money, lavish clothes, expensive cars, a flat in the West End and all the pretty boys he could manage; for a while he fell in love, and paraded his boy about as if he were a young mistress, tenderly calling him "son" and referring to himself as "your old Dad". But at heart he remained an unhappy and sick man. He despised the wealthy, confident clientele of the club. They made him feel insecure. He wanted an entourage of people he could control and began to attract a seedier variety of customer, offering hard-up nobility and habitual losers unlimited credit. Though the club's profits fell, it remained a goldmine, and its respectability was ensured for a time when they persuaded Lord Effingham – the first of a string of tame peers – to join the board of management. Charlie urged his brothers to invest their wealth quickly in clubs and betting shops, but Ronnie resisted. He knew that if the Krays became legitimate, he would cease to be of any significance.

While Ronnie now believed himself to be a reincarnation of Attilla the Hun and a Samurai warrior, read "Mein Kampf" and planned to create an army that would take the world by force, Reggie kept the business going and efficiently muscled into the protection rackets of the West End. He also established fruitful contacts with foreign organizations looking for a piece of the action in London and, aided by the ingenuity of Payne, the twins were able to execute a string of lucrative frauds. They began to expand outside London, taking over clubs in Birmingham and Leicester. They cultivated a reputation for philanthropy, giving generously to charity; they were not shy of publicity, and their faces were soon appearing regularly in national newspapers. They granted interviews to eminent journalists, and Ronnie approached one to ghost his autobiography, but the offer was declined.

In 1963, they made their first important political contact: Joan Littlewood, the legendary theatre director, introduced them to the influential and corrupt Tom Driberg, then Labour MP for Barking. A future Chairman of the Labour party, who later became a respected member of the House of Lords, Driberg was one of a number of eminent pederasts whom Ronnie was to form mutually rewarding relationships with. In return for support, Ronnie provided flesh to order. His parties became famous, and he began to receive invitations to stately homes outside London.

In the summer of 1964, the *Sunday Mirror* alleged the existence of a homosexual relationship between a prominent member of the House of Lords and a "leading thug in the London underworld". It also claimed that it had pictures to

When Reggie got out of prison he was in love with Frances Shea, the sister of a man the twins had known since their youth. She was sixteen, eleven years younger than Reggie. In prison he had written to her every day. He dreamed of a perfect marriage; with his fairy-tale bride he would at last lead the good life, free of the strain of crime, and free of Ronnie. His twin knew Frances was a threat. He hated her. At first, Reggie's society contacts and wealth impressed Frances and her parents. When he first proposed to her, in the autumn of 1961, she turned him down, on the grounds that she was too young. He persisted; he was possessive but also charming and generous, and courted her assiduously over the next four years. She married him on 20 April 1965, at St James, Bethnal Green. It was the East End wedding of the year. David Bailey photographed the wedding and the church was packed with journalists and voyeurs from the world of show business. Within eight weeks Frances, at last party to the truth about Reggie's life, could take no more. She fled back to her parents. Reggie could not leave her alone. She became frightened and withdrawn. She had a breakdown and tried to kill herself a number of times. She tried to get a divorce, but then agreed to attempt a reconciliation with Reggie, who claimed he was a changed man. On 6 June 1967 they booked air-tickets for a second honeymoon. That night, Reggie dreamed she had taken her life and, as dawn broke, went around to her parents where she was staying. It was true. She apparently died a virgin.

Ronnie met Ernest Shinwell, son of the Labour politician, who
interested him in a plan to build a new township costing several
million pounds in the bush outside an obscure Nigerian town.
Ronnie became obsessed with the plan, certain that it would
guarantee immortality, and visited the country as a VIP guest of
the Nigerian government. When the grandiose design collapsed,
he was bitterly upset. An old confederate of the twins had the
misfortune to catch Ronnie on a night after he had received the
bad news. He touched Ronnie for five pounds and made a
cheerful jibe about his weight. Ronnie took him into the bathroom and cut most of his face off. It took seventy stitches to put
him back together again.

prove it. Though they were not yet named, it was known that
the men referred to were Lord Boothby and Ronald Kray.

The twins were in two minds about the happening. There
was no such thing as bad publicity, but homosexuality was
illegal, and any investigation into Boothby might lead to their
activities. The police had long been looking for something that
would give them a hold over the Krays. But when the police
realized that a number of politicians might be involved, they
backed off. The photographer who had supplied the newspaper with the pictures suddenly wanted them back; Boothby
denied everything and received an apology and £40,000 from
the newspaper's parent company. Even Ronnie got an apology.
The editor of the *Sunday Mirror* got the sack.

The following January, a known associate of the Krays
entered a West End club, demanded money for the twins
and, when it was not forthcoming, smashed the place up.
The police believed that they at last had something on the
twins. They were arrested and charged with demanding money
with menaces. It is alleged that with Boothby's help, they were
able to command the services of the best criminal lawyers in
London, and Boothby even had the chutzpah to raise their case
sympathetically in the House of Lords. After two trials, and
amid whispers that both jurors and witnesses had been subject
to unseen pressure, the twins were acquitted. "To some extent I
share your triumph" wrote Boothby to Ronald Kray. No doubt
he had a considerable share in it. The twins walked free in a
blaze of triumphant publicity. Reggie married Frances Shea
almost immediately.

This perverse alliance of the Krays and respected establishment forces ensured that henceforth there was a virtual news-blackout on their criminal activities. They seemed unchallengeable, and were left alone to consolidate their hold on London. Over the next four years they re-organized protection rackets on a scale never seen in Britain, before or since. They dealt freely with the New York Mafia, marketing vast quantities of stolen US bonds, looked after the Mob's interests in London, and swindled and intimidated with absolute impunity.

In March 1966, at Ronnie's instigation, they found themselves in a rather unnecessary war with a lesser gang run by the Richardson brothers, scrap metal merchants from South London. Their interests should never have clashed. Ronnie got hold of a pair of Browning machine-guns, and the twins prepared for the bloody battle the "Colonel" longed for.

On 8 March there was an unrelated shoot-out when the Richardsons tried to steam-roller a local gang at Mr Smith's club in Catford. It left one man dead and another two seriously injured. The Richardsons came off worse, and there was clearly no need for the Krays to take any further action against them: they were finished as rivals.

But Ronnie wanted to have his say in the Richardsons' demise. There was a lesser Richardson member called Cornell, who he knew had once called him a "fat poof". Taking his Mauser 9mm pistol, Ronnie had himself driven to The Blind Beggar, the Richardsons' hang-out. He and his driver walked in; Cornell was sitting at the bar. The driver loosed off a couple of shots to clear the bar. Then, at point-blank range, Ronnie blew Cornell's head to pieces. It was the most satisfying moment of his career.

It would be two years before the police could persuade anyone to talk.

Reggie had to clear up the mess. He put his twin into hiding in an obscure flat in Finchley, where Ronnie was engulfed by another savage depression and bouts of waking nightmares during which he would turn violent or attempt suicide. But Reggie managed to contain him and still keep the business going, though the strain was telling. There was now an air of unnatural self-control about Reggie. Still good-looking, he had become thin and had dark rims under his bloodshot eyes. Ronnie was fat and swollen, his thickened face permanently distorted with anger.

By the spring of 1967, just as Ronnie was calming down,

Reggie's wife, Frances, committed suicide. Reggie went off the rails. He drank himself insensible and veered between violent self-reproach and utter hatred for her family who, he said, had turned Frances against him. After the funeral, Reggie became more like his erratic twin. Aside from the hour he spent at Frances's grave each day, talking to her ghost, he was drunk most of the time; with encouragement from Ronnie, he started looking for people he could hurt. The first was a former friend called Frederick, who he believed might have said something derogatory about his dead wife. Fuelled by a violent row with Ronnie, Reggie turned up at Frederick's house and shot him in the leg. He shot and wounded another man at a club in Highbury, then slit open the face of an old boxer with whom he had a vague dispute. One or two of the Firm's members went missing following disagreements with the twins.

Ronnie was still determined that his brother should kill a man in cold blood. The eventual victim was Jack "The Hat" McVitie. A criminal whose nerve had long gone, McVitie was a good-natured man who derived his courage from alcohol and pills. Ronnie heard that Leslie Payne had struck a deal with the police and was grassing on the twins' activities. He offered McVitie £500 to kill Payne. Jack "The Hat" bungled the attempt. Ronnie was furious, and wanted his money back; he issued threats. Reggie briefly smoothed things over. Then McVitie got drunk, and wandered into a club waving a shotgun and saying he was looking for the twins. Word of this reached Ronnie.

On a Saturday in October 1967 Reggie and Ronnie Kray told two of their henchmen to find McVitie and bring him to a party they had arranged in a dingy flat in the East End. The owner of the flat, a blonde girl they knew well, was happy to loan them her premises for the evening. Surprisingly, McVitie, who probably had no recollection of his previous behaviour, came willingly. As he walked in through the door, Reggie shot at him. The gun jammed. McVitie tried to dive through the window, but got stuck. Ronnie pulled him back; Reggie had taken a carving knife from one of the gang. McVitie looked at him in bewilderment; Ronnie insisted; Reggie struck the point of the knife into his head below the eye. As McVitie sank to the floor, Reggie stabbed him repeatedly in the stomach and then impaled him through the throat to the floor. The twins took a holiday in Suffolk. The body was never found.

Detective Chief Inspector "Nipper" Read of Scotland Yard

had a long-standing battle with the twins. They considered him highly dangerous and had done all they could to ruin his career. His failure to get them convicted on charges of extortion two years previously had nearly done for him. He was happy to stay away from them, but on being posted to Scotland Yard in 1967 was promptly put in charge of their case. It was an unenviable task. There was very little documentation of their activities. Any possible conviction was wholly dependent on persuading victims and villains to talk and the criminal code of silence had ensured this had not happened.

But Read was convinced that if he could persuade one to talk then many would follow. Leslie Payne had heard about the offer Ronnie had made to McVitie, and was the first to agree. Once he had outlined the Krays' activities in a statement two hundred pages long, Read knew that he had the basis of a case. With exacting slowness, his team began to pick up corroborating statements from reluctant witnesses. Read hoped that once people saw the Krays were under lock and key they would be happier to come forward. In particular, the barmaid at The Blind Beggar, who had witnessed the shooting of Cornell, might at last talk.

It was 9 May 1968 before they felt they had sufficient evidence to hold the twins. It was a gamble, but they could delay no longer. At 7 a.m., the police smashed in the doors of the house where the twins were staying and dragged them out of their beds. They had been out drinking until 5 a.m.. Ronnie was with his latest boy; Reggie, with a girl from Walthamstow.

With the twins awaiting trial, the police quickly rounded up the members of the already disintegrating Firm. With no Firm, the twins had no way of reaching those who talked and the wall of silence that had protected them collapsed. Their sources of money vanished; their support melted away; they had to apply for legal aid. The barmaid from The Blind Beggar did speak as a witness for the prosecution. Reggie was charged with being an accessory to that killing, and Ronnie as an accessory to the McVitie murder. On 8 March 1969, at the end of the longest and most expensive criminal trial in Britain, Mr Justice Melford Stevenson sentenced them to life imprisonment, and recommended that this should be not less than thirty years each.

They were only thirty-four years old. Apart from attending their mother's funeral, they have remained in prison ever since. Reggie is in Parkhurst on the Isle of Wight. A "Category A" prisoner, his life is spent in solitary confinement. He now suffers from acute depression and is haunted by the past. He hopes that he will still live to re-marry and settle in the country, but there is no parole for Category A prisoners. Ronnie was originally with him in Parkhurst, but was certified insane and transferred to Broadmoor. He lives well, dresses nattily and has become rather keen on art and health food. Although sedated by drugs, he still considers himself the Colonel, and has broad fantasies about his importance. He has plenty of hopes for the future, and no regrets about the past.

chapter eight

JACK SPOT AND BILLY HILL: THE LONDON VILLAINS

For many years before the Kray twins brought their particular brand of American-style organized crime and violence to London, the sprawling, fog-bound city of the 1930s and 1940s was run by two legendary villains: Jack Spot and Billy Hill.

At various times close friends and bitter rivals, both claimed the title of "King of London's Underworld". Although violence was endemic in their circles, it rarely erupted onto the streets or involved the public, and so long as they remained discreet, the police – many of whom formed close relations with the villains – were content to leave the criminals to themselves.

Far better the devil you know, the argument went. Underpaid bobbies on the beat were frequently accused of "rolling" those too drunk to resist, and stealing their possessions. This is the origin of the saying: "If you want to know the time, ask a policeman". Policemen were never without a watch, often donated by an unsuspecting drunk.

Guns, although increasingly available after the First World War, were rarely used and killings were less frequent than they would become under the Krays. The old gangs rarely indulged in the spectacular gun battles that American gangsters were so fond of. Enemies and traitors were not machine-gunned from cars but visited by the "chiv-man", who would carefully slice a face up with his taped-down cut-throat razor, or chop through their collar bones with his little hatchet.

In a fight, gangs used knives, razors, pick-axe handles, hatchets and the fist and the boot. But, for generations, their favourite weapon was the beer-bottle. If you carried a gun or a knife, you could be in serious trouble if the police stopped you. But an innocuous beer-bottle was entirely legitimate. Quite apart from providing suitable sustenance before an affray, it made an excellent club. It could quickly be smashed and its broken, jagged edges thrust into the face of an opponent with devastating results. It also made an excellent missile.

The English underworld in the early part of the century provided a number of illegal but nevertheless essential services. It supplied prostitution, gambling and out of hours drinking facilities to the public. The men who ran the illegal rackets were "wide-men"; the them, the respectable, hard-working populace were "mugs", waiting to be fleeced.

During the years of acute poverty, and particularly in the 1930s, prostitution was rampant in London, as women discovered that they could make a comparatively good living on the streets. They could get through twenty or thirty clients in a shift of four hours, and as they charged from ten shillings to a pound a time, the wages of sin were quite decent. Many

In the 1920s many major criminals in London tended to be men renowned for their sheer masculine toughness rather than as businessmen-gangsters. East End villains such as Jew Jack "The Chopper King", Wassle Newman, Jimmy Spinks and Dodger Mullins (who was later to become something of a mentor to the Krays) were legendary for their displays of brute force. Newman was reputed to toughen his fists by tossing bricks in the air and punching them as they came down; but he was no master of organized crime. He simply enjoyed being a bully, and would go into pubs and take away the customers' beer, daring them to protest. Mullins was notorious for his perfunctory views on the fairer sex, and once disposed of a girlfriend he had tired of by pushing her out of a moving car. She broke her back. Spinks was a bully like Newman; when actually asked to pay for some fish and chips he was guzzling, he tossed the cat belonging to the shop's owners into the chip-fryer. One Glasgow "hard man", Jimmy "Razzle Dazzle" Dalziel, was so afraid of having his masculinity questioned that he would always dance with a member of his gang, the "Parlour Boys", rather than be seen being sentimental with a woman.

prostitutes came from abroad. Marthe Watts, a French woman, hated the English climate, but was surprised at the
leniency of the police. She was also perturbed by the sexual
tastes of the average Englishman. She once said she was
astonished at the number of men who wanted her to tie them
up and beat them. Those who controlled the prostitution
rackets also tended to come from abroad: until 1929, the
principal racketeers were a Frenchman, Casimire Micheletti,
and a Spanish dancer, Juan Antonio Castanar. When "Mad
Emile" Berthier, a known associate of Castanar, mistook a
French pimp called Charlie "The Acrobat" for Micheletti and
slashed him to death in a seedy Frith Street dive, the police
deported the rival pimps. The prostitution racket was taken
over by "Red Max" Kessel, a heavily scarred Latvian, whose
bullet ridden body turned up in a ditch in Hertfordshire.
Another infamous pimp was Eddie Manning, a Jamaican dope

The use of hard drugs such as heroin and cocaine became more
common in the 1920s. The "Bright Young Things" of the
"Roaring Twenties" were often young women determined to
live the bright life and take their chances with death. They were
known as "dopers" and lived lives which consisted principally of
drugs and parties. Countless "Bright Young Things" began to
succumb to drug overdoses. Among these were many aspiring
actresses and society hostesses. Billie Carleton, a popular
actress much sought after (not only for her acting skill), died
of cocaine poisoning after attending the victory celebrations in
November 1918. Freda Kempton, who was a hostess at a club run
by the legendary "madame" Kate Meyrick, died of an overdose of
cocaine in March 1922. The actress Brenda Dean Paul was
crippled by her addiction. These – and many other casualties
– were laid at the door of "Brilliant" Chang, an immaculately
groomed Chinese man, who owned two restaurants in the heart of
the West End. He was strongly suspected of being a substantial
gangster specializing in the opium trade, and his close liaisons
with beautiful young women caused outrage and indignation. As
late as the 1950s one national newspaper remembered him as
"an arch-fiend, who would stop at nothing to gain his mastery
over beautiful women". Chang was arrested in 1924, but only
imprisoned for fourteen months. On his release he was deported,
but in exile he was still thought to have a substantial interest in
the London drugs trade.

dealer. Being black he was viewed, in keeping with the morals of the time, with particular horror, because of the power he exerted over white women. Manning was called the "wickedest man in London". After imprisonment in 1929 he died of a cocaine habit.

In the nineteenth century, betting on racehorses became a national past-time. But it remained illegal to lay a bet anywhere other than at the racecourse. This was to remain the case until the Betting and Gaming Act of 1960. Despite the illegal status of off-course bookmakers, there were well over 15,000 of them practising in the 1920s, and it was estimated that illegal bookmaking had an annual turnover of between £350 and £450 million. The police and the bookmakers had an unofficial arrangement, whereby the police would satisfy the public desire to see an occasional prosecution by periodically rounding up a number of bookmakers. They would be compensated by their fellows for any lost earnings. In return the police could expect to be well treated, receiving regular payments, and the odd case of whisky.

Criminals are almost exclusively attracted to sources of money, and such a vast business naturally invited the attention of protection gangs. These, apart from charging a book-maker for his "pitch" at the racetrack and taking a substantial percentage of his profits from illegal off-course betting, would protect him against theft and ensure that his debtors paid up. The last was most important. Gambling debts were not enforceable by law, and losses were vast. Between 1918 and 1956, the underworld was largely dominated by the race-gangs. Jack Spot ran one of these.

The son of Polish Jews who had come to England in the 1890s, Jack Spot, who generally gave his real name as Jack Comer, was born in Whitechapel in 1912. It was an industrious, hard working and law-abiding community, and from an early age Spot, who was restless and aggressive, stood out. His brothers and sister were employed in tailoring and dressmaking but Spot hung around the local boxing clubs and gyms, where the local ne'er-do-wells would congregate.

He established a reputation as a fearless fighter and, in those days of rising anti-Semitism, he soon found himself inundated with pleas for protection from Jewish bookmakers, businessmen, promoters and shopkeepers who were threatened by the activities of fascists. When Sir Oswald Mosley attempted to march through the East End with his Blackshirts in 1936, Spot and his entourage happily decimated Mosley's bodyguard.

The tongs were probably the first largescale protection racket in America, and this was largely because they organized the lives of their fellow citizens in this foreign country, and got them to pay a proportion of their wages. If a Chinaman established himself enough to want to bring his wife to America, the tong demanded a certain payment.

The tongs had a simple way of enforcing their will: murder. Their assassins preferred hatchets - hence the term 'hatchet man' - but also carried. a silk rope around the body, like the Thugs of India. Their 'protection' was genuine, like that of the Mafia in Sicily. In San Francisco in 1875, a hatchet man named Ming Long, of the Kwong Dock Tong, came upon Low Sing, a member of the Suey Sing Tong, holding the hand of a pretty 'slave girl' named Kum Ho, and split his skull with a hatchet.

Before he died, Low Sing gasped out the name of his killer to the head of his tong. Formal challenges were sent, and the next day at midnight the deadliest hatchet men of both tongs met in a certain street in Chinatown, and fought earnestly and bloodily until the police - mostly Irish - arrived with their whistles and night-sticks. No one was killed - although some died later. The Suey Sings were held to have won, because they had injured a large number of the enemy.

Payment was made to Low Sing's relatives; Ming Long was formally ejected from the tong, which meant that he was fair game for any hatchet man, and fled to China, where the tongs did not exist. The historian of San Francisco, Herbert Asbury, points out that both the tongs and chop suey were invented by the Chinese in America

Darby Sabini and his brothers Joe, Charles, Harry Boy and Fred came from Saffron Hill, Clerkenwell, the heart of London's Italian community. In the early 1920s they wrested control of the lucrative South of England racecourses from Billy Kimber and his Birmingham gang, with considerable assistance from the Flying Squad (then one of the first mobile police units) with which Darby Sabini had reached an "understanding". For fourteen years Sabini and his brothers maintained a discreet but all-powerful hold over the racing world. Their shootings and stabbings went largely unreported, but the police were quick to swoop on affrays instigated by the vengeful Birmingham mob, or one of the other London race-gangs. Once Sabini was attacked at the Fratalanza Club in Great Bath Street by a rival gang, the four Cortesi brothers, who blazed away at the gangster and his family. It was their first attempted shooting, however, and they missed. The four men were quickly rounded up. But only two of them were found guilty of "attempted murder", and the judge held that this was an internecine dispute, unworthy of public concern: the men only received three years each. In the end Sabini fell from grace as a result of a lost libel case. A newspaper called him "Britain's leading gangster". Sabini sued, and then failed to turn up in court. He lost and was ordered to pay modest costs, which, being a profligate, he couldn't manage, and he had to declare himself bankrupt. The excessive publicity he received perpetually discredited him in the eyes of his fellow criminals.

He was increasingly drawn to the lucrative world of the racetracks and the "spielers": the small, illicit gambling clubs that were widespread throughout Soho and the West End. These were the scene of many confrontations between Jewish and Italian gangsters. Though Spot took his fair share of beatings – he was thrashed to the point of death with billiard cues by a mob from Islington – he earned a reputation for his almost foolhardy courage.

By the early 1940s Spot, backed by his ferocious race-gang, was the emerging force in the criminal underworld. Following a police clamp-down on the "spielers" in 1940, Spot and his cronies found themselves dragooned into the army. Spot hated it, objecting to the bad pay, rotten food, harsh discipline and rampant anti-Semitism. He had no compunction about belting his superiors and, after three torrid years, the marine regiment admitted failure and discharged him as mentally unstable.

Spot returned to the Blitz-devastated East End to find that his parents were dead and his family long dispersed. He became involved with the spivs, but after an altercation with a local hard man (in which he nearly succeeded in killing him with a tea-pot), he fled to Leeds, the black-market capital of the north, and a haven for deserters, gamblers and racketeers.

Here his strength, lack of fear and his alcoholic abstinence quickly gave him an advantage over the local gangsters. He looked after club-owners and bookies, and after the war moved back into London's gambling clubs. High wages, the profits of crime and the recklessness induced by realizing one was still alive created a vast boom in post-war gambling.

From a club in St Botolph's row, on the outskirts of the City, Spot also ran his extensive racetrack business. After a pitched battle with the Islington mob, which brought him control of Ascot race-course, his only serious challengers were the White gang. But the White gang had grown soft, and met their Waterloo at the Stork club in Sackville Street, where Spot and his men coshed and "chived" them into bloody submission.

Spot's gang were also involved in lorry hijacking and big "project" heists. It was thought that he was behind the abortive 1948 Heathrow airport robbery, when ten men armed with lead pipes and with nylon stockings over their heads drove up to the airport in a lorry, coshed the security guards into submission, and broke into a warehouse which was reputed to contain ten million pounds in gold ingots. Unfortunately it was a Flying Squad trap, and they were assaulted by a phalanx of psyched-up policemen. After a brutal battle, the police got eight of the men. One of the villains – Franny Daniels – escaped by clinging to the underside of a police van, eventually falling off when it stopped outside a West London police station. Daniels crawled away into the night. There was insufficient evidence to incriminate Spot.

One morning in late 1949, Jack Spot went to the gates of Wandsworth gaol to meet a released prisoner. It was Billy Hill, now middle aged. Once a major gangster, he had of late fallen on hard times.

Billy Hill was born in 1911 in Seven Dials, on the north side of Covent Garden. It was not then a fashionable area, but a rookery of the poor and criminal. His mother was a "buyer of bent gear", and his father could barely pass a policeman without hitting him, a compulsion which had brought him five or six convictions. There were twenty-one children in the family. Those who survived generally turned to crime. Young Billy started his working life as a grocer's delivery boy in Camden Town, but looked upon it largely as an opportunity to feed a relative tasty information about prospective targets for burglaries. He was soon doing his own, preferring "drumming" (the wholesale ransacking of a house in its owners' absence) to "creeping" (burglary while the occupants slept). Drumming was increasingly popular among criminals; there were many new, quiet suburbs, whose occupants were out during the day, and drumming tended to be more leniently viewed by the courts than creeping.

Over the years, Hill specialized in domestic theft and smash and grab raids. When the Second World War broke out, he evaded military service and with his gang found that the confusion of war-time offered new opportunities for making easy money. He broke into post-offices and opened up safes with a custom-built giant tin-opener; the black-out meant that he went undisturbed, and a depleted police force lacked the man-power to keep tabs on him. Though Hill was overtly as proud as the next man to be British, and talked of the war-time camaraderie, he became an important figure in the vast spiv-ridden world of the black market, selling stolen goods and ration cards, and keeping the well-heeled supplied with everything from petrol and nylons to fresh salmon and bacon.

The profits were huge. Hill was making £3,000 a week from burglaries and many times that from his black-market activities. He never went on the town without a "monkey" (£500) or a "grand" (£1,000) in his pocket. He wore forty-guinea Savile Row suits, silk shirts and hand-made shoes.

Though not yet an ally of Spot's, Hill was also involved in the violent demise of the White gang. Shortly afterwards he was nicked by the police. Hill had spent nearly 15 years inside, and

> Teetotal Spot often had the mickey taken for drinking only lemonade. He didn't mind and favoured attacking his opponents when the alcohol had rendered them incapable of retaliation. He liked to attack the opposition in West End pub toilets. As he said himself: "I used to knock 'em out in the lavatory, that was my surgery. I used to follow 'em into the toilet and bomp! Leave 'em in the piss."

objected to being imprisoned for a crime of which he claimed to
be wholly innocent. He was indignant, and on bail decided to
leave England. Pretending to be a policeman, he relieved a pair
of crooks of their haul of parachute silk, and with the proceeds
headed for South Africa. In Johannesburg he opened a gambling club. But he was soon involved in a battle with Arnold
Neville, the emperor of South African crime. Neville was found
in a pool of blood outside a night-club. He had been sliced from
head to toe with razors, and needed over a hundred stitches.
Hill was arrested, but his polite demeanour and respectable
appearance earned him a light sentence. Afraid of extradition,
he jumped bail and headed back to England. But he was sick of
running, and finally gave himself up and went to Wandsworth
gaol.

When Spot took Hill under his wing, it was not for altruistic
reasons but because Spot's roster of trusted lieutenants had
been depleted by injury and police action. Hill was a useful
man, and Spot put him in charge of the spielers. He could be a
cold, hard man, and it was said that his eyes were like "black
glass". He was an excellent gambler, and tolerated no trouble in

---

Motorized crime and car theft began to boom in the 1920s. Fast
transport and the prospect of a swift getaway widened the
prospective criminal's catchment area. Two of the most famous
motor bandits were "Ruby" Sparks and his long-time lover and
side-kick the "Bobbed-Haired Bandit". Ruby earned his nickname while working as a cat-burglar: he unwittingly stole a
priceless cache of rubies from an Indian prince, but believing
they were fake, gave them all away. With the "Bobbed-Haired
Bandit" he turned to motorized smash and grab raids. The first
time he tried throwing a brick at a window it bounced back at him,
but he soon developed a successful technique, though it often
meant that he lacerated his arms. He would hold the gashes
together with bulldog clips until the "Bobbed-Haired Bandit"
sewed him up. The police admired the "Bobbed-Haired Bandit",
a Jewish girl from a respectable family who had turned to crime
after an unhappy love affair. She drove a Mercedes and sported a
black beret. After five years she and Ruby were caught, but got off
with light sentences. After Sparks escaped from a spell in prison
in 1940 they teamed up again. But they were old and tired. She
had grey in her hair and wore spectacles. After a few abortive
raids they finally retired.

the clubs he ran, though his propensity for violence elsewhere
often caused Spot embarrassment. Hill fell for the charms of
Gypsy Riley, a tempestuous temptress and noted good-time
girl. When her ex-pimp, "Belgian Johnny", tried to put her back
on the game, Hill marched into a restaurant where Johnny was
eating with his Belgian friends and publicly slashed his face to
shreds. Spot had to work hard to persuade the Belgian to keep
his mouth shut.

Spot had married a young Irish girl named Rita, and in 1951
he planned to retire. But he could not wholly trust his chief
henchmen to preserve peace in the underworld and in the end
he worked out a power-sharing arrangement with Hill where
the latter had control of the spielers while Spot kept a firm
grasp on the race-track.

But the world of gambling was changing. The Betting and
Gaming Act of 1960 would legalize many of the illicit areas
which the gangsters derived their wealth from. In the run-up to
it, the race-course authorities went about cleaning up the
activities on the courses, licensing and policing the bookmakers themselves. By the mid-1950s Spot had lost much of
his authority. His less scrupulous partner was looking for
opportunities to expand.

Hill had grown up when the legal system only meted out
modest sentences for petty crime and theft. Such stints were
regarded as an occupational hazard. The Criminal Justice Act of
1948 changed his attitude. Now he and others like him were to
be regarded as "continual reoffenders", and would face longer
and longer spells in jail. Hence, the rewards from petty
burglary and shifting bent gear no longer justified the potential
penalties. He cast around for bigger and bigger "project"
crimes. In his autobiography he as good as boasted that he
was responsible for the 1952 mailbag robbery, in which
£287,000 in used notes – a massive sum in those days – was
stolen from post office vans ambushed between Paddington
Station and the sorting office in the City. The following year a
lorry carrying £45,000 in gold bullion on behalf of KLM Air-
ways was hijacked in Holborn. Hill never had to worry about
money again.

Despite dallying with retirement, Hill still took violence
seriously, and in 1953 nearly got into serious trouble when
he viciously chived a young East End tearaway called Tommy
Smithson, who had given offence to his beloved Gypsy. That
same year Spot and Hill met two young, polite and promising

lads from the East End, Ronald and Reginald Kray. The twins later said that they never had much time for Spot, but Hill certainly aided their rise to prominence.

In 1954, Hill had the nerve to begin serializing his memoirs for *The People*. The first episode blatantly explained how the KLM bullion hijack had been executed. In the ensuing public outcry, Hill decided to emigrate to Australia. When he got there he was sent straight back. Spot was, as he put it, "well pissed off" with Hill's high profile and his claims to be the emperor of crime. They fell out, and Spot, who blamed Webb for fostering Hill's delusions of grandeur, personally put on his favourite knuckleduster and beat up the journalist. The subsequent court case did nothing for his public image, and when he too tried to serialize his memoirs, they received scant attention.

By 1955, Spot was losing what little influence he still had on the racecourses to a bunch of Italian bookies and their strongmen. It was at this time that the Krays saw him again at Epsom races, at his invitation; they were happy to be noticed but decided that they would ultimately be wrong to ally themselves with such a spent force. Hill had returned from his abortive attempt to emigrate, and at that same Epsom race meeting publicly allied himself with the Italians. Soon afterwards, Spot was strolling through Frith Street in Soho when he came across Albert Dimes, a genial Italian, whom Hill had

Billy Hill found an unlikely ally in the crusading journalist Duncan Webb, who described Hill as "a crook, a villain, a thief, a thug", but also "a genius and a kind and tolerant man". It was Webb who wrote a series of exposés for *The People* which brought about the demise of the Messina brothers, who had taken over running London's prostitution rackets. Of mixed Egyptian, Sicilian and Maltese descent, the Messina brothers ran an efficient operation in which their women worked strictly regulated hours and were limited to ten minutes per customer. One prostitute reckoned that between 1940 and 1955 she earned £150,000 for the gang; on VE Day she got through forty-nine clients. In the course of his investigations, Webb was constantly threatened by the Messina thugs. Then he met Hill, got on amicably and thereafter enjoyed the freedom of the underworld that so fascinated him. In return Webb ensured that Hill had a favourable press and even ghosted his autobiography called, with typical modesty, *Boss of Britain's Underworld*.

employed as a bodyguard. They began brawling outside the Bar Italia. Spot clouted Dimes on the chin. Dimes fled and tried to hide in a greengrocers shop. Spot, his temper up, seized a potato knife and stabbed Dimes with it several times before the proprietor of the shop, a formidable woman called Mrs Hyams, hit him over the head with a scoop from a set of scales. As he lay stunned, Dimes retaliated and slashed wildly at him with his knife. In the end, both men staggered off, cut to shreds. Although badly injured, they survived. But as Spot lay in hospital, the last vestiges of his criminal empire vanished.

He also ended up in court, charged with instigating the affray. Though he was acquitted, it subsequently came to light (largely as a result of work by Duncan Webb egged on by Billy Hill) that Spot's principal witness in his defence, an old and genteel clergyman called Parson Andrews, was popularly known as the "knocking Parson". Though he had a sanctimonious exterior he habitually swindled bookies and his ecclesiastical career had been devoted to whisky, gambling and women. This decrepit character had been recruited by Spot as a witness, and he and a coterie of Spot's associates and his wife Rita were eventually charged with conspiracy to pervert the course of justice. The case went badly for Spot, and this and a subsequent perjury case involving another witness ruined him.

Hill always kicked a man when he was down. One night in May, Spot and his wife Rita were strolling back to their flat in Hyde Park Mansions when they were set upon by a large group of men armed with razors, knives and coshes. Spot knew what was coming and tried to get his wife inside the door to the flats, but she refused and clung to him, screaming. Together they fell to the floor, and the men closed in on them. Rita was not cut, but Spot had seventy-eight stitches and a blood transfusion. He considered breaking the underworld code and revealing the identity of his attackers, but in the end decided not to. Although they had no respect for him, the Kray twins were looking for an opportunity to whip up a gang war in which they could assert themselves by brute force on the world of the West End, at that time still closed to them. They visited Spot in hospital, and urged him to let them start shedding blood in revenge. But such rash conflicts were anathema to Spot, and he said nothing in reply, but rolled over in his bed and faced the wall.

Rita had no qualms about talking to the law and took her husband's assailants to court. In the end, three of Hill's henchmen went to jail.

In the aftermath of the endless trials, Jack Spot was finally declared bankrupt and evicted from his Bayswater flat. Rita made a little pile of money from selling her life story and opened the Highball Club, which quickly became a popular haunt for the glitterati. But Hill didn't want Spot around in any form, and the club was constantly plagued by fires and pointless vandalism. Spot gave up and emigrated. He wanted to go to Canada, but when he was refused admission he settled for Ireland. Here he retreated into comfortable obscurity, working as a bookie's runner in Dublin and Cork. His marriage survived and his daughters went into show-business. Later, he returned to England, and lived a quiet life, making occasional appearances as a celebrity at sporting events.

Hill also assumed a lower profile, bought a villa in Marbella and delegated the handling of many of his affairs. Many of his gang drifted off to join the Richardson gang from South London, and became involved in the subsequent dispute with the Krays. Throughout the sixties Hill enjoyed a period of prosperity and respectability. He became close to the Kray twins, to whom he was invaluable as a guide to the low-life of London's West End and Soho. He was friends with journalists other than Duncan Webb and the rising media personalities of the era. He hob-nobbed with nobility, and gambled with Perac Rachman and Mandy Rice-Davies. Based for the most part in Spain, he was far removed from the unfavourable Kray-instigated scandals of the London underworld in the 1960s.

In the early 1970s he got fed up and returned to England, opening a night-club in Sunningdale. In 1976 he split up with his long-standing moll, Gypsy, and took up with a black singer, with whom, to his surprise, he fell deeply in love. It was late in the day to discover such tender feelings, and when, three years later, she committed suicide, Hill sank into depression and misanthropy and shut himself up in his flat. He was cursed to live until 1984, and died a lonely and unhappy man. Jack Spot described him as "the richest man in the graveyard".

• chapter nine •

"JUNGLE W11": RACHMAN AND MICHAEL X

"Jungle W11" was the name the London police gave to the Notting Hill area of West London in the 1950s. Now gentrified and hugely fashionable, the haunt of publishers, journalists, actors and the like, the area was once considerably run-down and seedy. The Notting Hill police station area stretched from the expensive genteel houses off Notting Hill Gate and Holland Park to the large, run-down and overcrowded properties of North Kensington and Paddington. In the poorer areas settled the West Indian immigrant population. The proximity of the area to the West End and the fact that at that time street prostitution extended from Marble Arch, all along the Bayswater Road, to Shepherds Bush, meant that the crumbling properties of Notting Hill had become coveted bases for organized operators in the field of vice. Illegal drinking clubs and rip-off joints were widespread, and the area was a bastion of the drug trade.

The immigrant West Indian community was easy prey for racketeering landlords, most notably Perac Rachman, whose name has become synonymous with rent extortion: "Rachmanism" is now in the dictionary.

Perac Rachman was born in Poland in 1920 and came to England as a penniless refugee in the wake of the Second World War; by the time he died in 1962, aged only forty-two, he was a millionaire.

When he arrived in London he started off by doing casual

work in the East End, then obtaining a job as a clerk at an estate agent's office in Shepherds Bush, a little further west than Notting Hill. The 1957 Rent Act made it possible for landlords to charge much higher rents than those hitherto paid by existing sitting tenants whose low rents were legally protected. However, Rachman had an astute mind and saw that the new Rent Act, the severe post-war shortage of housing, and the influx of immigrants desperate for accommodation offered a considerable opportunity to make money. The immigrants were a particularly vulnerable group; they had arrived in Britain to find that there was little rented accommodation available and that they were a low priority for council housing. Ignorant of the laws of the country, they would take whatever accommodation they were offered.

Rachman began to buy up large Victorian terraced properties, often on short leases, in North Kensington and Paddington. He obtained the capital principally from the Eagle Star Building Society, which in 1957 lent Rachman nearly sixty per cent of its total loans for the year, amounting to nearly £60,000; by the end of 1959 the company had lent Rachman and his associated companies – the police identified about thirty-three of which he was director and principal shareholder – over £220,000. The extent of the society's involvement was not discovered until much later, as none of Rachman's concerns was lent more than £25,000 and only details of the loans above this figure had to be disclosed in the society's annual returns.

Having purchased a property, Rachman's first move was to get rid of its existing sitting tenants. Initially he would offer them a modest pay-off to quit. If that was refused, life would become unpleasant for the tenants. Rachman would install some of his trusted henchmen in adjoining rooms, and suggest that they have a few all-night parties, turn the music up as loud as possible, let rubbish pile up in the communal areas and generally make living conditions as intolerable as possible for the existing tenants. If they still refused to go, strong-arm men would cut off the water and electrical supplies, smash up communal toilets and remove the external locks to the house, leaving it unsafe. The tenants would be left in no doubt that physical violence would follow.

Some courageous tenants did take their cases to local rent tribunals or considered legal action, but the majority tended to be poor people, for whom the complexities of civil law were a mystery. Furthermore, it was impossible to find direct evidence linking Rachman to the intimidation. Most sitting tenants quit their flats. Rachman then sent in the cowboy builders, subdivided the flats still further, made a few cosmetic repairs and re-let the accommodation at a still higher rent, either to immigrant families or to prostitutes looking for working space.

Rachman was living in a vast house in the exclusive area of Hampstead. He had a full time domestic staff, and was chauffeured around London in a Rolls-Royce, while his poverty-stricken tenants were crammed together in squalid, tiny flats, their exorbitant rents collected by men who had little time for excuses and quickly resorted to physical intimidation. A short, podgy, bespectacled and prematurely balding individual, he hardly looked like an emperor of crime and had a rather incongruous reputation as a ladies' man.

By 1959, allegations about Rachman's often violent methods were beginning to trouble the authorities, but since he avoided personal contact with tenants, it seemed impossible to mount a sustainable case against him. His financial affairs were targeted; his companies certainly owed tax, and a prosecution by the Inland Revenue would have forced him into bankruptcy. But, as his companies' shares had only a nominal face value, sometimes of a few pounds, it would have done him little damage. As much of his accommodation was let to prostitutes the police tried to get a conviction for brothel-keeping and living on the earnings of prostitutes, but could not gather sufficient evidence; Rachman was a cunning operator. The police tried again, and came sufficiently close to rattle Rachman. He sold his Notting Hill interests, and kept a low profile until his death three years later.

Rachman employed some of London's seediest types as enforcers. Among them were Raymond Nash, a Lebanese who later developed an interest in Soho's clubs and was finally barred from Britain after a conviction abroad for smuggling gold, and George Pigott, a well-known armed robber, currently serving a life sentence for his alleged involvement in the contract killing of "Italian Toni" Zomparelli, who was blown away in a Soho amusement arcade in 1974.

The most infamous of Rachman's henchmen was Michael Campbell De Freitas, a Trinidadian, who later reinvented himself as a black-power leader in the style of Malcolm X, and called himself Michael X. During the 1960s he acted as an agent for Rachman in the now prestigious areas of Colville Terrace and Powis Square in Notting Hill. He was heavily

The classic 'con' case of modern times is undoubtedly that of Count Victor Lustig's sale of the Eiffel Tower - not once, but twice. Lustig was in Paris when he saw a newspaper item reporting that repairs to the Eiffel Tower would cost thousands of francs. Some days later, several rich financiers received letters from a government department inviting them to a secret conference at the Hotel Crillon. The 'director deputy-general' who received them was actually Victor Lustig. He began by assuring them that this business was classified as top secret - hence the hotel suite instead of his office.

The government has decided, he told them, that the Eiffel Tower is too expensive to maintain; it is to be sold for scrap metal ... They gaped. 'Would you gentlemen care to submit your bids to me?' He had already noted the man who was the obvious 'mark', Andre Poisson, a man who clearly felt socially

inferior to the others. A few days later, Lustig rang him and told him that his bid was the highest - several million francs - and that if he would bring a cern fled cheque to the hotel, the deal could be concluded. Poisson was not entirely happy - until Lustig apologetically asked for a bribe, to ensure that negotiations would go smoothly.

That convinced Poisson that this was a genuine government official; he handed over the cash. And later, when it became clear he had been swindled, he was too ashamed to go to the police and make himself the laughing stock of France. The result was that Lustig was able to repeat the same trick a few years later.

The second part of Lustig's life was an anticlimax - an observation that applies to most confidence tricksters. In America in the early 1930s, he turned to the distribution of counterfeit money; the F.B.I. finally caught up with him, and he was sentenced to twenty years in gaol, dying in Alcatraz in 1947. The Federal agent mainly responsible for his capture, James P. Johnson, wrote the classic book on his career under the title *The Man Who Sold the Eiffel Tower.*   -

involved in a number of vice rackets, and for the right money arranged working accommodation for prostitutes. He was convicted for keeping a brothel, but though he had a fearsome reputation as a pimp and extortionist, he got off with a conditional discharge and a nominal fine.

Inspired by Malcolm X, he then became a Muslim, going under the name of Abdul Malik, later Michael X. He founded the "Racial Adjustment Action Society", and became the self-appointed Messiah of a black-power commune on the grimy Holloway Road in Islington, North London. De Freitas attracted a number of wealthy and influential followers, and found himself a hit with young, middle class white women, notably the ill-starred Gale Benson, daughter of the Conservative MP for Chatham. The enthusiasm of his followers did not wane when he was imprisoned for twelve months after publicly urging the shooting of any black girl seen with a white man.

His organized criminal activities continued throughout his immoderate political career. In 1969, De Freitas and four of his associates were put on trial at the Old Bailey, accused of robbery and demanding money with menaces. The proprietor of an employment agency in Soho had been subject to extortion, and when he had expressed a reluctance to pay, De Freitas had put a dog collar on his neck and forced him to crawl around the floor, begging for mercy.

De Freitas jumped bail and headed back to Trinidad, where he was followed by some of his supporters, including Gale Benson. There De Freitas formed a black-power party, and joined up with local criminals, creating a gang that was to prove a constant source of fury to the authorities. In 1972, a member of the gang, a man called Joseph Skerritt, refused to obey De Freitas's orders and carry out a raid on a local police station. De Freitas announced to his gang that he needed to improve the drainage in his garden, and ordered a number of them, including Skerritt, to dig a long trench. When this was done, De Freitas decapitated Skerritt with a cutlass and threw him into the trench. The other members of his gang became worried about their esteemed leader's erratic behaviour, and with good reason. Shortly afterwards, another of their number mysteriously drowned, and Gale Benson vanished. When De Freitas and his wife went away on a lecture tour, one of his henchmen set fire to his bungalow. While investigating the arson, a police inspector rooted around De Freitas's garden and became suspicious of some abnormally tall and horribly yellow lettuces. They began digging, and soon found the corpse of Skerritt. Two days later, Gale Benson's body was found, five foot underground. The pathologist deduced that she had been stabbed with a six-inch blade, but that it had not killed her outright. She had been buried alive.

Two of De Freitas's gang were convicted and hanged for her murder. Though De Freitas himself was indicted for the murder of Gale Benson, he was never tried for the crime. Convicted of the murder of Skerritt, he went to the gallows in 1974.

• chapter ten •

DRUG BARONS

Outside the Mafia, the international drugs trade is often controlled at its roots by a series of powerful individuals, drug barons, whose power base is the source of production within often lawless and poor countries, much of whose gross national income is connected to narcotics.

Colombia's economy has for many years depended largely on the export of cocaine; at one stage it was estimated that Colombia was exporting something like 100 tons of cocaine annually with a street value in excess of sixty billion dollars, representing forty per cent of the country's gross national product. With no alternative source of revenue in the impoverished and mountainous rural areas, government attempts to tackle the problem have met with stiff and violent local resistance; the impetus to drive out the drug producers has come largely from America, which has offered military training, equipment and financial incentives to the South American governments.

Trafficking in Colombia has long been controlled by a few powerful and wealthy dynasties. In the drug capitals of Medellin and Cali live the families of Escobar, Lehder, O'Campo and Ochoa, who have run the country with the liberal use of graft and the gun. One of the most prominent of these families is the Escobar clan. It has been claimed that Pablo Escobar, its head, a man in his early forties, is among the ten richest individuals in the world. Based in Medellin, where he runs five homes, Escobar's official status as a wanted man has done little to persuade him to keep a low profile. A public benefactor, his grandiose gifts to the poor – including building thousands of new homes – have given him the status of a hero and guaranteed that the slum-dwellers and the starving of Colombia are unlikely to surrender him to the authorities. The government does not have the funds to match the generosity of the criminals, and those politicians who refuse to be bought are murdered with impunity. In Medellin, a comparatively small regional capital city of a million people, there are nearly ten murders a day, principally drug-related, the result of quarrels between cartels, or of the enforcement of drug-law. In Colombia, it is quite customary for a cartel to kill not only an offender, but his entire family. In such surroundings of grinding poverty human life is seen as cheap.

Although Colombia is the leading exporter of cocaine, much of its output is actually grown elsewhere in South America, with Colombia forming a centre for refinement and distribution. Bolivia and its own drug baron, Roberto Suarez, are responsible for a substantial slice of the actual coca crop from which the cocaine is extracted. Suarez is unusual in that, far from being a gangster who has struggled out of the gutter, he is an educated and affluent man from a rich family. Once a cattle rancher, he discovered that his remote land holdings in the regions around Beni, Chapare and Santa Cruz could be far more profitably used for growing the stunted, wiry coca bushes.

Possessing an annual income in the region of one billion dollars, Suarez acquired a favourable public image in the accepted fashion, buying the hearts of the poor with lavish beneficence, building roads, schools and hospitals. Suarez was alleged to have had his own private army, the so-called "Fiances of Death", whose leader was reputed to be a mild-mannered German who went under the name of Klauss Altmann, better known to the world as the one-time Gestapo officer, Klaus Barbie, the "Butcher of Lyon", a resident of Bolivia since 1951.

After decades of de facto rule, the drug barons of Bolivia were disconcerted when, in 1978, the country democratically elected Silus Zuazo to the position of president. His predecessor, Hugo Banzer, had been a substantial trafficker in his own right, but Zuazo promised the Americans he would take on the cocaine kings. It was unlikely that he would have much effect, but to guarantee his failure, Suarez instigated a military coup led by disaffected officers eager for power and money. Colonel Luis Arce Gomez (a cousin of Suarez) was paid $800,000 to effect the necessary introductions, and General Luis Garcia Meza, head of the armed forces and the leader of the insurgency – the 189th coup in the short history of the Bolivian state – received a sum well in excess of one million dollars as a down payment on his future cut of the action. The coup, on 17 July 1980, was a success and Suarez became the effective ruler of Bolivia; his paid killers worked openly alongside the armed forces to suppress and exterminate civil opposition. Within two weeks of the takeover, 500 civilians had died, and several thousand more were imprisoned and subject to beatings and torture. Such authority also gave Suarez licence to break up and absorb the smaller rival cocaine cartels throughout Bolivia.

Meza's brutal and corrupt regime devastated the already tottering legitimate economy. The dictates of the International Monetary Fund were wholly ignored, inflation reached three figures and the United States suspended all aid. Perturbed by the bad reputation his nation was acquiring, and fearful of military intervention by the United States, Suarez encouraged Meza to mount a suitable weak, cosmetic and stage-managed campaign against a few minor cartels. It was enough to silence the Americans temporarily. Within the year, however, Suarez, the puppet-master of Bolivian politics, decided to bestow the crown of the bungling Meza elsewhere. In September 1981, he engineered yet another coup and replaced Meza with General Torrelio Villa, who in turn was discarded in favour of General Guido Calderon, who made the usual promises of democratic elections.

Suarez profited while Bolivia went to ruin. Finally, in the face of public unrest, Calderon was forced out of office and Zuazo returned from exile to confront the mess: a nation with no industry, massive unemployment and the highest murder rate in the world. Zuazo did good things. He deported Klaus Barbie back to Europe to face trial; he purged the army and put Gomez, Meza and a host of others to flight. But the problems of cocaine growing required dealing with at a fundamentally economic level; the poor farmers had to be financially encouraged to grow something other than coca. He turned to the Americans for help, and they created the crop substitution programme, offering forty million dollars in subsidies to farmers prepared to renounce coca in favour of legitimate crops. But no crop has such a good profit margin, and once the subsidy is

In 1803, at about the same time that De Quincey was taking his first dose of laudanum, a young German chemist's assistant named Friedrich Wilhelm Sertürnes was experimenting with opium in an attempt to isolate its 'sleep-giving' component. One day, he poured ammonia over the opium, and was startled to see white crystals forming in the liquid. He tried this white powder on his dog, and it fell asleep. He then invited three friends to join him in an experiment; they sat around a table, and each took half a grain of the powder. It produced a sense of warmth and delight. A second half a grain made them feel deliciously sleepy and happy; a third half a grain put them into a deep sleep, from which they woke up vomiting. They had taken an overdose of morphine - for this was the name that Sertürner gave to his drug, from the Greek word 'morpheus' - sleep.

So, for the first time, men became aware of the deadly nature of the magical painkiller. Those who took repeated quantities built up a resistance to it, and needed larger doses. If withdrawn from it, they went through agonies; and if they continued feeding themselves increasingly larger doses, they degenerated and died.

In the 1850's, there were sudden hopes of a solution to the problem of morphine addiction. A German doctor called Scherzer came back from Peru with some leaves of a plant called 'coca'; the Indians of Peru would chew this, and could then endure the most severe fatigues. Dr. Albert Niemann isolated its basic constituent in the laboratory, and gave it the name cocaine. American doctors tried using the drug on morphine addicts - and it seemed to free them of the craving for morphine. Until they realized that it did this by setting up a new addiction to cocaine.

accepted there is little way, in the mountainous terrain of
Bolivia, to ensure that the farmers actually switch crops. For
the past decade the authorities have fought an increasingly
bitter battle against the cocaine barons, with only a small
degree of success.

For a long time, cocaine was not seen as a major problem in
the same way as heroin. It was a social drug. "Cocaine" said
one American "is God's way of telling you that you're too
rich". That was once true; the cocaine economy depended upon
the criminal manipulation of a wealthy First World, for whom
cocaine was the consumer drug *par excellence*, and the poverty
of the Third World, where conditions allowed unfettered
production. The rich got their kicks, the poor made a living
and the organizers were as wealthy as Croesus. But the over-
production of cocaine by the greedy South American barons led
to an excess on the streets; not even the huge white middle class
of America could snort all that powder. With the street price
plummeting, it was necessary to make the cocaine accessible to
the huge market of the vast underclass; to put it in competition
with heroin. Crack – the drug of poverty and of violent escape –
was created.

The traditional source of heroin is the Golden Triangle, 80,000
square miles of mountainous jungle at the point where Thailand, Laos and Burma intersect. Bounded by the Mekong and
Mae Si Rivers, it is virtually impassable except to the native
inhabitants, the Shan, the mountain people. It is unpoliceable
terrain.

The Shan, in turn, feel little allegiance to the three national
powers that hold sway over the territory. Theirs is still a feudal
society, and their lords are individuals like Khun Sa, the
world's biggest opium producer. The son of a former Colonel
in Chiang Kai Shek's Chinese Nationalist army, Khun Sa's
power stems from the vagaries of American foreign policy in
Asia. When the Nationalist army was defeated and driven into
Burma by the Communists, it remained largely intact and was
welcomed first by the Shan tribesmen as a buffer against the
local government in Rangoon, and then by the Americans, who
saw the continued presence of the exiled Nationalists in Burma
as a bulwark against the spread of Communism. The Americans kept them supplied with arms and money for more than a
decade.

In the late 1950s, the Burmese government, hitherto tolerant of the Nationalist presence, decided that they were now too powerful, and pushed them out towards Thailand and Laos. The Americans gradually cut off the flow of aid, although covertly the CIA continued to support them for another fifteen years. But, with their sources of revenue seriously disrupted, the Nationalists began to look for alternative income, and moved into the cultivation of opium poppies, which have for centuries been a staple cash crop of the region, a situation largely ignored by the Burmese government.

Young Khun Sa grew up to become the Nationalists' main link with the CIA, supplying them with information about Communist insurgency while exporting massive amounts of heroin to the USA. The situation was entirely hypocritical; the American administration was openly at war with Khun Sa and his compatriots while their principal intelligence organ was employing him as an agent. During the Vietnam War, as many as one in seven American soldiers took heroin, probably supplied by Khun Sa, the same man who the CIA regarded as an ally. The American soldiers disliked the coarse, brown, smoking heroin the locals used and Khun Sa obligingly turned to manufacturing heroin in the form of a fine white powder suitable for intravenous injection.

In the 1970s, Khun Sa expanded his operations, encouraging Thai farmers to increase their output of raw opium base, and began to ship heroin to Bangkok, where he had formed a link with the Triads, Chinese gangsters.

When the American servicemen went home, Khun Sa began dumping his stocks on the streets of America's cities. His profits were enormous; a kilo of raw opium base costing $3,000 at source could fetch up to three million on the streets. The operation was run with corporate efficiency and Khun Sa had his hooks in most of the authorities; the Thai police have even been known to run some of his heroin manufacturing laboratories. In 1978 he even had the nerve to propose to the American Government that they could solve the nation's heroin problems by buying 500 tons of opium base a year off him, at a cost of fifty million dollars; but the Americans decided that he had sufficient supplies to sell this to them and still flood the streets.

In 1980, the Americans put a price of $25,000 on his head and furiously urged the Thai authorities to do something about his activities. In 1982 they finally did, launching a huge, American-sponsored assault on his hilltop fortress at Ban Hin Taek, a small Thai mountain village. The attack force of 2,000 troops supported by helicopter gunships killed over 200 of Khun Sa's private army and captured ten tons of weapons, but the mastermind was gone. He and the bulk of his forces slipped across the border into Burma where he immediately went into the heroin business with Communist insurgents. Two years later, he returned to Ban Hin Taek, and there he has remained; the Thai government has now become quite desperate in its struggle against the drug traffickers – one in fifty of its own population is an addict – and customarily awards the death penalty for trafficking. But the Golden Triangle remains impossible to police and the Shan tribes are still adamantly uncooperative. A quarter of them use the drug and all of them rely on it financially. To stop the heroin, and oust Khun Sa, would require a bloody war or an aid programme of monumental proportions.